New Labour's for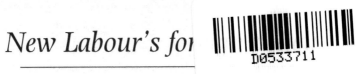

New Labour's foreign policy

A new moral crusade?

edited by Richard Little
and Mark Wickham-Jones

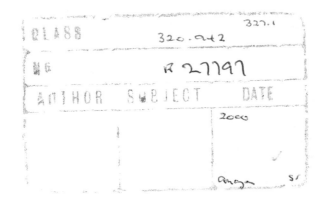

MANCHESTER UNIVERSITY PRESS

Manchester and New York

distributed exclusively in the USA by St. Martin's Press

Published by Manchester University Press
Oxford Road, Manchester M13 9NR, UK
and Room 400, 175 Fifth Avenue, New York, NY 10010, USA
http://www.manchesteruniversitypress.co.uk

Distributed exclusively in the USA by
St. Martin's Press, Inc., 175 Fifth Avenue, New York,
NY 10010, USA

Distributed exclusively in Canada by
UBC Press, University of British Columbia, 2029 West Mall,
Vancouver, BC, Canada V6T 1Z2

British Library Cataloguing-in-Publication Data
A catalogue record for this book is available from the British Library

Library of Congress Cataloging-in-Publication Data applied for

ISBN   0 7190 5961 5 *hardback*
       0 7190 5962 3 *paperback*

First published 2000

07 06 05 04 03 02 01 00   10 9 8 7 6 5 4 3 2 1

Typeset by Ralph J. Footring, Derby
Printed in Great Britain by Bell & Bain Ltd, Glasgow

Contents

Contributors

Will Bartlett is a Reader in the School for Policy Studies at the University of Bristol and author of articles on economic development in the Balkans and Sout East Europe.

Angela Bourne is a graduate student in the Department of Politics at the University of Bristol.

Jim Buller is Lecturer in Politics at the University of York.

Michelle Cini is Lecturer in Politics at the University of Bristol and co-author of *Competition Policy in the European Union* (Macmillan, 1998).

Neil Cooper is Lecturer in Politics at the University of Plymouth and author of *The Business of Death: Britain's Arms Trade at Home and Abroad* (Tauris Academic, 1997).

Igor Cusack completed his PhD thesis at the University of Bristol in 1999.

Michael W. Doyle is Professor of Politics and International Relations at Princeton University and author of *Ways of War and Peace* (Norton, 1997).

Tim Dunne is Senior Lecturer in International Politics at the University of Wales, Aberystwyth, and author of *Inventing International Society: A History of the English School* (Macmillan, 1998).

Vicky Harrison is a graduate student in Political Science and International Studies at the University of Birmingham.

Vernon Hewitt is Lecturer in Politics at the University of Bristol and author of *The New International Politics of South Asia* (Manchester University Press, 1997).

Richard Hodder-Williams is Professor of Politics and Pro-Vice Chancellor at the University of Bristol and co-editor of *Churchill to Major: The British Prime Ministership since 1945* (Hurst and Co., 1995).

Darren Lilleker is a graduate student in politics at the University of Sheffield and Lecturer in History and Politics at Barnsley College of Further and Higher Education.

Richard Little is Professor of International Politics at the University of Bristol and co-author of *International Systems in World History* (Oxford University Press, 2000).

Davina Miller is Senior Lecturer in Peace Studies at the University of Bradford and the author of *Export or Die: Britain's Defence Trade with Iran and Iraq* (Cassell, 1996).

Kevin Theakston is Professor of British Government at the University of Leeds and author of *Leadership in Whitehall* (Macmillan, 1998).

Rhiannon Vickers is Lecturer in the Institute for Politics and International Studies at the University of Leeds and author of *Manipulating Hegemony: State Power, Labour and the Marshall Plan in Britain* (Macmillan, 2000).

Nicholas J. Wheeler is Senior Lecturer in International Politics, University of Wales, Aberystwyth, and author of *Saving Strangers: Humanitarian Intervention in International Society* (Oxford University Press, 2000)

Mark Wickham-Jones is Senior Lecturer in Politics at the University of Bristol and author of *Economic Strategy and the Labour Party* (Macmillan, 1996).

Preface

The essays collected in this book address whether Tony Blair's New Labour government has made a difference to the conduct of foreign policy and what role ethical issues have played in policy formation. The authors are not, of course, agreed about the answers to these issues, nor do they reach a firm conclusion about what New Labour should have done or should do in the future. Rather the volume is designed to further understanding and analysis of Labour's foreign policy. The collection is not inclusive: space has precluded a detailed discussion of some areas of Labour's foreign and defence policy. For example, issues surrounding debt relief and the work of the new Department for International Development are not explored.

Since May 1997, Labour's 'ethical' dimension has been subject to considerable discussion. Since 1998, Tony Blair's pursuit of a 'Third Way' has been an added element of that debate. Much of this discussion has been polemical. The various analyses of the nature and import of the Third Way have been focused on assessing its domestic significance. The chapters provide an opportunity to begin the process of understanding Labour's contribution to foreign policy at the end of the twentieth century and start of the twenty-first.

The volume is organised into four distinct parts. The first provides an introduction to the analysis of New Labour's foreign policy. Mark Wickham-Jones outlines the background, including the content of Robin Cook's mission statement in May 1997 and Tony Blair's articulation of a Third Way. Rhiannon Vickers explores some of the difficulties that Labour's attempt to construct a distinctive strategy in foreign affairs has encountered.

The second part deals with theoretical perspectives on foreign policy. Michael Doyle gives an analysis of ethical conduct in foreign affairs. Tim Dunne and Nicholas Wheeler give an account of the 'Blair doctrine': they argue that Labour has pursued a distinct strategy in foreign affairs. Jim Buller and Vicky Harrison discuss the nature of good international citizenship and scrutinise its meaning for making foreign policy.

Part III provides political and historical perspectives on these issues. Mark Wickham-Jones explores the political context of Cook's ethical turn and assesses the party political dynamics that have shaped New Labour's foreign policy since 1994. Kevin Theakston studies Labour's relations with Whitehall and in particular with the Foreign Office.

Part IV contains a series of case studies of Labour's foreign policy in office since 1997. The cases deal with the war in Kosovo, arms sales, British and European relations with China, Iran, Labour's relations with India, the Blair government's defence policy and, finally, the nature of the 'special relationship' between the United States and the United Kingdom. In each case, the question of what role an ethical dimension has played is addressed alongside an analysis of how Labour's policy has differed from that of the outgoing Conservative administration. In the conclusion, Richard Little returns to some of the central themes identified here. He discusses the difficulties of pursuing an ethical dimension in foreign policy and addresses the role played by values in policy formation. Finally, Igor Cusack provides a comprehensive chronology of the development of Labour's foreign policy since 1983.

Acknowledgements

In many ways the production of this volume has been a team effort. Most of the chapters in this book were given as papers either at a series of panels at the 1999 Political Studies Association conference in Nottingham and at the 1999 American Political Science Association meeting in Atlanta (for the British Politics Group) or at a workshop on Ethics and Foreign Policy funded by the British International Studies Association and held at the University of Bristol, 8–9 June 1999. The workshop coincided with Michael Doyle's appointment at Bristol as a Visiting Benjamin Meaker Professor. The idea to hold the workshop came from our colleague Molly Cochran. By the time it took place, however, Molly had taken up a new appointment at the Georgia Institute of Technology in the United States. We are grateful to her for her work in planning the workshop, her interest in the project and for making the application for funds to the British International Studies Association.

We are also grateful to those who participated at the workshop: Chris Brown, Mervyn Frost, Eric Herring and David Sanders. William Wallace participated at an earlier stage in the project with his visit to Bristol, as a Benjamin Meaker Professor, in November 1999. We must also express thanks to the following who have helped us in a variety of ways with comments on chapters, details of references and access to a plethora of material: James Landale, Ruth Levitas, Camilla Leonelli, Eric Shaw and Andrew Wyatt. Igor Cusack worked tirelessly to produce the chronology that appears in the Appendix to this book. Eric Herring's paper for the workshop on economic sanctions against Iraq was a useful source in the compilation of this calendar of events. We are grateful also to the staff at Manchester University Press, including Nicola Viinikka, the former politics editor at the press. Ralph Footring did a fantastic job copy-editing and setting the text. Stuart Quayle helped immensely in constructing the index. Our thanks to both of them. Mark Wickham-Jones thanks those who gave up time to talk to him about Labour's foreign policy, including John Kampfner and Tony Lloyd, MP.

The British International Studies Association and the University of Bristol Benjamin Meaker Fund provided financial resources which we are pleased to acknowledge: without such support the workshop could not have taken place. Mark Wickham-Jones's contributions to the volume have benefited from earlier research grants, one from the Nuffield Foundation and one from the Harold Wincott Foundation: both are gratefully acknowledged. His work on the comparisons between 'old' and 'new' Labour was supported by an Arts and Humanities Research Board grant, which is also recorded with appreciation. In Mark Wickham-Jones's case, Rosa Tarling, Madeliene Tarling and Harry Tarling provided enjoyable research distractions.

Richard Little and Mark Wickham-Jones

Note on web sources

The ministerial speeches and official statements and reports referenced in the following chapters are generally available from the website of the Foreign Office: http://www.foc.gov.uk. The site maintains a full text database of foreign policy speeches by Foreign Office ministers and others, including the prime minister and secretary of state for defence. The website of the Department for International Development (http://www.dfid.gov.uk/news/speech.asp) also contains relevant material. Editions of *Hansard*, reporting all parliamentary debates, are available from 1988 for the Commons (http://www.parliament.the-stationery-office.co.uk/pa/cm/cmhansrd.htm) and from 10 June 1996 for the Lords (http://www.parliament.the-stationery-office.co.uk/pa/ld199697/pdvn/home.htm).

Speeches are also recorded at some news websites, such as *The Guardian*'s (http://www.guardian-unlimited.co.uk) and that of the *Daily Telegraph* (http://www.telegraph.co.uk) and the Labour party's site may also be helpful in this respect (http://www.labour.org.uk). News sites such as the BBC's (http://news.bbc.co.uk) are also a good source of contemporary commentary on events.

Abbreviations

APEC	Asia-Pacific Economic Cooperation
CASOM	Conventional Armed Stand-Off Missile
CFSP	common foreign and security policy
CND	Campaign for Nuclear Disarmament
CPRS	Central Policy Review Staff
DFID	Department for International Development
DTI	Department of Trade and Industry
ECGD	Export Credit Guarantee Department
EEC	European Economic Community
EU	European Union
FCO	Foreign and Commonwealth Office
FRY	Federal Republic of Yugoslavia
GIC	good international citizen
HIPC	highly indebted poor country
IMF	International Monetary Fund
JKLF	Jammu and Kashmir Liberation Front
KLA	Kosovo Liberation Army
LPACR	*Labour Party Annual Conference Report*
MoD	Ministry of Defence
MTCR	missile technology control regime
NATO	North Atlantic Treaty Organisation
NEC	National Executive Committee
NCRI	National Council of Resistance of Iran
NGO	non-governmental organisation
OECD	Organization for Economic Cooperation and Development
OSCE	Organisation for Security and Co-operation in Europe
PUS	permanent under-secretary
SALT	Strategic Arms Limitation Talks
START	Strategic Arms Reduction Treaty
UDC	Union of Democratic Control
UN	United Nations

UNDP   United Nations Development Programme
UNESCO   United Nations Educational, Scientific and Cultural Organization
UNHCR   United Nations High Commission for Refugees
UNMIK   United Nations Interim Administration Mission in Kosovo
UNSCOM   United Nations Special Commission

Part I

The context of New Labour's foreign policy

1

Labour's trajectory in foreign affairs: the moral crusade of a pivotal power?

Mark Wickham-Jones

Introduction

On 12 May 1997, less than a fortnight after Labour's crushing election victory over John Major's Conservatives, Robin Cook, the new foreign secretary, launched a mission statement for his department. The announcement of the statement was not unduly controversial. The idea that the Foreign Office should adopt such a document, a conventional feature of modern business strategy, was unremarkable. Introducing it, Cook opened, 'Every modern business starts from a mission statement that sets clear objectives. New Labour is determined to bring a businesslike approach to government' (Cook, 1997a). The mission statement was taken by some as evidence of the new government placing considerable weight upon the packaging of policies and less upon their substantive content. This emphasis was unsurprising. It simply represented the party's persistent concern with 'spin', the way in which proposals were conveyed to the electorate. Many commentators concluded that Labour's near obsession with communicating issues to voters in a direct and popular fashion was the defining feature of the party led by Tony Blair (see, for example, Oborne, 1999).

Robin Cook's brief mission statement outlined four goals. Three were straightforward: the Foreign Office would promote security and prosperity for the United Kingdom while seeking to enhance the quality of life. The last goal, however, proved to be contentious and much debated. It stressed Labour's commitment to mutual respect: 'We shall work through our international forums and bilateral relationships to spread the values of human rights, civil liberties and democracy which we demand for ourselves' (Foreign and Commonwealth Office (FCO), 1997). Cook was categorical: in a passage subsequently much quoted, he argued, 'The Labour government does not accept that political values can be left behind when we check in our passports to travel on diplomatic business. Our foreign policy must have an ethical dimension and must support the demands of other peoples for democratic rights on which we insist for ourselves' (Cook, 1997a). Of course, quite what an ethical approach amounted to in practice and how it differed from the policies of the outgoing Conservatives remained uncertain.

Media observers quickly noted the foreign secretary's insistence that foreign affairs under Labour would have an explicit moral dimension. The new administration, they concluded, was adopting an 'ethical foreign policy'. Cook later disassociated himself strongly from the phrase. He claimed a much more modest interpretation of his enunciation, that there would be a moral contribution to foreign policy. In the summer of 1997, however, the notion of an ethical foreign policy captured the image projected by spin doctors at the Foreign Office to portray the government's policies. Commentators concluded it to be at the heart of Labour's stance on foreign affairs. Government press officers did not dispute that characterisation (at a time when they were happy, by and large, to correct what they considered to be mis-interpretations of policies – John Kampfner, interview, October 1999).

The mission statement was an ambitious initiative. Cook asserted that the document signified a major realignment of UK foreign policy, claiming, 'It supplies an ethical content to foreign policy and recognises that national interest cannot be defined only by narrow *realpolitik*' (Cook, 1997a). He insisted that the statement defined a 'new direction', a phrase he used thrice at the launch (Cook, 1997a). The BBC later reported, 'It was an occasion when senior diplomats looked on in amazement' (BBC news website, 29 April 1998). *The Observer* reported that the defence industry was 'reeling' following the announcement (18 May 1997). One Labour MP claimed later, 'The mission statement was driven by a strong wish to be different, a desire to break with a tired policy of drift and anti-Europeanism' (interview, November 1999). Tony Lloyd, then a newly appointed minister of state at the Foreign Office, described it as 'an attempt to give a clear sense of direction to the Foreign Office and the wider public about what Labour intended to do. The last government did not have a foreign policy ... The Tories were afraid of the issues' (interview, November 1999).

The implication of the foreign secretary's argument was that any consensus between the leading political parties in the United Kingdom over the conduct of foreign policy had been abandoned. A significant re-orientation was underway, one that which broke with the trajectory established by the Conservatives during the successive administrations of Margaret Thatcher and John Major between 1979 and 1997. Put starkly, New Labour would have a new foreign policy. One of the distinctive features of the new approach would be the emphasis placed by the new government on the moral stance of its policy. The claim that Labour has adopted a new foreign policy has been echoed since May 1997 by prime minister Tony Blair's assertion, made frequently in 1998 and 1999, that his administration is pursuing a Third Way, a trajectory that is distinct from those taken by Labour and Conservative governments alike in the past.

The weight placed in the mission statement on an ethical dimension took the press by surprise. *The Observer* termed it 'Cook's ethical bombshell' (18

May 1997). *The Guardian* described the mission statement as 'unprecedented' (13 May 1997). A *Financial Times* leader called the ethical angle 'the most striking innovation' of the goals laid out by the foreign secretary (13 May 1997). Joe Rogaly, a respected commentator on the paper, described it as a 'startling' development (17 May 1997). *The Times* reported, 'Labour is anxious to set a new tone: on human rights and arms sales the shift is substantial' (13 May 1997). *The Economist* concluded, 'In Mr Cook, the moral dimension goes deep' (17 May 1997).

Labour's articulation of an ethical angle, combined with the claim that it would pursue a distinctive foreign policy, was also unexpected by academics. Many had anticipated that a bipartisan outlook would define the new government's approach. Tony Blair's risk-averse political strategy, designed to reassure the middle-class electorate, effectively ruled out any potentially problematic policy proposals than might alienate voters. Yet Cook's course appeared to chart new territory, including a firm commitment that moral values would be at the centre of foreign policy.

The chapters that follow examine Labour's foreign policy during the first years after the party's return to office in 1997. Together, they give an account of the programme adopted by the new government. They address the ethical character of the administration's measures and they assess whether Labour has re-orientated the conduct of foreign policy away from the path established by the Conservatives. A series of case studies comprising part IV of the book explores the nature of a moral dimension to foreign policy. In this introductory chapter, I outline the background to Labour's ethical turn. I discuss briefly the consensus over foreign policy, Cook's initiative and Blair's articulation of a Third Way in international affairs. Finally, I give an overview of Labour's foreign policy in practice, looking at some of the criticisms that have been made and some of the defences of it that have been offered.

New Labour and consensus politics

Tony Blair was elected leader of the Labour party in July 1994. Just over two months later, at the party conference in Blackpool, he launched 'New Labour'. The epithet was deliberate, explicit and provocative. His claim was that the previous initiatives to modernise and transform the party under his predecessors, Neil Kinnock and John Smith, had been piecemeal, compromised and insubstantial. They had failed, directly as a result, to complete the basic reforms to Labour's structure and policy outlook that were a precondition of the party regaining office. In contrast, Blair proceeded to make a series of changes to Labour's organisation and programmatic commitments. The actual character of Blair's measures and the extent to which they broke with the trajectory of his predecessors, rather than built on the foundations laid by them, is open to question. In the eyes of many scholars and observers, however, the new leader was perceived to introduce a series of radical and far-reaching reforms. He held this perspective himself, asserting boldly, 'My leadership of the party is based on the judgement that to become a serious party of government again, the Labour party needed not a series of adjustments but a quantum leap' (Blair, 1995: 11).

The Labour leader claimed to be guided by a coherent set of values and principles. He was blunt, however, about the necessity of the party meeting electoral preferences, if it was to take power again. Labour had to respond to the aspirations, desires and fears of ordinary voters. Old Labour, Blair claimed, 'lost contact with the electorate' (1996a: 17). Indeed, New Labour can be characterised by Blair's determination to locate the party within what might be termed the middle ground of British politics. (More formally, Blair's intention, arguably at any rate, was to place the party to the right of the median voter so as to ensure electoral victory by depriving the Conservatives of some of their core support; see Downs, 1957.) By the time Blair visited New York in April 1996, he was describing Labour as a party of the 'centre' and 'centre-left', a characterisation he continued to deploy (Blair, 1996b: 1).

The result of the leader's initiative was that the party adopted an extremely moderate set of policy proposals. Some scholars concluded that a new consensus, one heavily influenced by the years of the Thatcher and Major governments, had emerged between the Labour and Conservative parties. At an extreme, in the search for electoral victory, Labour had aligned itself to a Thatcherite framework of ideas and policies (see, for example, Hay, 1994, 1998). In their account of the 1997 general election, for example, David Butler and Dennis Kavanagh argued, 'Tony Blair openly accepted the essentials of Thatcherism' (1997: 64). Patrick Seyd commented, 'Much of the Conservative party's political clothing was stolen [by Labour] in the bid to reassure voters that a vote for change would not be a vote for instability or political lunacy' (1998: 64).

Foreign and defence issues, for many analysts at any rate, were an integral part of the consensus between the Labour and Conservative parties. There was a straightforward electoral dynamic for Labour seeking a bipartisan approach over such matters. In the early 1980s, the party had articulated a radical defence policy based around unilateral nuclear disarmament and strong antipathy to the continuance of US military bases in the United Kingdom. This stance was perceived to be electorally problematic and it was ruthlessly exploited as such by the Conservatives at the general elections of 1983 and 1987 (see Butler and Kavanagh, 1984: 282; 1988: 103–5). George Robertson, a moderate who became defence secretary after Labour's election victory in 1997, was later scathing about the party's defence policy in the 1980s:

> The Labour party suggested that perhaps we should not be playing the part in the world that has generally been suggested by the people. And it's only been ... by rebuilding our trust with the British people, by coming into synch

with what the British people want us to do as a nation, that we've managed
to get elected with the size of majority we have. (Robertson, 1997: 2)

David Clark, Labour's defence spokesperson in opposition, noted that during
the 1980s the party broke with the 'traditional consensus' surrounding
defence and security issues (Clark, 1997: 8).

Labour's defence policy was also responsible in part for the disastrous
outcome of a visit by Neil Kinnock to the Reagan White House in March
1987. Disagreements gave way to an undignified dispute as to how long
Kinnock had been given by the White House for his appointment. Its
spokesperson was dismissive afterwards about the Labour leader and the trip
failed to foster Kinnock's credentials as a potential head of government. In
1989, as part of the party's general policy review, Kinnock formally abandoned
unilateralism, a platform with which he had been closely associated for many
years. The decision to reformulate radically the party's defence policy appeared
straightforward, as a simple necessity of electoral competition. It was, however,
an emotional and painful choice for those who had invested much in the
unilateralist cause (see Hughes and Wintour, 1990: 104–27). Two members
of Tony Blair's 1997 Labour cabinet, Margaret Beckett and David Blunkett,
opposed the decision to renounce unilateralism. Two others, Robin Cook and
Clare Short, supported it with great reluctance. There were non-electoral
reasons for Labour's decision to abandon unilateralism. The end of the Cold
War, symbolised in 1989 by the demolition of the Berlin Wall, provided a
new opportunity for multilateral strategies (see for example Kinnock's speech
to the 1989 party conference; *Labour Party Annual Conference Report* (*LPACR*),
1989: 61–2). Gorbachev's programme of perestroika, coupled with improvements in relations between the United States and the Soviet Union during
the mid-1980s, raised new possibilities for disarmament. To some previous
adherents, Labour's unilateralism looked emblematic of a past era.

By the mid-1990s academics studying foreign policy concluded that there
was little difference between the outlooks of the two main parties. John
Garnett and Lawrence Martin argued that there was a consensus: 'most
Labour and Conservative politicians would sign up to a set of principles which
underlay foreign policy' (quoted by Wheeler and Dunne, 1998: 849). For
both electoral and substantive reasons, Labour had broken with its unilateralist
past before Blair became leader. He had no incentive to depart from the
bipartisan approach that had emerged since the late 1980s. Although briefly
a member of the parliamentary Campaign for Nuclear Disarmament (CND),
Blair's desire to locate Labour within mainstream opinion was manifest. (Blair
listed membership of CND proper on his curriculum vitae in 1983 when
seeking the nomination for the Sedgefield parliamentary seat for which he
subsequently became MP, something later denied by Labour party officials;
see Sopel, 1995: 64–5.) His statement for the Labour leadership in 1994
touched only briefly on foreign policy: 'Britain must adopt a foreign policy
that is clear and consistently applied in order to regain influence in the world.'

The issues noted were Europe, the role of the United Nations (UN) and the North Atlantic Treaty Organisation (NATO) and the need for improved north–south trade. It was an utterly unremarkable and bland stance (Blair, 1994: 1).

The Labour leader gave little attention to foreign policy when leader of the opposition between 1994 and 1997, making few speeches or interventions on the topic. (In chapter 6 Mark Wickham-Jones examines Labour party policy-making before its 1997 general election victory.) To the extent that Blair did take note of international affairs, his concern was with globalisation and the impact it had on national economic policy-making. His 1996 book *New Britain* was, as the title suggests, focused on domestic matters, and there were only two references to foreign policy in the index (Blair, 1996a: 70, 263–4). Both referred to Britain's role in Europe. Though the volume touched on some wider issues, there were only two entries in the index to defence. The contents of the only significant document published by the party on foreign policy in this period were unsurprising and provoked little comment in the press (Labour party, 1996).

By the time of the May 1997 election, Blair offered a ten-point contract with the people in Labour's manifesto. Only one (point ten) touched on international matters. It did so in an insipid and indistinct manner: 'We will give Britain the leadership in Europe which Britain and Europe need' (Labour party, 1997a: 5). The manifesto pages on foreign policy gave little indication that Labour would follow a new approach in office, other than in the United Kingdom's relations with Europe. These relations were the only foreign affairs issue to be subject to any debate during the general election campaign. On this matter there were differences between Labour and the Conservatives. Often clouded by rhetoric, the gap between the parties was nothing compared with that within the Conservative party. It was an issue on which the party turned inwards, self-destructing, as Conservative candidates publicly opposed each other's stance on the single European currency and relations with Europe generally, giving way to an orgy of mutual recrimination. The differences between Conservative candidates mirrored those in John Major's government. Labour characterised it as an administration paralysed by the disagreement and unable to act, while the media focused on the rows almost as a purely internal matter. In his one speech on foreign policy during the campaign, Tony Blair was forthright: 'Over the past six years we have seen a relentless decline in our effectiveness. Throughout this period the country has had no real foreign policy at all' (Blair, 1997a: 4).

Aside from Europe, those studying the 1997 general election campaign had good reasons for assuming that there would be considerable continuity in foreign affairs in the (widely expected) event of a change in government. In the run-up to the election, Labour frontbenchers emphasised the need for a consensus on defence. John Reid, a member of the shadow defence team, said, 'I believe more than ever we need to try to build a national consensus on national security. Neither the country nor the armed forces can any longer afford the type of yah-boo politics which has for so long marked the defence debate.' He went on, 'The reality is that this country has managed to sustain such a consensus for most of the period since 1939 and it would be an enormous benefit if we were to reconstruct it' (Reid, 1997). Likewise, David Clark stated, 'I believe in a consensual approach to the main defence and security issues facing us today. It seems obvious to me that we ought to be able to agree across the main political parties on the basic principles governing our national security' (Clark, 1997: 1–2). During the election campaign, *The Times* commented, 'There has been little debate about foreign policy in the past five years ... Douglas Hurd [Conservative foreign secretary between 1989 and 1995] attempted to steer a bipartisan course ... Labour gave low priority to a field so barren in opportunities for partisan advantage' (7 April 1997).

Cook's ethical turn

On the weekend of Labour's election victory, Cook gave a long interview to Will Hutton and Patrick Wintour of *The Observer*. He gave four priorities for the new government: to make the United Kingdom a leading player in Europe; to encourage trade (which he claimed to be the prime concern for British embassies abroad); to promote human rights and environmental issues; and to synthesise foreign and domestic policy (4 May 1997). It is noticeable that Cook's priorities do not correlate precisely with those set out in the mission statement just over a week later and that, other than the briefest of references to human rights, no emphasis was placed by him in the interview on a turn to ethics in foreign policy. In contrast, Cook ended his statement at the launch of the mission statement in an emphatic fashion by announcing his intention to 'make Britain once again a force for good in the world' (Cook, 1997a: 3).

Commentators pointed out the difficulties of adopting such a strong commitment to moral values in designing a foreign policy. The BBC later reported, 'Within the Foreign Office, there were serious doubts about launching with such a fanfare a policy which diplomats knew would be impossible to deliver' (BBC news website, 29 April 1998). However, one senior Labour politician commented, 'There was a good feeling in the Foreign Office about Labour, after the way in which the Conservatives had treated it. Officials felt beleaguered, especially over Europe. They were keen for a new direction' (interview, November 1999). Another stated, 'The mission statement was trying to up-date the Foreign Office' (interview, November 1999).

It was by no means obvious by what yardsticks Cook's promises would be judged. Indeed, one of the aims of this volume is to explore the notion of what an ethical foreign policy is, in both theory and practice. The notion marshalled by Cook on entering office was simultaneously vague and strong. Philip Stephens concluded, 'It will be fiendishly difficult for Robin Cook to add an ethical dimension to Britain's foreign policy, but it is good to know he will give it a shot' (*Financial Times*, 16 May 1997). John Lloyd noted that, once such a pledge was made, any and every concession would be highlighted as a departure from the government's apparently strong promises: 'The promulgation of high principle leaves low compromise ever vulnerable. From now on, every time the Foreign Office agrees to look the other way ... Mr Cook will be in the hypocrite's dock' (*The Times*, 15 May 1997). The *Financial Times* suggested that the policy abstracted from the reality of foreign affairs: 'In truth most foreign policy is based on complex trade-offs in which moral absolutes must contend with other less noble priorities' (13 May 1997). Within months the press argued that the government's policy was less clear than its rhetoric. On the publication of new arms guidelines, *The Times* concluded, 'The Sir Richard Scotts of any future enquiry into a breach of government policy will have their work cut out to find precisely what the policy is' (10 July 1997). (Sir Richard Scott chaired an inquiry into arms exports to Iraq and the relationship of the firms concerned to the Conservative government.)

There was great potential for inconsistency in adopting moral standards, given the importance of the arms industry for the UK economy (worth, according to some estimates, around £5 billion a year): 'The stronger the principled commitment to human rights, the greater the risks of being pilloried for double standards' (*The Times*, 13 May 1997). Would human rights come before arms sales and trade deals? The United Kingdom was responsible for nearly a quarter (around twenty-two per cent) of the world's arms exports (*The Guardian*, 16 October 1997). Estimates suggested that up to half a million jobs were tied up in arms manufacture (Kampfner, 1999: 142). The *Financial Times* noted in response to the mission statement, 'Taking a tough moral stand in such cases may mean sacrificing export orders and jobs at home. That is a legitimate choice, but one which the government must have the political courage to defend if its approach is to be credible' (13 May 1997). Before the 1997 general election, Tony Blair had told workers at British Aerospace, 'the defence industry base is an integral part of Britain's overall manufacturing capacity, and Labour's commitment to a strong defence industry is an integral part of our security thinking' (Labour party press release, 7 February 1997). A week later the party had published tough new proposals for arms exports (Labour party, 1997b). The threats posed to the domestic economy by the ethical initiative were especially ironic given Cook's self-proclaimed status as the standard-bearer of Labour's left wing within the Blair administration and his commitment to full employment as a key objective of economic policy. John Lloyd commented, 'Cook, of all the senior ministers the most concerned to retain the old Labour virtues of high employment and the fight against poverty, could easily be seen as the minister most threatening to jobs' (*New Statesman*, 25 July 1997).

The Conservatives were quick to attack Cook's initiative. Their criticism reflected in part a genuine anger that the foreign secretary was implying they had acted unethically when in office. One ex-minister, Tony Baldry, wrote, 'the implication [of the mission statement was] that in some way the previous Conservative government's foreign policy had not been ethical' (Baldry, 1998/99: 32). Moral considerations had always, senior Conservatives claimed, been an integral part of foreign policy. (In chapter 5 Jim Buller and Vicky Harrison discuss the difficulties of implementing an ethical foreign policy.) Donald Anderson, a Labour MP and chair of the Foreign Affairs Committee, noted, 'The framework [for foreign policy] was therefore already in place when the Labour government arrived. Moreover, previous British governments have included ethical considerations in their foreign policies, so we must ask whether the Labour government is justified in claiming to have effected a change since they came to power' (Anderson, 1999: 3). He concluded, however, that there was a new emphasis on ethical issues.

Despite warnings, the idea of an ethical foreign policy remained at the centre of New Labour's actions during the administration's first months in office. In May 1997 Cook promised 'searching questions' on the issue of existing arms sales to Indonesia (*The Guardian*, 24 May 1997). The foreign secretary stated, 'We must make sure that the arms trade is responsible and that there is responsible regulation of it' (BBC news website, 12 May 1997). The government moved quickly to ban landmines. In July 1997 Cook gave a major set-piece speech on the theme of human rights. He outlined a twelve-point plan to ensure the administration's commitment to the issue: 'These are rights which we claim for ourselves and which we therefore have a duty to defend for those who do not yet enjoy them' (Cook, 1997b). The measures proposed included sanctions, arms control, bilateral dialogue, better training of military personnel, the establishment of an international criminal court and the publication of an annual report on human rights.

It was not all plain sailing for the government's new approach, even in the first months of office. One cabinet member's wife claims in her account of the period that Alistair Darling, the chief secretary to the Treasury, wrote to the defence secretary, 'People rescued by the British from Zaire should be sent a bill. Before we enter any peacekeeping operation, any manoeuvre, any rescue it should be costed and considered' (Jones, 1999: 84). New Labour had entered office, of course, with an austere economic programme.

A concern with human rights was not the only characteristic of the administration's interest in an ethical dimension. Back in May 1997, *The Times* had defined Cook's initiative by four features: alongside the emphasis on human rights stood tougher controls on arms exports, greater environmental protection and the use of development aid to tackle poverty (13 May 1997). Two other aspects of Labour's foreign policy that could be located within the ambit of an ethical approach were the weight placed by the administration on the use of international institutions and on co-operation with partner states. These two components suggested a commitment to multilateral action. Later the administration came to emphasise external interventions as moral choices. Taken together, this package can be held to define the ethical dimension in Labour's foreign policy. (Michael Doyle explores the nature of moral foreign policies in chapter 3.) For the first year of office, the key elements of the ethical dimension, in terms of government spin and media attention, were the foreign secretary's promise to 'put human rights at the heart of our foreign policy' and the commitment to stricter controls on arms sales (Cook, 1997a: 2). The focus of most of the case studies in this volume is on arms exports, human rights and British intervention in external conflicts.

When questioned in July 1997 about the sale of Hawk aircraft to Indonesia, for many a defining issue in the pursuit of an ethical approach, Cook hinted at tough controls and a change in direction: 'If we have evidence that any particular weapons system – of which that is one – is being used for internal repression, we will not give an export licence for it' (BBC news website, July 1997). He claimed that jobs would be safe with an ethical foreign policy (incidentally, it is noticeable that he did not challenge the deployment of that phrase in the interview): 'A business with no ethical dimension is a business that is going out of business fast' (BBC news website, July 1997). His words echoed those of Clare Short when launching a charter for ethics in business as opposition spokesperson on overseas development in March 1997: 'Business realises that it is not just ethically right to introduce ethics into company practice, but that it makes good economic sense' (Labour party press release, 10 March 1997). In effect, to be ethical was to be self-interested.

A few weeks after Cook's interview, on 28 July 1997, the same day that revised arms guidelines were announced, the government revealed that the sale of the Hawks would, after all, go ahead. It was a considerable dis-appointment to many, including 136 Labour MPs who criticised the decision in an early day motion (Kampfner, 1999: 144). Cook's claim was that Labour could not annul a contract entered into by the previous government without compensating the relevant British firms. It would also, one Labour politician suggested, have given the wrong signals about the United Kingdom's com-mitment to the arms industry (interview, November 1999).

By the time of the Labour party conference in October 1997, the setback over the Hawks notwithstanding, Cook was triumphant: 'Britain is leading again by cleaning up the arms trade ... We fought the last election on the commitment that we would not give any more licences for arms exports that would conspire with conflict or abet oppression. We have carried out that commitment. We have put in place tougher criteria that are biting and are delivering our policies' (*LPACR*, 1997: 133). Only at the last minute was a passage noting the part played by the arms industry in the UK economy added to the foreign secretary's speech (Kampfner, 1999: 172).

A further indication of the government's new approach to foreign policy was given in 1998 with the formation of the Foreign Policy Centre, an independent think-tank designed to help the construction of policy from outside the formal mechanisms (and control) of the Foreign Office. A noticeable feature of the party's policy-making under Blair's leadership was the decreasing reliance of Labour upon once well established sources of ideas and proposals. In 1987 the party's international department had been re-organised within its policy directorate. Over the next decade, the policy directorate was reduced in scope and size as resources were transferred to frontbench spokespersons in the House of Commons (the leader's office grew considerably in size). The policy directorate's function was re-orientated towards the dissemination of policy ideas as opposed to their formation. In place of party officials, and alongside their own researchers, senior Labour politicians came to utilise more informal and unorthodox sources, ones less bounded by either the conventions of party politics or traditional commitments. In part, this process built on the establishment of the Institute for Public Policy Research in 1988 but New Labour often drew on the work of two other groups, Demos and Nexus. Demos, a think-tank founded in 1993, deliberately eschewed partisan and ideological policies, while focusing on unusual and imaginative solutions to difficult issues. Nexus consisted of a loosely structured group of academics. Such groups provided a direct strategic input to Blair and senior figures within the party, often on the basis of close personal links. They helped the Labour leadership by-pass traditional sources of policy, which were regarded as inflexible, ideological and conservative. (Vernon Hewitt and Mark Wickham-Jones discuss Labour's policy-making process in relation to Kashmir in chapter 12.)

On entering the Foreign Office, Cook announced his intention to establish a new body to tackle external matters. Ten months later, the Foreign Policy Centre, directed by Mark Leonard, an ex-Demos researcher, was set up to extend the process of policy formation to international affairs. Its launch statement claimed that, 'to be effective, foreign policy must be thought about and "done" differently' (Foreign Policy Centre, 1998). Even if it had been fully trusted, the party's international department had long been amalgamated with its domestic arm: the available resources were a fraction of what they had been during Labour's last term in office between 1974 and 1979. At the same time the party was not entirely at ease with the contribution of well established think-tanks in the realm of foreign affairs such as the Royal Institute for International Affairs (Chatham House). *The Times* commented, 'in opposition Robin Cook, then shadow foreign secretary, was known to have been irritated that Chatham House paid little attention to his views. He was biting in his criticism of a body that he dismissed as a graveyard of ex-diplomats' (24 September 1999). *The Guardian* reported, 'Chatham House never thought of trying to prepare for New Labour' (9 July 1999). The Foreign Policy Centre provided senior figures within the government with an alternative source of policy to that from Foreign Office researchers. Blair was patron of the new Centre, while Cook was its president. The Centre attracted press attention within weeks of formation for its claim that a successful foreign policy required the rebranding of British identity. Its initial focus on the packaging of policy seemed entirely compatible with New Labour's emphasis on spin.

The Third Way and foreign policy

Tony Blair's claim that Labour has pursued a distinct agenda in foreign policy from that of the Conservatives is linked to his espousal of a 'Third Way'.

The term itself is, of course, not original to Blair. His articulation of the concept is frustratingly elliptical and vague. He has used the term in different contexts with different meanings. During the 1997 general election campaign he deployed it to distinguish a path between the corporatism of the 1960s and the neo-liberalism of the 1980s in terms of the United Kingdom's post-war economic development (Blair, 1997c; see also Blair, 1998a). On other occasions he has intended the Third Way to define both a strategy between the old left and the new right, and one between the European model and that of the United States (see Blair, 1999a). The values by which Blair has defined the Third Way are also inconsistent. Speaking to the French national assembly, the prime minister declared that the Third Way comprised, among other features, an emphasis on solidarity and tolerance (Blair, 1998c). Later, in a Fabian pamphlet, these elements were dropped. In their place, mutual obligation, internationalism, equal worth and responsibility were added to liberty, opportunity, community and justice (Blair, 1998b). Blair's insistence that the values of the Third Way are those that Labour held in the past and that it is simply the means that have changed does little to reassure those who criticise the approach as one being defined by pragmatism.

Despite these inconsistencies, commentators and academics have given much attention to Blair's pursuit of a Third Way (Giddens, 1998; Hargreaves and Christie, 1998). Many have seen it as an attempt to provide some coherent theoretical underpinning for his administration's policies, one driven by a fear on Blair's part of being labelled opportunistic and utterly pragmatic. Some observers have concluded it to be doomed to failure; others assert that the prime minister is simply trying to give a new gloss to the neo-liberal agenda he has made his own.

The Third Way's alignment with domestic politics can be noted: much of the original debate surrounding it focused exclusively on national and sub-national issues. William Wallace and Neil Stockley charged that the Third Way was of little use in explaining foreign policy: 'The Third Way is at its woolliest here ... There is no sense of a coherent approach to foreign policy' (1998: 23). One Labour MP stated, 'I've no idea about the Third Way: it's an elastic concept' (interview, November 1999). (Rhiannon Vickers looks at the difficulties in using the Third Way as a basis for strategy in chapter 2.)

It is striking, however, that since 1998 Tony Blair has located the Third Way within an international context and has sought to flesh it out as a guide to British foreign policy. Tim Dunne and Nicholas Wheeler discuss this agenda in chapter 4. In their earlier work they represented the Third Way as an attempt to define a model of good international citizenship (Wheeler and Dunne, 1998). Though much of Blair's discussion of the Third Way has concentrated on a domestic agenda, it is noteworthy that his analysis of it has emphasised consistently the transformations to society and to the economy brought about by globalisation. In his Fabian pamphlet, Blair referred to the importance of international co-operation, though in a rather indistinct and bland fashion (1998b: 18). Since its publication, the prime minister has asserted in several speeches his commitment to internationalism in much greater depth. He has justified external intervention in the affairs of nation-states as part of the Third Way: in his speech in Chicago, on the doctrine of the international community, he presented it as an attempt 'to redefine a political programme' (Blair, 1999a). In effect he gave his vision of the kind of good international citizenship that Wheeler and Dunne have identified. In so doing, he adopted a broad definition of what are the United Kingdom's strategic interests.

In Cape Town, in January 1999, Blair accepted that the Third Way was not a purely domestic political phenomenon: 'The Third Way is not just about what happens in our own countries. The political debate today is shaped as much by how a country sees its place in the world as by internal ideological debate' (Blair, 1999b). In Chicago, Blair was blunt in outlining his commitment to intervention and claiming a moral underpinning for such acts: 'our actions are guided by a more subtle blend of mutual self-interest and moral purpose in defending the values we cherish. In the end values and interests merge' (Blair, 1999a). He concluded, 'We are witnessing the beginnings of a new doctrine of international community ... national interest is to a significant extent governed by international collaboration' (Blair, 1999a). The prime minister articulated a consequentialist justification for NATO's action over Kosovo: 'One of the reasons why it is now so important to win the conflict is to ensure that others do not make the same mistake in the future' (Blair, 1999a).

The Third Way provided Blair with a normative explanation for intervention in international crises and for direct interference in what might be considered the sovereign affairs of other nations, even without the support of the international community. Articulating an evidently controversial claim, he argued in his South African speech that action was necessary on occasion:

> The international community has a responsibility to act ... Sometimes, if collective action cannot be agreed or taken in time [this will be] through countries with a sense of global responsibility taking on the burden. People say you can't be self-appointed guardians of what's right and wrong. True, but when the international community agrees certain objectives and then fails to implement them, those who can act, must. (Blair, 1999b)

Between 1994 and 1997, Blair's political vision as leader of the opposition frequently emphasised the mutual interdependence of rights and responsibilities. One of his early set-piece lectures was entitled 'The rights we enjoy reflect the duties we owe'. In such speeches as the Chicago and South African ones, he extended the logic of this approach to the international arena. Nations that wanted rights must accept responsibilities. This claim echoed one made in his 1997 general election speech in Manchester: 'We believe that membership of the international community carries with it responsibilities as well as rights. And that is why we will work with others to ensure the promotion of democratic values, respect for human rights, the rule of law and the protection of the global environment' (Blair, 1997a: 9).

In office, Blair sought to enforce such responsibilities, utilising force where it was required, most obviously in the case of Kosovo. He was blunt about such interventions. Articulating an ambitious objective, Blair proposed that Labour would shape the norms of international behaviour according to what it considered to be moral. It would act, where necessary, without the UN; other institutional arrangements such as NATO or bilateral agreements, for example with the United States, would suffice as the basis for interventions. The war in Kosovo was 'a just war, based not on territorial ambitions, but on values' (Blair, 1999a). The prime minister was resolute in instigating NATO's military offensive against Serbia and in defending the action on moral grounds. Press reports suggested he was tougher than US president Bill Clinton, who was constrained by public hostility to any deployment of ground troops. Writing in *Newsweek* for an American audience, Blair criticised Major's Conservative government for prevaricating over the Balkans: 'In Bosnia we waited for years before taking action decisively ... NATO has not made the same mistake in Kosovo' (Blair, 1999c). Blair reiterated his consequentialist claims about the war in strong language: 'In this conflict we are fighting not for territory but for values. For a new internationalism where the brutal repression of whole ethnic groups will no longer be tolerated. For a world where those responsible for such crimes will have nowhere to hide' (Blair, 1999c). In June 1999, again in *Newsweek*, he repeated his claims of a new internationalism and argued that NATO's actions represented 'a new moral crusade' (Blair, 1999d).

Blair was not alone in taking a broad view of the United Kingdom's interests. George Robertson, Labour's defence secretary, said, 'I want our armed forces not only to defend our country, but to be a force for good, in a very complicated and a very difficult new world that we're facing' (Robertson, 1997: 2). Robertson went on to commit Labour to spend money 'even when our national interests are not directly engaged'. How different such a strategic orientation is to the claim of post-war administrations that the United Kingdom should 'punch above its weight' is an unresolved matter. Some argued that such interventions were not the basis for a new approach: one Labour politician concluded, 'Intervention is not new. Sovereignty has been breached before. Third Way advocates might seek to take it on. But it is not new. It tells you more about the prime minister' (interview, November 1999). Others disagreed: Tony Lloyd argued, 'International law was based historically on the rights of the nation state. Nation against nation. But new conflicts are not like that ... Tony Blair was saying that we must redesign the antennae of the international community ... a recognition that you can't sit on the sidelines and say that it is nothing to do with you' (interview, November 1999). Denis MacShane, a Labour MP, claimed, 'what happens within a state is no longer a private matter for the sovereign ... Historically, the most interesting aspect of New Labour's foreign policy was Robin Cook's quiet burial of the doctrine of non-intervention' (MacShane, 1998/99: 23).

One other feature of Blair's interest in the Third Way worth noting is his close relationship with Bill Clinton, the US president between 1992 and 2000 (see King and Wickham-Jones, 1999). The two enjoyed an intimate friendship that flourished in meetings before Blair became prime minister. New Labour copied many of the features of Clinton's 'New Democrats' that had helped him to election victories in the United States in 1992 and 1996. In office this relationship was confirmed. A few weeks after the May 1997 election Clinton addressed the new Labour cabinet. This meeting was followed by further talks in Washington in February 1998, which included a 'brain-storming session' on the future of the centre-left. Further meetings, among others, on the theme of the Third Way were held in Washington in September 1998 and Florence in November 1999. As noted above, Blair was strongly supportive of US foreign policy, more so than many European states. Clinton backed New Labour's initiative to re-energise the Northern Ireland peace process, culminating in the 'Good Friday' agreement of 1998. The overall result was that Anglo-US relations were warmer than for many years (despite a trade dispute between Europe and the United States in 1999). Clinton and Blair's special relationship went beyond that enjoyed even by Ronald Reagan and Margaret Thatcher in the 1980s. Likewise Cook established a close though somewhat tempestuous relationship with his US opposite number, Madeleine Albright. (UK–US relations are scrutinised by Richard Hodder-Williams in chapter 14.)

Just how closely Tony Blair's Third Way corresponds to Robin Cook's ethical initiative is an open question (and is addressed in several of the contributions to this volume). On the face of it there appears to be a manifest tension between the two. In foreign policy, Blair's Third Way provides a justification for interventionist acts. Cook's ethical turn of May 1997 focused more on human rights and the regulation of arms sales. Blair gave only one speech on foreign policy during his first year of office and a reference to its ethical dimension was added only at the last minute: 'human rights may sometimes seem an abstraction in the comfort of the West but when they are ignored, human misery and political instability all too easily follow' (Blair, 1997b; see Kampfner, 1999). There have been persistent press reports of tensions between the prime minister and his foreign secretary. Despite these apparent strains, both have widened the concept of an ethical foreign policy to include such issues as drugs, crime and terrorism.

Robin Cook was one of a few ministers within the government to pick up on the concept of the Third Way. He did so in both a domestic and an international context (Cook, 1998a, 1998b). His deployment of the term was in part a reflection of his own political weakness at that time. The foreign secretary argued that the entrenchment of ethical objectives within foreign policy was an indication of the Third Way at work: 'It [the Third Way] is not to accept the polarisation of blazing rows about human rights or else leave your values behind in Britain and go out simply to seek commercial contracts. You can pursue economic co-operation without being

silenced on human rights' (*New Statesman*, 1 May 1998). In his review of
the first year in office, the foreign secretary concluded, 'We have shown that
in foreign policy as well as domestic policy, there is a Third Way. We have
emphatically not sought to lecture or hector. We have instead built genuine
partnerships, that make a practical difference in improving the observance
of human rights' (Cook, 1998b: 5). The foreign secretary argued that the
Third Way was about promoting co-operation, not conflict. Hence, a new
and realistic dialogue over human rights was an important part of policy.
As such, the Third Way could be taken as a manifestation of his ethical
dimension.

Cook's emphasis on an ethical dimension is also compatible with the
emphasis placed by New Labour on a duty to intervene. Arguably, the weight
placed by Cook on dialogue and that by Blair on intervention were compatible
as different strategies, both suited to appropriate circumstances. Over Kosovo,
the two politicians had an agreed and clear view of what should be done:
negotiations were to be followed, if necessary, by a NATO offensive. Cook
proved to be as tough as Blair in taking military action. Like Blair, he
suggested that the Conservatives had been too weak during the early and
mid-1990s. John Lloyd reported, 'He [Cook] believes, too, that the Dayton
accord negotiated with Slobodan Milosevic appeased and encouraged Milosevic
when he should have been confronted and beaten' (*New Statesman*, 5 July
1999). The foreign secretary adopted a form of consequentialist argument,
close to that of Blair: 'Around the world tyrants and dictators will see what
happened here and may reflect more closely before they defy international
norms on human behaviour' (quoted by Lloyd, *New Statesman*, 5 July 1999).
Cook claimed a humanitarian impulse for military action. He told the 1999
Labour party conference, 'Gross breaches of humanitarian law are the
business of all humanity ... What prompted us to intervene, what motivated
us to maintain the resolve of the alliance, was our values – freedom, justice,
compassion, basic human decency' (Cook, 1999a: 9). At that conference,
a similar line, combining intervention with a humanitarian stance, was
articulated by Labour's National Policy Forum: 'In this global community
we can no longer separate what we want to achieve within our borders from
what we face across our borders' (National Policy Forum, 1999: 6).

Though tensions remain over such matters as arms sales, from this
perspective Blair's Third Way can be reconciled with Cook's ethical approach.
One Labour MP concluded, 'On actual policies, there is not much practical
difference between Cook and Blair. A different vocabulary perhaps ... Robin
has to preserve his credibility ... Blair has to reconcile different departments'
(interview, November 1999). The commentator Donald MacIntyre went further
and said of the foreign secretary's performance over Kosovo, 'Most importantly,
Mr. Cook's much derided promotion of an ethical foreign policy has found
its cause, one that Mr Blair has also pursued using remarkably similar
language' (*The Independent*, 10 June 1999). John Kampfner argued that Cook's
ethical initiative 'was retrospectively given a new military interpretation –

in effect, armed action was a legitimate means of imposing western liberal values on those who violated democracy' (Kampfner, 1999: 253).

Nicholas Wheeler and Tim Dunne (1998) argued that the ethical dimension could be combined with the Third Way and suggested that New Labour had adopted a new trajectory in foreign policy. They defined this trajectory by the new identity projected by the Blair administration, the language deployed, a commitment to an ethical dimension, support for human rights and variations to the policy-making process. Of course, other scholars were much less certain about the extent to which the tensions in an ethical approach could be resolved. In part, this judgement reflected the view that the new administration had not delivered its promised re-orientation of foreign policy. Widely different interpretations of Labour's record in office have been articulated.

In the autumn of 1999, at the Lord Mayor's banquet, Blair outlined his vision of the United Kingdom's role in the world:

> Nearly forty years ago Dean Acheson's barb – that Britain had lost an Empire but not yet found a role – struck home. Successive generations of British politicians tried –unsuccessfully – to find a way back ... However, I believe that search can now end. We have a new role ... not as a superpower but as a pivotal power, as a power that is at the crux of the alliances and international politics which shape the world and its future. (Blair, 1999e)

The concept of a pivotal power was one Blair had raised in November 1997 (Blair, 1997b). Two years later it was at the centre of his speech. He claimed that his Chicago speech had outlined 'an agreed framework for intervention'. There were, he accepted, limits to what the United Kingdom could do. Over Russian action in Chechnya, intervention was 'neither feasible nor desirable'. The United Kingdom's response to Indonesian action in East Timor (contributing to the peacekeeping force), however, illustrated the validity of the criteria laid out in Chicago. Blair concluded, 'we can be a power that is pivotal, dynamic and capable' (1999e).

Labour in office: foreign policy in practice

After Cook's initial enthusiasm on entering office, Labour's determination to ensure that there was an ethical dimension to foreign policy proved problematic and controversial. In part, the government's difficulties were political and personal. In the summer of 1997, on the eve of a holiday in the United States, Cook split up with Margaret, his wife of many years, as a tabloid newspaper revealed he was having an affair with his secretary. The split proved to be a bitter one as his by then ex-wife publicly questioned the foreign secretary's judgement and abilities in a series of very public revelations. The effect of Cook's divorce was to weaken considerably his political standing within the government, leaving him, for a time at any rate, as a very isolated figure.

Much more substantively, several of Labour's initiatives proved to be disappointing in their apparent ethical content. (Persistent critics included Nick Cohen of *The Observer*.) As noted above, the administration endorsed existing arms exports to Indonesia on the grounds that it was impractical to backdate changes to the rules. Tony Lloyd told the Foreign Affairs Committee that the existing licences were 'a matter of inheritance, not a matter of ambition' (Foreign Affairs Committee, 1998: vol. II, 150). Later the government's interpretation of the brief concerning existing contracts was challenged: 'Advice by Whitehall lawyers that the incoming Labour government could not revoke the contracts is now widely regarded as inaccurate' (*The Guardian*, 8 September 1999). New guidelines were issued in July 1997. Those seeking tough controls were disappointed. Cook's new criteria for the sale of arms included giving full weight to 'the protection of the UK's essential strategic industrial base' (Cook, 1997c). The phrase 'might be used' replaced 'likely to be used' in the existing guidelines covering weapons that could be used for internal repression (Kampfner, 1999: 146). Draft guidelines for a European Union (EU) code of conduct on arms sales, prepared during the UK presidency, were criticised by both Oxfam and Amnesty International (BBC news website, 24 May 1998). They were finally agreed in June 1998.

Labour in opposition had promised stricter rules to control the diversion of arms exports from their original destination to a third country. It was an issue that had been central to the Scott inquiry. Both Robin Cook and Tony Lloyd pursued the theme before the 1997 general election. Discussing a case involving Zaire, Cook concluded, 'There is clearly a need to change the law to ensure that companies do not evade arms embargoes by shipping supplies of weapons from third countries' (Labour party press release, 19 November 1996). When arms went from the Isle of Man to Rwanda, Lloyd said, 'The government must take action to close the legal loopholes which allow British companies to evade arms embargoes by exporting arms through third countries' (Labour party press release, 21 January 1997). In February 1997, the final point of eight in a Labour party policy statement read:

> The Scott Inquiry Report demonstrated the extent of diversionary routes used by Iraq to acquire defence equipment through third countries using false end-use certificates. Labour will strengthen monitoring of the end-use of defence exports to prevent diversion to third countries and to ensure that exported equipment is used only on the conditions under which the export licence has been granted. (Labour party, 1997b)

Once elected to office, Lloyd flagged the issue: 'We shall also take steps to strengthen the monitoring of end-use of defence exports to prevent diversion to third countries' (Lloyd, 1997). However, slow progress was made on the issue. Oxfam criticised the government over its failure: 'much more can and needs to be done' (BBC news website, 15 December 1998; *Sunday Telegraph*, 11 October 1998). In the summer of 1999, Geoff Hoon, a Foreign Office

minister, admitted that 'no formal mechanisms exist at present for systematically monitoring the use of British defence equipment once it has been
exported' (*The Guardian*, 8 September 1999).

Critics claimed that the pattern of arms exports from the United Kingdom
under Labour appeared little different from that established under the
Conservatives. A memo from the Campaign Against the Arms Trade for the
Foreign Affairs Committee compared January–June 1996 (under the Conservative government) with May–November 1997 (under Labour) for licences
to export to Indonesia and Turkey. Under the Conservatives, three licences
were refused for Indonesia and one for Turkey. Forty-three and sixty-three
respectively were granted. Under Labour, four were refused for Indonesia and
one for Turkey. Twenty-two and seventy-two were granted respectively (Foreign
Affairs Committee, 1998: vol. III, 273–4). The *Sunday Times* reported in
March 1999 that under Labour even more arms were going to Indonesia
than had been the case under the Conservatives, as a result of an increase
in the sales of small arms (14 March 1999).

It took time for the government's promised annual report on arms exports
to appear: that for 1997 was published in March 1999, that for 1998 in
November 1999 (FCO, Department of Trade and Industry (DTI) and Ministry
of Defence (MoD), 1999a, 1999b). The figures for 1998 were: just under
10,000 standard individual export licences granted, seven revoked and 122
applications rejected. The government had consulted other countries over
seven applications. The report was informative, though the detail included
in it was not as explicit as had been intended originally. Arguably, the new
guidelines, despite the concerns over human rights and internal conflict,
were being interpreted in a weak fashion: 'a significant number [of licences]
were to countries which have been accused by human rights organisations
of abuses' (*The Times*, 4 November 1999). The estimated value of military
equipment exports in 1998 was just under £2 billion (FCO, DTI and MoD,
1999b: 131). This figure represented a fall from £3.3 billion in 1997 (FCO,
DTI and MoD, 1999a: 111). Sales to Saudi Arabia fell from £1.6 billion to
£800 million. The overall fall may have reflected the economic crisis in the
Far East as much as the impact of the new rules. (Interestingly, Richard
Norton-Taylor gave a much higher figure of £6.25 billion for arms exports
in 1998 – *The Guardian*, 2 September 1999.)

In opposition Cook had criticised the proportion of export credits related
to the defence sector: 'Under the Tories, the percentage of ECGD [Export
Credit Guarantee Department] cover for military equipment has increased
from seven per cent of all capital goods cover to a staggering forty-eight per
cent' (Cook, 1997d). He did not promise to reverse the proportion but he
did offer better regulation of the arms trade. The proportion of capital goods
cover fluctuates between the defence sector and other areas from year to year.
In 1998/99, it is striking that fifty-two per cent of new cover for capital goods
went to defence (ECGD, 1999: 5). This proportion was higher than any given
in the previous four years (which saw defence at around twenty per cent).

Chris Brown suggested that Labour had abandoned the argument that the United Kingdom should continue to sell weapons because 'if we do not do it someone else will' (1999: 22). Since entering office, Labour has been concerned to ensure that arms manufacturers in other countries do not meet any demands where the UK government has rejected licence applications. The European code was designed with this intention. Launching new UK controls, Cook couched his argument in slightly different language while making the same point: 'It will be important to avoid a situation in which our policy of seeking to prevent certain regimes from acquiring certain equipment is undermined by foreign competitors supplying them' (Cook, 1997c). Later he noted, 'It will not work if we are the only ones to follow these standards' (Cook, 1998c).

Arms sales to Indonesia were a particular focus for critics of the government ('The great blot on the credibility of Mr. Cook and the government' – The Independent, 16 September 1999). The Observer (5 September 1999) reported that only 2.4 per cent of applications to sell to Indonesia had been rejected in 1998. It was only under mounting pressure, as the crisis in East Timor (annexed by Indonesia in 1975) worsened, that Labour took action in September 1999. Nick Cohen concluded polemically, 'Robin Cook is finished as a serious politician' (The Observer, 12 September 1999). Arms exports were finally suspended after the United States had introduced similar measures. In a reflection of differences within the Labour administration, it was reported that Cook, having pushed for the decision for a week, was 'where he wanted to be after personal unhappiness' at the original stance taken by the government (The Guardian, 13 September 1999). The Observer commented, 'Large moral claims have to be backed by action, even if costly, and there has to be consistency'. It concluded, 'We have sabre-rattled but dragged our feet as soon as any decision involved hard cash' (12 September 1999). An Independent leader was scathing: 'The Labour government, by contrast [to the Conservatives] likes the moral high horse – while seemingly doing under-the-table deals with as much enthusiasm as the Tories ever did. In short: no change, except for an added dose of hypocrisy' (16 September 1999). It went on: 'Certainly the words are more impressive than the deeds. The ethical foreign policy now looks threadbare at best.'

It had been stated earlier that the DTI had helped reschedule debt to help fund the Hawks (The Times, 15 September 1999) and that Stephen Byers, the secretary of state at that department, had overruled civil servants on aid to Indonesia (The Guardian, 15 September 1999). Press stories indicated that diplomats as well as officials at the MoD and the DTI had opposed the suspension of arms sales: The Times commented, 'Diplomats argued that cancellation looked provocative. But as European partners pushed for a general arms embargo and the United States adopted a harsher tone, Britain looked out of step' (23 September 1999). The disagreements led to an extraordinary outburst from Ken Purchase, a Labour MP and Cook's parliamentary private secretary:

In the end, all of these are a compromise. Robin did everything he possibly could to progress with policies which he felt were right. In the end you make an agreement with your colleagues. The DTI was very anxious to be a friend of business and industry. Business and industry mercilessly exploits that position. At the end of that rearguard action, or whatever you call it, reason has, I believe, prevailed. (Quoted by *The Independent*, 17 September 1999)

Inter-departmental conflict was unsurprising: press reports between 1997 and 1999 suggested splits between the foreign secretary and his prime minister over arms sales and the guidelines that regulated them. John Kampfner reported that Saferworld, a non-governmental organisation (NGO), had proposed that the guidelines should take a tough line on weapons that might be used for internal repression and that there should be a presumption of rejection for certain countries of concern (Kampfner, 1999: 145–6). Some of these proposals were included in a draft set of guidelines. Downing Street insisted on watering down the content and tone of the guidelines. In September 1997, when the Foreign Office blocked two contracts to Indonesia, Downing Street was reported to be infuriated at both the decision and the publicity as Cook claimed, 'It certainly does demonstrate that we have put in place tougher criteria' (Kampfner, 1999: 171). The DTI and the MoD moderated the details to be included in the annual report on arms exports on the grounds that the original proposals would damage UK competitiveness (*Sunday Telegraph*, 11 October 1998). On another occasion the International Development Committee concluded, 'It is clear that the DTI has yet to take on board effectively the human rights and conflict concerns which are at the heart of development policy' (*The Guardian*, 5 August 1999).

The difficulties of operating strict guidelines as part of an ethical policy were brought into sharp focus in 1998 by the 'Sandline affair', also known as 'arms-to-Africa'. It emerged that a British company had exported weapons and supplied mercenaries to help restore the democratic government of Sierra Leone. The objective was laudable to most but involved an apparent breach of UN guidelines (which the United Kingdom had helped to draft) and government policy. Cook denied the Foreign Office had informed him of the situation (a stance that did not promote good relations with his staff). Critics claimed this showed that he was not in charge of his own department. Blair, by contrast, simply brushed aside criticisms with the observation that the desired ends had been secured. One Labour politician described Blair's comments as 'unfortunate', presumably because the prime minister did not address the means deployed in securing such an outcome (interview, November 1998). (Kevin Theakston discusses the episode in chapter 7.)

On some issues, such as over Iraq, the Blair administration proved its mettle, while on others, including, initially at any rate, alleged Serbian atrocities in Kosovo, it proved reluctant to sanction intervention. (Will Bartlett discusses the Serbian case in chapter 8.) Some commentators argued that the inter-ventionist stance adopted by Blair on some issues owed more to his close relations with the US president, Bill Clinton, than to the merits of the case

concerned. Blair endorsed US raids against alleged terrorists in the Sudan
and Afghanistan in August 1998. He was quick to support and participate
in US military initiatives against Iraq in December 1998 when Saddam Hussain
refused to comply over weapons inspections. On both occasions the United
Kingdom acted out of step with some of its European partners. (Its position
may have reflected better intelligence and an ability to act decisively in such
matters in the absence of coalition governments. France, of course, has
strong commercial and historic links with Iraq.) Over Serbian atrocities in
Kosovo, the United Kingdom was slow to support European sanctions. In the
summer of 1998 the government hesitated about the implementation of a
ban on flights to and from Yugoslavia, claiming it would take a year to implement because of contractual arrangements. An EU Commission official stated,
'this is really baffling from a government which claims to have an ethical
foreign policy' (*The Independent*, 16 September 1998). The Foreign Affairs
Committee commented, 'The British government alone of the EU member
states initially took the position that there were legal difficulties in implementing the ban straightaway' (1998: vol. I, xli). Cook instigated the ban on 16
September 1999. In the event of military action in the spring of 1999, the
United Kingdom played an important role in galvanising support within NATO.

A trip by Queen Elizabeth II to India in 1997 had earlier raised troubles
for the government when Cook became bogged down in the long-running
dispute between India and Pakistan over the status of Kashmir. In apparently
off-the-record comments, he offered to mediate between the two sides. The
Indian government responded unfavourably to Cook's intervention by snubbing
the Queen. Press reaction in the United Kingdom was adverse to the foreign
secretary's performance. (In chapter 12 Vernon Hewitt and Mark Wickham-
Jones assess Labour's policy towards Kashmir.) A further foreign trip by Cook,
this time to Israel in March 1998, went equally badly. The foreign secretary
enraged the Israeli authorities by visiting, apparently in breach of an earlier
undertaking, a controversial Jewish settlement and meeting (briefly) a leading
Palestinian official.

The United Kingdom's relations with Iran improved under Labour: previously they had been hampered by the fatwa or death sentence pronounced
in 1989 over the author Salman Rushdie, following the publication of his book
The Satanic Verses. Some commentators concluded, however, that the improvement owed less to the lifting of the fatwa (which remained shrouded in
uncertainty) than to a desire to advance the United Kingdom's trade performance (the issues are discussed by Davina Miller in chapter 11). In July 1999,
the United Kingdom and Libya resumed diplomatic relations after a break
of fifteen years. The resumption followed an agreement where the Libyans
accused of planting the bomb on a Pan Am jet which exploded over Lockerbie
in Scotland in 1988 would stand trial in the Netherlands under Scottish law.

The government's record on human rights was as disappointing to some
as its performance on arms exports. Cook placed human rights firmly on
Labour's foreign policy agenda. Of the measures outlined in his July 1997

speech, his emphasis was on dialogue. He claimed that dialogue provided the basis for a constructive engagement: his approach was, he argued, differentiated both from the unprincipled pursuit of self-interest through commercial deals and from the sacrifice of all other goals in order to take a purist position regardless of the cost in terms of trade. Many countries proved, however, to be unreceptive to this dialogue and to Cook's emphasis on human rights. At the time of an overseas visit by the foreign secretary, his Malayan counterpart stated, 'I think on human rights it is very difficult to have one common yardstick that is universally applicable' (BBC news website, August 1997). The Indonesian government proved equally impervious to Labour's initiative, threatening to buy arms elsewhere. Its foreign minister was defiant: 'We would have to look at other sources and those, I can tell you, are very much available' (BBC news website, August 1997). The Foreign Affairs Committee concluded of Labour's dialogue with Indonesia, 'While this policy may have been conceived with the best of intentions, its implementation seems to have been seriously flawed' (1998: vol. I, xliv). The Committee called for more co-ordination within government, clearer principles to provide a framework for policy and a greater analytical context to the administration's annual report on human rights. It was important that dialogue did not become an end in itself.

To further constructive engagement, the United Kingdom did not, as in previous years, back the annual resolution which criticised China at the UN Commission on Human Rights (Kampfner, 1999: 218). The failure to act against China led some to claim that the government's ethical dimension was subordinate to commercial concerns. Donald Anderson noted, 'It is easy to be tough on weak countries, or countries where we don't have significant interests, such as Myanmar, and soft on powerful countries such as China' (1999: 12). Malcolm Rifkind, Cook's predecessor as foreign secretary, commented, 'There has also been a curious inconsistency in the need for a stronger emphasis on human rights' (*New Statesman*, 23 October 1998). One dissident was blunter about Cook's claims: 'He obviously isn't as involved in fighting human rights as he makes himself out to be. If you make empty promises on human rights, that indicates that the ethical policy is no more than a political slogan' (quoted by Kampfner, 1999: 218). Mr Lee, of the Hong Kong Democratic party, was equally cutting: 'It looks like an economic foreign policy to me' (BBC news website, 10 October 1998). A visit by the Chinese leader, Jiang Zemin, in October 1999, which saw heavy-handed policing of human rights protesters, did little to reassure many that the priority in Sino-British relations was human rights and not trade.

The Labour government's record

Unsurprisingly, the Blair administration claimed a more positive record in its foreign policy. Cook wrote:

> Britain's foreign policy has changed dramatically since New Labour came to power on May 2, 1997. We have pushed human rights up our foreign policy agenda, strengthened our relationship with the Islamic world, toughened our stance on war criminals in Bosnia, and helped to broker the agreements on climate change in Kyoto and Buenos Aires. (Cook, 1999b: 84)

The government's first annual report maintained that Labour had improved relations with Europe, re-establishing British influence. Once again, the United Kingdom was able, Labour asserted, to provide leadership in the world. Tony Lloyd stated, 'By far the most important change in foreign policy has been towards Europe: there has been a quantum leap' (interview, November 1999). One Labour MP commented, 'We were totally isolated under the Conservatives. We had no serious influence ... Now we are seen as a team player, much more involved' (interview, November 1999). (Angela Bourne and Michelle Cini address Labour's relations with Europe in chapter 10.) In its annual report, the government also cited the decision to set up the Department for International Development and initiate a new approach to overseas aid (*Government's Annual Report 97/98*, 1998). A white paper, *Eliminating World Poverty*, was published on development in November 1997. It rejected any link between aid and trade: 'The Aid and Trade Provision (ATP) lacks poverty elimination as its central focus; no more applications will be accepted for ATP assistance, and the scheme will be closed down' (Department for International Development (DFID), 1997: 45). It also emphasised human rights and promised to reverse the decline in government spending on aid. The extent to which the programme marked a departure was open to question (see Burnell, 1998). Later initiatives on debt relief, sponsored by Gordon Brown, the chancellor, and Clare Short, as secretary of state for development, might also be seen as contributions to the government's ethical dimension.

The administration banned landmines and the export of torture equipment during its first year. It had introduced the new guidelines for arms exports, followed by a European code of conduct in 1998 and the publication of an annual report on sales of military equipment from 1999 onwards. A white paper on strategic exports in July 1998 took up some of the themes raised in the Scott report in exploring parliamentary accountability and what might be the basis for tighter procedures (DTI, 1998). Announcing the new guidelines in July 1997 Cook claimed that they, as well as other measures, meant the government had taken four of the steps it had laid out in opposition (Cook, 1997c). Tony Lloyd argued:

> We were aware of the problems of arms sales [in terms of their economic importance]. Opening the books was always going to be difficult but transparency is an important principle of any policy ... We now have probably the most transparent reporting of arms sales in the world. The debate has moved onto a terrain that was not available to previous governments. (Interview, November 1999)

Faced with the legacy of existing licences on entering office, by 1999 the impact of the new approach was tangible. Cook told *The Times*, 'Nobody in this government need be defensive over arms sales' (25 September 1999). In contrast to the *Sunday Times* report quoted above, he pointed to 'the collapse in sales to Indonesia over the last two years'. According to the annual report on arms exports, Indonesia bought £112 million worth of military equipment in 1997 and £72 million in 1998 (FCO, DTI and MoD, 1999a: 113; FCO, DTI and MoD, 1999b: 129). Peter Hain, minister at the Foreign Office, gave different figures: 'under the last full year of the Tory government, they sold £443 million worth of arms to Indonesia. Under the first full year of the Labour government that was £2 million' (BBC news website, 3 November 1999). Earlier, Cook had claimed that a different pattern of arms sales was emerging, complaining that regimes were still able to use equipment that 'would, of course, not have been sold under the new criteria which we have brought in' (BBC news website, 25 January 1999). He maintained, 'There has been a big difference in what we would sell' (*The Guardian*, 25 January 1999).

Labour's foreign secretary argued that the Balkans provided a significant contrast between his government's policy and that of the Conservatives: 'If I were to look for specific examples of what we have done in the past eight months which were different, first of all I would begin with Bosnia where we have taken a much more robust policy and focused much harder and taken tougher measures to save the Dayton accord' (Foreign Affairs Committee, 1998: vol. II, 46). Labour's approach was characterised by a determination to bring war criminals to justice (little progress had been made under the Conservatives on this matter). In its second annual report, in 1999, the government emphasised its actions in Kosovo. It cited the establishment of the International Criminal Court (about which the Conservatives had been very reluctant); the launch of the Defence Diversification Agency; and the agreement with Libya over the terms by which those suspected of the Lockerbie bombing in 1988 would be tried (*Government's Annual Report 98/99*, 1999). In many of these initiatives, such as Kosovo, the government took a leading role. Lloyd argued, 'Britain has been redefining its global role and is seen by others to be more significant in the world. Britain has been significant about this since May 1997, seeking maximum impact in its world role' (interview, November 1999).

Labour politicians argued that a new dialogue over human rights had been established with such countries as China and the Philippines: 'China shows the success of our Third Way in foreign policy' (Cook, 1998b). Tony Lloyd accepted that 'Human rights is a very difficult area. But we have opened up the debate. Doing so, of course, invites criticism ... We have tried to bring in a series of norms' (interview, November 1999). The government claimed that its policy of constructive engagement had raised the human rights agenda and made the issue a mainstream one. An annual report from the Foreign Office and the Department for International Development laid out what the administration had done and there was now a clear strategy within the government (FCO and DFID, 1998, 1999). Cook told the Foreign Affairs Committee, 'There is a much greater priority being given now within the Foreign Office to human rights' (Foreign Affairs Committee, 1998: vol. II, 46). He went on, 'If you want to actually improve human rights, if you want to help those who may be oppressed, the fact of the matter is you have to get into dialogue with those countries who require to be reminded of human rights principles.' *The Independent* quoted Cook: 'By seeking to engage rather than isolate potentially hostile countries, we are increasing our ability to convey our point of view and, however marginally, to influence events' (9 July 1999). The easy option for Labour would have been to downplay human rights issues: 'Clearly the foreign secretary could have avoided much criticism if he had avoided taking the moral high ground' (Anderson, 1999: 9). His was a 'courageous decision'.

Supporters of the government also claimed that there had been a different ethos and style to foreign policy (Labour MP, interview, November 1999). This shift was evidenced by the administration's attitude to NGOs: Cook offered 'a new programme to bring the expertise of groups like Amnesty into the Foreign Office' (Cook, 1998c). Under Labour, the Foreign Office has been much more receptive to groups such as Amnesty International and Save the Children. Briefings for diplomats, personnel exchanges and regular seminars have furthered the input of NGOs to foreign policy. Donald Anderson noted, 'This increased openness in the policy process is also evident in the increased involvement of NGOs in the formulation of policy' (1999: 6).

At the 1999 Labour party conference, Cook claimed a series of successes, including a resolution of the standoffs with Libya and Iran, and better relations with countries as diverse as Argentina and Cuba. The foreign secretary repeated his criticism of Conservative policy over Bosnia:

> Milosevic was beaten in Kosovo. If our predecessors in government had acted as decisively to stop him in the past then we would never have seen the tragedy of Kosovo. Or Bosnia. Since the Serb army pulled out of Kosovo there is a new spirit of hope in Bosnia. The rate at which Bosnian refugees are going back has trebled now they know Milosevic is not coming back. (Cook, 1999a: 1)

He went on to offer a defence of universalistic human rights: 'I find it offensive that the same people should insist on democracy and human rights for Europeans, but insist we should do nothing to defend the same rights of the peoples of Asia, or Africa.'

Commentators and pressure groups differed in their judgements. Some characterised Labour's overall record as mixed. The BBC's review of the government's first year concluded that Labour's trajectory 'might be described as [going in] an ethical direction' (BBC news website, April 1998). It noted the establishment of the DFID, the ban on landmines and the government's work on human rights. NGOs differed over a range of government policies. The Campaign Against the Arms Trade criticised policy on arms exports: 'fine words but at the end of the day nothing ever changes' (*The Independent*, 16

September 1999). Another NGO, Saferworld, praised the annual report on arms as 'the most detailed report published by any European country' (*The Independent*, 16 September 1999). Amnesty offered qualified praise of the Labour administration: 'It is clear that it has made a genuine and active commitment to human rights ... some media criticism has been unduly cynical about attempts to promote human rights' (Amnesty International, 1999: 5). It went on to criticise the DTI and to seek clarification about the importance of human rights policy in relation to trade.

In the autumn of 1998, Cook distanced himself from the concept of an ethical foreign policy, stating bluntly, 'I've given up trying to get this across. I've never used the phrase. I never said there would be an ethical foreign policy' (*New Statesman*, 13 November 1998). One Labour MP stated, 'All the government submitted was that it would ensure that ethical considerations were given higher weight than hitherto' (interview, November 1999). However, some government ministers did use the phrase. For example, Stephen Byers employed it in justifying his policy towards arms sales (*The Independent*, 16 September 1999), and it was deployed on occasion in government documents. For example, the development white paper in November 1997 stated, 'The government has already made clear its commitment to human rights and a more ethical foreign policy' (DFID, 1997: 16). The prime minister used the term in the context of Sierra Leone: 'When people say run an ethical foreign policy, I say Sierra Leone was an example of that' (*Financial Times*, 18 May 1998). The spin placed by the Foreign Office in its mission statement and picked up by the broadsheet press in the summer of 1997 was unmistakable. Moreover, even if Labour did abandon the notion of an all-embracing ethical foreign policy, the concept of a moral dimension remained and the administration continued to assert that its foreign policy marked a departure from that pursued by the Conservatives. Cook continued to deploy the language of human rights prominently in speeches and interviews.

Cook's attempt to distance himself from the concept of an ethical foreign policy proved to be ambiguous. He identified himself as a 'realist with principles' (Foreign Affairs Committee, 1998: vol. II, 51). In his address to the 1999 Labour party conference, quoted above, he returned to ethical themes in a direct and strong fashion. He wanted, he claimed, to 'put a myth to rest'. It was not, however, that he sought to deny Labour's ethical foreign policy – far from it. Cook's contention was that its arms sales policy had been ethical: 'our government has not sold weapons that would suppress democracy or freedom. We rejected every licence to Indonesia when the weapons might have been used for suppression. We refused them sniper rifles, we refused them silenced firearms, and we refused them armoured Land Rovers' (Cook, 1999a: 6–7). He quoted Amnesty International's praise for the government's record and went on to point to an indication of his interventionist commitment: 'no other nation has a higher proportion of its armed forces active on peacekeeping duties around the globe'. (He made a similar point to *The Times*, claiming that the United Kingdom 'makes a much higher proportion of its armed forces available for peacekeeping operations than other members of the security council', 25 September 1999.) The *Sunday Times* pointed out that this level of international activity was unsustainable in the long term, a point admitted in *The Times* by the new secretary of state for defence, Geoff Hoon (3 October 1999; 15 November 1999).

Whatever the detail of Cook's articulation of an ethical foreign policy, by the administration's mid-term point, the phrase and Labour's apparent commitment were established features of contemporary political discourse, used widely throughout the media. The following chapters explore some of the themes laid out above.

References

Amnesty International (1999), *UK Foreign and Asylum Policy Human Rights Audit* (London: Amnesty International).

Anderson, D. (1999), 'The ethical dimension in foreign policy – is there a change?', lecture, 3 February.

Baldry, T. (1998/99), 'New Labour, new foreign policy? A Conservative perspective', *Oxford International Review*, vol. 9, no. 1, 31–3.

Blair, T. (1994), 'Change and national renewal', statement.

Blair, T. (1995), 'Power for a purpose', *Renewal*, vol. 3, no. 4, 11–16.

Blair, T. (1996a), *New Britain. My Vision of a Young Country* (London: Fourth Estate).

Blair, T. (1996b), speech, British American Chamber of Commerce, New York, United States, 11 April.

Blair, T. (1997a), speech, Manchester, 21 April.

Blair, T. (1997b), 'The principles of modern British foreign policy', speech, Lord Mayor's banquet, 10 November.

Blair, T. (1997c), speech, London International Financial Futures and Options Exchange (LIFFE), London, 6 April.

Blair, T. (1998a), speech, Annual Friends of Niewspoort Dinner, the Ridderzaal, The Hague, The Netherlands, 20 January.

Blair, T. (1998b), *The Third Way* (London: Fabian Society).

Blair, T. (1998c), speech, French National Assembly, Paris, France, 24 March.

Blair, T. (1999a), 'The doctrine of the international community', speech, Economic Club of Chicago, United States, 22 April.

Blair, T. (1999b), 'Facing the modern challenge: the Third Way in Britain and South Africa', speech, Cape Town, South Africa, 8 January.

Blair, T. (1999c), 'A new generation draws the line', *Newsweek*, website, 19 April.

Blair, T. (1999d), 'A new moral crusade', *Newsweek*, website, 14 June.

Blair, T. (1999e), speech, Lord Mayor's banquet, 22 November.

Brown, C. (1999), 'On the relationship between ethics and foreign policy', paper presented at the Ethics and Foreign Policy Workshop, University of Bristol, 8–9 June.

Burnell, P. (1998), 'Britain's new government, new white paper, new aid?', *Third World Quarterly*, vol. 19, no. 4, 787–802.

Butler, D. and Kavanagh, D. (1984), *The British General Election of 1983* (Basingstoke: Macmillan).

Butler, D. and Kavanagh, D. (1988), *The British General Election of 1987* (Basingstoke: Macmillan).

Butler, D. and Kavanagh, D. (1997), *The British General Election of 1997* (Basingstoke: Macmillan).

Clark, D. (1997), speech, Defence Forum, London, 11 March.

Cook, R. (1997a), 'British foreign policy', statement, 12 May.

Cook, R. (1997b), 'Human rights into a new century', speech, 17 July.

Cook, R. (1997c), statement, 28 July.

Cook, R. (1997d), speech, Socialist Environmental Resources Association, London, 25 January.

Cook, R. (1998a), speech, Social Market Foundation, London, 24 April.

Cook, R. (1998b), 'The first year', speech, Mansion House, London, 23 April.

Cook, R. (1998c), 'Human rights: making the difference', speech, Amnesty International, London, 16 October.

Cook, R. (1999a), speech, Labour party conference, Bournemouth, 28 September.

Cook, R. (1999b), 'Clean slate Britain and Europe: a new start', *Harvard International Review*, vol. 21 (spring), 84.

DFID (1997), *Eliminating World Poverty. A Challenge for the 21st Century*, cm 3789 (London: TSO).

Downs, A. (1957), *An Economic Theory of Democracy* (New York: Harper Row).

DTI (1998), *Strategic Export Controls*, cm 3989 (London: TSO).

ECGD (1999), *Annual Report and Trading Accounts 1998/99* (London: TSO).

FCO (1997), 'Mission statement', 12 May.

FCO and DFID (1998), *Annual Report on Human Rights* (London: TSO).

FCO and DFID (1999), *Human Rights* (London: TSO).

FCO, DTI and MoD (1999a), *First Annual Report on Arms Exports* (London: TSO).

FCO, DTI and MoD (1999b), *Second Annual Report on Strategic Export Controls* (London: TSO).

Foreign Affairs Committee (1998), *Foreign Policy and Human Rights*, vols I–III, first report, HC369 (London: TSO).

Foreign Policy Centre (1998), statement (London: Foreign Policy Centre).

Giddens, A. (1998), *The Third Way* (Oxford: Polity Press).

Government's Annual Report 97/98 (1998) (London: TSO).

Government's Annual Report 98/99 (1999) (London: TSO).

Hargreaves, I. and Christie, I. (eds) (1998), *Tomorrow's Politics* (London: Demos).

Hay, C. (1994), 'Labour's Thatcherite revisionism', *Political Studies*, vol. 42, no. 4, 700–7.

Hay, C. (1998), 'That was then, this is now: the revision of policy in the modernisation of the British Labour Party, 1992–97', *New Political Science*, vol. 20, no. 1, 7–33.

Hughes, C. and Wintour, P. (1990), *Labour Rebuilt. The New Model Party* (London: Fourth Estate).

Jones, J. (1999), *Labour of Love* (London: Politico's).

Kampfner, J. (1999), *Robin Cook* (London: Phoenix).

King, D. and Wickham-Jones, M. (1999), 'Bridging the Atlantic. The Democratic (Party) origins of welfare to work', in Martin Powell (ed.), *New Labour, New Welfare State?* (Bristol: Policy Press), 257–80.

Labour party (1996), *A Fresh Start for Britain. Labour's Strategy for Britain in the Modern World* (London: Labour party).

Labour party (1997a), *New Labour Because Britain Deserves Better* (London: Labour party).

Labour party (1997b), *Labour's Policy Pledges for a Responsible Arms Trade* (London: Labour party).

Lloyd, T. (1997), speech, Chatham House, London, 9 June.

MacShane, D. (1998/99), 'New Labour, new foreign policy? A Labour perspective', *Oxford International Review*, vol. 9, no. 1, 22–30.

National Policy Forum (1999), *Report to Conference 1999* (London: Labour party).

Oborne, P. (1999), *Alistair Campbell. New Labour and the Rise of the Media Class* (London: Aurum Books).

Reid, J. (1997), speech, Royal United Services Institute, London, 19 February.

Robertson, G. (1997), *On the Record*, BBC website, 26 October 1997.

Seyd, P. (1998), 'Tony Blair and New Labour', in Anthony King *et al.*, *New Labour Triumphs: Britain at the Polls* (Chatham, New Jersey: Chatham House), 49–74.

Sopel, J. (1995), *Tony Blair the Moderniser* (London: Michael Joseph).

Wallace, W. and Stockley, N. (1998), *Liberal Democrats and the Third Way* (London: Centre for Reform).

Wheeler, N. and Dunne, T. (1998), 'Good international citizenship: a Third Way for British foreign policy', *International Affairs*, vol. 74, no. 4, 847–70.

2

Labour's search for a Third Way in foreign policy

Rhiannon Vickers

Introduction

Given the current state of a rather nebulous debate on the 'Third Way', and the beginnings of an attempt to apply it to Labour's foreign policy with its new ethical dimension, it seems timely to highlight the recurring nature of Labour's quest for a principled foreign policy. The Labour party has traditionally argued in opposition that it would pursue a more principled stance in world affairs than the government, if only it was in office. Upon gaining office it is then faced with the dilemma of how to develop a workable foreign policy agenda. This chapter argues that current attempts by the Labour government to develop a Third Way in foreign affairs reflect recurring initiatives and problems that the Labour party has with foreign policy, and places Labour's search for a Third Way into its wider domestic and international political context. It argues that while the Labour government under Blair has attempted to project itself on to the international stage in a fairly systematic way, and to appear to be proactive rather than reactive when it comes to foreign affairs, 'New Labour' is still largely a domestic project and the Third Way provides little real guidance for making foreign policy.

Labour's foreign policy

As Richard Crossman pointed out, 'Labour policy has always been an amalgam' (1952: 2). Nowhere has this proved as much a problem as in the area of foreign affairs. The Labour party, unlike the Conservatives, has always had a problem concerning the fundamental purpose of UK foreign policy. The Conservative party has been content to present foreign policy as the pursuit and protection of UK interests, as the playing out of power politics. There may be disagreements over how to implement this – for example whether to be inside or outside of European integration – but the underlying values remain the same. While Thatcher introduced a more ideological stance to foreign policy with her 'megaphone diplomacy', at the heart of this was the protection of UK interests (Byrd, 1988: 2). The Labour party, however, has historically had a problem with this conception of foreign policy, wanting to go beyond it with a call for foreign policy to be based upon moral purpose. This has been for two main reasons.

First, the Labour party has tended to encompass a wider spectrum of political opinions than the Conservative party and, with its emphasis on party democracy, has given greater importance to its extraparliamentary institutions of policy-making. This has acted as a constraint on the party leadership (Rose, 1980: 146). Given the Labour party's ideological and representational beginnings and, particularly in its early years, the belief that the principles guiding domestic policy could be projected on to the international arena, different factions within the party have pulled foreign policy in different directions. For believers in class struggle, the Labour party's role was to protect working-class interests, internationally as well as nationally. The Liberal influence on the Labour party resulted in the belief in self-determination, international justice and the workings of international organisations, such as the League of Nations, the UN and, more recently, the desire for an international criminal court. For the ethical socialists and nonconformists, pacifism has been an important component of their world view. Thus, as Morgan has pointed out, 'From its earlier history, and especially from the thirties, Labour had inherited a confused bundle of sensations, socialist, populist, neo-pacifist, anti-imperialist, deeply suspicious of reality and power in world affairs' (Morgan, 1987: 154).

The second main reason for Labour's search for a foreign policy that involves more than the protection of national interests has been that, for extensive periods in the twentieth century, Labour's foreign policy has developed while the party has been in opposition rather than in power. As such, it has developed more as a response to the internal dynamics of the party, the tensions between left and right factions, rather than as a response to international events. The result of this has been that Labour has tended to promise an alternative foreign policy when in opposition, seeking a new formulation of foreign policy based on principles that reflect party opinion. It then finds that, once in power, the opinions of rebellious backbenchers become rather less significant compared with the pressures that governments come under from other nations, international organisations and powerful interests such as the arms industry, resulting in a changed foreign policy stance. Such changes should not be overstated, for the adversarial nature of the British party system means that 'What the government does and says, the opposition must usually oppose, if only to keep their supporters happy and maintain their distinctive position' (Bulpitt, 1988: 187). But, despite periodic claims to the contrary, Labour's foreign policy in office has tended to side with realism rather than idealism, however much the party has sought a new formulation for foreign policy while in opposition.

The tensions over foreign and defence affairs have been apparent through-out the Labour party's history, and reveal themselves in recurring issues and themes. One has been over the need to find a new foreign policy position. In the late 1940s this resulted in the idea of the United Kingdom providing a 'Third Force' or 'Third Way' between US capitalism and Soviet communism. Though largely a call from the Labour left, the notion of a Third Force was forwarded and seemingly supported, though briefly, by the Labour leadership (see Schneer, 1984). Another issue has been over Labour's ambivalence towards the use of force. Whether to back the use of force always causes heated debate, as can be seen in the cases of the Boer War, Korea, Vietnam, the Falklands, the Gulf and the former Yugoslavia. Another recurring issue is that of arms sales. There has historically been a conflicting pull between the desire to take the moral high ground by taking a stance against militarism and limiting arms sales on the one hand, and the need to protect jobs within the arms trade on the other. This bifurcation has resulted in both positions being taken at the same time. For instance, as the parliamentary Labour party was voting against the 1936 defence estimates put forward by the Conservative government, Sir Thomas Inskip (the minister for the co-ordination of defence) pointed out in the House of Commons that MPs from both the Labour front and back benches 'besought me to place orders for munitions of war in their constituencies' (*Hansard*, 20 July 1936, cols 315 and 74). During the 1960s Labour had vociferously condemned the sale of arms to South Africa when in opposition. At the Labour party annual conference in 1963, Barbara Castle, speaking on behalf of the National Executive Committee (NEC), declared that:

> I am proud that we have taken an unequivocal stand on this question of an embargo on the export of arms. We accept the Security Council resolution; we intend to operate it ... We know that Buccaneer aircraft are still being made in British factories for South Africa. The order has not been cancelled. We say that a Labour government would cancel that order and substitute a better one. (*LPACR*, 1963: 223)

However, once in power, 'faced with the loss of overseas earnings from the Buccaneer contracts at a time of international financial pressure, plus the legal problems of withdrawing from the contracts, Wilson and his Cabinet colleagues in November 1964 agreed to permit the existing orders to be met' (Wrigley, 1993: 125). This situation has been repeated with the Blair government. In opposition, Robin Cook told the 1995 Labour party conference that 'a Labour government will not license the export of arms to any regime that will use them for internal oppression or external aggression' (*LAPCR*, 1995: 191). In power, it was left to Tony Lloyd to explain to the House of Commons that it would not be 'practical' to backdate the new criteria for arms sales to apply to decisions on licences already taken by the previous administration (Kampfner, 1998: 144).

Another recurring theme is that of the United Kingdom's moral leadership and of a search for a new approach to foreign affairs. At the 1932 Labour party conference, it was emphasised that a Labour government could carry the 'moral leadership of the world' (*LPACR*, 1932: 321). Harold Wilson 'had an almost Gladstonian belief in his own righteousness', which was transferred to foreign policy to the extent that Wilson 'had too high an opinion of Britain's moral and other weight in world affairs – a delusion he shared with many leading CND activists who equally believed that a moral lead by Britain would have a major impact on others' (Wrigley, 1993: 126).

Thus Labour's recent attempts to develop an ethical foreign policy, as part of a Third Way in foreign affairs, are not new, merely the latest development of this tendency, the latest attempt by a Labour government to present a foreign policy that is both credible in the world and acceptable to party members, and that fits intra-party dynamics at leadership level. Neither is the attempt to produce a new foreign policy focus confined to the United Kingdom.

New Labour, the United States and the Third Way

Tony Blair came to power promising a new political standpoint, with a move away from tribal politics. At the heart of this has been his emphasis on the need for a Third Way in politics, beyond left and right. For Blair, the Third Way is 'an attempt to make realistic sense of the modern world. It is a world in which love of ideals is essential, but addiction to ideology can be fatal' (Blair, 1998a). The Third Way represents 'a new politics arising from the ashes of the struggles of the twentieth century between traditional views of capitalism and socialism'. It 'seeks to combine economic dynamism with social justice' (Blair, 1999a). In 1998 Blair held Third Way seminars in London and transatlantic policy seminars with Bill Clinton and some of his advisers. Time was taken at NATO's fiftieth-anniversary celebration to hold a meeting on the Third Way. This attempt to find a new political synthesis, a radical centre beyond left or right, a middle way, is not new, nor confined to the United Kingdom.

The politics of the Third Way contains two aspects, the first of which is the application of systematic political marketing to the issue of centre-left politics. It is the political/electoral strategy of triangulation proposed by Dick Morris, former presidential strategist. In 1994 he was pressing Clinton to 'Triangulate, create a third position, not just in between the old positions of the two parties but above them as well.' 'The president needed to take a position that not only blended the best of each party's views but also transcended them to constitute a third force in the debate' (Morris, 1997: 80).

The second aspect of the politics of the Third Way is the attempt to find an intellectual grounding for and sense of moral purpose to New Labour's policies. While the pursuit of power was an end in itself, having gained power New Labour needs to attach itself to a grand project, a belief system to provide its point of reference, in order to avoid being seen as a purely pragmatic government. Thus developing the new Third Way political trajectory has been 'urgent' for both Blair and Clinton 'because it gives a narrative to both administrations: to Clinton for what he has done, to Blair for what he is about to do' (Lloyd and Bilefsky, 1998: 33). This is reflected in the work of Anthony Giddens, Blair's academic guru, whose book on the Third Way attempted to put 'theoretical flesh' on the 'skeleton' of policy-making by the Labour government, in order 'to provide politics with a greater sense of direction and purpose' (Giddens, 1998: 2).

The politics of the Third Way reflects a somewhat uneasy meshing of these two aspects. Whether and how Labour can apply the Third Way to foreign policy depends on which aspect is seen as the more important. The suspicion is that it is the former of the two elements, the Third Way as electoral strategy, which dominates the Third Way as an intellectual project (see Gould, 1998). This version of the Third Way did not help Clinton come up with a credible foreign policy.

Clinton came to power without having shown much interest in, or having had much experience of, foreign affairs. He 'had no special vision of his foreign policy. He reacted, more or less reluctantly, to global concerns when they intruded so deeply into America's politics that he had to do something' (Morris, 1997: 245). This was demonstrated by the lack of a clear policy or position in Bosnia, Somalia or Kosovo. Unlike Clinton, Blair has, from the start of his administration, attempted to emphasise New Labour's grip on foreign policy. Much of this has drawn on the impact of globalisation. Indeed, he has said that 'The driving force behind the Third Way is globalisation' (Blair, 1999a). The result is an increased commitment to internationalism. Robin Cook, presenting the Foreign Office mission statement, opened with 'This is an age of internationalism' (Cook, 1997) and proceeded to emphasise how the global economy and the information revolution meant that 'We live in a world in which nation states are interdependent. In that modern world foreign policy is not divorced from domestic policy but a central part of any political programme. In order to achieve our goals for the people of Britain we need a foreign strategy that supports the same goals' (Cook, 1997). However, exactly what globalisation, internationalism and the Third Way mean in terms of foreign policy prescription remains unclear, and the thinking behind such statements is that foreign policy is important because of its potential impact on domestic politics and the New Labour project, rather than in itself. In Giddens' book on the Third Way, large sections are devoted to globalisation, as 'Social democrats should seek a new role for the nation in a cosmopolitan world' (Giddens, 1998: 129). However, there is no attempt to translate this into policy terms and there is no mention of either foreign policy or foreign affairs in the book.

Blair has emphasised that the United Kingdom can play a pivotal role in the world but that that means 'charting a new course for British foreign policy':

It means realising once and for all that Britain does not have to choose between
being strong with the US, or strong with Europe; it means having the confidence
to see that Britain can be both. Indeed, that Britain must be both; that we
are stronger with the US because of our strength in Europe; that we are
stronger in Europe because of our strength with the US. (Blair, 1998b)

This is perhaps the clearest statement to date on how the Labour government
views the role of the United Kingdom. However, this is not so very different
from foreign policy under the Conservatives, and Blair does not explain what
this means for British policy towards the EU and how this affects key decisions
such as whether to enter economic and monetary union. The lack of debate
over such key issues suggests that Blair really has little new to say on foreign
affairs. This is because New Labour, like the New Democrats, is a domestic
project, and is intellectually involved at the domestic level to the extent that
foreign policy is sidelined.

The Third Way and foreign policy

It is not immediately apparent how a Third Way can really be applied to
foreign policy, largely because it is so difficult to delineate a clear left/right,
capitalist/social democratic stance in foreign affairs. The Third Way does not
deliver instant solutions to practical problems. The main way that a new,
Third Way, approach to foreign policy has manifested itself so far has been
over the commitment to internationalism, through an increased focus on
ethics and human rights. Certainly the 'ethical dimension' to foreign policy
has been seen by some as a Third Way 'on the global level' (Lloyd, 1998b:
13). This ethical dimension to Labour's foreign policy was heralded in the
Labour party's 1997 general election manifesto, when it was stated that:

> Labour wants Britain to be respected in the world for the integrity with which
> it conducts its foreign relations. We will make the protection and promotion
> of human rights a central part of our foreign policy. We will work for the
> creation of a permanent criminal court to investigate genocide, war crimes and
> crimes against humanity. (Labour party, 1997: 39)

Such rhetoric, while strongly reflected in the Liberal Democrats' manifesto,
was not used by the Conservatives. It does, as has been pointed out above,
have historic antecedents in Labour's foreign policy.

Claims to morality, if not ethics, in foreign policy are not confined to the
United Kingdom. For instance, much of the current debate on an ethical
foreign policy has been predated by developments in Australian foreign policy
in the late 1980s and early 1990s, with its quest for an ethical position based
on good international citizenship (see below), which was in turn influenced
by similar discussions in Canada. The United States in particular has tended
to justify its foreign policy with reference to its moral content, drawing on

the language of freedom and rights to back up its more interventionist stance in the Cold War – the Truman doctrine and Marshall plan speeches being two of the most obvious examples. Jimmy Carter placed human rights on his foreign policy agenda. In the United Kingdom, David Owen wrote a series of speeches and articles that then appeared as a book on human rights while he was Labour foreign secretary in the late 1970s. As he pointed out, events 'have raised the profile of human rights in international affairs and have compelled those who formulate foreign policy – at least in those democratic countries where public concern cannot be ignored by Governments – to give a higher priority than ever before to human rights' (Owen, 1978: 14). It was under Major's Conservative government that the Foreign Office established a committee on human rights. Thus the use of language of human rights and an ethical or moral standpoint in world affairs is nothing new, and a commitment to an ethical or moral stance, however laudable, does not in itself provide the basis for a foreign policy agenda.

Robin Cook has been eager to draw on the Third Way as a point of reference for his foreign policy, though it is not clear to what extent this reflects an agenda laid out by Blair or by himself, and press reports indicate some tensions between the two. At the launch of the Foreign Office mission statement on 12 May 1997, Cook stressed the importance of political values and the need for British foreign policy to have an 'ethical dimension' (Cook, 1997). His stance was reiterated in the House of Commons when he announced on 14 May 1997 that 'The promotion of human rights worldwide will be our priority' (*Hansard*, 14 May 1997, col. 44). As a consequence of this, the Foreign Affairs Committee decided to hold an inquiry into foreign policy and human rights with the aim of examining 'how the Government implements its human rights objectives when formulating and executing foreign policy, both bilaterally and multilaterally, and to assess the extent to which such policy can be effective in preventing or remedying human rights abuses' (Foreign Affairs Committee, 1998: vol. I, v).

The inquiry heard from many academics and NGOs, such as Amnesty and Saferworld, which came up with forty-seven recommendations for British policy. This, along with a number of other developments, represents Labour's concern to take a more ethical standpoint than previous governments with regard to its international commitments. For instance, on 13 May 1997 Cook announced that the United Kingdom would rejoin the United Nations Educational, Scientific, and Cultural Organization (UNESCO). Cook and George Robertson, the defence secretary, announced on 21 May 1997 that the United Kingdom would 'ban the import, export, transfer and manufacture of all forms of anti-personnel landmines' (*Hansard*, 21 May 1997: col. 72). This was ahead of the international decision to ban landmines. There was a commitment to some form of stricter policy on the arms trade. The United Kingdom hosted the international conference on Nazi gold on 2 December 1997, at which Robin Cook gave a key speech. The United Kingdom, unlike the United States, backed the establishment of the International Court of

Justice in July 1998. Cook has continued to signal his belief in human rights through speeches and initiatives, such as members of Amnesty and Save the Children acting as advisers to the Foreign Office on human rights (Cook, 1998). Cook also promised 'a more open, inclusive approach' to the management of foreign relations, which were not to be left to the politicians, and laid out the government's 'commitment to foster a people's diplomacy to increase respect, understanding and goodwill for Britain among nations as well as governments' (Cook, 1997).

Cook has also found that he is not necessarily in a position to implement promises made in opposition and has had to tone down his commitment to an ethical dimension in foreign affairs. While he has promoted how the United Kingdom has been 'leading by cleaning up the arms trade' and has said that Labour has carried out its manifesto commitment not to give any more licences for arms exports that would 'conspire with conflict or abet repression' (*LPACR*, 1997: 133), arms have continued to be exported to Indonesia. Despite realising that 'Brutal, megalomaniac dictators tend to be rather poor at paying their invoices on time' (*LPACR*, 1997: 133), this area of policy has not proved so straightforward and the proposals for the new criteria for arms sales were repeatedly toned down before they were made public (Kampfner, 1998: 145–6; *Hansard*, 28 July 1998, cols 26–9).

The other main issue that has proved to be a recurring embarrassment has been policy towards Sierra Leone. The Sandline affair, where it was found, much to Cook's fury, that the Foreign Office had, at some level, known about the shipment of arms to Sierra Leone (which flouted UN resolution 1132), and the intervention of mercenaries to restore President Kabbah, shot a hole through his attempts to present the Foreign Office as working under a stricter regime than with the Conservatives. His response to this event suggested that he considered that the upholding of UN resolutions was the ethical position to take, whereas Tony Blair suggested that the ends justified the means in restoring Kabbah, who had been democratically elected, to power. Some of the British press agreed.

There have also been foreign policy decisions that do not fit well into this new ethical dimension, representing a gung-ho attitude at odds with a more measured interpretation of a Third Way in politics. Support for the threats, and the decision, to bomb Iraq over its refusal to allow access to the United Nations Special Commission (UNSCOM) weapons inspectors placed the United Kingdom firmly in the US camp. No other European state supported the United States' policy with anything like the same enthusiasm. However, Labour took the moral high ground as Cook and others wrote columns in *The Sun* with titles such as 'Why we dare not ignore terror arsenal' (5 February 1998). Cook presented the threat of the use of force as the 'ethical' option, arguing, 'Here is the link between our opposition to Iraq and an ethical base to foreign policy. We have taken a very strong line against nuclear, chemical and biological weapons. It would be totally inconsistent with that if we were to allow Saddam to remain in possession of weapons of mass destruction'

(Cook, cited in Lloyd, 1998a: 10). This does not, however, get over the problem of the accusation of double standards vis-à-vis Israel and Iraq.

Thus neither Blair nor Cook has yet revealed what the Third Way could really mean for foreign policy. As Wheeler and Dunne point out:

> To date, most of Cook's references to a third way relate to one aspect of the process, that of human rights diplomacy. Despite repeated public statements about the need to put human rights at the heart of foreign policy, the government has not elucidated a conceptual framework for deciding the priority and consistency of the various principles contained in the mission statement.

They propose that 'good international citizenship is the appropriate strategy for a foreign minister negotiating the third way in the world' (Wheeler and Dunne, 1998: 848 and 849). This proposal draws upon the development in Australia of the idea of an ethical foreign policy based upon good international citizenship, propounded in particular by Gareth Evans and the Australian Labor Party. Senator Evans stated that we 'have an interest in being – and being seen to be – a good international citizen'. Good citizenship is 'an exercise in enlightened self-interest: an expression of idealistic pragmatism' and a situation in which 'The balance between idealism and pragmatism in the pursuit of good citizenship will vary from issue to issue'. He called for a vision of Australia's role in the world 'which does not distinguish between internal and external policies, as if the rules of international behaviour are somehow different from the rules governing other human behaviour' (Evans, 1989: 12, 13, 15). Blair has started to develop a new angle on this with his statements on the Kosovo crisis, in particular with his Chicago speech, using the rhetoric of the international community rather than international citizenship.

The crisis in Kosovo and the prospects for an ethical foreign policy

The events in Kosovo highlighted Labour's lack of a clear foreign policy agenda, but also stimulated a new search for a basis for a foreign policy based on the values of the late twentieth century. While Clinton was left looking weak, indecisive, as the recipient of bad advice and as the victim of domestic opinion rather than a leader of it, Blair came forward with a stronger voice on foreign policy. By the time of the NATO Washington summit in April 1999, the American press was running headlines such as 'Blair grabs role as Alliance hawk'. It was said that Blair was not only pushing for a stronger line on Kosovo, but was 'proposing to rewrite the rules of global security for the 21st century' with 'a new doctrine of international community' (*International Herald Tribune*, 24–25 April 1999).

This 'doctrine of international community' was outlined at his speech to the Economic Club of Chicago on 22 April (Blair, 1999b). In this speech,

Blair emphasised that globalisation and increasing interdependence meant that 'We live in a world where isolationism has ceased to have a reason to exist ... We are all internationalists now, whether we like it or not.' As a result, 'We are witnessing the beginnings of a new doctrine of international community.' And, 'The principles of international community apply also to international security.' Further, 'Non-interference has long been considered an important principle of international order ... But the principle of non-interference must be qualified in important respects. Acts of genocide can never be a purely internal matter.' Thus, 'This speech has been dedicated to the cause of internationalism and against isolationism' (Blair, 1999b). The Chicago speech demonstrated more clearly than any other event the role that Blair sees for himself as the initiator of a new doctrine on international community, which in turn he sees as the basis of his foreign policy. This, of course, is as much old Labour as New Labour, being at the heart of many previous foreign policy initiatives. It was the belief in internationalism and an international community that led Labour to pursue its 'League of Nations' policy under Ramsay MacDonald and Arthur Henderson in the 1929–31 minority government. Belief in the international community was even written into the Labour party's constitution, with the commitment to 'the establishment of suitable machinery for the adjustment and settlement of international disputes by conciliation or judicial arbitration and for such other international legislation as may be practicable' (*LPACR*, 1918: 141).

While a new emphasis on international community may provide the basis for Labour's foreign policy, it risks highlighting internal contradictions at the heart of New Labour. At the same time as the Labour government was focused on the plight of the Kosovar refugees, its asylum bill was going through parliament. As one rather caustic article has emphasised, 'The Kosovar Albanians are the victims of the greatest crime of postwar Europe, but as soon as they cross the Channel, they grow horns and become scrounging frauds' (Cohen, 1999: 15). Further problems arise in that an emphasis on the international community, or good international citizenship, as it is currently understood, is not necessarily compatible with the proactive foreign policy stance that Blair is promoting.

First, good international citizenship has in the past been predicated on obeying the rules and laws of the international community and so suggests a rather passive stance to foreign affairs. The decision to make a humanitarian intervention to put a stop to ethnic cleansing in Kosovo by bombing Serb military targets, while reflecting the ethical impulse to prevent atrocities, was seen as breaking the norm of non-intervention. Such contradictions will need to be addressed whether one supports the action or not. Secondly, a focus on good international citizenship and the international community suggests some notion of equality between citizens, which does not fit with Blair's emphasis on the United Kingdom's moral leadership. For instance, in the name of good international citizenship it would make sense for the United Kingdom to relinquish its UN Security Council seat in return for a European seat. The United Kingdom has the option of either accepting its diminished role in the world or of holding on to its resources that provide it with residual power, such as the nuclear deterrent and its Security Council seat. The Labour government is clearly pursuing the second option. Thirdly, the Australian idea of an ethical foreign policy based on good international citizenship (or community) cannot simply be transposed to the United Kingdom, as the two nations have such different histories and expectations. A fourth problem is that the focus on the international community is still quite abstract and does not necessarily result in any answers to the questions of the United Kingdom's relations with its allies within the international community. Blair has pursued a very close relationship with the United States, the one country that could provide leadership in the international community but clearly does not want to. Neither does a focus on good international citizenship provide an answer to what is probably the most important long-term question for the United Kingdom – its role in Europe.

If those heralding a Third Way in foreign policy really got to grips with the last issue, they might conclude that the United Kingdom needs to chart a course that means it is more firmly inside the EU. However, the Third Way as electoral strategy would suggest that Labour should continue its policy of not alarming the voters when it comes to Europe. While Blair has the Third Way as an intellectual project firmly in mind, the desire to be at the head of the first Labour government to serve two full terms in office acts as a constraint on the way that policy is presented to the domestic audience. Chancellor Gordon Brown has touched upon one issue that may herald a Third Way in international affairs with his calls for a regulatory body for global financial markets. This is Third Way in its compromise between free market capitalism and protectionism, but this idea is the result of the domestic agenda being projected on to the global level. The choice of foreign secretary and the absorption of many aspects of the relationship with Europe into the domain of the Treasury and the prime minister's office in 10 Downing Street suggest that the current Labour government is actually trying to avoid delineating any major new foreign policy stance.

Conclusions

There are two features of the Third Way that are especially notable. First, it has been driven by electoral pressures and the domestic political agenda. Second, as a consequence, the Third Way as a solution to the age-old dilemma of what a Labour government is to do about foreign policy is problematic. The Third Way as a compromise between free market capitalism and social democracy has little guidance to offer at the international level. The Third Way as a new foreign policy process, which takes into account the ethical dimension, does not necessarily fit with the domestic concerns of New Labour. The idea of an ethical dimension to foreign policy can be criticised as little more than window-dressing because there has been no systematic attempt really to think through what the results of such a policy basis might be across government departments. For example, the foreign secretary can tighten up arms sales only if he has the support of the DTI, but this is resisted because the DTI has a very different set of priorities to the Foreign Office. Foreign policy will continue to be a problem for the Labour government unless some way is found to integrate it into the heart of the New Labour project and to reconcile the domestic and the international agendas. Creating a modern foreign policy adapted to the challenge of a globalised world will remain impossible unless it becomes feasible to provide 'joined up' government in the foreign policy sphere.

References

Blair, T. (1998a), speech, French National Assembly, Paris, France, 24 March.

Blair, T. (1998b), 'Britain's role in the EU and the transatlantic alliance', speech, one hundred and fiftieth anniversary of the Associated Press, London, 15 December.

Blair, T. (1999a), 'Facing the modern challenge: the Third Way in Britain and South Africa', speech, Cape Town, South Africa, 8 January.

Blair, T. (1999b), 'The doctrine of international community', speech, Economic Club of Chicago, United States, 22 April.

Bulpitt, J. (1988), 'Rational politicians and conservative statecraft in the open policy', in P. Byrd, ed., *British Foreign Policy Under Thatcher* (Oxford: Philip Allen), 180–225.

Byrd, P. (ed.) (1988), *British Foreign Policy Under Thatcher* (Oxford: Philip Allen).

Cohen, N. (1999), 'The great Balkan lie', *New Statesman*, 26 April.

Cook, R. (1997), 'British foreign policy', statement, 12 May.

Cook, R. (1998), 'Human rights: making the difference', speech, Amnesty International, London, 16 October.

Crossman, R. H. S. (1952), 'Towards a philosophy of socialism', in R. H. S. Crossman (ed.), *New Fabian Essays* (London: Turnstile Press), 1–32.

Evans, G. (1989), 'Australian foreign policy: priorities in a changing world', *Australian Outlook*, 43 (3), cited in P. Keal (ed.) (1992), *Ethics and Foreign Policy* (Canberra: Allen & Unwin).

Foreign Affairs Committee (1998), *Foreign Policy and Human Rights*, vols I–III, first report, HC369 (London: TSO).

Giddens, A. (1998), *The Third Way* (Oxford: Polity Press).

Gould, P. (1998), *The Unfinished Revolution: How the Modernisers Saved the Labour Party* (London: Little, Brown).

Kampfner, J. (1998), *Robin Cook* (London: Victor Gollancz).

Labour party (1997), *New Labour Because Britain Deserves Better* (London: Labour party).

Lloyd, J. (1998a), 'Ethics makes the world go round', *New Statesman*, 6 March.

Lloyd, J. (1998b), 'Cook's defence lies in the detail', *New Statesman*, 15 May.

Lloyd, J. and Bilefsky, D. (1998), 'Transatlantic wonks at work', *New Statesman*, 27 March.

Morgan, K. O. (1987), *Labour People: Leaders and Lieutenants, Hardie to Kinnock* (Oxford: Oxford University Press).

Morris, D. (1997), *Behind the Oval Office. Winning the Presidency in the Nineties* (New York: Random House).

Owen, D. (1978), *Human Rights* (London: Jonathan Cape).

Rose, R. (1980), *Do Parties Make a Difference?* (Basingstoke: Macmillan).

Schneer, J. (1984), 'Hopes deferred or shattered: the British Labour left and the Third Force Movement, 1945–49', *Journal of Modern History*, vol. 56, no. 2, 197–226.

Wheeler, N. J. and Dunne, T. (1998), 'Good international citizenship: a third way for British foreign policy', *International Affairs*, vol. 74, no. 4, 847–70.

Wrigley, C. (1993), 'Now you see it, now you don't: Harold Wilson and Labour's foreign policy 1964–70', in R. Coopey, S. Fielding and N. Tiratsoo (eds), *The Wilson Governments 1964–1970* (London: Pinter), 123–35.

Part II

Theoretical perspectives

3

Ethics and foreign policy: a speculative essay

Michael W. Doyle

Introduction

What should we make of statements such as the one by Vaclav Havel that the war in Kosovo was a (perhaps, he says, *the* first) humanitarian war, a war motivated by ethical concern? Havel, president of the Czech Republic, commented, 'This is probably the first war that has not been waged in the name of national interests but rather in the name of principles and values. Kosovo has no oil fields to be coveted ... [NATO] is fighting out of the concern for the fate of others' (*Boston Globe*, 5 July 1999: A14). In a speech before the Canadian parliament, he added: 'Decent people cannot sit back and watch systematic, state-directed massacres of other people. Decent people simply cannot tolerate this, and cannot fail to come to the rescue if a rescue action is within their power' (*Toronto Sun*, 2 May 1999: 38). How do we square the judgement of that widely respected, contemporary statesman with the words of William Wordsworth, that great earlier poet of democratic revolution, with his ever so devastating comment on his times: 'Earth is sick, / And Heaven is weary, of the hollow words / Which States and Kingdoms utter when they talk / Of truth and justice' (Wordsworth, 1814).

To many in our field of international politics, asking just what is the role of ethics in foreign policy is like asking what did Chopin's sonatas contribute to the success of the New York Yankees or Manchester United. But to wiser heads different questions and different answers arise. Arnold Wolfers, Michael Walzer, Stanley Hoffmann, Hedley Bull, Richard Ullman (see below) and a new generation of international relations scholars have identified important markers for the role of ethical judgement in international relations. (The group is becoming increasingly substantial: among these contributions are Brown, 1992; Finnemore, 1996; Frost, 1996; Linklater, 1990; Lumsdaine, 1993.) In 'Human rights and economic power: the US versus Idi Amin' Richard Ullman argued that ethically outrageous treatment by a state of its own citizens could breach national rights to non-intervention and give rise to justified international interference. Governments, especially those with a commitment to human rights, should be 'prepared to say that there are boundaries of decency beyond which other governments must not pass in their treatment of their own citizens' (Ullman, 1978: 540). In this case, Ullman argues, ethical concerns warranted a US boycott of Ugandan coffee, on whose sales the regime was especially dependent, particularly as the impact of the embargo would be felt mostly by the target regime and not by the already victimised ordinary Ugandans. Similar ethical concerns for the well-being and autonomy of people cut the other, non-interventionist, way when regimes with a claim to be furthering the well-being of their population were being interfered with for reasons that we could judge to be remote from an effort to promote the interests of the affected population. The 'not so covert' campaign by the United States against the Sandinistas in Nicaragua fits this latter instance as Richard Ullman showed in 'At war with Nicaragua' (1983). Moreover, by fostering emergency conditions in Nicaragua, the United States probably strengthened and hardened the Sandinista regime, harming the one potentially ethical goal that should have been and could have been a legitimate aim of another, more respectful US policy – a more democratic and less dominated Nicaraguan society. So whether it was the Carter administration's failure to interfere or the Reagan administration's intervention, ethical and pragmatic concerns should have been at the core of US policy (and were not) – and could have readily worked together.

The persuasive power of Richard Ullman's two essays rests on the under-appreciated conjunction of ethical concern and pragmatic, long-run, national self-interest. (For a discussion of the potential conjunction of ethics and interest see also Ullman, 1984.) The two do not always, of course, coincide and Richard Ullman's extensive discussion of international intervention in the Russian civil war explores many of the confusing tradeoffs that often arise in world politics between decent goals and absent means (as well as the common but unfortunate coincidences of exploitative ends and readily available means). In this vein, Richard Ullman has commented on the desperate search by British statesmen for 'moderates' – 'saner elements of the left' – with which to ally in their effort to manage the 1917 Russian revolution and consequent civil war. He then warned: 'Civil wars are polarizing experiences; leaders who can supply the discipline and efficiency necessary to win are not likely to be "moderate" (although they may be by most people's lights "sane") whether they come from the Right or the Left' (Ullman, 1968: 352).

Arnold Wolfers is another scholar who has highlighted the nature of the tradeoffs that Richard Ullman noted in Russia's civil war and the rarity of coincident ethics and interests. His famous essay 'Statesmanship and moral choice' begins: 'Nowhere does the contradiction between professed ethical principles and actual behaviour appear so patent and universal as in the conduct of foreign relations.' But he then ends in the spirit invoked by Richard Ullman: those 'who have non-perfectionist and non-nationalistic moral convictions dare not evade moral judgment whether of their own political acts or of the acts of others' (Wolfers, 1962: 47 and 63). The two statements are in such obvious tension that many argue they form the core of international ethics: in international relations, ethics are more than difficult but at the same time moral judgement should not and cannot be evaded. In this chapter, I discuss why ethical judgements should not and cannot be evaded, and end with why they are so difficult and troubling in international politics. I explore three issues:

- why international ethics should not and need not be evaded through three classic but dangerous simplifications, each of which serves as an excuse for dismissing ethical judgement;
- the roles that considerations of ends, means and consequences can play in ethical judgements of international politics;
- why ethical principles so often leave us far from ethical outcomes in international politics.

Contra-scepticism

First, why is it that international ethics should not and need not be evaded through three classic simplifications – simplifications that should be rejected as partial truths, so partial as to be dangerous? (For extensive discussions of scepticism in international relations see Cohen, 1984; and Beitz, 1979, chapters 1 and 2.) The three simplifications are:

- Ethics should be limited to private life, because public political life is necessarily a separate world of dirty hands. This is the Machiavellian problem.
- Ethics should be domesticated, seen as fit only for domestic politics and judged to be inherently absent from, and irrelevant to, international politics, which is the Hobbesian problem.
- Ethics should be dismissed as being inherently a set of hypocritical or merely self-serving political slogans. We could call this Wordsworth's problem.

The first and most prevalent reason why we are told that ethical judgement can be ignored is that it is inapplicable to political decisions. As Dean Acheson, former US secretary of state, once said, 'Moral talk was fine preaching for the Final Day of Judgment, but it was not a view I would entertain as a public servant' (quoted by Gutmann and Thompson, 1997: xi). This is often called the ethics of public responsibilities. Engaging in politics means, requires, 'learning to be cruel to be kind' (as Shakespeare's Hamlet intoned). It is Max Weber's argument in 'Politics as a vocation' (on this issue see Walzer, 1973). In political theory, this is the Machiavellian problem. 'A wise prince,' Machiavelli said, 'knows how to do wrong when it is necessary.' And it is often, very often, necessary to act, he adds, 'contrary to truth, contrary to charity, contrary to humanity, contrary to religion – if the Prince wishes to sustain his government' (Machiavelli, 1985: 14).

Ethics, some self-described Machiavellians say, are for stay-at-homes, those happy men and women who till their own gardens, secure in the knowledge that they are able to do so safely. But princes, it is added, have no choice but to be like the 'ferocious beasts', for the moral life available to private men and women is neither safe nor sufficient for them. 'Princes must be like a very savage lion and a very tricky fox.' But why 'must'? First, for themselves: for without beast-like force and fraud, they will be overthrown. Second, and more tragically for us: for without the political order of government we would all have to be beasts, too, or perish under the attacks of thieves and murderers. Our making ethical judgements of specific political acts is therefore inappropriate and an act of bad faith, so many simple realists have said.

But this is too simple. Machiavelli knew it was, and so should we. Princes can and should be making moral choices. Not every prince is the leader of a threatened coup, everywhere and with everyone at war. Old, traditional princes would do themselves harm if they acted like new princes, the successful coup masters. Rules and traditions are the bulwarks of traditional princes.

As importantly, we private men and women in our gardens can hardly claim the virtue the political amoralists grant us. Are we, in fact, free from moral conflict? Are we free from contrariness with respect to truth, charity, humanity and religion? Machiavelli, author of the *Mandragola*, knew we were not. In that racy, sexual comedy, the wily Callimacco, deeply in love, tricks old Nicias into allowing him to sleep with his beautiful young wife, Lucrezia. With Lucrezia's connivance, Callimacco invents a curse that the first man to sleep with her will suffer a painful death. Gullible Nicias allows Callimacco to 'suffer' for him. Private men and women – Callimaccos and Lucrezias – are as crafty and ruthless as any fox-like public prince.

Machiavelli thus says private life, too, is not without moral corruption and authentic moral conflict. So should we. Moreover, we do. We do not grant our politicians a moral hunting licence. Indeed, we may hypocritically hold them to standards we rarely meet. In short, we share a moral universe with politicians. If we endorse their ability to punish or even kill in the name of the state, it is because we allow ourselves to use force in self-defence. They can be said to do it for us, because we are prepared to do it for ourselves. We hope they will do it more impartially – for public ends – and are often disappointed. But both public and private individuals can make moral choices and often face dreadful tradeoffs. The world often requires some very hard tradeoffs where rules of moral conduct confront the moral value of public survival and these are choices both our leaders and we understand.

If all politicians are not inherently different, inherently absent from moral judgement, maybe, say the second set of critics, it is the *international* politicians who fall outside ethical standard. The minister of health and the town mayor are in the ethical world; Bismark, Kissinger, the foreign minister and the defence secretary are out. This is the Hobbesian problem.

Hobbesians argue that nation-states exist in a condition of international anarchy, with no superior world state to provide law and order. There follows a general struggle for power – all against all – fuelled by competing desires for scarce goods, by fear of what others might do, by hunger for glory. Internationally, nations have no choice but to compete, because the competition is for survival. Domestically, ethics can be established once a state establishes law and order. Then promises will be enforced, social norms will be decreed, and those norms will be taught to the young. Lacking an international government of law and order, all is uncertain. Anything goes in the struggle for survival. This is the condition of complete struggle that general William T. Sherman had in mind when he told the citizens of Atlanta, after he burned their city in the US civil war, 'War is cruelty and you cannot refine it' (Sherman, 1875: 119–20; for a discussion see Walzer, 1977: 32–3).

But, again, moral life is not so simple. International politics is not an absolute struggle of all against all. Contemporary relations between the United Kingdom and France, Germany and Belgium, and between the United States and Canada, bear no similarity to that Hobbesian model. Relations are safe from war and shaped by international law (Slaughter, 1992; Ullman, 1991). Even the genuine representation of citizens becomes mixed. Both the US Midwest and Canada cause acid rain, but Ottawa's greater concern for the consequences may better represent a downwind New Englander than does Washington. Even in war, most states have come to accept the principle that the struggle is not 'against all'. Rules of war forbid struggle against non-combatants, against children and against the ill in hospital. And some modern Hobbesians fail to ask what the meaning is of survival – national or state survival? States are artificial beings, not natural ones. They exist, as Wolfers has noted, for the purposes of their inhabitants, not their inhabitants for states (Wolfers, 1962). Some citizens shuck off their sovereign Leviathans, as the British did in 1688, the American colonists did in 1776 and the former Soviets did in 1991. Moreover, the moral meaning of survival is frequently contested – up for domestic political competition – as it was in France in 1940. Was France to survive physically and conservatively as it did under Marshal Petain's Vichy regime or be risked, grandly, as it would be under General de Gaulle's Free French Resistance (see Bloch, 1949)?

States represent, or can represent, not merely our fears (as Hobbes argues) but also our hopes and our ethical commitments. Goals and values therefore define what normal survival means, what is worth protecting in both domestic and international politics. US civilian and military officials, for example, swear to preserve the constitution, a set of principles. Our ends define what is worth sacrificing for and shape even the international behaviour of states.

The third objection to international ethics accepts the view that politicians can be as ethical as we are (or no worse), whether they are engaging in foreign or domestic affairs. But, as the sceptics like Wordsworth have said, politicians just about always choose not to be. Their international ethics is all ordinary cynical hype and nothing more. They can be ethical. They choose to be hypocritical, paying the small tribute vice pays to virtue. Preaching ethics to them is thus like preaching chastity in a bordello.

Speaking as former member of the United States Air Force and noting that some of my best friends were in the Navy, let me tell you of a truly pathetic instance of convenient political morality. In 1949, the Navy decried the A-bomb, then the sole property of the Air Force, as immoral. By 1951, two years later, as the Navy started to assemble its own atomic arsenal and plans for a nuclear submarine force, atomic bombs suddenly became necessary to the survival of the free world. Of course, neither their criticism nor defence were thought convincing.

Again, we should hesitate to generalise the hypocrisy. Ethical arguments need not be altruistic to be convincing and some seem even to masquerade as self-serving advantage. At the Tehran conference in 1943, Stalin suggested to Churchill that after the defeat of Hitler, all 50,000 of the German officer corps should be summarily shot by the Allies. Churchill replied, 'The British parliament and public will never tolerate mass executions. They would turn violently against those responsible after the first butchery had taken place' (quoted by Morgenthau, 1984). Churchill's fear of reprisals from the British public does not wash. Indeed, should we not suspect hypocrisy in reverse? Appalled by the indiscriminate slaughter Stalin proposed, Churchill invents the self-serving logic of electoral advantage and political survival to appeal to the ruthless Stalin and, perhaps, soothe his own discomfort with 'moral talk'?

Elements of international ethics

International ethics thus are not impossible because politicians unlike us must be beasts, nor because international politics is a universal jungle, nor because nothing but hypocrisy and partisan advantage can influence a politician. What then is international ethics? What can and should it be?

Like all ethics it is the inescapable judgement that precedes action. Not all judgement, however, is or need be ethical. Prudential judgement prescribes productive strategies in the pursuit of given ends for a given person. Aesthetic judgement asks what is best, good or beautiful. Ethical judgement combines prescription (like prudence), over-ridingness (what is best, like aesthetics) and impartiality (what should be done not just by or for me, but by or for anyone in the same position). You should, as I should, fulfil an ethical duty because it is designed to apply to us all, like the 'golden rule' of doing unto others as you would have them do unto you.

Three concerns shape ethical judgement. In a fine book on *Nuclear Ethics*, Joseph Nye calls them motives, means and consequences (Nye, 1986; see also Hare and Joynt, 1982). Let us call them ends, means and consequences.[1]

---

1 Motives are not quite the same as ends. My dentist may be motivated only by money when he drills my teeth, but what distinguishes him from the torturer also motivated by a generous salary is the end of the act he is performing – fixing cavities rather than coercing confessions. Motives are highly relevant for judging character; but for assessing the policy of complex institutions ends seem to serve better.

An ethical end is necessary. Only ends justify, if anything can, the means we employ. In simple terms, it is ends that make some wars just defensive wars when, that is, they seek to protect the borders, the territorial integrity and the political independence that allow people to determine their own lives freely. Related ethical arguments can justify some humanitarian interventions across borders to rescue peoples from genocide and other grievous and systematic violations of their basic rights. People cannot shape their lives collectively if they are being repressed and slaughtered.

Good ends, however, are not sufficient to justify our acts. The theologian Paul Ramsey has shown why not in a striking parable (1968). If we really, truly, sincerely, deeply wanted to end, once and for all, the deaths of and injury to tens of thousands each year in car accidents – a worthy end surely – there is a simple and sure-fire means. All we have to do is tie, in as comfortable a way as possible, babies to the front and rear of our cars. Can anyone doubt that, slowed to a fully moral crawl, as in Ramsey's example, our cars would successfully avoid thousands of traffic accidents?

The problem here is in the means: the anguish to innocent infants, and perhaps even more the anguish to parents, none of whom is individually responsible for the collective tragedy of traffic fatalities. Some ethicists have condemned nuclear deterrence for just these reasons: deterrence terrorises innocent civilians.

Third, even with good ends and acceptable means, we need to consider and anticipate consequences. Our sense of ethical ends (for example, national self-defence, national self-determination) and ethical means (for example, in war, respecting non-combatant immunity because non-combatants pose no direct threat) are powerful and inherited and learned intuitions. They are taught by parents, learned at our mother's knee (or, as Acheson once said, some other low joint). They are part of now-traditional, evolved social conventions.

We need to govern these intuitions or rules by a consideration of consequences. It is wrong to lie in ordinary morality, but only a fool would tell a known murderer the location of his prospective victim. Similarly, even if Henry Kissinger is correct that the United States would have been 'profoundly immoral' to have abandoned South Vietnam to a totalitarian tyranny from the North (and thereby to have weakened the strategic credibility on which the West relied) and even if the United States had fought the war justly, minimising where possible civilian non-combatant casualties, the war could and would have been morally flawed if the United States failed to consider the suffering that would result from trying to win against a guerrilla movement supported by a large fraction of the population in a culture that the United States did not understand for a local government that had little support from too few of its own people (see Kissinger, 1979: 228; for an extensive moral criticism of US policy in South East Asia see Shawcross, 1979; the last point is part of Michael Walzer's criticism of the US intervention in Vietnam – see Walzer, 1977).

A similar moral wasteland was emerging in Serbia in the spring of 1999 when NATO looked at the prospect of destroying, by October or November of that year, tens of thousands of non-combatant Serbs, through the disease and medical deprivation that in a modern society accompanies the destruction of electricity, transportation and trade – all traditionally legitimate targets for bombing. The ends and means were justifiable: rescuing and returning thousands and thousands of non-combatant Albanian Kosovars 'ethnically cleansed' from their homes and avoiding in the process, as much as was feasible, the bombing of non-combatant Serbs. It was the indirect consequences on the ability of the Serbian population to provide essential services needed for health that were becoming morally unacceptable. The Clinton administration was aware of this issue and the danger of replicating the moral morass that had emerged in Iraq after years of a debilitating sanctions regime. Special measures were taken to ensure that the destruction inflicted on power plants and electrical grids would be repairable before the onset of winter, including the use of chaff to short-circuit the grids, rather than bombs to destroy them (private communication with US National Security Council officials). Goals and means can become disproportionate when warriors find themselves destroying villages in order to save them or killing more non-combatants in order to save fewer non-combatants.

Unavoidably violent means need to be proportionate to legitimate ends. And to do this, we need to consider all the available alternatives and weigh the consequences of each.

International conditions

If ethics is not impossible in international relations and if ordinary ethical judgement is identifiable and applicable, why, as Wolfers said, do we find such a gap between ethical principles and actual behaviour in foreign relations?

The simplest reason is that the behaviour may or may not in particular instances be motivated by ethical principles. More troubling is that even when it is (and we often have little reason to assume not) it does not have the same civilising effects as ethical behaviour in domestic politics. It is much more constrained because international politics is conflictual, confused and un-controlled.

There are at least four reasons for this unfortunate outcome (I draw these distinctions from Locke and his discussion of the troubled 'state of nature'; see Doyle, 1997, chapter 6; see also Hoffmann, 1971, 1998):

- anarchy – no enforcement;
- moral diversity – conflicting values;
- uncertainty – as to adversary and intentions;
- uncertainty and lack of control over our responses.

International anarchy does not make ethical behaviour impossible. As noted, politicians are moral and immoral beings like the rest of us, but it does make ethical behaviour difficult and the international good problematic. The lack of a world government capable of enforcement means unethical behaviour lacks adequate punishment, and evil is insufficiently deterred. The Vietnam War was widely criticised in the 1960s. And Idi Amin met with widespread moral condemnation in Africa in the 1970s for his human rights violations. But as long as Washington was a superpower and Amin controlled the Ugandan army, arresting, trying and correcting wrongs meant war. Intervention against the United States would have been suicidal. Intervention against Uganda was unacceptable as long as invading Uganda was unacceptable to Ugandans and to Uganda's African neighbours. Until 1979, that is, when Amin finally provoked Tanzania – provoking in the process international intervention by an African neighbour. Given international anarchy, furthermore, even ethically motivated states need to take measures of self-help to defend themselves. These measures restrict the resources that might be otherwise spent in aiding the poor economically, or helping to enforce just behaviour among states.

Second, complicating international anarchy is moral diversity. There is not a practical international consensus on right and wrong. There are some nearly universally recognised values, including human dignity; various human rights specified in the Universal Declaration of Human Rights; and, in practice, avoiding nuclear war. But they are thin. States have diverse ideologies and values and these lead to conflicts (Michael Walzer discusses the implications of thin and thick moral conventions in Walzer, 1996). Sincere communists have much to disagree with when they meet sincere liberals. Marxists think they can identify progressive forces scientifically; liberals should be, but are often not, more sceptical. Fundamentalist Islam is said to be in a 'clash of civilisations' with the Christian West (Huntington, 1996). Even if exaggerated in its impact, differences between Islam and the West over women's rights and freedom of the press clearly occasion strife.

Even with a wider consensus on principles, ethical conflicts over application can be extreme, when social and environmental circumstances differ and when power and authority become involved. When desperately poor immigrant farmers seek to settle in the seemingly less than fully used lands of a society of nomadic hunters, both do and, perhaps, justly can claim rights: the farmers to settle and hunters to resist the destruction of their hunting and way of life. As Locke once said, in these circumstances one 'appeals to heaven' and thus wars ensue. In less extreme circumstances, and even when states share a broad consensus on basic human rights and the efficacy of market economies, the threat of foreign imposition – Washington dominance – leads to strife over national honour and independence.

Third, international politics, even more than domestic politics, is full of uncertainty. In one gruesome example, the casualties at Hiroshima and Nagasaki were five times more than expected, partly because US planners expected that the cities would take the protective measures other Japanese cities had taken when they were first bombed. But the lone atomic bombers failed to trigger the protections (Hare and Joynt, 1982: 90). The United States undoubtedly still would have bombed in any case, but the arguments made at the time in favour of a warning explosion were probably weakened by the false lower estimates of Japanese casualties.

Sometimes we do not know whether to support or oppose or ignore, not merely because other principles may be disputed but also because the facts are unclear. Liberals can wonder whether Cuba or China or Eritrea are socialist democracies (as some of their apologists claim) suffering trying times and tolerating restrictions on freedom such those that characterised US politics between 1776 and 1781, and 1861 and 1865. Or, are they dictatorships of the left consolidating autocratic rule? Or are they something else altogether?

It is hard enough to understand what is happening in Boston, New York, London or Chicago; do we know what to approve or condemn in Eritrea? Was the Vietnam War a civil war or did it represent North Vietnam's aggressive stance towards South Vietnam? Judgements such as those can make enormous ethical difference.

And fourth, we do not control our responses very well. When states wind up trying to punish the behaviour of other states that elements of their own bureaucracies have provoked, ethical behaviour loses its effectiveness, even its meaning. If the US Congress supported aid to the Contras in Nicaragua because and only because the Contras could help deter the Nicaraguans from external attacks on Honduras (where the Contras were based), and if it did not know that the Central Intelligence Agency funded the Contras and directed the Contras in cross-border raids against Nicaragua, then the first action (supporting Honduras), justifiable as it may be on its own terms, is undermined ethically by the covert actions that accompanied and preceded it, for the Nicaraguans were engaged in just reprisals when they crossed the Honduran frontier.

In short, as citizens outside the university and scholars within it, there is no need to refrain from ethical judgement of those who claim as public officials to act for us. Ethics is not impossible. But not all ethical arguments are equally convincing – we need to hold our public officials as well as ourselves to careful considerations of ends, means and consequences.

When we do so, we cannot be either optimistic or crusading. Ethical judgement and behaviour are difficult. We should not expect international good automatically to follow because many international conflicts are fought over ethical differences. And we cannot expect international good to follow because the circumstances of international anarchy, confusion and lack of control often leave us desperate, driving in the dark, without lights and with a loose steering wheel. All of which are grounds for cautious modesty in the practice of international ethics, but not for abandoning ethical judgement in international relations.

Note

An earlier version of this essay was delivered as the Benjamin Meaker Professorial Lecture at the University of Bristol, UK, on 6 June 1999. It will appear in a forthcoming festschrift for Richard Ullman, edited by Tony Lake and David Ochmanek. I am grateful to the various organisers and audience and to Amy Gardner, Richard Little and Mark Wickham-Jones for comments and suggestions.

References

Beitz, C. (1979), *Political Theory and International Relations* (Princeton: Princeton University Press).

Bloch, M. (1949), *Strange Defeat*, translated by G. Hopkins (Oxford: Oxford University Press).

Brown, C. (1992), *International Relations Theory: New Normative Approaches* (Columbia: Columbia University Press).

Cohen, M. (1984), 'Moral skepticism in international relations', *Philosophy and Public Affairs*, vol. 13, no. 4, 299–346.

Doyle, M. (1997), *Ways of War and Peace* (New York: Norton).

Finnemore, M. (1996), *National Interests in International Society* (Ithaca: Cornell University Press).

Frost, M. (1996), *Ethics in International Relations* (Cambridge: Cambridge University Press).

Gutmann, A. and Thompson, D. (1997), *Ethics and Politics* (Chicago: Nelson Hall).

Hare, J. E. and Joynt, C. B. (1982), *Ethics and International Affairs* (New York: St Martin's Press).

Hoffmann, S. (1971), 'International law and the control of force', in K. Deutsch and S. Hoffmann (eds), *The Relevance of International Law* (Garden City, NY: Anchor Books), 34–66.

Hoffmann, S. (1998), 'The politics and ethics of military intervention', in S. Hoffmann, *World Disorders* (Lanham, MD: Rowman and Littlefield), 152–76.

Huntington, S. (1996), *Clash of Civilizations and the Remaking of World Order* (New York: Touchstone).

Kissinger, H. (1979), *The White House Years* (Boston: Little, Brown).

Linklater, A. (1990), *Men and Citizens in the Theory of International Relations* (Basingstoke: Macmillan).

Lumsdaine, D. (1993), *Moral Vision in International Politics* (Princeton: Princeton University Press).

Machiavelli, N. (1985), *The Prince*, translated by H. Mansfield, Jr (Chicago: University of Chicago Press).

Morgenthau, H. (1984), 'Human rights and foreign policy', in K. W. Thompson (ed.), *Moral Dimensions of American Foreign Policy* (New Brunswick: Transactions Press).

Nye, J. (1986), *Nuclear Ethics* (New York: Free Press).

Ramsey, P. (1968), *The Just War: Force and Political Responsibility* (New York: Scribner).

Shawcross, W. (1979), *Sideshow* (New York: Simon and Schuster).

Sherman, W. T. (1875), *Memoirs* (New York: D. Appleton and company).

Slaughter, A.-M. (1992), 'Law among liberal states: liberal internationalism and the act of state doctrine', *Columbia Law Review*, vol. 92, no. 8, 1907–96.

Ullman, R. (1968), *Britain and the Russian Civil War* (Princeton: Princeton University Press).

Ullman, R. (1978), 'Human rights and economic power: the United States versus Idi Amin', *Foreign Affairs*, vol. 56, no. 3, 529–43.

Ullman, R. (1983), 'At war with Nicaragua', *Foreign Affairs*, vol. 62, no. 1, 39–58.

Ullman, R. (1984), 'Both national security and human rights can be served simultaneously', *Center Magazine*, March/April, 21–9.

Ullman, R. (1991), *Securing Europe* (Princeton: Princeton University Press).

Walzer, M. (1973), 'Political action: the problem of dirty hands', *Philosophy and Public Affairs*, vol. 2, no. 2, 160–80.

Walzer, M. (1977), *Just and Unjust Wars* (New York: Basic Books).

Walzer, M. (1996), *Thick and Thin: Moral Disagreements at Home and Abroad* (Notre Dame: University of Notre Dame Press).

Wolfers, A. (1962), *Discord and Collaboration* (Baltimore: Johns Hopkins University Press).

Wordsworth, W. (1814), *The Excursion* (London: Edward Moxon), book V, 'The pastor', lines 378–81.

4

The Blair doctrine: advancing the Third Way in the world

Tim Dunne and Nicholas J. Wheeler

Introduction

'We need to focus in a serious and sustained way on the principles of the doctrine of international community and on the institutions that deliver them' (Blair, 1999a). This doctrine advocated by the British prime minister echoes a foundational claim of the English school, whose members have long maintained that states share interests and values (Wight, 1966). Yet it is significant that these theorists were reluctant to use the term 'international community' for the reason that it suggested a greater consensus on values than the practice of international relations warranted. Their preference was for the term 'international society' as it signified the presence of a plurality of different communities while still holding on to the idea that being a member of that society meant upholding the rules (Bull, 1977: 13).

One of the tasks for this chapter is to ask whether Tony Blair is right to believe that the time has come for thinking about global politics in terms of the existence of an international *community*. Or is he mistaken in believing that there is a near universal agreement on the values we all share and what we should do if they are violently rejected? In other words, should Blair listen to Hedley Bull's concerns (made in the early 1980s) about the consequences of acting *as if* a consensus on the standard of good governance existed already? Bull cautioned us against using force to impose the will of the international community upon states that fail to live up to the principles embodied in the international human rights regime. He feared that this would 'jeopardise the rules of sovereignty and non-intervention', which, he believed, provide a tolerable degree of order in international society (Bull, 1984: 193). If the West were to set itself up as the judge, jury and executioner of what counts as a human rights violation, why should we not expect other great powers (and their coalitions) to do the same?

Hedley Bull clearly believed that the doctrine of the international community, or 'solidarism' as he called it, was premature. Advocates of the Third Way in foreign policy respond by arguing that the end of the Cold War has opened up the possibility for establishing a deeper consensus on the standard of civilised conduct expected of governments around the world. The question underlying the body of the chapter concerns the appropriate instruments for advancing the values of human rights and good governance that underpin the ethical dimension of New Labour's foreign policy. It is clear that Robin Cook in particular believes that promoting these values requires fundamental changes to the form and conduct of foreign policy. The next section discusses these changes in broad terms, before the chapter goes on to consider how far the diplomacy of human rights can promote the ends of a Third Way foreign policy.

The main part of the chapter addresses the vexed issue of whether it is justifiable for proponents of a Third Way to use force in defence of human rights, if all other non-forcible means have failed. This is an issue that New Labour did not address in its early policy documents, either in the run-up to the general election victory or in the first year of office. The crisis in Kosovo changed all that. Not only was the UK government at the forefront of making the argument that the world had to 'do something' to reverse the policy of ethnic cleansing, Blair's Chicago speech – delivered on 22 April 1999 – showed that during the war against the Federal Republic of Yugoslavia (FRY), the United Kingdom was taking the lead in developing criteria under which forcible humanitarian intervention could be legitimised. We need – Blair argued – 'new rules' of enforcement to implement the doctrine of international community (Blair, 1999a: 8). Does the humanitarian war in Kosovo suggest that the use of force for human rights has an important role to play in a Third Way foreign policy? Or is one of the central lessons of the intervention, as some critics argue (Booth, 1999: 11), that evil means very rarely bring about good ends?

A Third Way for UK foreign policy

New Labour's determination to plot a different course for UK foreign policy was evident from the ministerial speeches in the first few months of the government's tenure. In the much trumpeted 'mission statement' delivered on 12 May 1997, Robin Cook announced to an expectant audience that foreign policy was to be guided by the goals of security for all nations, prosperity, protection for the environment and 'an ethical dimension'. It was this part of the statement that dominated the media coverage the following day, but there were many other hints of a radical departure from the pragmatic conservatism that had dominated foreign policy in the preceding fifty years. New Labour's view of British identity seemed quite different from the jingoism that dominated the Thatcher governments. Sovereignty talk, which had become so loud under the previous government as to drown out all other issues, was nowhere to be heard. There was no mention of 'threats' to national security, no elevation of the principle of non-intervention in the United Kingdom's domestic affairs; in their place, we heard 'internationalism', 'promoting democracy', 'promotion of our values and confidence in our identity', 'a people's diplomacy' and so on.

The most significant discursive departure concerned the priority to be accorded to the promotion of human rights: 'Our foreign policy must have an ethical dimension and must support the demands of other peoples for the democratic rights on which we insist for ourselves. The Labour Government will put human rights at the heart of our foreign policy' (Cook, 1997). While Cook's predecessors would no doubt have concurred with the priority accorded to the goals of security, prosperity and protection for the environment – even if they would not have been so open in announcing these policy goals – they would definitely not have been comfortable with his crusading call to 'make Britain once again a force for good in the world' (Cook, 1997).

After a year in office, Cook made the first explicit link between the 'ethical dimension' to Labour's foreign policy and the government's ideology of a Third Way (*New Statesman*, 1 May 1998). Before then, the Third Way had been developed primarily as a political strategy for transcending the dualism between the old left and the new right. As a guide to political economy, it tries to avoid the injustices of the free market and the inefficiency of public ownership (Hutton, 1995). In our article offering a preliminary evaluation of the 'ethical foreign policy' one year into the government's term, we argued that neither the government nor its gurus had begun to think through the implications of the Third Way in foreign policy (Wheeler and Dunne, 1998).

Looking back at the context within which we wrote the essay, two factors stand out. First, and contrary to arguments put forwards by journalists, the Third Way has not been discarded. Arguably, the debate over the promotion of ethics in foreign policy has been stepped up. In fact, given its prominence, what is surprising is not that we thought it worthy of scholarly attention but that more members of the international relations community *did not* (Lawler, 1999: 2). The second aspect of our article that was prescient concerned our criticism of New Labour for ignoring the issue of precisely what principles should govern the use of force in defence of humanitarian values. In the light of subsequent events, Labour began to do this, as we discuss below.

Before exploring this issue further it is important to reflect on the content of a Third Way foreign policy. As Mark Wickham-Jones notes in chapter 1, the discourse has been fairly elastic. Both Giddens (1998) and Blair (1999b) see it primarily as a response to globalisation. In other words, the changing global context is inducing economic and social reform 'at home' as well as shining a spotlight on the 'common problems' facing all states and peoples. Blair's way of dealing with this challenge is by developing the institutions and rules for collective action among the members of the international community. As noted at the outset, the parallels with these arguments and an English school approach to international relations are striking (Lawler, 1999: 4).

Like the defence of international society, there is a 'Goldilocks' quality about the Blair doctrine, as it wants to reject a policy based purely on self-interest ('too cold') as well as steering clear of a form of cosmopolitanism that seeks to replace the states system with a universal community ('too hot'). What, then, is 'just right'? This middle position has been expressed by Chris Brown when he argues that it is an attempt to 'reconcile the national interest with the norms of international society' (Brown, 2000). But this must not be conflated with an instrumental view of norms. Former Australian diplomat Richard Woolcott illustrates exactly what the relationship *is not*. In his words, 'Some states participate in what are called "good international citizen" activities but only to the extent that their national interests are served and not undermined by such activities' (1995: 24). The key issue becomes one of judging what to do when the national interest and the norms of international society are in tension. Without an explicit criterion, the debate becomes something of a sterile one between politicians and diplomats defending the United Kingdom's 'interests' and the press believing that an ethical foreign policy means the consistent application of principles irrespective of widely divergent contexts.

A conceptual way of resolving what to do when the goals of an ethical foreign policy are in conflict has been suggested by Andrew Linklater. Ethical states are not required to sacrifice their vital security interests out of fidelity to the rules of international society but they are required 'to put the welfare of international society ahead of the relentless pursuit of [their] own national interests' (Linklater, 1992: 28–9). Given that respect for human rights is central to the 'welfare of international society', states that are good citizens not only have to place order before the pursuit of narrow commercial and political advantage but they are also required to forsake these advantages where they conflict with human rights.

Although Labour's foreign policy innovations range much more broadly than the promotion and protection of human rights, the test for the Third Way is ultimately whether it is willing to make sacrifices for the world common good. It is not possible to put human rights 'at the heart of our foreign policy', to borrow Cook's evocative phrase, without sometimes pushing realist goals out to the periphery. How, then, is a foreign policy of the Third Way going to promote human rights values in the United Kingdom's relations with non-liberal states? Let us examine the 'hard case' of Indonesia, the rock on which Australia's ethical foreign policy foundered (Lawler, 1999: 12).

Dialogue as an instrument

In his contribution to defining the Third Way in foreign policy, the foreign secretary claims he is mapping a course between the 'row' and the 'kow-tow' (*Daily Telegraph*, 15 November 1997). He rejects the low priority the previous government accorded to human rights and argues that more will be achieved through 'dialogue' than public confrontation. A genuine 'dialogue' is not an occasion for lecturing or hectoring (Cook, 1998a); rather it is an opportunity for an 'open exchange of views' (FCO and DFID, 1998). Given the intensity with which Cook has defended the universality of human rights rhetorically – 'demanding' that others have these rights too – it is not obvious what would count as a different 'view' and still be 'acceptable'. To the contrary, Cook's speeches suggest that he is reluctant to consider different understandings of human rights, for example which kinds of rights to promote and the priority to be accorded to rights over responsibilities.

If the purpose of a human rights dialogue is not to establish legitimate deviations from an agreed standard, then presumably what it signifies is the preference for diplomatic pressure over public censuring (or even sanctions). There is textual evidence to support this interpretation of what the government means by 'dialogue'. In the case of Indonesia, the foreign secretary said that 'diplomatic pressure' was 'important' (Cook, 1998b: 1). Dialogue is therefore an instrument for quietly persuading, even cajoling at times, recalcitrant governments to comply with 'democratic rights on which we insist for ourselves' (Cook, 1997). This tactic has been controversial from the outset given that Indonesia has one of the worst human rights records in the world, a bloody 'prize' for which there are far too many contestants. Many on the left argue that we should not have a dialogue with murderous regimes, a point the government seems to concede in the case of Myanmar (Burma) (Fatchett, 1999) but not Algeria, China or Indonesia.

The brutality of the Indonesian military was exposed for all to see in the days following the 30 August 1999 referendum in East Timor. There is considerable evidence that the military was supplying so-called anti-independence militias with weapons and in many cases participating in the destruction of the country (United Nations Mission in East Timor, 1999). It will be a while before the scale of the violence has been documented, but the pattern since 1975 suggests a deliberate policy of genocide and mass executions. On this occasion there was a UN presence on the island to record the horrors, aided by journalists and television crews. What these events reveal is the difficulty of engaging in a meaningful dialogue with a hard-line nationalist government dominated by a military whose primary aim is to quell all forms of dissent.

Given this background, how does the government's policy of a human rights dialogue bear up? There is no doubt that it has consistently maintained contact with the leaders of the East Timorese resistance movement. The late Foreign Office minister, Derek Fatchett, met Xanana Gusmao in prison a number of times, against the wishes of the Indonesian government. Robin Cook claims that Gusmao's decision to take refuge in the British embassy is evidence that 'for two years no other country with an embassy in Jakarta has done more for East Timor' (Cook, 1999). The government can also claim some credit for pressurising president Habibe to accept the deployment of

UN peace enforcers, although president Clinton's threat of sanctions was probably the biggest single reason for his capitulation. Just before travelling to the summit of the Asia-Pacific Economic Cooperation (APEC) in Auckland, Robin Cook issued a strong statement condemning 'the appalling brutality' and demanding 'an urgent response from the international community' (FCO, 1999a). It would be a mistake to underestimate the important role played by Cook and the Foreign Office in supporting a 'coalition of the willing' to intervene and, equally importantly, in the drafting of a chapter VII Security Council resolution mandating the Australian-led multinational forces to restore peace and security in East Timor.

When it became obvious that the Indonesian military was active in derailing the transition to democracy in East Timor, the UK government broke with the policy of a quiet dialogue with Indonesia over human rights. It was clear that events demanded a tougher response and, for the reasons noted above, the United Kingdom effectively used all the instruments available to it – including the deployment of troops – to put a halt to the barbarism. This was a very different kind of response from the one that Harold Wilson's government made in 1975, when Suharto's illegal annexation of the territory was thought by many in Whitehall to be in the United Kingdom's commercial interests (Pilger, 1999). Security concerns were the other principal reason why the West consented to Indonesia's occupation of East Timor; this was heightened by the sense of communist gains in South East Asia following the defeat in Vietnam. Both these factors suggest that, over two decades after Suharto's troops marched on Dili, the normative context that framed the government's relations with Indonesia had changed considerably, in line with the wider transformation in the conduct of international relations after the Cold War.

What had not changed over those two decades was the sale of armaments to Indonesia. In 1977, just as reports of Suharto's genocidal policy were being widely publicised, the then foreign secretary, David Owen, approved the sale of Hawk jets to the Indonesian government. In what will surely go down as the darkest episode of New Labour's ethical foreign policy, the government continued to supply weapons to Suharto's successors, ranging from jets to rapid-firing machine guns. The justification for this has been woefully inadequate. Baroness Symons, the defence procurement minister, claimed that Indonesia has a right under the UN charter to buy weapons for self-defence; but this is surely problematic given the overwhelming evidence that 'defence' forces have violently 'policed' a territory that has never been recognised as a *de jure* part of its sovereignty. Symons has not been the only member of the government to come up with slippery explanations for arms exports to Jakarta. In a radio interview, Robin Cook claimed that the existence of new guidelines for arms sales would not permit the export of equipment 'that will be used in internal repression' (Cook, 1998b). He was clinging to the wreckage of this policy even after ten days of anarchy in East Timor (Cook, 1999). What we have seen in the aftermath of the 30 August vote is proof enough that the Indonesian military has routinely used its British-made hardware for internal repression.

The contradiction that Indonesia exposes between the goals of a foreign policy centred on human rights and the persistent export of arms was eventually acknowledged by the UK government in the face of widespread condemnation by the left (Pilger, 1999) and ridicule by the right (Jones, 1999). On 11 September 1999, Cook announced that the government had suspended the planned sale of nine Hawk trainer/ground-attack jets. The foreign secretary said that the United Kingdom would 'support an EU arms embargo and will take national action to suspend further arms exports' (FCO, 1999b). Perhaps the best description of the UK government's Janus-faced policy towards Indonesia has been offered – fittingly – by an East Timorese activist: 'There is a profound contradiction between pushing for a peaceful solution and arming the Indonesian armed forces which are orchestrating the militia death squads and preventing a peaceful solution in East Timor' (Budiardjo, 1999).

Using force to defend human rights

NATO's intervention to protect Kosovar Albanians in March 1999 brought the use of force to the top of the government's foreign policy agenda as ministers grappled with the complex moral, legal and strategic dilemmas. During the crisis, Robin Cook resisted pressure to look into the crystal ball and predict whether this was a turning point in the construction of a new kind of global human security architecture. But his prime minister was less cautious. He chose a keynote address in Chicago on 22 April 1999, on the eve of NATO's fiftieth anniversary conference, to outline a checklist of five 'new rules' that should govern the resort to – and conduct of – so-called humanitarian wars. In his words, 'the most pressing foreign policy problem we face is to identify the circumstances in which we should get actively involved in other people's conflicts' (Blair, 1999a). These rules can be thought of as constituting a Third Way policy on humanitarian intervention. This section examines these five 'new rules' in the light of the Kosovo case to see whether this action met Blair's standard for judging the legitimacy of humanitarian intervention (Wheeler, 2000b).

Before beginning this analysis it is important to add a brief qualification about the dangers of overstating the importance of the British contribution to the war in defence of the Kosovar Albanians. In terms of actual hardware, the Americans were by far the most significant contributor to Operation Allied Force, launching *all* the Tomahawk cruise missiles and flying ninety per cent of the bombing missions. Judging by these figures, it was not, as some of New Labour's supporters portrayed it, 'Tony's war'. At the same time, there is no doubt that Tony Blair, Robin Cook and the defence secretary, George Robertson, enabled the United Kingdom to punch above its weight, in part because of their resolute attitude but also because Clinton was constrained from advancing a hawkish line owing to isolationist sentiments in Congress. This ambiguity was not lost on right-wing Republicans like Pat Buchanan, who dubbed Blair 'the mouse that roared' and suggested that if he wanted to play 'Globocop' he should do so with his own troops (Gordon, 1999).

The first requirement that the prime minister laid down is that force can be considered only when 'we are sure of our case'. There is no doubt that Blair did not waver in his belief that NATO's military action was justified. It was, in his words, a 'just-war based not on any territorial ambitions but on values' (Blair, 1999a). He believed that the United Kingdom would have forfeited any right to call itself a member of a civilised international community if it had not tried to end Milosevic's brutal policy of ethnic cleansing in Kosovo. To be 'sure of our case', intervention must be motivated by humanitarian goals. In contrast to some critics of the West's Balkan policy, we do not claim that the humanitarian rationale must be the sole or even the over-riding motive; what must be ruled out is the invocation of just cause in order to cover the pursuit of self-interest, and that any non-humanitarian reasons for action do not undermine the humanitarian purpose of the mission. In the case of Kosovo, had containment been the over-riding motive then critics would have been justified in questioning the reasons given by Blair and NATO leaders for their actions.

The certainty with which senior members of the cabinet judged the case for using force was both a strength and a weakness – a strength in that the belief in the justice of the cause helped to maintain alliance solidarity, but also a weakness insofar as it alienated other permanent members of the Security Council. This can be seen from the government's attempt in October 1998 to push through a resolution specifically authorising 'all necessary means' to end the killings in Kosovo. Two days later, Russian embassies around the world issued a statement 'that the use of force against a sovereign state without due sanction of the UN Security Council would be an outright violation of the UN Charter, undermining the existing system of international relations' (Warren and Lockwood, 1998). The implications of the legality or otherwise of the action are discussed further at the end of the section.

The second dimension of a Third Way policy on intervention is that all 'diplomatic solutions' must have been exhausted before force is resorted to. 'We should always give peace every chance,' Blair claimed, 'as we have in the case of Kosovo' (Blair, 1999a). Critics of the war argue that the Alliance foreclosed on diplomacy too early and that the initiation of the air campaign led Serb forces in Kosovo to escalate their policy of ethnic cleansing. This is a damning indictment of NATO strategy but the problem is that it does not address the obvious counter that had NATO *not* acted, the Serbs would have been able to implement the policy of ethnic cleansing with impunity anyway. The ink was not even dry on the 'October agreement' negotiated between Milosevic and NATO before Serb generals began implementing their plan for depopulating Kosovo of its Albanians. Consequently, when peace talks broke down at Rambouillet in February, the choice facing the Alliance was one of becoming militarily engaged in Kosovo or standing by and allow ethnic cleansing by stealth.

Are the pro-intervenors right to say that every diplomatic alternative to war 'was tried and failed' (Ignatieff, 1999: 21)? There are four responses to this position that need to be taken seriously. First, Western diplomacy was backed by force and this may have fostered an adversarial context within which a peaceful resolution to the crisis became impossible. As Robert Skidelsky argued, 'had NATO accepted from 1998 that force was ruled out without clear evidence of genocide or mass expulsion, the diplomacy would have been different' (1999: 19). Second, there is the realisation that Western leaders were wrong to have left out Kosovo from the previous Balkan settlement negotiated at Dayton. As one British official put it – off the record – 'it got put in the "too difficult and not absolutely pressing" in-tray' (Butcher and Bishop, 1999). Third, some argue that the end of the war was brought about by Russia's withdrawal of its diplomatic backing for the FRY (Butcher, 1999); if this is the case, then the failure to keep Russia on board begins to look like a serious miscalculation on the part of NATO leaders. The fourth and most ambitious response is that even if all diplomatic routes had been exhausted the same cannot be said for *all non-violent strategies* for ending the repression of the Kosovars. Thinking along these lines, the example of the fight against apartheid might be a better model of dealing with gangster states, in other words bringing severe international and domestic pressure on the Milosevic regime while offering economic incentives 'for a changed polity in Kosovo' (Booth, 1999: 10).

The third principle guiding humanitarian intervention should be whether there are military operations 'we can sensibly and prudently undertake' (Blair, 1999a). There are countless examples of state leaders abusing the rights of their citizens, many falling into the category of gross human rights violations. What happened in East Timor after the election on 30 August 1999 was a deliberate policy of systematic expulsion and vengeful repression. If we take international humanitarian norms as our guide, a humanitarian war against Indonesia would have been justified. But would it have been prudent? There must be serious doubts whether a multinational 'coalition of the willing' could have defeated Indonesia militarily; going to war against the fourth largest country in the world would have entailed huge risks to the intervening forces and would probably have further destabilised regional peace and security. For this reason, had we applied Third Way rules for evaluating the case for intervention without Indonesia's consent, the answer to the question of whether the 'willing' could have 'sensibly and prudently' undertaken anything would have been 'no'.

Clearly the balance of forces in the case of Kosovo was very different. NATO's awesome capability was available, even if it was held back for the first month (it took NATO twelve days to fly the same number of combat

operations that it flew in the first twelve hours of the Gulf War in 1991).
Military resistance from the FRY was non-existent. Whether the strategy of
air power was sensible remains hotly debated. Those who believe it worked
resort to the simple argument that before 24 March diplomacy had failed
and eleven weeks later Kosovar Albanians were returning to their homes
(Keegan, 1999). Those who believe it was a disaster point to the fact that
the stated aim of 'averting a humanitarian catastrophe' was undermined
by the bombing. As Ken Booth argues, while NATO was not to blame for
the ethnic cleansing, 'it can be held responsible though for creating the cover
of war for the ethnic cleansers, and for inflaming the latter's desire to extract
revenge against the defenceless Albanians they despised' (1999: 6).

In other words, the worry is that even when the strongest military
alliance in the world wants to 'enforce' civilised behaviour on a weak
government, it may not be prudent to use force. At this point, Blair's rules
need to be broadened somewhat to consider the 'just war' concern that the
use of force must be proportionate. In the case of Kosovo, did the level of
force employed exceed the harm that it was designed to prevent? This question
raises the issue of NATO's bombing of civilian targets and whether a different
NATO strategy could have prevented the ensuing humanitarian catastrophe.
Although the Alliance never targeted civilians deliberately, as the pressure
for a result grew NATO expanded its targeting of bridges, power stations
and factories in ways that produced civilian deaths. If we were to include
in our ethical audit of the war the damage done to the FRY's infrastructure,
and hence the quality of life of its citizens, the balance sheet on the
'proportionality' issue begins to look quite different.

During the course of the air war, these concerns were raised by Mary
Robinson, UN High Commissioner for Human Rights. She questioned whether
NATO was being sufficiently careful in its targeting; there is a need, she
said, 'not only to adhere to the principle of proportionality, but to err on
the side of the principle' (Bishop, 1999). Failure to do this could, she added,
undermine the humanitarian credentials of Operation Allied Force. The
reluctance to deploy ground forces to stop the ethnic cleansing and the
concomitant reliance on the air campaign reflected in her view a lack of
moral courage on the part of governments to ask the armed forces to place
themselves in harm's way in defence of our values. Those broadly in favour
of the humanitarian war would respond by pointing to the loss of civilian
life (measured in hundreds) as a direct consequence of the bombing campaign,
concluding that this was an acceptable price to pay for an end to ethnic
cleansing.

Were there other military options that were prudent and potentially better
suited to delivering the aim of protecting the Kosovars? Preventing the evils
of ethnic cleansing would have required a ground intervention from the
outset, but there was no political consensus in the Alliance for this given
the high risk of casualties. Consequently, NATO had to make do with an air
strategy that was ill-suited to the rescue mission that it had embarked upon.

Once it became clear that Milosevic was determined to implement his plan to expel the Kosovar Albanians, NATO's war aim was changed to ensure that all the refugees could return in safety to their homes. Consequently, the litmus test of a means–ends calculation shifted from averting a catastrophe to enabling the refugees to return home.

The fourth of Blair's rules is that the intervening force must be 'prepared for the long term'. Given the sizeable commitment in money and workforce to the early stage of the peace-building process, it would be reasonable to concede that the government has met this aim. There is, however, a long way to go before this criterion can be said to have been complied with in full. It is perhaps interesting to speculate how much more important this rule might loom in the minds of decision-makers facing demands to 'do something' about human rights crises. As Australia is about to find out in East Timor (at the time of writing, November 1999), once a country's troops have been committed to dealing with a trouble spot, there is an in-built incentive for the UN *not* to replace them with a multinational force under a UN banner. This touches upon the question of burden sharing and the need for peacekeeping and peace-enforcement to be consistent with member states' wealth and capabilities.

The final rule for a Third Way policy on humanitarian intervention is whether or not 'we have national interests involved'. Blair hints that it made a difference that the human rights violations were taking part 'in such a combustible part of Europe'. In a sense, he put the problem the wrong way around. The fact that NATO arguably had 'vital security' concerns in maintaining stability in the Balkans made it all the more easy to justify the use of force. But what happens when there are no national interests at stake? Blair's hope – and it is central to the ethos of a Third Way in foreign policy – is that there is a compatibility between 'mutual self-interest and moral purpose' (Blair, 1999a). Again, the case of the Australian-led intervention in East Timor is interesting because it is plausible to argue that this is an instance where national security and international obligations face in different directions. It would be hard to argue against the view that, had the former been prioritised over the latter, Australia would have turned a blind eye to the plight of a few hundred thousand East Timorese. Put simply, doing business with Indonesia was more important than defending the rights of the islanders. The fact that Australia chose not to play the realist game led directly to the Indonesian government abrogating the 1995 bilateral security treaty, considered by many to be a watershed in Australia's search for a constructive role in the region. It would be wrong to pretend that these choices can be made without paying a price – in this instance a renewed threat to Australia's security as well as the commercial opportunities that will now be foreclosed.

As we saw in the second section of the chapter, it is not satisfactory for proponents of the Third Way to move between two clusters of international norms *without* a clear justification of the grounds on which national interests trump humanitarian norms. This begs the counter-factual question of whether the United Kingdom would use force for humanitarian reasons *in the absence* of any claims to advance the national interest? Would a Third Way approach to humanitarian intervention have stood aside and watched Rwanda burn? Or would New Labour have sought to lead the argument that intervention was a duty given the genocidal slaughter that was taking place? The experience of Kosovo suggests that the United Kingdom would have been more energetic than previous Conservative governments in trying to mobilise some kind of multinational response, but whether it could have cajoled the United States into returning to Africa is another matter.

Having examined Blair's five considerations, it is appropriate to consider what he omitted. The most obvious silence concerns the question of authorisation. For intervention to have the force of law and legitimacy it should be authorised by the UN Security Council, since this is the only body that is empowered to mandate force for purposes other than self-defence. The Blair government has argued that its use of force has a secure basis in international law. It accepted that military intervention lacked express Security Council authorisation but claimed to be enforcing existing Security Council resolutions. Moreover, the British government argued that there are precedents supporting the legality of NATO's action in Kosovo. Baroness Symons claimed that the intervention in northern Iraq in 1991 to create 'safe havens' for the Kurds supports a new custom of intervention, a claim that is highly problematic (see Wheeler, 2000a).

The foreign secretary also defended the legality of the action over Kosovo. He was bold enough to tell the House of Commons Foreign Affairs Committee that 'all the legal advisers to the 19 member states in NATO' have concluded that the action was legal (Foreign Affairs Committee, 1999). Yet this was not widely shared within the Alliance, let alone outside it. His counterpart in Germany, Klaus Kinkel, was worried that the position taken by Russia and China in the Security Council made it very difficult to argue that existing Security Council resolutions authorised NATO's use of force (Guicherd, 1999: 26–7). On this point, the German foreign minister was spot on. Russia and China publicly argued that NATO was setting a dangerous precedent by acting outside the authority of the UN charter. Their view, shared by many non-Western states outside the Security Council, is that these 'new rules' conflict with the 'old rules' that protect states from unwarranted interference in their affairs. By analogy, one could ask how NATO states would respond if a coalition of willing Arab countries were to use force against Israel without the consent of the Security Council but with a host of condemnatory resolutions as their cover?

NATO is on weak grounds in claiming that there is a recognised right of humanitarian intervention in international law, but it has raised an important issue concerning the relationship between legality and legitimacy (Wheeler, 2000a). Underlying the justifications of Cook and Blair is the argument that the lack of explicit Security Council authorisation should not stand in the way of humanitarian rescue. Given that the UN charter is built upon the foundation of 'we the peoples', those opposing the action have to address the question of whether the threat of a Russian or Chinese veto should be allowed to block nineteen democratically elected states from upholding values that are endorsed by the wider community of states. This issue of authority is a deep and complex one that is not possible to address fully here. What we can say is that the position taken by the British government has at least advanced the argument that legitimacy does not reside solely with the Security Council. In this sense, New Labour could be said to have been acting as a 'norm entrepreneur' (Finnemore and Sikkink, 1998). How has this been received within the UN? The position of the UN secretary-general is interesting in this regard. Despite reservations about the lack of a mandate, Kofi Annan admits that where forceful intervention becomes necessary, the Security Council 'must be able to rise to the challenge' (Annan, 1999). The secretary-general put the dilemma of recent precedents clearly when he argued that 'The choice must not be between council unity and inaction in the face of genocide – as in the case of Rwanda – and council division but regional action – as in the case of Kosovo' (Annan, 1999). Where Annan and Blair are in definite agreement is that there is a 'developing international norm' of humanitarian intervention and that identifying the circumstances under which an armed response is justified poses a fundamental challenge to the international community.

Conclusions

We opened this chapter by asking whether there is sufficient solidarity among states to make a reality of an 'international community' as heralded by Blair in Chicago. Part of the enunciation of a Third Way in the world concerns the increased interdependence of global problems and their solutions. But we argued that the Third Way needs to have more focus than simply a synonym for globalisation; it must provide a moral compass for a government committed to strengthening human rights in the society of states. Recent reflections by the prime minister and by the foreign secretary suggest a growing awareness that responding effectively to the enemies of human rights and good governance is the key test for the Third Way.

The first point to note about this goal is its fallibility. No government can respond effectively to all the gangsters who routinely abuse their citizens. Yet New Labour often suffers the delusion of great power status, as though the United Kingdom had the economic and military capability to 'demand' that the values we cherish be respected by others. This is not to suggest the government has been inactive in its defence of human rights, with significant deployments of troops and resources in Bosnia and Kosovo; but New Labour's ability to do something about Algeria, Angola, Afghanistan, China, Myanmar and so on is severely limited.

Even if it does not have many aces in its hand, we still need to ask how well the government has played its cards. The United Kingdom's relationship with Indonesia illustrates the limits of a human rights dialogue with a murderous government. The good intentions of assisting the independence of the East Timorese have been undermined completely by the fact that Labour did not take a principled stand on the question of arms shipments to Jakarta. At this point, the motives for the dialogue begin to be questioned, so much so that even respected insiders, such as Martin O'Neill, MP, chairman of the Commons Trade and Industry Committee, have been moved to ask 'what an ethical foreign policy amounts to, and how different it is from that followed by the previous government, because it is not very clear' (Jones, 1999). What makes this failure more difficult to reconcile with the aims of the foreign policy is that, in economic terms, our interests are *so small*. In fact, in the case of Indonesia, British citizens are subsidising the export of weapons. A government committed to promoting Third Way values must rule out arms sales to governments that do not share these values. Gangster states cannot be trusted; the complicity of the Indonesian army in the tragedy of East Timor tells us that 'assurances' from importing countries that weapons will not be turned against their civilian population are worthless.

Like Indonesia, the human rights abuses by the FRY led to a humanitarian intervention (even if, strictly speaking, the Indonesian government 'consented' to the UN-mandated peace enforcers). Given the proximity of the FRY and the presence of NATO, this was a crisis that the government *could* do something about. The main part of the chapter examined the conduct of the humanitarian war in the light of the new rules for intervention suggested by Blair in April 1999. Here we lent our support to the government for opening up this important issue for further debate and elaboration. As the UN secretary-general is only too aware, the UN's experience of intervention since the end of the Cold War has provided an 'unsatisfactory model for the new millennium' (Annan, 1999).

Blair argued in Chicago that the UN and the rule of law should be at the heart of any doctrine of international community, but how far did his defence of the use of force against the FRY undermine international legality? In exceptional cases of human suffering where only a few states stand out against military intervention, and Kosovo fits this category, Blair was right to argue that the veto power of Russia and China must not be allowed to block the defence of human rights. But one of the consequences of eroding compliance with international law is that the doctrine of international community begins to look like an instrument for maintaining Western dominance. In the absence of a consensus on 'new rules' backed by the threat of enforcement, the view from the non-Western world is that these are a cover for a group of liberal-democratic states prepared to defend liberalism by force in their relations with non-liberal states. As we emerge out of the latest phase of the Balkan crisis, the challenge for the new doctrine is to put into practice the Third Way commitment to dialogue in the course of securing legitimacy for these 'new rules' of the international community.

Note

We would like to thank the editors, all the participants at the original workshop at the University of Bristol (May 1999) and Marianne Hanson for their very constructive advice on the redrafting of our original paper.

References

Annan, K. (1999), 'In a humanitarian crisis, world must accept the challenge of timely intervention', *The Australian*, 20 September.

Bishop, P. (1999), 'UN rights chief warns Nato on bombing', *Daily Telegraph*, 5 May.

Blair, T. (1999a), 'The doctrine of the international community', speech, Economic Club of Chicago, United States, 22 April.

Blair, T. (1999b), 'Facing the modern challenge: the Third Way in Britain and South Africa', speech, Cape Town, South Africa, 8 January.

Booth, K. (1999), 'The Kosovo tragedy: epilogue to another "low and dishonest decade"', unpublished lecture given at the South African Political Science Association Biennial Congress, held at the Military Academy, Saldanha, 29 June.

Brown, C. (2000), 'Ethics, interests and foreign policy', in M. Light and K. Smith (eds), *Ethics and Foreign Policy*.

Budiardjo, C. (1999), 'Fatchett and East Timor', *The Guardian*, 12 May.

Bull, H. (1977), *The Anarchical Society: A Study of Order in World Politics* (Basingstoke: Macmillan).

Bull, H. (1984), 'Conclusion', in H. Bull (ed.), *Intervention in World Politics* (Oxford: Oxford University Press), 181–95.

Butcher, T. (1999), 'Victory over Serb Forces was a close run thing', *Daily Telegraph*, 5 June.

Butcher, T. and Bishop, P. (1999), 'Nato admits air campaign failed', *Daily Telegraph*, 22 July.

Cook, R. (1997), 'British foreign policy', statement, 12 May.

Cook, R. (1998a), 'The first year', speech, Mansion House, 23 April.

Cook, R. (1998b), interview, BBC Radio, 14 May.

Cook, R. (1999), 'Britain is ready to pursue justice in East Timor', *The Observer*, 19 September.

Fatchett, D. (1999), 'Burma: outrage is necessary but not enough', speech, Regent's College, London, 15 October.

Finnemore, M. and Sikkink, K. (1998), 'International norm dynamics and political change', *International Organization*, vol. 2, no. 4, 887–919.

Foreign Affairs Committee (1999), 'Examination of witnesses, Rt. Hon Robin Cook MP and Mr Peter Ricketts', 14 April, question 154.

FCO (1999a), 'News: East Timor', 7 September.

FCO (1999b), 'News: East Timor, Britain to support EU arms embargo', 11 September.

FCO and DFID (1998), *Annual Report on Hunan Rights* (London: TSO).

Giddens, A. (1998), *The Third Way: The Renewal of Social Democracy* (Oxford: Polity Press).

Gordon, H. (1999), 'Americans recoil from bellicose Prime Minster', *Daily Telegraph*, 26 April.

Guicherd, C. (1999), 'International law and the war in Kosovo', *Survival*, vol. 41, no. 2, 19–33.

Hutton, W. (1995), *The State We're In* (London: Jonathan Cape).

Ignatieff, M. (1999), 'Is military intervention over Kosovo justified?', debate in *Prospect* (June), 16–21.

Jones, G. (1999), 'Ministers on defensive over arms', *Daily Telegraph*, 16 September.

Keegan, W. (1999), 'Please Mr Blair, never take such a risk again', *Daily Telegraph*, 6 June.

Lawler, P. (1999), 'The good citizen Britain? Tradition, ethics and British foreign policy', unpublished paper.

Linklater, A. (1992), 'What is a good international citizen?', in P. Keal (ed.), *Ethics and Foreign Policy* (Canberra: Allen and Unwin), 21–41.

Pilger, J. (1999), 'Blood on our hands', *The Guardian*, 25 January.

Skidelsky, R. (1999), 'Is military intervention over Kosovo justified', debate in *Prospect* (June), 16–21.

United Nations Mission in East Timor (UNAMET) (1999), 'High commissioner for human rights to make first-hand assessments of deteriorating situation in East Timor', press release, 9 September.

Warren, M. and Lockwood, C. (1998), 'Russia warns it will use veto to halt military action', *Daily Telegraph*, 7 October.

Wheeler, N. J. (2000a), 'Humanitarian vigilantes or legal entrepreneurs: enforcing human rights in international society', *Critical Review of International and Social Philosophy*, vol. 3, no. 1 (forthcoming).

Wheeler, N. J. (2000b), *Saving Strangers: Humanitarian Intervention in International Society* (Oxford: Oxford University Press).

Wheeler, N. J. and Dunne, T. (1998), 'Good international citizenship: a Third Way for British foreign policy', *International Affairs*, vol. 74, no. 4, 847–70.

Wight, M. (1966), 'Western values in international relations', in H. Butterfield and M. Wight (eds), *Diplomatic Investigations: Essays in the Theory of International Politics* (London: Allen and Unwin), 89–131.

Woolcott, R. (1995), 'The perils of freedom', *Weekend Australian*, 22–23 April, 24.

5

New Labour as a 'good international citizen': normative theory and UK foreign policy

Jim Buller and Vicky Harrison

Introduction

Arguably, the traditional emphasis of UK foreign policy has been one of power politics (see, for example, Sanders, 1990). Speaking in 1993, Douglas Hurd, the then foreign secretary, was clear on the matter: 'British foreign policy exists to protect and promote British interests. Despite all the changes in the world that underlying truth has not changed' (cited in Martin and Garnett, 1997: 61). While this statement would probably be met with general agreement from the British electorate, the 1990s witnessed a number of episodes that cast a shadow over some of the methods being used to promote 'British interests'. One could point to the Pergau Dam affair, where it was discovered that the Thatcher government had agreed to finance a dam project in Malaysia in return for the purchase of British arms, despite civil service objections about poor value for money. Alternatively, there was the Scott report into the arms-to-Iraq affair, which saw the Thatcher government secretly relaxing its policy on the sale of weapons to this dictatorship. By the 1997 election, such scandals seemed to be contributing to a more general image of sleaze that surrounded the Major government. Allegations about the conduct of Jonathan Aitken, a former defence minister, forced him to resign from the cabinet to fight a libel action against *The Guardian* newspaper (which he subsequently lost in dramatic fashion, having already lost his seat at the general election).

That such issues might generate political capital was not lost on the Labour party leadership during the 1997 election campaign. That said, while much emphasis was placed on cleaning up domestic politics in its manifesto, such sentiments did not appear to extend to foreign and defence policy. True, promises were made to reform the arms trade in response to the criticisms made by Sir Richard Scott. Moreover, the party announced its intention to initiate a ban on landmines. But these pronouncements represented the sum total of Labour's claim to extend 'the morality of government' into the sphere of statecraft. However, once in office, Robin Cook set out plans to inject an 'ethical dimension' into British diplomacy amid a blaze of media publicity.

This re-orientation of foreign policy recognised 'that the national interest cannot be defined only by narrow *realpolitik*' (Cook, 1997a). For good measure, Cook outlined a twelve-point plan for the promotion of human rights (Cook, 1997b).

In an article in *International Affairs* (1998) Nicholas Wheeler and Tim Dunne have attempted to set this ethical project within the broader literature on international relations (and see chapter 4). They begin by arguing that, over the last fifty years, there has been no public articulation of a conceptual framework through which the ends and means of UK foreign policy can be understood. It is in this context that the authors introduce the 'good international citizen' (GIC). This term originated in the speeches and writings of the Australian foreign secretary Gareth Evans, who rejected the traditional realist assumption that national interests and human rights always pull in opposing directions. For Evans, the GIC was not engaged in 'Boy Scout good deeds', but 'enlightened self-interest'. This entailed an internationalist agenda, addressing issues such as peacekeeping, human rights and arms control (quoted in Wheeler and Dunne, 1998: 854–5). The notion of the GIC was initially developed by Andrew Linklater (1992), who placed the concept on a more solid theoretical grounding by establishing criteria by which to enact and judge an ethical foreign policy. For Linklater, the GIC was required 'to put the welfare of the international society ahead of the relentless pursuit of [its] own national interests' (Linklater, 1992: 28). The purpose of Wheeler and Dunne's work is to apply the GIC to demonstrating the possibilities for an ethical Third Way in UK foreign policy.

This chapter is split into three main sections. The first outlines the concept of the GIC as used by Wheeler and Dunne. The second sets out a number of problems with using this concept to forge a new ethical Third Way in foreign policy. The third discusses the theoretical possibilities for injecting an ethical dimension into UK foreign policy, in the light of these criticisms.

The good international citizen and UK foreign policy

Wheeler and Dunne employ the concept of the GIC in at least two distinct ways. In the first instance, the authors clearly intend the GIC to be an analytical contribution to the debate on New Labour's foreign policy. In this sense, it represents an attempt to develop a conceptual framework through which the inter-relationship between Labour's main foreign policy principles can be explored. As implied above, the central question facing all policy-makers (and advisers) is how to reconcile a state's traditional concerns about security with a new emphasis on human rights. For Wheeler and Dunne, the GIC provides a way of ensuring the latter are not lost or by-passed in the general cycle of policy-making.

How does it do this? In line with Evans's argument, the GIC is capable of strengthening the ethical dimension of foreign policy because it rejects the conventional assumption that there is necessarily a dualism between the pursuit of national interest and the nation-state's obligations to the international community as a whole (Wheeler and Dunne, 1998: 848–9). Indeed, in the international system of the late twentieth century, there will often be mutual interdependence between the provision of national security and the strengthening of international order, particularly for a middle-sized power. Of course, there will be times when the two conflict and terrible moral choices will have to be made. In this instance:

> Good International Citizens are not required to sacrifice their *vital* security interests out of a fidelity to the rules of international society, but they are required 'to put the welfare of international society ahead of the *relentless* pursuit of [their] own national interests ... to place the survival of order before the satisfaction of minimal national advantages'. (Wheeler and Dunne, 1998: 855, quoting Linklater, emphasis added)

In making this statement, Wheeler and Dunne expound a view of international relations that rejects the dominant paradigm of realism in favour of the English school. More particularly, the authors identify themselves on the 'solidarist' wing of this approach, which maintains that state leaders 'are burdened with the guardianship of human rights everywhere' (Wheeler and Dunne, 1998: 856).

If the GIC is intended as an analytical contribution to the possibilities for a Third Way in UK foreign policy, the concept is also employed in a second sense, as a benchmark against which government action in this area can be evaluated. According to this criterion, Wheeler and Dunne go on to make the empirical claim that there has been a 'marked' shift in foreign policy since the 1997 election. In addition to a new emphasis on human rights the authors point to: a new forward-looking identity for the United Kingdom, which is less preoccupied with the age-old problem of managing decline and more concerned to promote the new values and self-assurance of 'cool Britannia'; a new language that is less reliant on outdated notions of sovereignty and more willing to embrace the challenges and opportunities of global interdependence; and a new emphasis on opening up the policy-making process, including greater consultation with NGOs (Wheeler and Dunne, 1998: 850–1). Put another way, Wheeler and Dunne give solace to supporters of the Blair project: New Labour has definitely made a difference in this area.

The work of Wheeler and Dunne provides an original and stimulating contribution to the literature on UK foreign policy in the 1990s. That said, the argument is not without its problems. In the next section, two lines of criticism are pursued. First, it is argued that, empirically, Wheeler and Dunne overestimate the amount of change that has taken place under New Labour. Indeed, despite an undoubted shift in elite discourse, evidence of continuity in foreign and defence policy is much more compelling. Second, as an explicit conceptual framework aimed at promoting an ethical Third Way in British diplomacy, we postulate that the GIC, as presently defined, is unlikely to make much impact. In particular, what might be termed the emancipatory possibilities of the concept remain constrained by an adherence to realist terminology.

A critique of the good international citizen

From an empirical point of view, Wheeler and Dunne overestimate the amount of policy change that has taken place under New Labour. As already noted, the authors state early on in the article that a 'marked shift' has taken place in British diplomacy since 1997. On closer inspection, this claim largely refers to the language of Labour ministers in office. However, for Wheeler and Dunne, change at this level can still have an important effect on policy outcomes:

> The constitutive role that language plays in international relations can be seen from the fact that other governments take seriously what is said to them and about them ... in every epoch, it [language] is central in shaping a range of permissible actions. 'International debate', as Cook argued, 'is shaped by foreign secretaries and the rhetoric they use'. (Wheeler and Dunne, 1998: 851)

In other words, when it comes to the question of understanding policy change, language appears to have been assigned a transformative capacity.

The problem with this argument is that, if language does indeed possess such capacity, evidence that this change in discourse has been translated into actual decisions on the ground is less impressive. Indeed, as Wheeler and Dunne are forced to admit at the end of their 'ethical audit', there has so far been 'inconsistency' in the application of such a policy by the Blair government. For example, one could point to the decision to proceed with the sale of Hawk aircraft to Indonesia, a ruling that the authors do not bother to defend (Wheeler and Dunne, 1998: 680–2). Alternatively, one could highlight the white paper on strategic export controls, introduced in July 1998 as part of Labour's response to criticisms of Conservative policy contained in the Scott report. These measures recommended the rapid replacement of a structure, created in 1939, under which the 'government has an unfettered power to impose whatever export controls it wishes and to use those controls for any purpose which it thinks fit'. Instead, these powers should be subject to parliamentary approval. However, the white paper rejected as impractical the idea of making every export control regulation and application for an export licence subject to parliamentary scrutiny (Nicoll, 1998: 10). Yet other successful arms-exporting nations have in place structures for such parliamentary scrutiny. Sweden, for example, operates a system whereby a parliamentary select committee vets sensitive licence applications.

The US administration has a legal requirement of prior and public disclosure. Any US company that seeks to export arms valued in excess of $14 million must give fourteen days' advance notice to Congress. Such a legal requirement does not seem to have damaged US companies' ability to compete in world arms markets.[1]

At the same time, the Blair government's promise to open up the foreign policy process can be criticised. To be sure, ministers have delivered on promises to involve NGOs in the formulation and implementation of decisions. For example, Harriet Ware-Austin from Amnesty International and Dan Seymour from Save the Children have been seconded to work at the Foreign Office. However, it is possible to highlight the real limitations of this goal if one considers the Foreign Office's conduct in the arms-to-Africa affair. This incident refers to allegations that the Foreign Office approved a shipment of arms by Sandline International (a British firm) to Sierra Leone, despite a UN embargo on such activities sponsored by the United Kingdom. Although ministers and officials were subsequently cleared of complicity, they hardly conducted themselves in a transparent way throughout the investigation. It was admitted that 'restricted' telegrams informing Whitehall of Sandline's activities had 'gone missing' (*Financial Times*, 14 May 1998). Ministers were confused and unclear in their answers to parliament concerning exactly when they were made aware of the customs investigation of this impropriety. Cook initially rejected the release of the remaining telegrams to the Foreign Affairs Committee, which was conducting its own inquiry into the subject. When summaries were finally provided, they were reported to be so brief as to be 'almost meaningless' (*Financial Times*, 17 July 1998). Finally, Ernie Ross, a member of the above-mentioned committee, admitted sending a draft copy of the resulting report to the Foreign Office before it was published (*Financial Times*, 25 February 1999). No wonder Cook was reported to have given up using the phrase 'ethical' foreign policy, complaining that it had been continually misrepresented (*Financial Times*, 12 November 1998).

The point of these examples is that they raise a more general theoretical problem with the GIC as a new conceptual framework for the conduct of UK foreign policy. In lauding the importance of language, Wheeler and Dunne give tacit support to some within New Labour who propagate the hyper-voluntarism of political will in transforming the context of UK politics.[2]

---

1 For more detail of arms export regulations within the United Kingdom see DTI (1998a); and Defence, Foreign Affairs, International Development and Trade and Industry Committees (1999b). The European code of conduct is detailed by Neil Cooper in chapter 9. For comparison with regulations in other countries, including the United States, see Foreign Affairs Committee (1998b). The above illustrations represent a number of the problems faced by the government. For more examples see, among others, Black and Fairwell (1997); Buchan (1998); Chittenden (1998); Evans (1998); Walker (1998) and Wallace (1997).
2 The authors would like to acknowledge the work of Peter Lawler in helping to clarify this point.

Of course, changes in language and tone are important, especially when it comes to winning the battle of political ideas within which future decisions concerning the direction of UK foreign policy will be made. However, discursive reconstruction is not enough to embed social, political and cultural change, especially in a policy area where the rights of individuals and groups have historically lost out to the need for flexibility and pragmatism in diplomacy. Changes in discourse need to be accompanied by an awareness of material constraints on policy prescriptions and a willingness to contemplate significant institutional reform. It is only when new ideas are combined with structural change in a way that can be presented as 'commonsensical' to the British public that new policies can become entrenched. Put another way, the discursive and the material are not ontologically separate: they are necessarily linked in a dialectical relationship, which changes over time.

If ethical concerns have failed to establish themselves consistently at the centre of New Labour's foreign policy, the question remains: what are the chances that the new conceptual framework of the GIC will help clarify and promote the conditions for this moral dimension? What follows is a sceptical response to this question. Despite the rejection of realism by Wheeler and Dunne, realist terminology continues to constrain the parameters of the authors' world view, thus limiting the 'emancipatory possibilities' of the concept. To recap, in the event of a conflict between the state's national interests and its international obligations, GICs are not expected to forgo their *vital* security interests, but are instead obliged to place the well-being of the international community ahead of the *relentless* pursuit of national aims and objectives.

If we accept that conflict between national interests and international obligations cannot be wished away, in many ways this statement represents the backbone of Wheeler and Dunne's conceptual framework. Yet it is shot through with ambiguity. For example, what constitutes a matter of *vital* national interest? How might the *relentless* pursuit of such interests be defined? When precisely is it legitimate for a GIC to ignore the welfare of international society? Can the latter be objectively determined?

Why is this conceptual ambiguity a problem? If not addressed, it runs the risk of giving policy-makers a licence to override ethical considerations whenever it is convenient for them. Take, for example, Wheeler and Dunne's discussion of New Labour's policy towards China. The authors accept that Cook's decision to engage China in a dialogue (as opposed to tougher action) might have had only a limited impact on the promotion of human rights in that country. That said, the Blair government's decision is defended because of the potential damage that may have accrued to the United Kingdom's 'vital security interests in terms of Asia-Pacific stability and the broader need for Chinese participation in multi-lateral security institutions' (Wheeler and Dunne, 1998: 865). However, it is notable that Wheeler and Dunne ignore a similar threat when they praise the United Kingdom's actions in Iraq, despite the fact that China (and other UN Security Council countries) expressed public opposition to the bombing campaign. What is not entirely clear is why the GIC, as employed by Wheeler and Dunne, makes a distinction between these cases and justifies opposite courses of action. The main point here is that there is no consistent, objective meaning of 'the national interest'. Appeals to this entity can and will be constructed and used by particular governments to avoid hard choices concerning the promotion of human rights in certain situations. Unless further attention is paid to defining the exact parameters of this concept, the GIC runs the risk of being used to justify continual abuses of human rights.

Indeed, one could go further and point to a more fundamental problem with the GIC. If we, as academics, continue to conceptualise the state as a unitary actor with national interests and if we accept that we cannot wish away conflicts between such interests and the promotion of more humanitarian concerns, of course the latter is going to lose out. At the same time, the 'emancipatory capacity' of the concept to free British policy-makers from their perennial concern with power politics is reduced and we find that the debate has not moved on very far. Brown captures this contradiction beautifully:

> Once one accepts the premise that the state ought to be the key actor in international relations it is rather difficult to go on and argue that the state ought, in fact, to behave as though it were not the key actor, as though humanity as a whole ought to be the moral reference point for state behaviour, rather than the interests of its citizens. If that is what one believes to be morally required, surely it would make more sense to promote the emergence of world government rather than to press for an ethical foreign policy? (Brown, 1998)

To put the same point in different terms, Wheeler and Dunne face a level-of-analysis problem in the sense that they seek to impose a 'society of humanity' concept on to a 'society of states'. We return to this point below.

Normative theory and the future of Labour's ethical foreign policy

In light of these problems, what are the future possibilities for promoting an ethical foreign policy within the context of UK politics? The rest of this chapter takes a more optimistic line. It begins from the premise that change is possible in international relations. The material and social structures that constrain the opportunities for action are relatively enduring, but not immutable. In certain circumstances they can be appropriated and reformed by individuals, groups and organisations consciously seeking to further their objectives. This discussion relates to a more general question that pervades the study of the social sciences: the agent–structure problem. Here our position is that agents, the discourses they employ and the structures within which they operate are necessarily implicated in a dialectical relationship, which unfolds across time and space. Agents are potentially purposive entities whose actions can reproduce and transform the society in which they live. Yet it is also true to say that society is made up of social relations that structure the interactions between agents. In short, both agents and structures are relevant to understanding the formulation and implementation of public policy. Ontologically, agents possess 'relative autonomy' from these structural constraints (see, for example, Dessler, 1989; Giddens, 1979; Hay, 1996; Wendt, 1987).

However, if the problem is to emancipate British policy-makers from their existing belief systems so that they consistently pursue their obligations to the international community, the first task is to clarify any structural constraints that inhibit such a project. What makes this task more difficult is the fact that the effect of structures can be disguised by the discourses that agents employ to understand the world. As Linklater has powerfully observed, before prescriptions concerning policy reform can be generated, agents must reflect on the social construction of the material world, a construction which helps conceal the role that knowledge plays in legitimising and reproducing these unsatisfactory arrangements (Linklater, 1996: 279). Part of this task will involve not only deconstructing the language of policy-makers but will also entail questioning the concepts that we, as academics, use to make sense of the process of making foreign policy. In this context, the chapter finishes by arguing that future attempts to promote a more ethical statecraft should begin by deconstructing the realist language that continues to constrain the parameters within which we view this issue. In doing this, we will begin to develop a clearer picture of the structural constraints (and opportunities) that may affect the possibilities of change in this area. Two realist concepts in particular are highlighted and discussed below: 'the state' and 'the national interest'.

One problem with Wheeler and Dunne's analysis is that it contains no explicit discussion of the process of making foreign policy in the United Kingdom. However, to posit continually that British diplomats face a trade-off between protecting the national interest and respecting their obligations to the international community is to imply a picture of the state as a unitary actor, consciously and objectively weighing up various options before deciding on a course of action. In this context, it is worth noting that a number of writers have challenged this approach by 'opening up' the 'black box' of the state and concluding that 'policy develops out of a highly political process in which the interplay of the power and interests of various organisations and government departments is at least as important a determinant of policy as are any cool calculations of national interest by Foreign Office mandarins' (Martin and Garnett, 1997: 66; see also Clarke and White, 1989; Smith, 1991). In other words, it might not be helpful to view the state as some sort of 'being' with its own identity and objectives: indeed, a number of academics have cautioned against such reification (Nordlinger, 1988). Instead, the state is better conceptualised as a related set of institutions, which provides a terrain on which agents manoeuvre in an attempt to secure their particular interests. This is not say that the institutional terrain will be neutral. It will be biased towards some strategies rather than others and may preclude some strategies altogether. Strategic action and institutional reform will be possible by some groups in particular spatial and temporal contexts. At the same time, the state's future shape and trajectory will not be set in stone.

To question the conceptual terminology of realism in this way helps us to bring the structural constraints facing the pursuit of an ethical foreign policy into sharper focus. By opening up the black box of the state, we can gain a greater appreciation of the way specific domestic institutions serve to frustrate progress in this area. Take the example of arms sales. As the Scott report argued, more effective control of activity by UK firms is inhibited by the fact that the DTI is responsible for both the promotion and the licensing of exports, a dual role that serves to structure outcomes in favour of the former function. To quote the report:

> The DTI's main departmental brief is the promotion of British business, trade and employment prospects. Exports play a vital part in that regard and it is one of the main functions of the DTI, subject to any constraints of government policy from time to time, to encourage and assist exporters, to smooth their path and, where possible, to remove obstacles standing in their way. Export controls are unquestionably an obstacle standing in the way of exporters. Export controls may, and do, serve a variety of purposes of importance to the FCO or the MoD or, indeed, to the government as a whole. *But the controls will inevitably run counter to the main departmental interests of the DTI.* It is to be expected, therefore, that, in individual cases, DTI officials will tend to be in favour of the granting of licences. (Scott, 1996: 111, emphasis added)

In many instances, Scott's warnings have been played out in practice. The failure of the Foreign Office to halt the sale of Hawk aircraft to Indonesia and the watering down of a Whitehall plan for rules on the disclosure of exports, for example, have plausibly been ascribed to pressure from other departments (Wintour, 1998). Embedded institutional interests are not only resident at the DTI. Despite Scott's comprehensive attack on the secrecy surrounding arms exports, the MoD responded to the criticism over its objections for increased transparency in arms exports by insisting that secrecy is vital. Without a hint of irony (in light of how the United Kingdom aided Saddam), the MoD argued: 'the national security of the UK may be jeopardised if a third country obtains details of an importing ally's defence inventory that potentially puts UK troops and civilians at risk during conflict' (Norton-Taylor, 1998).

This deconstruction of realist terminology also allows us to demystify the concept of 'the national interest' – so often invoked to revise or downgrade a concern with ethical priorities. As Weldes has convincingly argued, the national interest does not exist as an objective reality but is better understood as a social construct, reflecting the various beliefs and interests of state elites and other groups. It emerges out of the various 'intersubjective meanings', 'representations' or 'situation descriptions' through which these actors make sense of the mass of conflicting and *ad hoc* information that confronts them. Of course, such meanings will not be generated out of thin air. They will be crucially related to the shared experience of governing a particular territory over time (Weldes, 1996; see also Wendt, 1992; Milliken, 1999). However, to understand the national interest as a particular social construct, propagated by specific actors privileged by the institutional terrain on which policy-making is played out, is the first step to recognising that it is not an objective and immutable reality. Ideas, meanings and discourses can change as relations between agents and structures are played out across time and space.

If we 'unpack' these concepts in this way, it is clear that an important structural constraint facing the implementation of an ethical foreign policy is the *perceived* importance that *particular* state actors place on links between the defence industry and the broader interests of the UK economy. For example, a recent government green paper estimated that over 400,000 jobs within the United Kingdom were dependent on military expenditure and exports (MoD, 1998). Of course, the verities of these arguments have long been a matter of debate (see Coates, 1994: 193–201; Hartley, 1998; Jones, 1999). What is significant is that present government ministers believe these arguments (Edgerton, 1998). Reversing this particular construction of the national interest remains one of the biggest challenges facing normative theory in this area.

At the same time, the problem is not how to find a Third Way between the pursuit of national interest and human rights (in the likely event that they will conflict). Instead, the issue becomes how to promote and embed the political will for an ethical foreign policy that might exist in some pockets of the state apparatus. Put more grandly, how can you reconstruct the terrain on which you are working in order to make it 'strategically select' the ethical option more often than at present? One option of course is domestic institutional reform. An obvious example of change, which stems from the discussion above, is the removal from the DTI of responsibility for the allocation of arms export licences. For example, Amnesty International has recommended the establishment of a single, independent authority with responsibility for export licence applications and the enforcement of export control legislation. Unfortunately, exchanges between ministers and members of the Foreign Affairs Committee betray a lack of urgency on the issue of domestic institutional reform. Under investigation, Robin Cook and Tony Lloyd accepted that up to half a dozen other Whitehall departments would have a clear input into foreign and defence policy. Yet both seemed reasonably happy that no written rules existed concerning co-ordination in cases where human rights clashed with the interests of other departments (Foreign Affairs Committee, 1998a: 49–50, 54–9, 150–1 and 159–60). When asked about the diffusion of interests within the domestic institutional realm, Robin Cook's reply was simply that: 'The Foreign Office, by definition, is the lead department on all international issues and external policy of the United Kingdom' (Foreign Affairs Committee, 1998a: 61).

Conclusions

Much of the preceding argument has highlighted the role and importance of language (and, indeed, academic conceptual terminology) in understanding the UK policy-making process and the prospects for reform. What has become clear from this discussion is that it is important not to underestimate the continued obstacles facing the pursuit of a more consistent ethical foreign policy in the United Kingdom. As Kapstein (1995) has argued, despite being deeply flawed, realism is likely to remain the dominant intellectual paradigm in international relations, if only because no rival meta-narrative exists to take its place. Even then, if a paradigm crisis were to develop, realism remains important to policy-makers, partly because of the *governing advantages* it confers. As Weldes (1996: 276) has suggested, politicians will continue to find the concept of the national interest useful, both as a way of thinking about their goals and as a means of mobilising support for them. In other words, the national interest provides a convenient cloak for 'cruder' political or organisational objectives. Even then, if a paradigm shift, which rejected realism, was achieved at the policy-making level, changing the terms of the debate is only the first step. Institutional reform must follow: indeed, it is crucial to embedding a shift in policy goals and the new discourse that accompanies them. Since coming to power, New Labour has given the impression that it recognises the importance of altering the language concerning the way we understand the goals of foreign policy. However, this must be matched by institutional change. Put another way, the whole structure of the British process of making foreign policy must be 'problematised' and then reconstituted.

References

Black, I. and Fairwell, D. (1997), 'The arms trade: profits of doom', *The Guardian*, 16 October.

Brown, C. (1998), 'Mutual respect? Ethical foreign policy in a multicultural world', paper presented at the International Studies Association, Minneapolis, United States, March.

Buchan, D. (1998), 'Cook's human rights efforts undermined', *Financial Times*, 23 September.

Chittenden, M. (1998), 'Cook faces arms-for-trade row', *Sunday Times*, 29 March.

Clarke, M. and White, B. (eds) (1989), *Understanding Foreign Policy* (Aldershot: Edward Elgar).

Coates, D. (1994), *The Question of UK Decline: State, Society and Economy* (London: Harvester Wheatsheaf).

Cook, R. (1997a), 'British foreign policy', statement, 12 May.

Cook, R. (1997b), 'Human rights into a new century', speech, 17 July.

Defence, Foreign Affairs, International Development and Trade and Industry Committees (1999), *Appendices to the Minutes of Evidence*, 26 May (London: TSO).

Dessler, D. (1989), 'What's at stake in the agent–structure debate?', *International Organisation*, vol. 43, no. 3, 441–73.

DTI (1998), *Strategic Export Controls*, cm 3989 (London: TSO).

Edgerton, D. (1998), 'Tony Blair's warfare state', *New Left Review*, 230 (July/August), 123–30.

Evans, M. (1998), 'Britain selling Jakarta weapons of repression', *The Times*, 15 May.

Foreign Affairs Committee (1998a), *Supplementary Memorandum, Minutes of Evidence*, 17 February (London: TSO).

Foreign Affairs Committee (1998b), *Foreign Policy and Human Rights*, first report, HC369, vol. II (London: TSO).

Giddens, A. (1979), *Central Problems in Social Theory* (Basingstoke: Macmillan).

Hartley, K. (1998), 'Defence procurement in the UK', *Defence and Peace Economics*, vol. 9, 39–62.

Hay, C. (1996), 'Structure and agency', in D. Marsh and G. Stoker (eds), *Theories and Methods in Political Science* (Basingstoke: Macmillan), 189–206.

Jones, P. R. (1999), 'Rent seeking and defence expenditure', *Defence Peace and Economics*, vol. 10, 171–90.

Kapstein, E. B. (1995), 'Is realism dead? The domestic sources of international politics', *International Organisation*, vol. 49, no. 4, 751–74.

Linklater, A. (1992), 'What is a good international citizen?', in P. Keal (ed.), *Ethical and Foreign Policy* (St Leonards, Australia: Allen and Unwin), 21–43.

Linklater, A. (1996), 'The achievements of critical theory', in S. Smith, K. Booth and M. Zalewski (eds), *International Theory: Positivism and Beyond* (Cambridge: Cambridge University Press), 279–98.

Martin, L. and Garnett, J. (1997), *British Foreign Policy: Challenges for the Twenty-First Century* (London: Royal Institute for International Affairs).

Milliken, J. (1999), 'The study of discourse in international relations: a critique of research methods', *European Journal of International Relations*, vol. 5, no. 2, 225–54.

MoD (1998), *Defence Diversification: Getting the Most out of Defence Technological Proposals for a Defence Diversification Agency*, cm 3861 (London: TSO).

Nicoll, A. (1998), 'Arms exports may face stricter scrutiny by MPs', *Financial Times*, 2 July.

Nordlinger, E. (1988), 'The return to the state: critiques', *American Political Science Review*, vol. 82, no. 3, 875–85.

Norton-Taylor, R. (1998), 'The arms market: for sale (credit available for Iraqis)', *The Guardian*, 17 February.

Sanders, D. (1990), *Losing an Empire, Finding a Role* (Basingstoke: Macmillan).

Scott, R. (1996), *Report of the Inquiry into the Export of Defence Equipment and Dual-Use Goods to Iraq and Related Prosecutions*, vol. 1 (London: HMSO).

Smith, S. (1991), 'Foreign policy analysis and the study of British foreign policy', in L. Freedman (ed.), *Britain in the World* (Cambridge: Cambridge University Press), 42–73.

Walker, M. (1998), 'Anger as arms code is diluted', *The Guardian*, 26 May.

Wallace, W. (1997), 'The hole in the centre of our foreign policy', *The Guardian*, 18 November.

Weldes, J. (1996), 'Constructing national interests', *European Journal of International Relations*, vol. 2, no. 3, 275–318.

Wendt, A. (1987), 'The agent–structure problem in international relations theory', *International Organisation*, vol. 41, no. 3, 335–70.

Wendt, A. (1992), 'Anarchy is what states make of it: the social construction of power politics', *International Organisation*, vol. 46, no. 2, 391–425.

Wheeler, N. J. and Dunne, T. (1998), 'Good international citizenship: a Third Way for British foreign policy', *International Affairs*, vol. 74, no. 4, 847–70.

Wintour, P. (1998), 'New blow for Cook in ethics battle', *The Observer*, 11 October.

Part III

Political and historical perspectives

6

Labour party politics and foreign policy

Mark Wickham-Jones

Introduction

As shadow foreign secretary between 1994 and 1997, Robin Cook gave no indication that he would initiate an ethical dimension to UK foreign policy on entering office. He did not place any great weight upon moral issues: he rarely discussed such matters as arms controls and human rights. On 6 September 1996, the *New Statesman* published a long interview with the shadow foreign secretary that covered debates within Labour, the enlargement of the EU, the importance of global free trade and disarmament. Cook touched briefly on arms control, refusing to answer the specific question of sales to Indonesia, and mentioned child labour. In the same month, a *Sunday Times* interview focused on him as the leader of Labour's left: it dealt with his concerns over domestic issues including poverty, equality and party–union relations (29 September 1996). In neither interview, coming six months before the election campaign began, was emphasis placed on Labour's distinctive approach to ethical issues: no spin was placed on these matters as an integral element in foreign affairs. An earlier *New Statesman* interview had focused on Europe alone (9 February 1996). In three appearances for the BBC's *On the Record* programme, Cook discussed European issues (twice), devolution and the reform of the House of Lords (BBC website). In 1995, without going into details, Cook told *Tribune* newspaper, 'There can be a socialist foreign policy' (17 February 1995). The four pillars he laid out were a leading role in Europe, international solidarity, the environment and peacekeeping. A year later, a further interview with *Tribune* was taken up with the Scott investigation into arms for Iraq (9 February 1996).

In this chapter I examine the political background to the ethical initiative that Cook launched in May 1997. I explore three issues. First, I consider what kind of commitment Labour had offered on ethical issues over the previous fifteen years. I focus on two key aspects of Cook's strategy once in office: the control of arms exports and the promotion of human rights. Second, I outline public attitudes to some of the key features of Labour's foreign and defence policy, starting with its unilateralist stance of the early 1980s. Third, I appraise Cook's performance as shadow foreign secretary between 1994 and 1997. In the conclusion to the chapter I draw these themes together and sketch out a political explanation of Labour's decision to place so much emphasis on the ethical content of its foreign policy.

Labour's policy on arms exports and human rights, 1983–97

It may be that too much has been made of the surprise expressed by media commentators and others (noted in chapter 1) at the launch of the Foreign Office's mission statement (FCO, 1997). Two elements of Cook's ethical dimension in foreign policy were especially important in speeches and statements during Labour's first months back in government during the summer of 1997: they were a commitment to place human rights at the centre of the administration's policy agenda and a promise to implement a stricter stance on arms exports. In the party's manifesto for the 1997 general election, the section on foreign affairs stated that Labour would be 'an advocate of human rights and democracy' (Labour party, 1997a: 37). The party offered controls on arms exports: 'Labour will not permit the sale of arms to regimes that might use them for internal repression or international aggression. We will increase the transparency and accountability of decisions on export licences for arms. And we will support an EU code of conduct governing arms sales' (Labour party, 1997a: 38). There was a brief paragraph on human rights: 'Labour wants Britain to be respected in the world for the integrity with which it conducts its foreign relations. We will make the protection of human rights a central part of our foreign policy' (Labour party, 1997a: 39). These succinct statements, made before the 1997 election victory, flagged the central aspects of Cook's moral dimension to foreign policy. Of course, neither was given great emphasis in the battery of policies and promises deployed by Labour and there was no explicit mention of an ethical dimension.

The need to regulate arms exports has long been a theme of Labour party policy documents. The party's 1983 general election manifesto offered much the same commitment as did that of 1997: 'We will not supply arms to countries where the chances of international aggression or internal oppression would be increased' (Labour party, 1983: 37). It went further in stating, 'We are alarmed by the growth of the arms trade. Labour will limit Britain's arms sales abroad and ban the supply of arms to repressive regimes such as South Africa, El Salvador, Chile, Argentina, and Turkey' (Labour party, 1983: 37). These proposals built on those contained in the party's gargantuan policy document, *Labour's Programme 1982*. It also stated, 'We shall bring details of individual arms sales out into the open' (Labour party, 1982: 250). On human rights, the 1983 manifesto in its final section gave 'the highest priority to the protection of human dignity, civil rights, democracy and freedom' (Labour party, 1983: 39).

The party's stance on the arms trade was stronger still after the culmination of the two-year policy review in 1989. That year's document noted, 'Far too often arms-trading – either for power-brooking or for commercial advantage – by the larger nations is the cause of a dangerous spread of armed conflict among smaller or less powerful countries' (Labour party, 1989: 88). The policy review document promised measures 'stringently limiting the scope and scale of arms sales by Britain' (Labour party, 1989: 88). The economic implications of this proposal were not spelt out in explicit terms. It was apparent that the party expected jobs to be lost through disarmament: tighter control of the arms trade might be presumed to have the same outcome. The party proposed to establish an Arms Conversion Agency as part of its industrial strategy to create new jobs and to help transfer resources from the production of weapons to civilian uses. (In the context of British disarmament, arms conversion had been central to the party's 1976 programme; Labour party, 1976: 116–17.) The 1989 policy review repeated the pledge to refuse exports to any country 'which might use them [arms] for internal repression or international aggression' (Labour party, 1989: 88). The policy review's tough stance on arms sale was not matched by an interest in human rights, which received scant attention.

The firm approach to the arms trade was maintained in the run-up to the 1992 general election. Labour's 1990 policy document, *Looking to the Future*, concluded, 'We do not believe that selling more arms to poor countries is an acceptable or effective way of maintaining the British defence industries' (Labour party, 1990: 46). The emphasis on diversification away from weapons manufacture, with help for lost orders and retraining, was repeated. At the time, Labour toyed with the idea of some form of defence review. Unlike the strategic review promised in 1997, such an appraisal was, in part, directly conceived of as a cost-cutting exercise (in the wake of developments in Eastern Europe). Frontbench spokesperson Martin O'Neill concluded in an internal memorandum: 'Labour wants to initiate an immediate defence review upon taking office so that we are in a position to see in which areas we can reduce expenditure' (O'Neill, 1990). *Looking to the Future* also placed significance upon human rights: 'The Labour government will uphold these fundamental principles of human rights in all our policies and in our dealings with every country … All governments must accept the right of others to ask questions about compliance with human rights principles' (Labour party, 1990: 48). *Opportunity Britain*, passed at Labour's 1991 conference, added little to existing policy (Labour party, 1991).

In his introduction to the party's 1992 general election manifesto, Neil Kinnock argued, 'In this increasingly inter-dependent world there are no distant crises. The Labour government will therefore, as a matter of moral obligation and in the material interests of our country, foster the development and trade relationships necessary for the advance of economic security, political democracy and respect for human rights' (Labour party, 1992: 8). Five years later, when launching the mission statement, Robin Cook echoed Kinnock's claim, stating, 'we are instant witnesses in our sitting rooms through the medium of television to human tragedy in distant lands, and are therefore obliged to accept moral responsibility for our response' (Cook, 1997a: 1).

The 1992 manifesto was brief but moralistic on arms control: 'Selling more arms to poor countries is not an acceptable or effective way of maintaining Britain's defence industries. We will stop sales to countries which might use them for internal repression or international aggression' (Labour party, 1992: 27). Labour would monitor human rights, publishing an annual report on the subject.

Concerns about human rights pervaded Labour's internal policy-making during the mid-1990s. In 1993, Michael Meacher represented Labour at a Socialist International meeting held to draft a document for a forthcoming UN human rights conference. In an internal report to Labour's policy-making international committee, Meacher criticised the draft: 'Since this was a consensus document on a highly contentious subject, its anodyne content reflected the lowest common denominator of extremely divergent views. It had been watered down to secure the agreement even of the most offending states, and hence it lacked both specificity and any effective sanctions' (Meacher, 1993: 1). What is interesting about Meacher's report is that the emphasis he placed on the importance of developing effective sanctions resembles closely the arguments deployed by Tony Blair during the Kosovo crisis six years later. Meacher condemned the lack of teeth to deal with nations that violated human rights and called for the establishment of a UN tribunal to deal with crimes against humanity. He went on to endorse 'Military intervention, only as a last resort and only in the most extreme cases involving genocide or a complete breakdown of law and order and of all government institutions' (p. 2). He accepted that 'all this will require a re-formulation of the principle of sovereignty and the internal rights of nations' (p. 2). There was considerable difference between 'neo colonialist interference' and legitimate action, sanctioned by the UN.

In June 1994, Jane Cooper from Amnesty International gave a paper to the party's newly formed Policy Commission on Foreign Affairs and Security. Her argument emphasised 'the new threats posed by intra-state armed conflicts' (Working Group on Defence Policy, 1994: 1). David Clark, from the party's front bench, 'drew attention to the tension between the rigorous and consistent enforcement of human rights – by for instance, establishing human rights tribunals for war criminals – and the often over-riding priority to bring wars and armed conflict to an end – through say, negotiating with those leaders responsible for human rights abuses' (p. 1). The meeting went on to discuss when 'it would be legitimate to interfere in a state's internal affairs when human rights were being abused, particularly in circumstances that fell short of genocide' (p. 1). A meeting of the Commission's sub-group on defence policy concluded that 'the group needed to think carefully about the circumstances that might justify armed intervention for humanitarian purposes' (Working Group on Defence Policy, 1994).

Policy-makers within the party also came to accept that defence expenditure could not easily be reduced given the United Kingdom's existing commitments (cuts in military spending were a standard demand at Labour party conferences). Mike Gapes argued at the Working Group on Defence Policy (1994: 1) that 'further defence cuts would be incompatible with our role as an influential force in world affairs and with the continuance of our permanent seat on the Security Council'. (Incidentally, members of the Policy Commission on Foreign Affairs and Security noted at this time that 'we should not allow Labour party policy to be too driven by NGOs'; Working Group on Defence Policy, 1994: 1.)

The most significant party document on foreign policy published between 1992 and 1997 was produced in 1996 as part of the stream of publications that fed into Labour's draft manifesto (on which, for the first time, individual party members voted). Tony Blair had been leader of the party for nearly two years by the time *A Fresh Start for Britain. Labour's Strategy for Britain in the Modern World* was launched (Labour party, 1996a). Much of the debate about the document surrounded his endorsement of the United Kingdom's nuclear deterrent. The document was explicit about both human rights and the arms trade:

> Labour believes that the values that inform our domestic programme must also form the basis for our foreign policy. That is why this statement puts forward a strong commitment by Labour to promote human rights and to support good governance through our participation in the world community. We cannot pride ourselves on our democratic traditions if we fail to help those who are demanding the same democratic rights for themselves. (Labour party, 1996a: 1–2)

The document promised that human rights would be a key part of foreign policy: as in the 1992 manifesto, it offered the publication of an annual report. It was qualified about humanitarian intervention, though it did emphasise the role of the UN.

The party's existing stance on arms exports was fleshed out: 'In government, Labour will not issue export licences for the sale of arms to regimes that might use them for internal repression or international aggression. Nor will we permit the sale of weapons in circumstances where this might intensify or prolong existing armed conflicts or where these weapons might be used to abuse human rights' (Labour party, 1996a: 14). In a reflection of the recent Scott inquiry, the party also concluded, 'There is a clear need to increase transparency and impose more stringent controls over the export of arms and dual-use technology' (Labour party, 1996a: 14). Cook told *Tribune*, 'I would expect a Labour government to implement the Scott Report recommendations. We have also stated repeatedly that Labour will not sell arms to regimes that use them for external aggression or internal repression. We have made it plain that this is a test which we would apply to Indonesia and any other government' (9 February 1996).

Labour's *Policy Handbook*, also published in 1996, repeated the party's stance on the arms trade and human rights. However, it also noted the importance of the arms industry for the well-being of the British economy: 'Labour recognises that the British defence industry is integral to Britain's overall industrial base and of vital importance to the nation's economic performance ... Labour will support our defence industry as an economic and a strategic asset' (Labour party, 1996b: section 5.2.3). In 1994, an NEC statement had stated, 'Conference notes that over 100,000 jobs have been lost in the defence industries since 1990 and believes that reductions in defence expenditure need to be properly managed if they are not to result in further mass unemployment. Conference believes that government has a direct responsibility to play an active role in managing defence cuts' (Labour party, 1994: 2). A year later, in *Strategy for a Secure Future*, Labour was more positive about the arms industry, arguing that arms exports were important not only for the United Kingdom's economy but also for efficient provision to the country's armed forces. The document was largely concerned with the arming of UK troops. In terms of arms exports, it stated, 'The export of British defence goods is vital for the long-term prosperity of the UK defence industrial base as it permits British companies to lower development costs through larger production runs' (Labour party, 1995: 20).

In the six months leading up to the 1997 general election, Labour gave little attention to either foreign policy or defence. Robin Cook continued to harass the government over arms exports, criticising sales to Zaire and Rwanda. Clare Short, shadow spokesperson on overseas aid, criticised alleged links between arms sales and aid to Indonesia: 'Britain's aid programme must not be tainted by connections with the arms trade' (Labour party press release, 22 January 1997). A couple of months later, Short launched a charter for ethics in business. It promised that, as a priority, the new development department would 'emphasise the role of ethics' (Labour party, 1997c). Among other points, Short called for a code of conduct for transnational companies (Short, 1997). (Once in office, research was commissioned on this issue by Short; see Ferguson, 1998.)

Labour's last major pronouncement on military sales before the 1997 general election came in February that year with the publication of an eight-point plan to regulate arms exports (Labour party, 1997b): stricter criteria about internal repression and external aggression (including no sales that 'might intensify or prolong existing conflicts'); greater transparency, including an annual report; a European register; a stronger UN conventional arms register; a European code of conduct; a ban on torture equipment; a ban on landmines; and stronger monitoring of end-user certificates to stop weapons getting to third countries by different routes. It was suggested that the annual report would included the details of licences granted and refused. Cook argued that such transparency was essential: 'we will break down the walls of secrecy behind which the Tories tried to hide the arms-to-Iraq scandal' (Cook, 1997c; see also *The Guardian*, 14 February 1997). Overall, it was a tough package that suggested a Labour administration would introduce tight controls on exports. At its launch, Cook accepted the legitimate role of the arms trade: 'Britain is a leading arms exporter. We have a right to maintain our competitive edge in this market, but we must also accept our responsibility to ensure that the arms trade is regulated' (Cook, 1997b; see *Financial Times*, 14 February 1997). In the same month, Cook was reported as stating that Labour would make human rights central to its foreign policy (*The Times*, 15 February 1997).

Three points can be noted from this review of Labour's policy documents of the last fifteen or so years. First, Labour has been consistent about both the need to regulate arms exports and, to a lesser extent, its desire to raise the status of human rights issues in foreign policy. The party has repeatedly stated that exports of weapons or equipment for internal repression or international aggression will be stopped. This phrase was used in the 1992 and 1997 manifestos. A variant of it was also used by Jack Cunningham, then shadow foreign secretary, at the party's 1994 conference and by Robin Cook at the 1995 conference. Unsurprisingly perhaps for a left-wing party, Labour has articulated a tough stance on arms control over the last fifteen years. Though they have received less attention, the party has not neglected human rights issues. In the 1990s the party began to discuss the circumstances in which military intervention might be justified. Often Labour's policies on these issues have either been touched on only briefly or gone unmentioned altogether in the media: *The Times* did not report the party's February 1997 arms exports plan. During the election campaign, the newspaper claimed that Labour's concern with human rights and development was a straightforward reflection of Conservative weaknesses on such matters. At other times, the press has noted the party's interests. At the launch of *A Fresh Start for Britain*, the *Financial Times* reported, 'It also promises that a Labour government will put human rights and developmental issues at the forefront of diplomacy' (26 June 1996). Of course, the idea that social democrats should be concerned with the arms trade and human rights should be of no surprise given the values that they seek to uphold. Both the Palme Commission (an independent body which examined disarmament issues, chaired by Olof Palme, the Swedish social democrat) and the Socialist International, among others, worked on these matters during the 1980s and 1990s (see Vivekanandan, 1997: 83 and 93).

Second, despite the party's consistency, an important shift in Labour's attitude towards arms exports took place during Blair's first years as leader. In a break with its existing approach, the party recognised explicitly the positive role played by the defence industries in the UK economy. Under Kinnock's leadership, the party indicated that the dependence of the economy and the balance of payments upon the arms trade would be severely reduced by a Labour administration. Considerable emphasis was placed on defence diversification, the conversion of arms industries to civilian usages. Restructuring the economy might be difficult but it was a necessary element of the party's promises over the arms trade (and, of course, disarmament).

Blair, by contrast to Kinnock, went to considerable lengths to reassure arms manufacturers about the intentions of a Labour government towards them. Just before the launch of the policy proposals on arms exports, Blair told the British Aerospace in-house magazine: 'Winning export orders is vital for the long-term success of Britain's defence industry. A Labour government will work with the industry to win export orders' (Labour party press release, 7 February 1997). Blair went on, 'Of course, the export of defence goods must reflect Britain's foreign and security interests and priorities, and should be regulated through the export licence process'. Far from being constrained by sweeping regulations that the party had proposed during the 1980s, New Labour indicated that arms manufacturers would receive government support in the promotion of exports. Labour gave little attention to how support for the arms sector could be reconciled with the pursuit of even the modest restrictions to military exports that a moral approach demanded.

The shift in Labour's policy approach can be illustrated in the development of the party's commitment to an Arms Conversion Agency. In 1989, Labour promised such an agency as a necessary part of the economic restructuring. The proposal was repeated in subsequent documents. In 1990, however, the agency was renamed a Defence Diversification Agency (it was briefly called a Defence Conversion Agency – see Labour party, 1994: 2). It would be responsible for helping those 'affected by changes in British defence policy' (Labour party, 1990: 47). By 1996, the rationale for the agency had been moderated in a striking fashion. The party's *Policy Handbook* proposed the agency was needed 'so that where there is excess capacity due to shifting procurement needs, the skills of our defence workers are, whenever possible, retained for use in either alternative areas of the defence industry or in the civil manufacturing sector' (Labour, 1996b: 5.3). The agency would be helping the defence sector in response to changing market requirements. Its role would not be determined by government policy and it would not be responsible for the conversion of defence production, unless circumstances dictated it to be appropriate. In 1997 the remit for the agency was altered again. As a reflection of the high level of expertise in the defence sector, the agency should help disseminate those skills: 'its [the defence sector's] expertise can be extended to civilian use' (Labour party, 1997a: 38). Under Blair's leadership its title was usually given in lower case; under Kinnock it had been capitalised. The agency had been transformed from that originally envisaged by Labour in the 1980s. The transformation reflected the importance of the arms sector in terms of employment and the balance of payments. It also indicated the limitations of arms: at a meeting of the party's Working Group on Defence Policy in June 1994, 'Donald Anderson drew attention to the need for more in-depth work on defence diversification. He stressed that some of the old ideas – that weapons producers could be transformed into producers of hospital equipment etc – were quite unrealistic' (Working Group on Defence Policy, 1994: 2). When Labour published a green paper on the defence diversification agency in March 1998, George Robertson, the defence secretary, was frank: 'We are not in the business of running down defence production facilities and converting them to civilian use' (Kampfner, 1999: 215).

Third, despite the consistency of Labour's concerns over the arms trade and human rights, there was no articulation before the 1997 general election of either an ethical dimension or a moral content to policy. At no point did the party self-consciously claim to be pursuing a package of measures that were inherently ethical. (The nearest to such a stance was Clare Short's specific pronouncements on development and the role of ethics in business.) From this perspective, Robin Cook's claim to have initiated an ethical dimension was an innovative one, even if individual aspects of his approach were much in line with the party's existing trajectory as outlined in opposition before 1997. The question remains as to why so much emphasis was placed by the new administration on the theme of ethics.

Public opinion and Labour's policy: from unilateralism to an ethical dimension

At the time of the 1983 general election, Labour trailed the Conservatives by thirty per cent in opinion polls concerning which party had the better defence policy. Fifty per cent of respondents approved of Conservative policy, barely twenty per cent backed Labour (*Political Social and Economic Review*, no. 83, June 1983: 15). Only one in three Labour voters supported unilateral disarmament. Only sixteen per cent of the electorate endorsed such an approach (it had enjoyed higher levels of support a couple of years earlier). Labour's perceived weakness was not helped by internal disputes within the party over the nature of its unilateralist commitments. Differences of opinion created confusion as to what exactly was the substance of the party's non-nuclear defence policy.

Between going into opposition in 1979 and the spring of 1983, Labour's ruling NEC indicated little interest in public opinion polls. The party made little attempt to meet the perceived policy preferences of the electorate on such issues as defence. Instead, it engaged in a period of 'ideological policy formation', in which the party's programme was driven by values and beliefs (see Wickham-Jones, 1996: 191). Such an approach was not necessarily irrational: many within the party perceived public opinion on a variety of economic and defence issues to be malleable. They hoped to change voters' perceptions about what was feasible and desirable. Geoff Bish, secretary of Labour's research department, commented in October 1982 that the party had little time 'to achieve a huge and sustained shift of opinion within the electorate' (Bish, 1982: 2). Another memorandum concluded that Labour needed 'to generate understanding and support for these policies' (Wickham-Jones, 1996: 190).

Whatever the practicality of Labour's electoral approach in 1983, many commentators assumed that in the aftermath of what was a cataclysmic defeat there would have to major changes to the party's policy commitments, including defence. Many figures were, however, passionately attached to non-nuclear defence. It was by no means apparent how the party's uni-lateralism could be reversed while sustaining the credibility and integrity of its senior policy-makers, including the new leader, Neil Kinnock. Between 1983 and 1987, the party persisted in its non-nuclear approach to defence. Labour's proposals regarding the full extent and detailed timing of disarma-ment were uncertain. Many members of the parliamentary Labour party were wedded to multilateral approaches. At the 1987 general election, the party's difficulties were repeated: the saliency of defence increased during the campaign as (already limited) support for the party's approach crashed (Butler and Kavanagh, 1988: 134).

The party's third defeat provided the context for a detailed rethink of its policy programme, including defence. A central feature of the review was a sustained attempt to ascertain the electorate's preferences on a variety of issues (though the party had utilised polls after the 1983 defeat). One party document in 1988 concluded, 'At no stage in the last five years has more than a quarter of the electorate felt that Labour's views on defence came closest to their own' (Labour party, 1988: 12). By the late 1980s the leadership of the party accepted that public opinion could not be ignored in the construction of defence policy. Kinnock later bemoaned that it took so long to ditch the unilateralism to which he had once been so firmly wedded. In 1988 he stated in a television interview that there was 'no need for a something-for-nothing' unilateralism. His comments were ambiguous: they could be taken as a normative statement (that is a break with unilateralism) or as a reflection of the realities that confronted the party in the emergence from the Cold War era (that is unilateralism was no longer needed). Kinnock equivocated. His words echoed those of the party's former leader, James Callaghan, when he had attacked unilateralism during the general 1983 election. Discussing British nuclear weapons, Callaghan had stated, 'We should not give them up unilaterally for nothing' (Butler and Kavanagh, 1984: 96). At the time both Robin Cook and Neil Kinnock entered the row initiated by Callaghan's comments. Cook claimed that the election offered a choice between more American missiles and an end to the arms race. History would not, he claimed in ponderous fashion, forgive those who muddied this judgement (*The Guardian*, 27 May 1993). Kinnock was more straightforward, declaring, 'The Labour party has a non-nuclear defence policy and the Labour govern-ment will implement the policy' (*The Times*, 27 May 1983).

By 1989, after laying the groundwork carefully in the policy review and at conference, Kinnock was able to ditch the party's unilateralism. The decision was motivated in large part by public opinion. It was also shaped by the thawing of the Cold War and by Kinnock's experiences trying to sell unilateralism to leaders in other states and voters alike. Changed relations between the superpowers meant that Kinnock could claim 'the log jam is broken' (*This week*, 9 February 1989; Kinnock papers, box 256).[1] Kinnock's

1 Kinnock papers, Churchill College, Cambridge University.

personal preference should not be ignored: echoing words used at the NEC, he told the Welsh Labour conference in 1989:

> What bothered me most was the undisguised puzzlement on the faces, both East and West, at the policy which meant that we would give up our weapons unconditionally and without seeking anything in return. I have seen the same puzzlement ... elsewhere. I have seen it on the faces of the ordinary people of this country. People simply could not support the idea that we could give so much without seeking anything in return. I'm not going to do that again. (Quoted by Neil Stewart, a member of the Labour leader's office, 20 June 1989; Kinnock papers, box 580)

The decision was confirmed at the 1989 Labour conference: what many commentators perceived to be a major impediment to electoral victory had been finally removed.

Labour's break with unilateralism did not result, however, in an improved opinion poll rating for defence. (We should not, of course, assume a direct and simple link between policy change and the electorate's preferences.) At the 1992 general election Labour trailed the Conservatives fifty-two to twenty-two per cent as to which party handled defence better (*Gallup Political and Economic Index*, no. 380, April 1992: 6). By now, neither foreign affairs nor defence were perceived to be salient issues by voters. Five years later, the importance of these matters remained equally negligible. Voters mentioned neither as an urgent issue during the 1997 general election campaign. Only in December 1998 did peace and international affairs appear as topics demanding immediate attention in opinion polls. In March 1999, eight per cent of those polled ranked peace as the most pressing issue confronting the government and five per cent recorded Bosnia. The poll came just before the outbreak of the Kosovo conflict. In May 1999, twenty-four per cent rated Kosovo as the most urgent problem; peace fell to two per cent and Bosnia to one per cent. What is striking from these data is the lack of salience accorded by voters to international affairs and defence, except in relation to specific crises.

New Labour was unable to reverse the Conservatives' historic lead in opinion polls over defence policy. But the gap between the parties was narrowed. By May 1997 forty-three per cent of voters endorsed the Conservatives' defence policy, twenty-nine per cent backed Labour (*Gallup Political and Economic Index*, no. 441, May 1997). On Europe, another matter in which Labour had trailed the Conservatives, Blair was able to establish a slight lead at around thirty-five to thirty-one per cent. In the months that followed, polling indicated that central elements of Cook's ethical initiative proved to be extremely popular (few data are available). Ninety per cent approved the decision to re-open the question of compensation for those suffering Gulf War syndrome and eighty-nine per cent supported the decision to ban landmines (*Gallup Political and Economic Index*, no. 442, June 1997). These were the two most popular responses for Labour from a list of ten issues on which respondents were questioned. Interestingly, with regard to the troubles that Labour found itself in over its policy towards Kashmir, a poll in September 1997 indicated that fifty-four per cent of respondents (to forty-four) felt that the United Kingdom should leave former colonies to run their own affairs (*Gallup Political and Economic Index*, no. 445, September 1997: 9). In May 1998, there was support for the decision to sign up to the European Convention on Human Rights. One opinion poll in October 1998 indicated that seventy-seven per cent of respondents thought there was too much secrecy in arms sales (*Sunday Telegraph*, 11 October 1998). Cook proved to be a surprisingly popular foreign secretary, given tabloid interest in his private life. In October 1997, of those who knew his position in the government, five times as many thought he was doing a good job as opposed to a bad one (*Gallup Political and Economic Index*, no. 446, October 1997: 10). Six months later, fifty-nine per cent approved of his performance, while thirty-one disapproved (the figures fell subsequently).

Public opinion was supportive of the Blair government's tough stance towards Iraq and Serbia. In March 1998, over eighty per cent concluded Saddam Hussain to be a threat to world peace. Though there was backing for the use of diplomatic pressure, if the government decided that force was necessary sixty-two per cent supported the use of air attacks; fifty-six per cent sanctioned the deployment of ground forces (*Gallup Political and Economic Index*, no. 451, March 1998: 6). Respondents favoured attacks on military targets rather than civilian ones and accepted that there might be civilian casualties. In March 1999, fifty-eight per cent of respondents approved of NATO's action in Kosovo while one-third disapproved (*Gallup Political and Economic Index*, no. 464, April 1999: 7). There was less support for the use of ground troops. In April, the approval figure rose to over seventy per cent, though it dipped slightly subsequently. At the start of the war, sixty-nine per cent of those questioned concluded that Serb actions in Kosovo constituted a humanitarian outrage that demanded action. Only twenty-three per cent saw it as an 'internal matter'. The figures for the conflict in Kosovo can be contrasted with those recorded over the Bosnia crisis. In September 1993, as the crisis intensified, forty-six per cent of respondents were dissatisfied with the Major government's handling of Bosnia and only thirty-two per cent were satisfied (*Gallup Political and Economic Index*, no. 397, September 1993: 42). Two years later the gap had widened: fifty-five per cent disapproved and only twenty-two per cent approved.

By 1998, Labour had finally reversed the Conservatives' lead on which party handled defence better, by forty-two to thirty eight per cent (*Gallup Political and Economic Index*, no. 453, May 1998: 7–8). At each election between 1983 and 1997 the Conservatives had received more support than Labour. In the summer of 1999, the Blair administration held on to this lead (*Gallup Political and Economic Index*, no. 467, July 1999: 7).

This brief excursion through attitudes to defence and other foreign affairs issues indicates how the public opinion constraint that once confronted

Labour has been transformed. In 1983 the party's commitment to uni-lateralism was at odds with electoral preferences. By the late 1990s, aspects of Labour's ethical initiative and the party's commitment to intervention in what were perceived to be humanitarian crises were popular. New Labour as an electoral machine has always placed considerable emphasis on the need to meet the perceived preferences of the electorate. The available evidence indicates that Cook's ethical dimension realised such a condition: it was popular. The government's interventionist stance over Kosovo was much admired. John Kampfner, Cook's biographer, argued that the foreign secretary 'felt that the British public was ahead of official thinking. British voters were exercised about human rights and NGO-type issues' (interview, October 1999). In short, there was an electoral incentive for New Labour to break the existing bipartisan consensus over foreign affairs and defence issues.

Intra-party politics and foreign policy

After Labour's 1992 general election defeat, Robin Cook was given the trade and industry portfolio in the shadow cabinet. For two years, until 1994, he determined the party's industrial policy, advocating a *dirigiste* approach. He thereby came into direct conflict with the party's shadow chancellor, Gordon Brown. The party's then leader, John Smith, was largely unperturbed at some antagonism between the shadow chancellor and the spokesperson for trade and industry. Himself something of a combination of 'macroeconomic conservative' and 'microeconomic radical', he may have seen such a blend as creative and potentially successful. Cook was relatively content: to be sure, he would rather have been shadow chancellor but he had considerable latitude over industrial policy. Brown was much less happy with this state of affairs and concluded Cook's interventions to be a significant obstacle to his own attempts to recast the party's economic policies.

In May 1994 Smith died unexpectedly. Both Brown and Cook considered standing for the party leadership, equivocated and then withdrew from the contest before it had begun. Brown's departure was important: it opened the way for Blair to stand as the sole candidate of the party's so-called modernising wing. In exchange for standing aside, the shadow chancellor pressed for effective control of the party's economic and industrial policy-making (Kampfner, 1999: 103–4). In the shadow cabinet reshuffle following Blair's victory in July, the new leader moved Cook from the trade and industry to the foreign affairs portfolio. Although ostensibly a promotion to one of the big three (shadow) offices of state, he took it to be a 'shunt upstairs' (Kampfner, 1999: 104). Cook had little interest in foreign affairs. His replacement at trade and industry was the previous shadow foreign secretary, Jack Cunningham, whom Blair saw as a 'safe pair of hands' for the more important (in electoral terms) trade and industry portfolio. One commentator wrote, 'the critical move in the reshuffle is that of Robin Cook

... At first sight a promotion ... To the left's chagrin, it reduces the influence on economic policy of the last remaining senior spokesperson with an economic portfolio who is critical of shadow chancellor, Gordon Brown's ultra-cautious economic strategy' (Paul Anderson, *New Statesman*, 28 October 1994).

There was considerable press speculation that Cook was unhappy about the switch with Cunningham. Cook had performed well in the 1994 elections to the shadow cabinet (coming top of the poll) and it was reported that he had hoped to be offered the shadow chancellor's position. In her memoir, his ex-wife wrote of the period that Cook 'sank further into misery, feeling that he was being sidelined' (Cook, 1999: 217–18). The foreign secretary's biographer concluded, 'Initially Cook was very disappointed by the move to the Foreign Office. Nominally he had got a more senior position but he realised it would take him out of the economic policy loop – which was exactly what Gordon Brown wanted' (John Kampfner, interview, October 1999). One fear of Cook was that the new brief would involve considerable foreign travel, thus inevitably sidelining him from important debates about the party's domestic programme.

In arguing unsuccessfully to hold on to his domestic portfolio, Cook insisted that he retain his place on the shadow cabinet's economic committee (alongside the party's left-inclined deputy leader, John Prescott). While much of his attention was devoted to foreign affairs in the remaining years in opposition, he sought to influence the party's domestic policy as well. He chaired Labour's National Policy Forum and was in charge of overall policy co-ordination. He took a variety of responsibilities both in the long run-up to the 1997 general election and during the campaign itself. He harried the Conservatives on Europe but continued to speak on domestic issues. In February 1997 he told the trade union Unison conference that Labour would restore a national framework to National Health Service pay. He was the Labour chair of a bilateral committee set up with the Liberal Democrats to investigate constitutional reform. Nor was Cook confined to foreign affairs during the election campaign: he criticised the sleaze associated with the Major government and Conservative splits on Europe. He flagged food safety, constitutional issues, water privatisation and 'fat cat' employers at press conferences and in press releases.

With little experience of international relations, it took time to establish himself in his new job and to work up enthusiasm for it (Kampfner, 1999: 104). *The Times* commented later: 'For almost a year after his appointment, Robin Cook gave every indication that he did not want the job and was itching for a return to the cut-and-thrust of domestic politics' (7 April 1997). The *New Statesman* noted, 'He spent his first year as shadow foreign secretary repositioning Labour on Europe' (9 February 1996). Cook gave four set-piece speeches in 1995. Only the first, on Europe, received much press attention. His great parliamentary triumph between 1994 and 1997 concerned the Scott inquiry: he attracted considerable praise in the media during 1996 for the skill with which he persistently tackled the government over the arms-to-Iraq affair. But responsibility for the issue did not go with the foreign affairs portfolio: it was a trade and industry matter, but one that he had insisted on keeping when reshuffled in 1994.

The shadow foreign secretary's persistent concern with domestic issues, especially economic matters, between 1994 and 1997 was evident. Speaking at one conference, he gave three themes for a Labour government's foreign policy. Alongside peacekeeping and disarmament, he argued that Labour should seek 'The provision at a global level of the kind of structures of political intervention that we have – or in the case of Britain used to have – for intervention in our economy and society to ameliorate the adverse effects of economic forces' (Cook, 1995: 20). Speaking to *Tribune*, he was blunt, 'My intention is that Britain under a Labour government should have a distinctive industrial policy to underlie our foreign policy. The two elements are in parallel – a foreign policy which reflects our domestic policy' (17 February 1995). In the *New Statesman*, Cook argued: 'At the domestic level Labour's "big idea" is that a strong community is essential if we are to provide an environment in which individuals can succeed. The same principle applies to our international perspective' (Cook, 1995: 20). Paul Anderson predicted that on Cook becoming foreign secretary, 'He'll want the job description changing to give him an economic policy role' (*New Statesman*, 27 October 1995). In his interview with *The Observer* on taking office, Cook stated that integrating foreign affairs into domestic debate was a key priority (4 May 1997). Will Hutton and Patrick Wintour took this stance to signal 'his intention not to be sidelined from domestic politics' (*The Observer*, 4 May 1997). By 1997, as it was apparent that he would be offered the post of foreign secretary in a Labour administration (and offered only that post), Cook became more reconciled to the outcome. The *Sunday Telegraph* reported that he still hoped to have some say on economic strategy and he was determined to sustain his political profile within the party (30 March 1997).

One explanation for Labour's ethical initiative is, therefore, in terms of intra-party dynamics. Having been given the foreign affairs portfolio, a politically low-profile though prestigious job, Cook needed to develop a distinctive approach in order to demonstrate his own left-wing credentials. The ethical dimension did just that: it raised Cook's profile both in the party and in the country generally through the articulation of a new and potentially radical policy. John Kampfner argued, 'Much of the trouble that Cook got into later with the mission statement was a direct consequence of his feeling that he had to stamp his own identity on the government quickly after the election' (interview, October 1999). Some commentators were quick to note that the mission statement was launched a week after Gordon Brown, Cook's historic rival in the party, had given the Bank of England independence over the setting of interest rates – a move that took observers by surprise (Kampfner, 1999: 135). The articulation of the foreign secretary's ethical dimension can be interpreted as an attempt to capture the political imagination and demonstrate the determination of the new administration. In a sense it was part of the euphoria that pervaded New Labour's stunning election victory and transition to power: 'At the time it seemed that the government could do no wrong' (John Kampfner, interview, October 1999).

Cook's intention may have been to raise his own profile and avoid the pitfalls that previous foreign secretaries had encountered through becoming entrenched in a series of time-consuming but politically unrewarding activities. Traditionally, foreign policy is politically unexciting. John Kampfner felt that 'Ever since 1994, Cook had tried to marry foreign policy which had always been seen as an offshoot of government, albeit an important one, with his need to be at the heart of the administration' (interview, October 1999). In this sense, the mission statement was an attempt to set himself apart from his predecessors and offer more political criteria by which he should be judged. Some commentators had concluded that he had been sidelined in the run-up to the election. At the same time, though, he was the standard bearer of what remained of the party's left. A *Guardian* profile noted that Cook 'will carry into government ... the hopes of Labour's traditional leftwing supporters, who see him as the politician who did not sell out and who will push a radical line' (21 April 1997). The support among party members for an ethical dimension would not be lost on Cook, conscious of his role as the standard bearer of the left. On Labour entering office, the *Independent on Sunday* concluded, 'His aims are to make the Foreign Office a big player on the domestic front, embracing issues such as the environment, defence and exports, and to strike a chord on the left' (18 May 1997).

Conclusions

Assessing Cook's first year in office, Malcolm Rifkind, his predecessor as foreign secretary, commented acerbically, 'When Cook lectured Binyamin Netanyahu [the Israeli prime minister], Franjo Tudjman of Croatia or the Indonesians there was the slight feeling that it was being done partly for dogmatic Labour party reasons and partly to make the foreign secretary feel better' (*New Statesman*, 23 October 1998). Cook's first twelve months in office had proved to be extremely difficult. He was subject to considerable tabloid press attention because of his private life and some of his initiatives ran into trouble, most notably his offer to help India and Pakistan mediate over Kashmir. The BBC commented that, by May 1998, he had been left in a 'dramatically weakened position' (BBC news website, 12 May 1998).

Cook's attempt to synthesise foreign and national policies, always poorly defined, came to little. His desire to have some input into domestic policy formation was equally unsuccessful. Once in government, he was not included on any of the cabinet committees concerned with economic issues. He chaired only two (in comparison, Gordon Brown chaired five and John Prescott took four). He was included on the constitutional reform committee but played little role in the Scottish and Welsh referendums over devolution. For the first eighteen months of office, he was not especially involved in discussions over European economic and monetary union and the United Kingdom's potential membership of it. Thereafter he became more involved. His articulation of a Third Way at home, in a speech to the Social Market Foundation (Cook, 1998), came to nothing. The speech itself was a reflection of the foreign secretary's desire to rehabilitate himself after the political setbacks he had encountered.

In the summer of 1998, some commentators concluded that Cook was a strong candidate to be reshuffled (*The Independent*, 10 June 1998). The conflict in Kosovo changed perceptions about his vulnerability. Cook's perform-ance during NATO's action impressed colleagues within the government, the British media and senior figures within the Clinton administration. By the summer of 1999, he was re-established within the Blair cabinet. In some ways, however, he had less impact on the course of foreign policy: one result of the Kosovo crisis was that Tony Blair took fresh and considerable interest in such matters. Kampfner described the foreign secretary as an 'ever-loyal executor of a foreign policy made in Downing Street' (Kampfner, 1999: 254).

In this chapter, I have made three inter-related points about the politics of Labour's foreign policy. First, I have argued that there is continuity between some of the party's previous policy commitments and some of the measures at the centre of Cook's ethical dimension as it was launched in 1997. There is less continuity between party policy documents and the kind of military intervention that the Blair administration undertook in Kosovo. Previously Labour was wedded to international action through the offices of the UN. The party did, however, discuss in the mid-1990s the conditions for legitimate intervention to protect human rights. Second, I have suggested that, insofar as evidence is available, both Cook's ethical dimension and Blair's moral interventionism are electorally popular, in marked contrast to Labour's unilateralist commitments of the 1980s. Last, I have claimed that Cook's ethical turn was motivated, in part at any rate, by a desire to raise his political profile within the Blair administration as a different kind of foreign secretary.

My last point does not resolve debate about whether Labour's foreign policy has been driven by either realist or idealist concerns. It does not validate the different perspectives laid out by either Dunne and Wheeler in chapter 4 or Buller and Harrison in chapter 5. The political explanation I have advanced is compatible with each, rather different, approach they adopt. I hope that it serves to provide an extra dimension in understanding the administration's policy. Labour's foreign policy can be characterised as a kind of two-level game in which international concerns must be linked with a domestic agenda, in this case essentially a party political one (see Putnam, 1988). The political dimension to Labour's foreign policy is important. It provides an explanation for some of the difficulties that Cook's initiative subsequently encountered. Why did the government make such a strong claim about the nature of its foreign policy in May 1997? How could the claim about an ethical dimension be reconciled with the continuance of arms manufacturing, an industry so important for the UK economy? In retrospect, disappointment seemed inevitable. I have argued here that Labour's ethical turn was a political development: it reflected significant intra-party dynamics. Wider issues about either the exact nature of an ethical foreign policy or the implementation of such matters as stricter controls on arms exports given the structure of the UK economy were not given due consideration.

References

Bish, G. (1982), 'The general election campaign: a note on priorities', RD:2522/ October. Internal party memorandum (London: Labour party).

Butler, D. and Kavanagh, D. (1984), *The British General Election of 1983* (Basingstoke: Macmillan).

Butler, D. and Kavanagh, D. (1988), *The British General Election of 1987* (Basingstoke: Macmillan).

Cook, M. (1999), *A Slight and Delicate Creature* (London: Orion Books).

Cook, R. (1995), 'Global tasks', *New Statesman*, 30 June.

Cook, R. (1997a), 'British foreign policy', statement, 12 May.

Cook, R. (1997b), press statement, 13 February.

Cook, R. (1997c), speech, Dutch Labour party, The Hague, The Netherlands, 15 February.

Cook, R. (1998), speech, Social Market Foundation, London, 24 April.

FCO (1997), 'Mission statement', 12 May.

Ferguson, C. (1998), 'A review of UK company codes of conduct, report commissioned by Social Development Division', DFID website.

Kampfner, J. (1999), *Robin Cook* (London: Phoenix).

Labour party (1976), *Labour's Programme 1976* (London: Labour party).

Labour party (1982), *Labour's Programme 1982* (London: Labour party).

Labour party (1983), *New Hope for Britain* (London: Labour party).

Labour party (1988), *Labour and Britain in the 1990s* (London: Labour party).

Labour party (1989), *Meet the Challenge, Make the Change* (London: Labour party).

Labour party (1990), *Looking to the Future* (London: Labour party).

Labour party (1991), *Opportunity Britain* (London: Labour party).

Labour party (1992), *It's Time to Get Britain Working Again* (London: Labour party).

Labour party (1994), *International Affairs and Security*, NEC statement (London: Labour party).

Labour party (1995), *Strategy for a Secure Future* (London: Labour party).

Labour party (1996a), *A Fresh Start for Britain. Labour's Strategy for Britain in the Modern World* (London: Labour party).

Labour party (1996b), *Policy Handbook* (London: Labour party)

Labour party (1997a), *New Labour Because Britain Deserves Better* (London: Labour party).

Labour party (1997b), *Labour's Policy Pledges for a Responsible Arms Trade* (London: Labour party).

Labour party (1997c), *An Ethical Charter for a New Development Department* (London: Labour party).

Meacher, M. (1993), 'Socialist International preparatory meeting for the World Human Rights Conference, 14 May 1993', PD (I):3339/June. Internal party memorandum (London: Labour party).

O'Neill, M. (1990), 'The defence expenditure implications of the recent events in Eastern Europe', PD (I):2374/January. Internal party memorandum (London: Labour party).

Putnam, R. D. (1988), 'Diplomacy and domestic politics. The logic of two-level games', *International Organisation*, vol. 42, no. 4, 427–60.

Short, C. (1997), speech, launch of Labour policy document, London, 11 March.

Wickham-Jones, M. (1996), *Economic Strategy and the Labour Party* (Basingstoke: Macmillan).

Working Group on Defence Policy (1994), minutes, Labour party, 16 June.

Vivekanandan, B. (1997), *International Concerns of the European Social Democrats* (Basingstoke: Macmillan).

7

New Labour and the Foreign Office

Kevin Theakston

Introduction

Labour party politicians love to hate the Foreign Office. From Hugh Dalton's cutting remarks about the 'Palsied Pansies of the F.O.' (Pimlott, 1985: 294) to Brian Sedgemore's claims about a 'Vichy mentality' in the department (Hennessy, 1989: 400), with Joe Haines (Harold Wilson's press secretary) chipping in to allege that 'the Foreign Office prepares new orchestrations of "I surrender, dear" to every demand or demarche made to it' (Haines, 1977: 31), MPs, party advisers and even ministers have queued up to denounce the department. The precise charges vary. At times the argument is that the Foreign Office is a sinister, secretive and powerful block on a 'socialist' or radical foreign policy – the idea, as E. D. Morel, of the Union of Democratic Control (UDC), put it in 1923, that the Foreign Office is 'the most undemocratic institution in the world' (Cline, 1967: 134). Tough-minded types, like David Owen (1991: 264–5), complain that 'the culture of diplomacy elevates splitting the difference into an art form' and suggest that British diplomats lack 'backbone'. Then there are criticisms of the class character of the diplomatic service; as Tony Benn put it in the 1960s: 'It is the final end of the public school man now that the Empire has gone – to finish up in British Embassies around the world, representing all that is least dynamic about British society' (Benn, 1987: 367). As with the civil service generally, there are different strands of Labour thinking and no single, coherent 'Labour party view' about the nature and problems of the Foreign Office and the diplomatic service or their reform (Theakston, 1992).

Robin Cook's relationship with the Foreign Office since he came into office in 1997 has certainly been problematic. Some of the difficulty has been due to his style and method as a politician, and his prickly, impatient and sometimes arrogant manner. He has been suspicious of the Foreign Office culture and, like some other New Labour ministers, has kept some of his officials at arm's-length (Theakston, 1998). With a left-wing, CND background, and as a very 'political' foreign secretary, he was perhaps bound to have a rocky ride in a department which has been well described as 'the least ideological, the least amenable to change and the least hospitable for a politician wanting to make his mark in Westminster' (*The Times*, 31 January 1998). Personal gaffes and a hostile media have taken their toll on the strong political reputation he had built up in opposition.

This chapter aims to put the tensions and problems experienced by Robin Cook and New Labour in relation to the Foreign Office and the diplomatic service into historical perspective, and brings out the differences and continuities from earlier Labour administrations. The chapter surveys Labour's relations with and thinking about the Foreign Office in three stages. First, it reviews the experience in office of Labour foreign secretaries and explores their relationship with their officials, discussing also the issue of Foreign Office scepticism about an 'ethical' foreign policy. It then discusses the long-running Labour concern about the class make-up of the diplomatic service. Before concluding, the chapter discusses the reform (or non-reform) of the Foreign Office machine under Labour governments.

Ministers and officials

It is difficult to generalise about the relations between Labour foreign secretaries and their officials in the Foreign Office and the diplomatic service. On the officials' side, 'the mythically "anti-Labour Foreign Office" is, of course, a simplistic caricature', as Geoffrey Moorhouse (1977: 154–5) noted. The diplomats were undoubtedly anxious about the advent of a Labour government and the first Labour foreign secretary back in 1924: the then permanent under-secretary (PUS), Sir Eyre Crowe, is said to have 'found his Labour party ministers only slightly less disagreeable than the Bolshevists' (Jones, 1989: 146). Pre-Thatcher, there was sometimes talk of 'a more natural relationship' between the Foreign Office and a Tory government. Paul Gore-Booth (1974: 231), PUS in the 1960s, recalled that 'in general Conservatives tend to be less touchy about advice than their opponents' – but then he did work with George Brown!

In the Labour party, there is manifestly a deep suspicion of the Foreign Office. Harold Wilson mistrusted the department and at times felt it was pursuing its own agenda. The charge that – like the Treasury – there is a determination that the opinion of the machine should prevail is constantly flung at the Foreign Office. Dalton believed in 1929 that the diplomats wanted to be 'not civil servants, but civil masters' (Pimlott, 1985: 192). Labour ministers' initial relations with Foreign Office officials can be wary – when Callaghan arrived in the department in 1974 he remarked that he supposed the Foreign Office was pro-Arab, pro-Catholic and pro-Europe to a man; like Henderson in 1929, he handed out copies of Labour's manifesto so that there was no misunderstanding about party policy. (That said, he went on to establish an excellent and effective working relationship with his officials.)

Ministerial–official relations were particularly strained during the tenures of George Brown (1966–68) and David Owen (1977–79). It was certainly a roller-coaster ride with Brown, a weighty politician who had the potential to be a great foreign secretary, but whose flashes of political brilliance were more than counterbalanced by his weakness for the bottle, his class resentments and inferiority complex, and his abominable personal behaviour and bullying of officials (Paterson, 1993). When Brown complained that the department was resistant to policy change, the international 'facts of life' as understood by the Foreign Office were put to him:

> Whatever politicians may say when they're in Opposition, they soon find out when they get into office and read the confidential papers that they can't possibly do what they said they would do and must instead follow the line of their predecessors in office, because there's just no other line any Government can follow. (Moorhouse, 1977: 157)

David Owen, too, was distrustful of the diplomatic machine and his abrasive personal style won him few friends. Although pro-European, he felt – like Margaret Thatcher later – that British diplomats did not fight hard enough in Europe for British interests; the Foreign Office Europeanists, he claimed, were strongly resistant to political control:

> Here was a very determined department [he recalled] which thought that its view was the right view ... they seemed to want to carry on conducting foreign policy on the lines that they thought were right, irrespective of what ministers wanted. That did lead to quite a number of clashes ... [and] some [senior] officials ... would fight the implementation of a decision taken by the Secretary of State. (Jenkins and Sloman, 1985: 103; see also Owen, 1991: 246–8)

Owen insisted on installing as ambassador to France Reginald Hibbert (previously the Foreign Office's man in Outer Mongolia) because he wanted a tough and robust negotiator in that post. Thatcher was in due course amazed to find someone on her wavelength in the Paris embassy and wondered how he had ever been appointed (Owen, 1991: 281).

Establishing a good relationship with the diplomats can make a Labour foreign secretary vulnerable to the charge of abandoning party principles, as Bevin found in the 1940s. Left-wingers like Laski complained of him falling 'an immediate victim to the worst gang in the F.O.' and being 'fooled with fantastic ease by the professionals who capture him'. But the idea that Bevin was some kind of puppet, with conservative diplomats manipulating the strings, carries no historical credibility (Bullock, 1983).

All the same, standing for bipartisanship, policy continuity and the ongoing 'international realities' can sometimes set the Foreign Office against ministers. The Foreign Office clearly hated Labour's policy of 'renegotiating' the terms of entry to the European Economic Community (EEC) in 1974. In the early 1980s there were signs that Labour's commitment to take the United Kingdom out of Europe and its non-nuclear defence policy would have caused ructions with the foreign policy and defence establishments had a government led by Michael Foot ever come to power (Hennessy, 1989: 402–3).

As far as an 'ethical' foreign policy is concerned, the Foreign Office has a record of scepticism or hostility towards Labour initiatives. Moorhouse's study in the 1970s described the diplomats as being 'very impatient with an emphasis on morality purveyed by Labour politicians', the department striving to counter what it regarded as these 'eccentric ... tendencies' and uphold what it believed was its own 'realism' (Moorhouse, 1977: 157–8). Former ambassador Sir Nicholas Henderson (1984: 89–91) testifies to the Foreign Office's dislike in the 1960s of Labour ministers' talk of the United Kingdom setting an example to the world and giving a moral lead in international affairs. At the time this involved issues like possibly waiving the veto in the UN, taking a principled stance on the rule of law in international life, the distribution of overseas aid to countries most in need without regard to a possible tie-in with UK foreign policy interests, and nuclear disarmament. Sir Con O'Neill, one of the Foreign Office's top brass, could barely contain himself, telling Henderson: ' the weaker we are, the more we seem to expect people to follow our example. It's almost as though it were a substitute for power. Yet what a nonsense it is. Can you think of a single example in history of one country following a good example set by another? There are plenty of instances of countries following bad examples.' In the same vein, during the 1974–79 government, Ted Rowlands, a Labour minister of state responsible for policy towards Latin America, found that his desire to prioritise human rights was constantly thwarted and undermined by Foreign Office officials and ambassadors whose instinct was to try to maintain 'good relations' and get on with their host country's government: 'don't you think [minister] that in the interests of trying to influence the events in Chile we might soften our attitude in this respect or that respect?' (Jenkins and Sloman, 1985: 103–5).

In the Foreign Office, as around Whitehall in general, there was considerable goodwill towards the incoming Labour government in 1997. Younger members of the Foreign Office in particular apparently felt undervalued and humiliated by Tory xenophobia and Euroscepticism (Kampfner, 1998: 151). But in an interview a Foreign Office minister explained that the department had experienced a 'culture shock':

> Change was difficult in terms of our new style. [Officials] were very comfortable with the Tories. Eighteen years makes a really comfortable relationship ... Therefore, there was an uncertainty as to what was going to happen – some [officials] have been able to live more easily with that, others have found it a challenge they cannot manage, and have been difficult. There have been examples of ambassadors trying to redefine what we've been saying ... It will take a little time to work through.

Robin Cook was reported to be suspicious of the 'establishment' culture of the Foreign Office and the diplomatic service. He has tried to introduce new ideas by reaching out to groups that might previously have been regarded more as thorns in the Foreign Office's side: a human rights adviser was recruited from Amnesty International and a children's rights adviser from Save the Children; Amnesty also now provides human rights briefings for newly appointed ambassadors.

Relations between Cook and Foreign Office officials have not been trouble free. Cook himself has said: 'There is no *maquis* somewhere in the underground trying to resist the policy that I'm putting through.' Sources close to him insist that claims that the Foreign Office is up in arms against the much-trumpeted 'ethical dimension' in foreign policy are exaggerated (Lloyd, 1998). In the Whitehall tussles over arms sales and export licences, for instance, the real arguments have been with Number 10, the MoD and the DTI, which have wanted to tone down the 'ethical' policy and reassure the defence industry (Kampfner, 1998: 145–6, 171, 213). Ministers have sometimes given conflicting signals. All the same, there have been reports that some senior officials – disliking Cook, viewing the 'ethical' foreign policy with cynicism and dubious about the trendy talk of 'rebranding' the United Kingdom's image – were privately pleased to see him damaged by the political storm over his ousting of the diary secretary in his private office and the claims that he had considered appointing his mistress to the job. The arms-to-Africa affair further strained relations between ministers and diplomats, and raised questions about the running of the Foreign Office, as Cook appeared to blame officials for not keeping him properly informed and distanced himself from staff failures and administrative mistakes. There was controversy over whether officials had deliberately kept ministers in the dark about the Sandline arms shipments, or whether ministers had failed to brief themselves properly. Cook was alleged to be sometimes neglectful of the detailed dossiers in his ministerial red box.

The media had another field day in January 1999 when Sir David Gore-Booth, who as High Commissioner to India had not hit it off with Labour ministers, retired early from the diplomatic service complaining that Cook had 'lost the trust' of senior diplomats. There was renewed speculation about poor relations between Cook and his senior officials, but the difference between problems with particular disgruntled diplomats and determined institutional resistance or obstruction within the Foreign Office is an important one, and there is little reliable evidence of the latter.

Cook brought with him into office two special advisers – now a familiar species in Whitehall – from his opposition staff. (A third was funded by Labour.) Though hardly a 'counter-bureaucracy', these advisers can provide a useful source of alternative advice, as well as links to outside organisations and experts, and can have a 'mine-detector' role, alerting ministers to possible party trouble or sensitivities about certain issues. The idea of reinforcing a Labour foreign secretary against the Foreign Office by making these sorts of appointments can in fact be traced back to the fall-out from the Zinoviev letter incident in 1924. Supporters of the UDC within the party had been pressing for some time for a 'clean sweep' of existing senior Foreign Office staff and the appointment, as PUS and as ambassadors in the principal missions, of outsiders who were in sympathy with Labour's international ideas (Young, 1918, 1920; Labour party, 1921). Before Labour took office, MacDonald had been warned that 'he must have someone he could trust in charge of the private secretariat, of publicity, and of Russia' (Morris, 1977: 164). He ignored this advice and E. D. Morel argued that the 'Red Letter' affair showed 'the powerlessness of a Labour government to control the permanent officials of the Foreign Office and to protect itself against their incapacity or worse' (Taylor, 1957: 168). (The real culprits seem to have been renegade MI6 agents, acting in cahoots with Tory Central Office, as the recent official study commissioned by Robin Cook suggests; see Bennett, 1999.)

In 1925 the party's Advisory Committee on International Questions drew up a radical plan to appoint a 'political' private secretary to control the ministerial private office, bring in a Labour journalist as head of the publicity department, set up a League of Nations branch in the Foreign Office to be headed by a party supporter and appoint Labour sympathisers to head crucial diplomatic posts abroad. MacDonald, however, would have no truck with anything like an American-style 'spoils' system (it would be 'a complete reversal of all our ideas regarding the Civil Service', he insisted), and intervened to tone down and effectively kill the plan (Theakston, 1992: 45–7).

Bevin, after 1945, upheld the MacDonald line too, refusing to carry out the sort of purge of the Foreign Office urged by left-wingers in the party. He told the 1946 party conference that he was determined to 'stick to the career man'. Where political appointments might have been made – to the UN or to the Washington embassy, which Harold Laski was pitching for – he chose career diplomats instead, and his decision to allow the former Tory minister Duff Cooper to remain as ambassador to France (until 1947) was controversial in the party (Bullock, 1983: 72–4). Subsequent Labour governments have occasionally made 'political' ambassadorial appointments, such as John Freeman as High Commissioner to India and then ambassador to the United States in the 1960s, and in the 1970s Ivor Richard as ambassador to the UN and Peter Jay, Callaghan's son-in-law, as ambassador to the United States. However, the massive media and political storm over the Jay appointment shows that there can be a political price to pay. Certainly, when Cook in opposition floated his plan to advertise ambassadorial posts to attract private sector business people (see below) Labour stressed that there was no intention of introducing a 'spoils' system or of undermining Whitehall's tradition of political neutrality and that there would be no outside *political* appointees – no more Peter Jays. Cook did not want an 'outsider' as ambassador to the United States, and Christopher Meyer, an archetypal Foreign Office high-flyer and former press secretary to John Major, got the job in 1997. There was some speculation that Sir Stephen Wall, UK permanent representative to the EU and a close confidant of John Major's, might face the axe under Labour but Blair signalled before the election that he intended to keep him on. The PUS chosen by Blair in 1997 to head the Foreign Office, Sir John Kerr, had also been a prominent and influential figure during the Conservative years, another sign that New Labour did not plan to overthrow the diplomatic service or break its grip on the machine.

Labour attacks on the 'unrepresentative' Foreign Office

The unrepresentative, class character of the Foreign Office and diplomatic service has long been a target of Labour party criticism. A system of exclusion meant that a member of the working class's party could become foreign secretary but would not be considered 'good enough to become a First Secretary', claimed one of Labour's early foreign policy advisers (Young, 1918: 8). Laski-style attacks on the Foreign Office for being a 'nest of public-school singing birds' always found a ready audience in the party.

The 'representative bureaucracy' argument rests on the claim that the policy preferences of the Foreign Office can be 'read off' from the (elitist) backgrounds of its official personnel. As a Fabian study argued in 1930: 'a Foreign Service containing representatives of all social classes should produce a type of official more sympathetic to public opinion ... A Foreign Service manned by those drawn from the privileged classes will remain antipathetic to the new internationalist ideals' (Nightingale, 1930: 18). Labour has regularly been urged to take positive steps to encourage more recruits from varied social backgrounds into the diplomatic service. Spreading the net wider was necessary to make the Foreign Service more responsive to the demands of radical change in foreign policy, it was argued, for 'the social base of the Foreign Office is such as to make it at the worst antithetical, and at the least indifferent, to the aspirations of Labour' (Fielding, 1975).

During the Second World War Bevin had urged the 'democratisation' of Foreign Office recruitment. But as foreign secretary he firmly rejected suggestions of class bias in Foreign Office personnel or policy. The working-class Titan was himself, apparently, free from class prejudice, except, that is, for his violent dislike and mistrust of middle-class left-wing intellectuals. One of his Foreign Office aides recalled that a public school background was no disadvantage with Bevin, who was in fact 'a warm admirer of Eton and Harrow' (Barclay, 1975); diplomacy could not do without Etonian recruits, he once remarked (Moorhouse, 1977: 175). He believed that the post-war system did make the diplomatic service open to all, irrespective of social or educational background, though the 1940s–60s recruitment data tell a different story (Davis, 1954: 350–1; Moorhouse, 1977: 59).

For all Labour's suspicions, however, a straightforward connection between diplomats' class backgrounds and their public school/Oxbridge education and a policy outlook supposedly hostile to, or at odds with, the party's views is more easily alleged than proven. 'The "Laski view"', as Geoffrey Fry (1982: 4–5) noted, 'tends to be expressed in a sufficiently generalised form to be incapable of substantiation – or refutation.' There is a widespread assumption that the bulk of the Foreign Office staff traditionally vote Conservative, though one former career diplomat and ambassador claimed (just before the Social Democratic party split from Labour in 1981) that 'it was common knowledge that two-thirds of the Foreign Office and Service voted Labour nowadays' (Jackson, 1981: 80). A mid-1980s study noted 'the aversion many diplomats feel towards Mrs Thatcher's brand of radical Toryism'. Rather than a simplistic class-based or partisan bias, however, the bias – as in any bureaucracy – is probably better characterised as a resistance to or scepticism about 'risky policy innovations' (Jenkins and Sloman, 1985: 105–6).

Although Alistair Campbell, Blair's press secretary, has been quoted denouncing 'plummy-voiced Old Etonian diplomats' (*The Times*, 19 October 1998), Labour's concern in the 1990s about the social arithmetic of the diplomatic service (and Whitehall generally) focused on principles of equal opportunity in a wider sense – broadening the recruitment base and making the higher posts more accessible to women, ethnic minorities and people with disabilities. Under Robin Cook, the Foreign Office has appointed Whitehall's first ethnic minorities liaison officer, and 'open days', attended by hundreds of young people, have been held in an attempt to dispel the 'old school tie' image. Baroness Symons, the Foreign Office junior minister pushing these changes, says that New Labour is determined to make the department's staffing 'better reflect the diversity of modern British society' (*The Guardian*, 21 June 1997). To underline the point, a black female barrister, Baroness Scotland, and the first minister of Asian descent, Keith Vaz, received junior ministerial appointments in the department in 1999.

There is certainly a long way to go at official level. Only three and a half per cent of Foreign Office staff in 1998 were from ethnic minority backgrounds and two-thirds of those were to be found in the bottom grades of the service, with only one out of 443 officials in the top four grades of the 'senior management structure' from an ethnic minority. Only seven per cent of staff (thirty) in the top four grades were women in 1998 (thirty-six per cent of all Foreign Office staff being female) and there were seven women ambassadors/heads of mission. The department trumpeted the progress made in fast-stream recruitment, women accounting for fifty-two per cent of the successes in 1998 (compared with thirty-six per cent in 1997) and ethnic minority recruits increasing from none to nine per cent. But perhaps it is too Old Labour to wonder why the Oxbridge percentage actually increased from forty-eight in 1997 to sixty-five in 1998 and to point out that among the 'under-represented groups' in fast-stream diplomatic recruitment are the ninety-three per cent of the population attending state schools – the seven per cent attending independent schools providing sixty-one per cent of the 1998 intake (FCO, 1999: 79–81). Realistically, it may be some time before we see changes on a significant scale to the composition and character of the senior ranks of the diplomatic service under New Labour.

Reforming the Foreign Office machine

In the case of the Foreign Office – as with the rest of Whitehall and the home civil service (Theakston, 1992) – socialist intellectuals and Labour party pamphleteers and policy pundits have over the years been active in devising reform schemes and re-organisation blueprints, but these have often been just paper exercises because the party leadership has not taken them up or made them a high priority. In office, Labour governments – from MacDonald's to Callaghan's – have usually been institutionally conservative.

Before becoming prime minister, Ramsay MacDonald had insisted that the Foreign Office needed a 'thorough overhauling' – 'we must destroy the old methods of Foreign Offices', he argued, calling for 'open windows and fresh air' to end the traditional secret diplomacy (MacDonald, 1920: 124–9). There was in fact no shortage of practical Labour proposals for reform of the Foreign Office in the 1920s but, in government, MacDonald and Henderson were at best lukewarm about them and more often either not interested or too frightened of offending official susceptibilities. Thus the imaginative plan of the party's International Advisory Committee to merge the foreign and consular services and to introduce specialised regional services to meet the changed conditions of the post-1918 international scene was simply ignored (Theakston, 1992: 79, 148–9). There was also no progress on the long-standing Labour and Radical Liberal pledge to create a parliamentary Foreign Affairs Committee, though in 1924 the 'Ponsonby rule' was established, giving an opportunity for MPs to debate a treaty before it was ratified. (A House of Commons Foreign Affairs Committee did not finally appear until 1979 – illustrating Labour ministers' executive orientation, George Brown in the 1960s had considered the idea but rapidly dropped it when he realised that MPs on such a committee would want to investigate policy questions.)

Bevin had a key influence over the landmark 1943 white paper *Proposals for the Reform of the Foreign Service*, published by Anthony Eden during the wartime coalition. The key reforms all featured in a 1940 Bevin memorandum, including the appointment of labour attachés; widening of recruitment; and the merging of the Foreign Office, diplomatic, consular and commercial staffs into a single service (Bullock, 1967: 199–202). (Bevin also wanted equality between men and women in the foreign service – something that Eden fudged.) Ideas like these had been around a long time, of course, and had been part of the programme of the party's Advisory Committee on International Questions in the 1920s. Reform was long overdue. The changes, introduced by Bevin after 1945, would in time transform the Foreign Office, he believed. The Eden–Bevin reforms were widely supported in the Foreign Office at the time. But perhaps this was because the innovations did not in practice herald a radical break in recruitment patterns, personnel or the basic character of the foreign service, as Bevin's left-wing critics recognised. Bullock (1983: 101) notes Bevin's institutional conservatism, arguing that the reforms he made 'were adaptations designed to make [the Foreign Office and foreign service] work more efficiently rather than to change them'.

Labour's unwillingness seriously to contemplate or push through a radical shake-up of the diplomatic machine was, again, very apparent in the 1960s and 1970s. The establishment of a unified diplomatic service at the beginning of 1965, following the (1964) report of the Conservative-appointed Plowden Committee, and the series of departmental amalgamations which produced in 1968 the merged Foreign and Commonwealth Office, were certainly important developments (in the latter case the fashion for bigger Whitehall departments and the turn to Europe in 1966–67 overcoming lingering Labour party hostility to such a merger). But on two occasions when the diplomats might have felt that they had their backs to the wall, Labour governments backed off from major reform.

George Brown claimed that he had had 'high hopes' of the Duncan Committee (1968–69), but felt that its report was 'possibly the most missed opportunity of quite several decades to bring about a genuine reform of the Foreign Service' (Brown, 1972: 57). The Duncan inquiry was unwelcome to the Foreign Office, and was largely inspired by Treasury demands for expenditure cuts in the aftermath of the devaluation of the pound and the decision to withdraw military forces from east of Suez. At a cabinet meeting in January 1968, according to Tony Benn, there had been:

> a long discussion about the extravagant level at which British diplomats lived abroad, and the cost of Embassies ... Harold Wilson pointed out that it wasn't necessary to have massive political intelligence when you hadn't got the power to make use of the information, and he urged that we group our Embassies and concentrate almost entirely upon commercial work. (Benn, 1988: 12)

Evidence that the staffs of British posts abroad were up to twenty per cent larger than their French equivalents and double the size of West German missions suggested that there was plenty of scope for cutbacks (Watt, 1969).

The Duncan report duly came up with proposals for expenditure savings and cuts in the size of the diplomatic service (involving the premature retirement of serving officials). It emphasised the over-riding importance of commercial work and export promotion (leading a critic to quip that the committee believed a diplomat was a man who goes abroad to sell washing machines for his country). Most controversial of all, however, was the committee's central analysis of the basic nature of the United Kingdom's diplomatic interests – involving a distinction between an 'area of concentration' and the rest of the world – and its consequent recommendations about 'comprehensive' and 'selective' missions in countries falling into one or other category (Review Committee on Overseas Representation, 1969).

Duncan was 'spell[ing] out, belatedly, the logic of the end of Empire', insisted Andrew Shonfield, a member of the committee (Shonfield, 1970: 247). But the report caused something of a storm in the press and went down badly in the Foreign Office itself. At a meeting of the Labour cabinet's Overseas and Defence Policy Committee in November 1969, foreign secretary Michael Stewart said he did not like the over-blunt distinction between the 'area of concentration' and the 'outer area', which Harold Wilson also condemned as dividing the world 'literally into black and white' (Castle, 1984: 729). Parliament was told that the government broadly accepted 'the Duncan principles' but believed that the two-category division of diplomatic operations it envisaged had been 'too sharply drawn' and was over-rigid. Major changes in the export promotion effort and a downgrading of political reporting were also ruled out (House of Lords debates, *Hansard*, 19 November 1969: cols 941–54). Within a year, Labour had lost office and the report was quietly shelved.

Ironically for an institution regarded with some suspicion by Harold Wilson in 1974 as a 'Tory Trojan Horse' and attacked by Tony Benn as a tool of a conspiratorial bureaucracy, it was the Central Policy Review Staff (CPRS) think-tank's 1976–77 *Review of Overseas Representation* exercise which was to canvass the most radical surgery and to call into question the continued survival of the diplomatic service in its existing form. It was only to be expected that the Foreign Office would be vehemently opposed to a report that criticised its social tone, complained about over-staffing, extravagance and unnecessary perfectionism, urged the need for greater specialisation, and proposed the closure of over fifty overseas missions or posts and the abolition of a separate diplomatic service and its merger with the home civil service (CPRS, 1977). The think-tank's recommendations regarding the BBC external services and the British Council helped to ensure a devastating 'establishment' counter-attack. Labour ministers were well aware that senior diplomats were behind the anti-CPRS propaganda campaign and press leaks (Blackstone and Plowden, 1988).

In the event, the Callaghan government opted for a quiet life and ditched the CPRS's main recommendations. The prime minister (though he had commissioned the study late in 1975, when he had been foreign secretary) apparently had no appetite for the detailed discussion of a 400-page report. If on the big issues the Foreign Office was spared the think-tank's axe, many of its detailed recommendations were in fact accepted and implemented in a low-key way over the next few years and into the 1980s, such as staff economies, the closure of posts, the introduction of 'mini-missions' and other organisational improvements. But the whole episode confirmed that Labour in the 1970s was essentially supportive of the Whitehall status quo. 'Thinking the unthinkable' about the Foreign Office had no supporters in the 1974–79 Labour cabinet.

As Labour's opposition foreign affairs spokesperson in the House of Lords in the 1990s, Tessa Blackstone was still canvassing a CPRS-type reform. The DTI should do export promotion in support of business at home and abroad, she argued, deploying trade experts rather than generalist diplomats, as done by other countries. Foreign Office staff numbers had been cut from over

9,000 when Thatcher took office in 1979 to 6,000 by 1994, but Blackstone believed that there was still considerable scope for streamlining in posts overseas: 'in too many places the Foreign Office runs a Rolls-Royce service where something more modest would do the job'. 'Radical pruning' of overseas missions was still possible (*The Guardian*, 21 May 1993). Interestingly, Blackstone was moved sideways, into the education department, after the election, being replaced in the Foreign Office ministerial team by Baroness Symons, a Blairite and friend of the prime minister.

Robin Cook seemed keener to stress his concern to make the Foreign Office less 'stuffy' and to highlight his plan to hire private sector business people as ambassadors (*The Times*, 6 October 1995; *The Guardian*, 11 June 1996). This proposal always sounded more radical than it really was because Labour made it clear that there would only be a few (four or five) 'business-ambassadors', on temporary contracts and targeted at specific countries (the emerging markets of Asia and the Pacific rim were cited). In office that plan quietly gave way to a scheme for 'short-term business attachments', with around twenty private sector executives spending three to six months in UK embassies abroad, with (at a more senior level) various 'captains of industry' signed up as informal roving 'ambassadors for British business' (an ill-defined and rather symbolic role). The Conservatives had also had a business secondment scheme and none of this really threatens the Foreign Office. Some Foreign Office trade promotion jobs have even been advertised externally, including that of director of the British Trade and Investment Office in New York, but this post went to a career diplomat, not a business executive. And the Foreign Office's position was, if anything, strengthened rather than diminished by the outcome of the (1998–99) Wilson review of export promotion, which resulted in the creation of a new body, British Trade International, which brings together the trade development and export promotion work of the Foreign Office and DTI under a single chief executive, who turned out to be a career diplomat and former ambassador, not a businessman (*Financial Times*, 11 May 1999).

Cook deftly presented the Legg report (Sierra Leone Arms Investigation, 1998) as a catalyst or a lever, enabling him to boost and accelerate the 'modernising' changes he wanted to make to the Foreign Office anyway. Legg (and a follow-up report by the Foreign Affairs Committee, 1999) certainly painted a damning picture of Foreign Office errors and misjudgements, poor communications, deficient (domestic) political sensitivities and management failures. Cook has restored the dedicated sanctions-enforcement unit in the Foreign Office, abolished by the Conservatives in 1996; he has put in place new guidelines for contacts with private military companies and new arrangements for handling intelligence reports; and he has revised the guidelines for briefing ministers, including for parliamentary appearances. All these changes directly tackle faults and problems uncovered by Legg. Reversing the long-running pattern of staff cuts, Cook saw off Treasury demands for savings in the Foreign Office's budget and secured increased resources, permitting the recruitment of 375 more staff (staff overload was a contributory cause of what went wrong, according to Legg).

Significantly, Legg's co-investigator was Sir Robin Ibbs, previously head of Thatcher's Efficiency Unit, and architect of some of the key civil service management reforms of the 1980s. The Whitehall management revolution of the Conservative years had, arguably, not been fully felt in the Foreign Office. Cook has launched a programme of Foreign Office modernisation involving sixty separate measures to improve management, including plans to bring in outside expertise in personnel management; reducing the hierarchy in the department to enable officials to take more responsibility sooner; the introduction of performance targets, linking resources and objectives; new information technology and telecommunications systems; and targets for service standards (for example, time taken to reply to letters or provide information). The Foreign Office information technology department has been 'benchmarked', a contract has been drawn up for outsourcing pay-roll services, work has been proceeding on developing an 'internal market' for Foreign Office support services – all these are now standard 'new public management' practices in Whitehall. With the Foreign Office owning assets (chiefly properties overseas) valued at over £1 billion, the hunt is also on for 'under-performing assets' that can be sold and the money re-invested (a £90 million target has been set). While the Foreign Office is, managerially speaking, catching up with the rest of Whitehall, Cook is continuing the well established trend to devote more resources to trade and export promotion, and strengthening commercial and economic work (FCO, 1999: 76–7, 86–9). Whatever the eventual fate of his 'ethical' foreign policy, Cook's tenure of office is likely to have a significant impact in terms of making the Foreign Office itself up to date, well managed, efficient and properly resourced.

Conclusions

The relationship between Labour and the Foreign Office is complex and always potentially fraught. One suspects that in large part this is because the two 'sides' do not fully understand each other – the cultures, the organisations, the methods and the fundamental objectives are perhaps too different. Geoffrey Moorhouse (1977: 159) noted the 'divergent philosophies, the implicit challenges, the careful sparring and the eventual compromises that exist when the diplomats find themselves serving a Labour government'. When the history of the Blair government and its 'ethical' foreign policy comes to be written, the same story is likely to be told.

Looking ahead to the possible longer-term impact of the New Labour government on the Foreign Office and the diplomatic machine, three issues seem crucial. The first concerns Europe. In the 1980s Thatcher toyed with the idea of carving out a separate Ministry for Europe and in opposition some of Blair's advisers considered breaking up the Foreign Office in this way, too, but Blair ruled it out before the 1997 election. A Labour minister admitted in interview: 'With so much of the FO's time and resources devoted to European issues, there was no way the bureaucracy was going to allow Europe to be hived-off separately. The FO would lose its big "in" in Whitehall. Europe is the FO's way of getting involved in a whole range of other issues.' But critical aspects of European policy since Labour came to power have been driven by Number 10, the Cabinet Office and the Treasury; the Foreign Office (and Cook) have been marginalised. As European integration speeds up, the Whitehall boundaries here may well come under review again.

Related to this is the fashionable issue of 'joined up government'. The Foreign Policy Centre think-tank is assessing the future role of the Foreign Office, talking about 'joined up foreign policy', with each government department engaging internationally to achieve its goals, and changing the culture of the foreign service to make it more open to new ideas and more effective at learning from its mistakes (the Foreign Office as a 'learning organisation') (*Independent on Sunday*, 28 February 1999). The Foreign Office will want to go along (or appear to go along) with a lot of this, at least while ministers seem interested. But the big institutional threat it faces is that 'joined up government' could put the merger of the diplomatic service and the home civil service back on the agenda, sparking a re-run of the arguments provoked by the CPRS's report in 1977.

The third issue impacting on the future of the Foreign Office is devolution. The UK government will remain responsible for international relations, including relations with Europe. But the government wants (and needs) to involve the devolved administrations in Scotland, Wales and Northern Ireland in the development of policy on those international issues that also have implications for devolved functions (and this will be particularly the case in relation to EU issues). 'Concordats' have been negotiated to provide a framework for co-operation, committing the Foreign Office to keep the devolved administrations informed on relevant international/EU developments, and committing the devolved administrations to keep the Foreign Office informed about relevant policy proposals and proposed contacts. In theory, the Foreign Office will be the formal channel for relations with other countries (and the United Kingdom is the formal EU member state and member of international organisations), but it is recognised that Scotland, Wales and Northern Ireland will set up their own offices in Brussels, for instance – from the Foreign Office's point of view, the tricky issue is ensuring that these complement rather than cut across its own diplomatic activities. In the areas where international/EU negotiations touch on devolved matters, there will be a Joint Ministerial Committee, with underpinning official support, to broker agreements and hammer out a co-ordinated UK 'line' (Quin, 1999). How this will all work out in practice on highly charged political issues is anyone's guess. Devolution is not just about domestic politics; it will complicate the United Kingdom's international/EU relations and make the Foreign Office's life more difficult. The period ahead is likely to be a critical one for the Foreign Office.

References

Barclay, R. (1975), *Ernest Bevin and the Foreign Office* (London: Latimer).

Benn, T. (1987), *Out of the Wilderness: Diaries 1963–67* (London: Hutchinson).

Benn, T. (1988), *Office Without Power: Diaries 1968–72* (London: Hutchinson).

Bennett, G. (1999), 'A Most Extraordinary and Mysterious Business': The Zinoviev Letter *of 1924*, History note no. 14 (London: FCO).

Blackstone, T. and Plowden, W. (1988), *Inside the Think Tank: Advising the Cabinet 1971–1983* (London: Heinemann).

Brown, G. (1972), *In My Way* (Harmondsworth: Penguin).

Bullock, A. (1967), *The Life and Times of Ernest Bevin, Vol. II, Minister of Labour* (London: Heinemann).

Bullock, A. (1983), *Ernest Bevin: Foreign Secretary* (London: Heinemann).

Castle, B. (1984), *The Castle Diaries 1964–70* (London: Weidenfeld and Nicholson).

Cline, C. (1967), 'E. D. Morel and the crusade against the Foreign Office', *Journal of Modern History*, vol. 39, 126–37.

CPRS (1977), *Review of Overseas Representation*, cmnd 7308 (London: HMSO).

Davis, E. (1954), 'The foreign and commonwealth services', *Political Quarterly*, vol. 25, no. 4, 347–59.

FCO (1999), *Departmental Report*, cm 4209 (London: TSO).

Fielding, R. (1975), *The Making of Labour's Foreign Policy* (London: Fabian Society).

Foreign Affairs Committee (1999), *Sierra Leone*, HC 116–I (London: TSO).

Fry, G. (1982), 'The British diplomatic service: facts and fantasies', *Politics*, vol. 2, no. 2, 4–8.

Gore-Booth, P. (1974), *With Great Truth and Respect* (London: Constable).

Haines, J. (1977), *The Politics of Power* (London: Coronet).

Henderson, N. (1984), *The Private Office* (London: Weidenfeld and Nicholson).

Hennessy, P. (1989), *Whitehall* (London: Secker and Warburg).

Jackson, Sir G. (1981), *Concorde Diplomacy* (London: Hamish Hamilton).

Jenkins, S. and Sloman, A. (1985), *With Respect, Ambassador: An Inquiry into the Foreign Office* (London: BBC).

Jones, R. A. (1989), *Arthur Ponsonby: The Politics of Life* (London: Christopher Helm).

Kampfner, J. (1998), *Robin Cook* (London: Gollancz).

Labour party (1921), *Control of Foreign Policy: Labour's Programme* (London: Labour party).

Lloyd, J. (1998), 'Cook's defence lies in the detail', *New Statesman*, 15 May.

MacDonald, J. R. (1920), *A Policy for the Labour Party* (London: Leonard Parsons).

Moorhouse, G. (1977), *The Diplomats* (London: Cape).

Morris, A. J. A. (1977), *C. P. Trevelyan 1870–1958: Portrait of a Radical* (Belfast: Blackstaff Press).

Nightingale, R. (1930), *The Personnel of the British Foreign Office and Diplomatic Service 1851–1929* (London: Fabian Society).

Owen, D. (1991), *Time to Declare* (London: Michael Joseph).

Paterson, P. (1993), *Tired and Emotional: The Life of Lord George Brown* (London: Chatto and Windus).

Pimlott, B. (1985), *Hugh Dalton* (London: Macmillan).

Quin, J. (1999), 'Devolution and foreign affairs', speech, Belfast, 26 February.

Review Committee on Overseas Representation (1969), *Report of the Review Committee on Overseas Representation 1968–1969*, cmnd 4107 (London: HMSO).

Shonfield, A. (1970), 'The Duncan report and its critics', *International Affairs*, vol. 46, no. 2, 247–68.

Sierra Leone Arms Investigation (1998), *Report of the Sierra Leone Arms Investigation*, HC 1016, 1997–98 (London: TSO).

Taylor, A. J. P. (1957), *The Trouble Makers: Dissent over Foreign Policy 1792–1939* (London: Hamish Hamilton).

Theakston, K. (1992), *The Labour Party and Whitehall* (London: Routledge).

Theakston, K. (1998), 'New Labour, New Whitehall?', *Public Policy and Administration*, vol. 13, no. 1, 13–34.

Watt, D.C. (1969), 'Overseas representation', *Political Quarterly*, vol. 40, no. 4, 485–90.

Young, G. (1918), *The Diplomatic Service: What It Has Done To Us, and What We Should Do To It* (London: National Labour Press).

Young, G. (1920), *The Reform of Diplomacy: A Practical Programme* (London: Labour party).

Part IV

Labour's foreign policy in practice

8

'Simply the right thing to do': Labour goes to war

Will Bartlett

We are doing what is right, for Britain, for Europe, for a world that must know that barbarity cannot be allowed to defeat justice. That is simply the right thing to do. (Blair, 1999a)

Introduction

Until recently the territory of Kosovo in the southern Balkans was the epitome of a 'far-away country of which we know little'. Almost coincidentally with Labour's election victory in 1997, this small province in south-west Serbia was thrust into the limelight as a vicious civil war developed between Albanian insurgents and Serbian security forces. The Albanian majority in Kosovo, comprising almost ninety per cent of the two million population, had waged a campaign of passive resistance against the repressive policies of the Serbian regime since the late 1980s. That regime, led by Slobodan Milosevic, had come to power in Belgrade in 1987 on a wave of Serbian nationalist hysteria, directed initially largely against the alleged growth of Albanian nationalism in the province, although subsequently also directed against other non-Serb groups within Yugoslavia.

In 1997 Albanian resistance developed into a guerrilla war of national liberation. It broke out into open conflict in early 1998, as an armed insurgency led by the Kosovo Liberation Army (KLA) was met by a full-scale counter-insurgency operation by the Serbian security police. Serbia regarded its policy in Kosovo as an internal matter. NATO countries argued that it was a matter of international concern because of both the perceived threat of a wider regional conflict erupting and the related humanitarian crisis. The conflict revolved around a clash between Albanian demands for some sort of independence and Serb assertions of national sovereignty. The UK Labour government, along with NATO allies, argued ultimately that Serb actions to police the province and manage the conflict were unacceptable. In March 1999, military action was taken against Serbia, with Labour at the forefront of those demanding such an outcome. In this chapter, I look at Labour's policy towards Kosovo during its first two years in office. I note the shift in the Blair administration's approach that led to war in 1999. I go on to discuss the justification for the war and assess its aftermath. In my conclusion I locate the military campaign within the overall context of the Labour government's foreign policy.

Background to the crisis

Historically, Kosovo had been part of the old mediaeval Kingdom of Serbia. The region is divided between Muslim Albanians and Christian Serbs. Following on from the 1974 Yugoslav constitution, the predominant Albanian population enjoyed considerable autonomy (though insufficient to satisfy all). In such circumstances, some of the minority Serb population felt unfairly discriminated against. In the late 1980s, Milosevic sought to reduce the province's autonomy through constitutional amendments, so fuelling tensions between the two polarised populations. During 1989–90 protests aimed at the Serbian authorities became widespread. Albanians sought the rights of other republics within Yugoslavia. The Serbs wanted to prevent Albanian domination of Kosovo and in 1990 the province's status was redefined as a region of Serbia. The government in Kosovo refused to co-operate and declared itself independent unilaterally, thus precipitating a decade of repression.

These difficulties did not occur in isolation. A series of conflicts erupted across Yugoslavia, most notably, of course, in Bosnia. The response of the Conservative government in the United Kingdom to this evolving crisis was slow and uncertain. Following the Dayton accord of 1995, British troops went to Bosnia as part of the UN peacekeeping force.

Labour's policy in the first year of office: a neutral stance

In 1997, following the belated recognition of the FRY by the EU, the conflict was radicalised by an armed Albanian faction calling itself the KLA. The EU recognition of the FRY highlighted the failure of the non-violent and peaceful road to independence mapped out by Ibrahim Rugova,[1] since it enshrined the constitutional status of Kosovo as a mere region of Serbia. Radical nationalist Albanians concluded that armed struggle would be the only way to liberate their country from, as they saw it, the colonial occupation of the Serbian government. They had the example of the Bosnian Serbs to encourage them who, following the Dayton accord, had created a *de facto* republic in Bosnia through the use of military force (Vickers, 1998: 286–7; Chandler, 1999).

The Labour government became directly involved in the Kosovo crisis in January 1998, when the United Kingdom took over the presidency of the

---

1 Ibrahim Rugova was the leader of the Democratic League of Kosovo and the unofficially elected 'president' of Kosovo.

EU. As a member of the six-nation Contact Group established in 1995 (consisting of the United States, the United Kingdom, France, Germany, Italy and the Russian Federation), it took a leading role in co-ordinating international efforts to resolve the conflict peacefully. Initially, it insisted on working through the UN. In early February, the Serbian Interior Ministry police forces, backed by the Yugoslav army for the first time, launched a major offensive against the KLA. The offensive resulted in fifty deaths, and Adem Jashari, an important KLA leader, was killed. Robert Gelbard, senior US envoy to the Balkans, described the KLA as a terrorist organisation. Robin Cook was also lukewarm towards it (Gumbel, 1998). As the crisis intensified, he hosted an emergency meeting of the Contact Group in London on 9 March 1998, the first for two years. The US secretary of state, Madeleine Albright, called for strong action against Belgrade. The Contact Group threatened to freeze Yugoslav assets held abroad, adopted a visa ban on those responsible for war crimes and decided to seek an arms embargo through the UN (which was eventually passed by the UN Security Council as resolution 1160 on 31 March 1998). A proposed ban on investment in the FRY was resisted by Italy largely because Fiat had just won a lucrative contract to renovate the Zastava car factory, while Italian companies had also participated in the sale of the Serbian telecommunications network in 1997 (Fox and Stephen, 1998). In issuing the joint declaration of the meeting, Cook denounced both the repression by the Serbian forces and the use of terrorism by the KLA (Youngs and Dodd, 1998: 24).

Milosevic claimed domestic democratic legitimacy for his policy towards the international community over Kosovo. In a referendum held on 23 April 1998, Serbs voted overwhelmingly to reject international diplomatic interference in the crisis (Fox and Petrie, 1998). Following a second meeting of the Contact Group which took place in Rome on 29 April 1998, Cook set out the government's position: 'we do not support independence for Kosovo, but we believe that its present status must be enhanced through meaningful autonomy. We are therefore determined to promote political dialogue on an enhanced status for Kosovo between Belgrade and Pristina as the only course that is likely to produce a stable, peaceful outcome' (Youngs and Dodd, 1998: 30). Subsequently, US diplomats Richard Holbrooke and Robert Gelbard held talks in Belgrade with Milosevic. The Serb leader declared his willingness to admit international monitors under the auspices of the Organisation for Security and Co-operation in Europe (OSCE), as a result of which, on 18 May 1998, the Contact Group lifted the threat of an investment ban (Youngs and Dodd, 1998: 26).

While the Contact Group was debating the appropriate policy response to the crisis during May, a further Serbian offensive was launched in the border region with Albania. The operation was designed to stop the inflow of arms across the border but had the effect of giving the KLA a huge boost in support and KLA fighters became openly visible throughout the province (Steele, 1998). No longer a rag-tag army of peasant rebels, it now acquired modern weapons, including rocket-propelled grenades and mortars. *The European* commented, 'In Kosovo, Serbs and Albanians alike know that the war has begun' (Fox and Petrie, 1998).

Labour's policy in the second year of office: the swing to the KLA

Meeting in early June 1998, NATO foreign ministers decided to prepare plans for a joint air–land operation in Kosovo with the aim of forcing Serb police and troops to withdraw. A NATO-led peacekeeping force would replace them. Elections would be held for an autonomous government within a year. NATO sources reported that the United States was opposed to sending in ground troops without a settlement. Once agreement was reached, the United States accepted that there should be a peacekeeping force (Evans, 1998). NATO members favoured autonomy because continued fighting meant that there would be increasing numbers of refugees seeking asylum in Western Europe. They opposed independence since it might unlock unrest in Macedonia and even a wider conflict involving Greece and Turkey.

On 8 June 1998 the EU Council of Ministers called for a withdrawal of special police and army units from Kosovo. Cook wanted to fend off a German and Dutch proposal for the threat of military force. He asked EU ministers not to tie his hands before the British-drafted UN resolution authorising 'all necessary means' was agreed with the Russians (Martin Walker, 1998). By early June, the second Serb offensive had been concluded after four weeks (and 250 deaths). The Serbs followed it by planting landmines along the Albanian border, claiming the measure was an anti-terrorist operation and asking for understanding from the international community. The UNHCR announced that there were 50,000 internally displaced persons who had fled their homes, 12,000 of whom were in Albania and 7,000 in Montenegro (Mather and Petrie, 1998). Tony Lloyd, British Foreign Office minister and the newly appointed EU envoy to Kosovo, visited Pristina on 12 June 1998. He told Rugova's advisers that the West was resolved to avoid a repeat of the Bosnian war, in which ethnic conflict between Serbian nationalists and Bosnian Muslims and Croats had caused enormous loss of life earlier in the decade (Tom Walker, 1998). As Serb troops prepared a new offensive in the south-west of Kosovo, Fehmi Agani[2] told Lloyd that air strikes were the only means to resolve the crisis, adding that the Albanians were not willing to negotiate with the Serbs (Tom Walker, 1998). A large demonstration by 25,000 Albanians took place in Pristina with placards announcing 'NATO, Kosovo is Burning!' (Mather and Petrie, 1998). NATO studied its options.

The Contact Group held an emergency meeting in London on 12 June 1998. Klaus Kinkel, the German foreign minister, pushed for immediate

---

2 Fehmi Agani was deputy chairman of the LDK. He was killed in the early days of the war.

military intervention. The United Kingdom argued against, aware that its commitment in Bosnia meant that its armed forces would be over-extended (Mather and Petrie, 1998). The US State Department was hawkish, accusing Milosevic of ethnic cleansing. Collectively, the Contact Group demanded that Serbia: cease all action by its security forces and withdraw them; allow unimpeded access to international monitors; facilitate the return of refugees; and make progress in dialogue with the Albanian leadership. The investment ban was re-imposed and all Yugoslav and Serbian government assets abroad were frozen. Cook asserted that 'in the event of President Milosevic failing to carry out the action plan we have mapped out, we will consider further measures that will be different in quality and will include those measures that may be authorised by a UN Security Council resolution' (Black, 1998). Cook persisted in stalling over the use of force. Furthermore, if the use of force proved necessary, the government hoped that a resolution backing it could be pushed through the UN Security Council. On 15 June, at the Council of Ministers, the EU agreed a ban on flights to the FRY. In late June, the first informal contacts between Richard Holbrooke and the KLA took place, endorsed by Cook (Youngs and Dodd, 1998: 29). British policy had begun to swing away from neutrality towards support for the Albanian nationalist cause. At this stage, however, the United Kingdom was not a hawk and hoped the conflict could be resolved through UN intervention.

In July 1998, an offensive restored Serbian control over most of the province (Youngs, 1998: 8). It resulted in 250,000 refugees being forced from their homes. Two hundred villages were destroyed (*The Economist*, 24 October 1998). Both sides committed atrocities, including summary executions (*Human Rights Watch*, October 1998). On 23 September, the UN Security Council called for a cease-fire by all parties and a withdrawal of Serb troops (resolution 1199). Disagreements remained as Russia and China opposed the use of force to back the demand. In the absence of agreement, NATO went ahead unilaterally without UN support and issued an ultimatum to Milosevic (Youngs, 1998: 12). It set a deadline of 27 October by which the Serbs should comply with the UN resolution or face air strikes. Following intensive negotiations with Holbrook in Belgrade, Milosevic agreed to comply with NATO's demands that he meet the terms of the Security Council resolution. The Serbs would be required to reduce their forces to the pre-conflict levels of February 1998. A 2,000-strong verification force was to be deployed under the auspices of the OSCE. The allies did not demand a full withdrawal of Serbian forces, as they were aware that this would effectively allow the KLA to take over the province. The Contact Group's aim was administrative autonomy for Kosovo within Serbia (Youngs, 1998: 17).

Cook told the House of Commons, 'Britain played a leading part within the international community in putting pressure on President Milosevic that made these agreements possible ... President Milosevic [would not] have made such a commitment if the diplomatic efforts backed by the contact group had not also been backed by the credible threat of military action by NATO'

(Youngs, 1998: 23). The threat of force was made by NATO without formal UN backing: it represented an important change in British policy, which had hitherto insisted that the use of force or the threat of its use should have the authorisation of the Security Council.

By 26 October, the Yugoslav army had met the conditions laid out. It was uncertain whether the special police forces had fully complied. The 250,000 displaced people began to return home from hiding and the UN verification mission entered Kosovo.

The Rambouillet ultimatum

Despite the presence of international monitors, low-level fighting between the KLA and Serb security forces continued. In response to KLA activity, the Serbs once again increased their forces' presence in the province, a violation of the October agreement. A massacre of forty-five Albanian civilians at Racak in January 1999 triggered the adoption of a much more aggressive policy towards Serbia from NATO countries, although subsequently a Finnish forensic team that investigated the killings concluded that it was impossible to pass judgement on who had been the perpetrators (Youngs *et al.*, 1999: 11).

New talks were opened at Rambouillet, co-chaired by Robin Cook and Hubert Védrine, his French counterpart. The Albanian and Serb delegations were presented with a plan drawn up by the Contact Group. It proposed a three-year period in which the province would gain extensive autonomy while remaining part of Serbia. After three years, an international conference would negotiate a final settlement. The two parties were told that the plan was largely non-negotiable. Serb troops were required to withdraw and the KLA would be demilitarised. NATO would deploy a peacekeeping force of 30,000 troops, including a Russian contingent. Neither side signed up immediately to the plan as the talks became bogged down (Youngs *et al.*, 1999). By mid-March, the Kosovo Albanians agreed reluctantly to accept the deal. They anticipated that the Serbs would reject it and that NATO would enter the conflict on their side. The Serbs had already accepted the political conditions but they balked at NATO leadership of the proposed international peacekeeping force for Kosovo and at the military annex that would have allowed unimpeded access for NATO forces throughout the whole of the FRY (Contact Group, 1999). They refused to sign up to what was effectively an ultimatum (Krauthammer, 1999; Youngs *et al.*, 1999: 17).

The OSCE monitors began to withdraw on 20 March 1999. The Serbs stepped up their campaign against the KLA fighters (Bird, 1999). Some days later, reports of systematic ethnic cleansing by the Serb forces filtered through into the Western media (Lloyd, 1999). Within days, more than 80,000 people were reported to have fled their homes (*The Economist*, 20 March 1999: 51). In a last-minute attempt to persuade the Serbian government to give way, Richard Holbrooke held talks with Milosevic, but his initiative failed. On 25

March, air strikes were launched with a wave of cruise missile attacks from warships in the Adriatic against targets throughout Serbia.

Between June 1998 and March 1999 Labour's policy on Kosovo had changed. Originally, the United Kingdom had followed a cautious line based on negotiation. Its approach was neutral between the two sides. The threat of military force was an option to be considered only reluctantly, if at all, and in any case should be underpinned by UN resolutions. But by March 1999, Labour rejected dialogue. Its policy had swung towards support for some, at any rate, of the Albanian demands. It was based on the assumption that reasoned negotiation with Milosevic was impossible: only ultimatums, backed by threats of force, would work. Such threats needed to be coherent and plausible. If necessary, NATO would have to go it alone, without UN support. Subsequently, Labour argued as if it had taken such a tough stance all along. Ministers claimed that the Tories had appeased Milosevic during the early and mid-1990s, in contrast to Labour's robust position. In fact, Labour's policy towards Serbia was re-aligned in office. By March 1999 the British conciliator had become a hawk.

Labour during the war: ethics to the fore

In an emergency statement to the House of Commons on 23 March, Tony Blair made three points to justify the air war against the FRY (Blair, 1999a). First, he claimed that all possible diplomatic efforts had been exhausted: 'We tried for six long months to keep Milosevic to the agreements he made' (Blair, 1999a). In fact, the two sides had come close to an agreement at Rambouillet (Youngs *et al.*, 1999: 13). It is possible that the Serbs would have signed the deal if the allies had not insisted on both NATO leadership of any peacekeeping force and the unfettered movement of NATO troops throughout the whole territory of the FRY. Control of the peacekeeping force by the OSCE might have been acceptable to the Serbs (*The Economist*, 27 February 1999: 41). The draconian nature of the military annex was probably an unnecessary obstacle to an agreement (Jenkins, 1999).

Second, Blair claimed that the air strikes were morally justified: 'To those of you who say the aim of military strikes is not clear, I say it is crystal clear: it is to curb Milosevic's ability to wage war on innocent civilians ... Fail to act now, and the conflict unleashed by Milosevic would not stop. We would have to deal with the consequences of spiralling conflict and hundreds of thousands of refugees' (Blair, 1999a). Tragically, the air strikes failed to prevent such an outcome. Some commentators suggested they precipitated the result that they had been intended prevent. Jonathan Eyal (1999) noted that comparisons with Bosnia concerning the effectiveness of air power were irrelevant. In Bosnia, the Serbs were beaten by a combined offensive including the Bosnian and Croatian armies on the ground, and not by air power alone. He predicted accurately that the Serbs would retaliate against the Albanians, causing a huge wave of refugees to stream out of Kosovo: 'The West is justifying the operation as necessary in order to avoid a humanitarian disaster. In fact, the biggest humanitarian disaster will unfold when the air attacks start' (Eyal, 1999). In April, Conservative members of the Foreign Affairs Committee, John Stanley and Peter Luff, argued that the NATO air strikes had worsened the plight of the Kosovo Albanians, a proposition vigorously rejected by Robin Cook.

Third, Blair claimed a legal justification for military action: 'To those who say NATO is striking at a sovereign nation without justification, I say it is Milosevic who scrapped Kosovo's autonomy' (Blair, 1999a). Although widely accepted, this justification for attacking a sovereign nation had its critics. Tony Benn pointed out that 'an ultimatum has been announced amounting to an all-out air war, and possibly a ground war against a member state of the United Nations which under article 51 has the right to self-defence. By doing so, the British Government and other NATO governments are defying the charter, to which we are committed and breaking international law' (quoted in Youngs *et al.*, 1999: 41). Likewise, William Rees-Mogg concluded, 'NATO has no authority in international law for the bombing'. He continued: 'at least in theory, the NATO leaders, under the Nuremberg ruling, are open to a similar indictment which has been brought against President Milosevic' (Rees-Mogg, 1999).

As the air campaign progressed seemingly without success, the moral aim of the war emerged as the key justification of NATO's action. The allies faced a dilemma: should they lose credibility by admitting failure (and stopping the campaign), or should they step it up (with increasing intensity and a wider range of targets, including those that were questionable militarily but of economic and psychological importance). The ethical dimension of what was increasingly seen as a 'humanitarian war' came to the fore. The media focused on stories of terrible brutality and human tragedy suffered by the Kosovo Albanians, hundreds of thousands of whom were expelled from their homes and driven from the country by the indiscriminate Serbian offensive against both the KLA and the civilian population. George Robertson, defence secretary, emphasised the moral justification above any other war aims: 'As internationalists, we cannot stand idly by when entire villages are being torched, when women and children are being herded to trains at gunpoint and when men are being murdered simply because they are Albanian. We have a responsibility to do all we can to halt the bloodshed and help alleviating the humanitarian disaster which is unfolding here' (Robertson, 1999). As Eyal (1999) observed, the NATO air strikes and the withdrawal of the OSCE monitors had given Milosevic the opportunity to carry out exactly such a campaign of ethnic cleansing. But Robertson would have none of it, arguing that 'NATO did not cause the ethnic cleansing, Milosevic did' (Robertson, 1999).

Repeated relentlessly by the government in the months ahead, the moral argument became the main justification for the war. It neglected mounting evidence that atrocities had been committed on both sides before the NATO campaign began. It glossed over the divisions between the peaceful resistance of the Albanians led by Ibrahim Rugova and the violent methods of the KLA. Possibly KLA tactics had been designed to pull NATO into a war with Serbia, and so lead to independence for the province (*The Economist*, 27 February 1999). In the period before Rambouillet, tension and violence were much diminished compared with the previous year. There were relatively few refugees and most displaced people remained within Kosovo. It is unlikely that, had the OSCE verification mission stayed in the province, the violence would have increased markedly (Krauthammer, 1999). The world media would have been in place, of course, to observe any conflict.

The war was presented to the British public as a humanitarian one. The new concept of humanitarian war gelled well with the pronounced intention to pursue an ethical dimension in foreign policy. It was a war fought for a higher moral purpose rather than narrow self-interest. Air strikes, aided by modern technology, would deliver pinpoint accuracy against purely military targets, so avoiding civilian casualties. They were to be delivered by remote engagement, by missiles and aircraft flying beyond the reach of the enemy defences. The war was ostensibly fought not against the Serbian people but primarily against an abstract embodiment of evil, personified in the form of one individual, Slobodan Milosevic, the 'dictator' of Serbia. In *The Sun*, Blair wrote stridently, 'This is now a battle of good against evil ... our cause is just. In the battle between good and evil, we are on the right side. And we will win' (5 April 1999).

The new concept of humanitarian war suffered from inherent contra-dictions since the means of waging war were to be limited to avoid unnecessary civilian casualties on the enemy side and military casualties on the allied side.[3] As Charles Krauthammer has observed, 'humanitarian war requires means that are inherently inadequate to its ends' (1999). Against expectations, the Serbian regime did not succumb to the initial wave of attacks against air defence systems, military headquarters and empty barracks within Serbia. After several weeks of strikes intended, in the words of General Wesley Clark (in a televised statement at the start of the air campaign), to 'disrupt, diminish, degrade and ultimately destroy' the Serbian armed forces, NATO had failed to achieve its initial aim – to protect the Albanian civilians within Kosovo. The war aims were revised to include the reversal of the wave of ethnic cleansing and to secure the *return* of the refugees to their homes (Rose, 1999). The air attacks against Serbia were stepped up. Civilian infrastructure targets were attacked. Less regard for civilian casualties was observed as the campaign was drawn ineluctably into a phase of generalised strategic bombing

3 In answer to questions put to him by the House of Commons Committee on Defence on 24 March, George Robertson replied that 'Our objective ... is to use strategic precision bombing on military targets' (minutes of evidence, para. 375) but that while 'we are conscious that we do not want to add to the miseries of [the civilians] who are in that location ... we would obviously still be conscious of our own force protection necessities' (para. 367).

with the intention of crippling the Serbian economy. To achieve domestic political support, the moral argument was given increased emphasis during this intensification. This case was furthered by the public outrage at the treatment of the Albanian civilian population by the Serbian forces within Kosovo, visible nightly on television screens and in extensive media coverage. It is unlikely that the Western alliance would have held together through the eleven weeks of continuous bombing against Serbia without the popular domestic support for the campaign that was fuelled by the cruel treatment of the refugees. But civilian casualties of NATO's bombing campaign also mounted. Presented as 'mistakes', these were nevertheless the inevitable consequences of its intensification. In addition, attacks against the economic infrastructure resulted in widespread destruction of public utilities within Serbia, depriving the population of access to water, electricity and transport. Numerous bridges were destroyed, which blocked the Danube, bringing water-borne trade to a halt not just within Serbia but also badly damaging the economies of neighbouring countries that depend on the waterway as a major trade route.

In addition, the bombing campaign inflicted severe damage on the environment. A UN study revealed that mercury and dioxins had leaked into the Danube, threatening the safety of water supplies as far away as Bulgaria and Romania, while the use of depleted uranium munitions posed severe health hazards in Kosovo (Balkans Task Force, 1999). A spokesman for the World Wide Fund for Nature commented, 'By bombing oil refineries and chemical factories NATO was conducting a highly dangerous chemical experiment with unknown and possibly devastating consequences' (Brown, 1999). These means are questionable not only in their failure to meet the immediate objectives set by NATO but in their own right in terms of the wider environmental consequences of their use.

The ethical credentials of the Labour government were jeopardised by official policy towards the 800,000 refugees who had fled to Albania and Macedonia. The exodus was unprecedented. Local families took in many refugees but were burdened by the added economic cost of caring for the migrants. Most refugees were confined in cramped conditions in the new tent cities hurriedly constructed with aid from the allied countries. Calls grew for the allies to take the refugees into their own countries. However, Labour argued that it would be better for them to remain within the region to facilitate their eventual return home (Schaefer, 1999). Anne Clwyd, a backbench Labour dissident, encountered claims, during a visit to the camps, that some refugees were being barred from entry into the United Kingdom. She told the House of Commons that 'they have been told that Britain didn't want them. I found that a very worrying statement indeed and I don't know whether it is true or not. But so far we have only been told that two hundred and fifty Kosovo refugees are coming to this country' (Schaefer, 1999). The burden of hosting the refugees was enormous for Albania and Macedonia. In the latter state, it threatened to disturb the fragile ethnic accommodation between the Albanian and Macedonian communities and political parties, and so further destabilise the region. It highlights the way in which the issues surrounding regional stability were over-simplified before and after the war. The preservation of regional stability was a war aim (Blair, 1999c). But the effects of the conflict and the subsequent breakdown of trade and economic activity within Macedonia and other countries may give rise to far more regional instability in the future than would have been likely if more strenuous efforts to achieve a diplomatic solution had been pursued in the first place.

After the war: ethics abandoned

Labour supported the hostilities against Serbia on the grounds that NATO was fighting a humanitarian war against the scourge of ethnic cleansing. For Robin Cook, 'This war was fought in defence not of territory but in defence of values ... we have struck a blow for human decency' (*New Statesman*, 5 July 1999). Having failed to prevent a humanitarian disaster, the eventual aims of the war shifted to a more limited one of creating the conditions in which the refugees could return home (Rose, 1999). To reconstruct the region, a Marshall plan for the Balkans was proposed (Blair, 1999c). It was formalised through the promise of $2 billion of aid and the institution of a stability pact for the region announced at a donors' conference in Brussels and at an intergovernmental meeting in Sarajevo in July (Murray, 1999). Cook insisted that, as long as Milosevic remained in power, Serbia was to be excluded from this aid (*New Statesman*, 5 July 1999). However, as a central economic unit within the region, any efforts at reconstruction cannot make headway with economic sanctions continuing against Serbia.

Tony Blair was unable to resolve this dilemma. In a speech in Sofia in May 1999, he announced his government's intention to assist regional reconstruction:

> Rebuilding the region will be an enormous task. But I give you my personal pledge that it will be completed successfully. Britain and its allies have not launched this campaign simply to withdraw and leave others to pick up the pieces. The conflict changed the political geography of South Eastern Europe for a generation. Politicians across Europe need to accept this new reality. People ask where are the new leaders to replace Milosevic. I don't know. (Blair, 1999b)

The Serbian opposition has been weak and divided: a main contender to replace Milosevic is Vojislav Seselj, leader of the Serbian Radical Party, an even more demagogic nationalist than Milosevic.

Following Milosevic's eventual capitulation, a peace agreement was signed on 9 June 1999. Yugoslav forces withdrew in their entirety from the province in good order within ten days of its signing. Following a brief delay, which saw a potentially disastrous confrontation between Russian and NATO troops at Pristina airport narrowly averted, NATO armies entered Kosovo and took over responsibility for military defence and policing within it. The UN, through the creation of an interim body known as the United Nations Interim Administration Mission in Kosovo (UNMIK), assumed the civilian administration. The OSCE accepted responsibility for organising future elections and for restoring the institutions of civil society.

The moral component of the war aims, ending the ethnic cleansing, was thwarted by the actions of the restored Albanian population. Terrible atrocities had occurred during the war and the suffering of the Albanian population had been immense (OSCE, 1999a). Damage assessments by the UN revealed that as much as one-fifth of the housing stock in Kosovo had been destroyed or badly damaged, mainly by Serbian forces in their campaign of ethnic cleansing (Bremner, 1999). The enormous psychological impetus to the revenge attacks must be recognised. In this atmosphere, they perpetrated their own wave of ethnic cleansing directed against the indigenous Serbian population (OSCE, 1999b). Murders, expulsions and intimidation resulted in the rapid departure to Serbia and Montenegro of as many as 100,000 Serbs from the province within a few weeks. Unwelcome reminders of defeat, the new refugees were treated with callous disregard by the Serbian authorities. NATO troops could do little to prevent the disorder within the province in the absence of the promised international police force (Kraja, 1999). Perhaps they could not prevent revenge attacks. But, as the weeks went by, few words were heard by way of condemnation of these activities from Labour's spokespeople.

In Serbia the damage inflicted by the bombing campaign was estimated by the independent G17 group of economists in Belgrade to be about $29 billion, including the losses due to an estimated two-fifths fall in gross domestic product (G17, 1999). Infrastructure damage was estimated at around $4 billion, with the destruction of factories and offices leaving over 200,000 people without jobs (Prentice, 1999). Serbia has been effectively excluded from the aid provided for reconstruction. The allies expected that the economic isolation of Serbia would cause hardship among the population and give rise to an opposition movement to oust Milosevic. The equally probable outcome is to provide the regime with an excuse for the poor living conditions in the country, which can easily be blamed on the actions of the international community.

Conclusions

The United Kingdom played a key role in the Kosovo conflict and was intimately involved in the development of policy. Strategy emerged jointly with allies in NATO, the EU and the Contact Group. Labour influenced these bodies but did not enjoy a decisive role. The UK government was bound by collective decisions and was unable to pursue an independent line.[4] Only to the extent

4 There were some areas in which UK policy was relatively autonomous, for example in relation to the treatment of refugees, the level of forces committed and the supply of aid to refugees and to Kosovo and the region after the conflict.

that the international community's policy was moral could Labour claim to be pursuing an ethical approach. In what sense was the policy ethical?

It is difficult, if not impossible, to define an ethical foreign policy, especially in relation to the Balkans. No definitive conclusions can be reached concerning whether the policy adopted by the allies was ethical, had an ethical core or had ethical elements within it. Nevertheless the government did make a large number of statements indicating that this was how it should be seen and how they themselves viewed it. For Tony Blair it was a war of good against evil. It was a war, uniquely, fought not for territorial gain or national interest but out of a concern for 'our fellow human beings' (Blair 1999a). But there is some evidence to suggest that the war contained elements that were distinctly non-ethical. Pacifists would argue that war can never be ethical, while the Church of England, among others, sets out conditions for a just war. It is not the purpose of this chapter to enter into this debate. But there are a number of internal contradictions between policy statements and the policies pursued to cast doubt on the idea that this was an example of ethical foreign policy in action. Foremost among these was the difference in the reaction to ethnic cleansing of Serbs by Albanians after the war; the lack of concern for the suffering of civilians in Serbia; the unwillingness to commit ground troops; the priority to attack command and control rather than to make high-risk attacks in Kosovo to stem the ethnic cleansing; the lack of consideration that the policy of air strikes would itself provoke a humanitarian disaster; and the negative attitude to the migration of refugees and asylum seekers – in which the United Kingdom performed worse than its allies. In each of these areas Labour's approach might be found wanting in terms of its ethical foundations.

Labour's policy towards Kosovo has been to support autonomy for the province but at the same time to resist Albanian calls for independence. This position was linked partly to concerns for regional stability and partly to a need to stem the flow of refugees into Western Europe. The ethical non-violent Albanian resistance movement led by Ibrahim Rugova had been persistently sidelined in the post-Dayton period when the United Kingdom was courting Milosevic, a policy that Labour failed to challenge while in opposition. Initially neutral between the Serbs and the KLA, the Labour government moved closer to the Albanian position, even though the KLA was fighting for outright independence. As the Contact Group position developed, Cook became more and more firmly attached to the US insistence on a firm stand against Milosevic. The Rambouillet talks, co-chaired by Cook, eventually presented the Serbian side with an ultimatum, which was presented in such a way that the use of force by NATO was virtually inevitable. The contradiction between implicit support for the KLA and the policy of autonomy resulted in a fudged peace agreement that has left Kosovo formally still a part of Serbia and the FRY and therefore bereft of effective government. This state of virtual anarchy bodes ill for future stability in the region (Rexhepi, 1999).

It is noteworthy that Labour's policy did not emerge as a deliberate set of measures driven by ethical concerns. Rather the party drifted in response to the crisis. Labour's shift to support for the Albanian cause mirrors some aspects of New Labour. The Blair government has introduced devolution for Scotland and Wales. It has disavowed its past identity as Old Labour, which had traditionally been supportive of the integrity of Tito's Yugoslavia. It has been dismissive of its opponents and the legitimacy of their arguments. New Labour did, in a rather contradictory fashion, resort to the Old Labour values of anti-fascism and anti-colonialism by drawing polemical parallels between Milosevic and Hitler, an argument repeated on several occasions by both Robin Cook (*New Statesman*, 5 July 1999) and Tony Blair (1999c). Blair and Cook referred to Milosevic as a 'dictator', ignoring the fact that the Socialist Party of Serbia has repeatedly been returned to power through open elections although, as in some other East European and Balkan countries, the level of democratic practice is far below that in the West, gerrymandering and election abuses are commonplace and democracy is far from the stage of consolidation (Pridham, 2000).

The Kosovo war was Labour's first real excursion into putting the ethical dimension of foreign policy into practice. It was justified as a moral war, with the government explicitly on the side of good against evil. But the humanitarian credentials of the war were dubious. The initial aim to prevent a humanitarian disaster was confounded in the first weeks of the war while the choice to pursue a military solution arguably contributed to the refugee crisis that evolved. Since the war, the ethical imperative has lost much of its force as the ethnic cleansing of Serbs from Kosovo received little attention in the Western media. The main aim of post-war policy has been to isolate Serbia and to ignore the plight of the population of that country. As winter approached in the autumn of 1999, the economy of Serbia lay in ruins, its people deprived of basic conditions of existence through the imposition of an oil blockade, continuing financial sanctions and a refusal to assist the reconstruction of the destroyed infrastructure until and unless Milosevic is deposed. While the ethical foreign policy as applied to the Balkans was a well intentioned exercise in populist politics it failed to achieve the goals of either protecting the Kosovo Albanians from a humanitarian catastrophe or of establishing a democratic multi-ethnic society in Kosovo after the war ended. The legacy of the ethical approach is likely to be continued instability and immiseration in the region for decades to come.

References

Balkans Task Force (1999), *The Kosovo Conflict: Consequences for the Environment & Human Settlements* (Geneva: United Nations Environment Programme and United Nations Centre for Human Settlements).

Bird, C. (1999), 'Kosovo villagers flee as monitors leave', *The Guardian*, 20 March.

Black, I. (1998), 'NATO pins hopes on Yeltsin to get Serbs to listen over Kosovo', *The Guardian*, 13 June.

Blair, T. (1999a), 'Full text of prime minister's speech to the nation on Kosovo', *The Guardian*, 27 March.

Blair, T. (1999b), 'The Kosovo conflict: a turning point for South Eastern Europe', speech, Atlantic Club of Bulgaria, Sofia University, 17 May.

Blair, T. (1999c), 'There can be no compromise in Kosovo', *The Times*, 7 May.

Bremner, C. (1999), 'US and EU clash over Kosovo cost', *The Times*, 14 July.

Brown, P. (1999), 'Danube study questions warfare that bombs polluting targets', *The Guardian*, 27 October.

Chandler, D. (1999), *Bosnia: Faking Democracy After Dayton* (London: Pluto Press).

Contact Group (1999), *Interim Agreement for Peace and Self Government in Kosovo. Appendix B: Status of Multi-National Implementation Force*, Rambouillet, France, 23 February 1999. Full text available from JURIST website: http://www.jurist.law.pitt.edu/ramb.htm#Chap7

Evans, M. (1998), 'Defence ministers give go-ahead for Nato airstrike', *The Times*, 11 June.

Eyal, J. (1999), 'The aerosol myth', *The Guardian*, 24 March.

Fox, R. and Petrie, C. (1998), 'War machine warms up', *The European*, 11–17 May.

Fox, R. and Stephen, C. (1998), 'Sanctioning slaughter in Kosovo's fertile land', *The European*, 4–10 May.

G17 (1999), *Economic Consequences of NATO Bombing: Estimates of Damage and Finances Required for Economic Reconstruction of Yugoslavia – Summary* (Belgrade: G17) (available at www.g17.org.yu)

Gumbel, A. (1998), 'Cook plea falls on deaf ears as Serb police blitz villages', *The Independent*, 7 March.

Jenkins, G. (1999), 'An offer Serbia couldn't refuse', *Socialist Review*, 231 (June), 8–9.

Kraja, G. (1999), 'A violent peace breaks out in Kosovo', *Balkan Crisis Report No. 80* (London: Institute for Peace and War Reporting).

Krauthammer, C. (1999), 'The short, unhappy life of humanitarian war', *National Interest*, vol. 57 (fall), 5–8.

Lloyd, J. (1999), 'Hit-and-run attacks slow Serb advance', *The Times*, 24 March.

Mather, I. and Petrie, C. (1998), 'Nato fiddles, Kosovo burns', *The European*, 8–14 June.

Murray, A. (1999), '£1.3 bn pledged to rebuild Kosovo', *The Times*, 29 July.

OSCE (1999a), *Kosovo/Kosova: As Seen, As Told* (Warsaw: OSCE Office for Democratic Institutions and Human Rights).

OSCE (1999b), *Kosovo/Kosova: As Seen, As Told, Part II, June to October 1999* (Warsaw: OSCE Office for Democratic Institutions and Human Rights).

Prentice, E.-A. (1999), 'Cost of NATO damage estimated at $29 bn', *The Times*, 23 July.

Pridham, G. (ed.) (2000), *Experimenting With Democracy: Regime Change in the Balkans* (London: Routledge).

Rees-Mogg, W. (1999), 'Flying above the law', *The Times*, 31 May.

Rexhepi, F. (1999), 'Kosovo seized by lawlessness and crime', *AIM Press*, Pristina, 29 October.

Robertson, G. (1999), 'I say to the Left: our bombs are not making it worse. We must win this', *The Guardian*, 16 April.

Rose, M. (1999), 'Nato's "failure" to achieve its aims', letter, *The Times*, 14 July.

Schaefer, S. (1999), 'Refugees say "Britain does not want us"', *The Independent*, 23 April.

Steele, J. (1998), 'Serbian onslaught pushes Albanians together under banner of resistance', *The Guardian*, 9 June.

Vickers, M. (1998), *Between Serb and Albanian: A History of Kosovo* (London: Hurst).

Walker, M. (1998), 'Nato planners prepare for air–land operation', *The Guardian*, 9 June.

Walker, T. (1998), 'EU envoy warns Serbs against Kosovo violence', *The Times*, 12 June.

Youngs, T. (1998), 'Kosovo: the diplomatic and military options', House of Commons Library Research Paper no. 98/93.

Youngs, T. and Dodd, T. (1998), 'Kosovo', House of Commons Library Research Paper no. 98/73.

Youngs, T., Oakes, M. and Bowers, P. (1999), 'Kosovo: NATO and military action', House of Commons Library Research Paper no. 99/34.

9

The pariah agenda and New Labour's ethical arms sales policy

Neil Cooper

Introduction

The Conservative government rejected at the polls in May 1997 had been dogged by a succession of arms scandals (the arms-to-Iraq affair and the associated Scott inquiry, the Pergau Dam affair, the al-Masari controversy, the Iraqi supergun and BMARC). Even the Jonathan Aitken affair, ostensibly a scandal over the question of whether the then minister had or had not paid his own hotel bill, turned out to be connected to the issue of arms sales. The cumulative impact of such incidents had contributed to the general impression of an amoral and sleaze-ridden administration that in turn was a major factor in New Labour's landslide election victory.

Before the election Labour had been keen to exploit each and every arms scandal, losing no opportunity to paint the Conservative approach to arms sales as ethically challenged. Consequently, Labour arrived in power committed to cleaning up government in general and to introducing an ethical dimension to arms exports in particular.

This chapter assesses Labour's policy on arms sales. It begins by examining the rhetoric of New Labour and then assesses its formal policy statements both in opposition and in government. It is suggested that Labour's arms control agenda principally emphasises the restraint of arms sales to pariah states and restrictions on pariah weapons. Labour's commitment to even this narrow agenda has been weak. This conclusion is illustrated via an examin-ation of policies towards pariah weapons and pariah states. The chapter goes on to outline the way in which New Labour's policy is rooted in a post-Cold War security discourse that, ironically, serves to legitimise high levels of defence expenditure and the development of high-tech weaponry that can be produced economically only if exported. The chapter then examines the new challenges to arms control presented by the twin forces of globalisation and technological revolution; it argues that Labour's current arms control agenda largely fails to address such challenges, and maps out a set of 'structural arms control' initiatives designed to address these new challenges.

New Labour, new language?

While there have been different judgements made on the conduct of foreign policy under Labour, most commentators have acknowledged that what Brown refers to as 'the mood music' (1999: 23) has changed. For some, such as the former foreign secretary Douglas Hurd, this is all that has changed: Labour has simply perpetrated a public relations charade while changing actual policy by no more than a few degrees (Foreign Affairs Committee, 1998). For others, however, the new language of foreign policy is itself of significance. For instance, while Wheeler and Dunne take the government to task over its failure to conform with their principle of good international citizenship on the question of arms sales to Indonesia, they also argue that to dismiss Labour's ethical language is to ignore the fact that:

> [the] view of language as instrumental has become increasingly discredited by philosophers and sociologists who point to the constitutive aspect of language in the production of meaning. The constitutive role that language plays in international relations can be seen from the fact that other governments take seriously what is said to them and about them. (Wheeler and Dunne, 1998: 851)

It is certainly the case that the body language of ministerial pronouncements has changed (for an example of the Conservatives' language see Foreign Affairs Committee, 1981: 45 and 52). However, Labour's commitment to a responsible arms trade has, at the level of rhetoric at least, been 'constituted' as a sub-set of its human rights agenda. What this has meant is that for Labour (with the arguable exception of its commitments on transparency) the arms trade problem has largely been framed with reference to the problem of inhumane weapons and inhumane actors.

This interlinking of Labour's agenda on human rights and values with its commitment on arms sales was demonstrated in a rash of speeches and policy initiatives produced in the immediate aftermath of the party's election victory in 1997. Indeed, the very day after coming to power Robin Cook announced that New Labour would 'put human rights at the centre of our policy concerns'. This was followed on 7 May 1997 by a trilateral statement with France and Germany promising to 'give particular priority' to the early conclusion of an international agreement to ban landmines (*The Guardian*, 8 May 1997). On 21 May Labour announced a review of arms export criteria. The same day, Cook asserted that the United Kingdom would destroy its stock of anti-personnel landmines by 2005 and impose an immediate moratorium on their use until an effective international agreement entered into force, or until 2005, whichever came first (*The Guardian*, 22 May 1997). The key event in this period, however, was the production of a mission statement – the first ever – on 12 May. In his speech accompanying its launch, Cook's rhetoric was high-flown. He asserted, 'The global reach of modern weapons creates a clear national interest in preventing proliferation and promoting international control of conventional weapons' (an implicit distinction being made between the need *prevent* the proliferation of weapons of mass destruction and the need to *control* the proliferation of conventional weapons). He noted that Labour would 'give a new momentum to arms control and disarmament' (Cook, 1997a). Noticeably, it was the trilateral statement on landmines that was cited as an example of Labour fulfilling this commitment in office.

Two months later, Cook returned to these themes in a speech on human rights, stating that 'Britain will refuse to supply the equipment and weapons with which regimes deny the demands of their peoples for human rights ... We will not supply equipment or weapons that might be used for internal repression' (1997b). A few weeks later, on 28 July, Labour announced both the results of its review of export licence criteria and that it was implementing its commitment to ban the export of torture equipment. Notably, although the former resulted in a wide-ranging document (see FCO, DTI and MoD, 1999: 3–6) that, in principle at least, identifies a number of constraints on arms sales, ministers have consistently emphasised its role in delivering on the commitment not to export pariah weapons or to sell to pariah actors. Thus, as Cook noted at the 1997 Labour party conference, 'Britain is, again, leading by cleaning up the arms trade ... we fought the election on the commitment that we would not give any more licences for arms exports that would conspire with conflict or abet repression. We have carried out that commitment.' He also noted that one lesson of the arms-to-Iraq affair was that 'brutal megalomaniac dictators tend not to pay their invoices on time' (Cook, 1997c) – conveniently ignoring the fact that even if poverty-stricken democracies do pay their bills on time this may not actually be in the interests of their long-term economic development.

Of course, an approach to the arms trade that concentrates on the issue of pariah weapons or on the question of sales to pariah actors is not *necessarily* an unethical one. It can be painted as an effective way of bridging the tension that exists between a state's right to self-defence and the growing concern to protect global society from the negative effects of weapons proliferation. However, ministerial speeches on the arms trade are only the first part of a two-stage process by which the arms trade problem has been framed. The second stage has consisted of the wording of formal policy documents.

New Labour's formal policy

What is notable about Labour's formal policy statements is that while these address a much wider range of concerns related to weapons proliferation – for example the impact on regional security or a recipient's economic development – they have also been constructed in language that is far more permissive than that used (*à la* Wheeler and Dunne) by foreign secretaries in their speeches. This language is not only much less ambitious than that contained in ministerial speeches but it is also less ambitious than a number of other criteria against which it might be judged.

A comparison of Labour policy in the 1980s with that of today highlights the way in which formal policy on arms exports has become more permissive. Labour's 1983 general election manifesto declared 'we will not supply arms to countries where *the chances* of international aggression or internal oppression *would be increased* ... We are alarmed by the growth of the arms trade. Labour will *limit Britain's arms sales abroad* and *ban the supply of arms* to repressive regimes such as South Africa, El Salvador, Chile, Argentina and Turkey' (Wickham-Jones, 1999: 6, emphasis added). In contrast, by 1997, both the general commitment to limit arms sales abroad and a specific list of countries to which arms sales would be banned had been dropped. Labour merely promised it would 'not permit the sale of arms to regimes that might use them for internal repression or international aggression' (Labour party, 1997: 38).

Labour's declared policy on arms sales is also more permissive than that of a number of other Western countries. Both Germany and Sweden, and in some respects the United States, have more restrictive policies than does the United Kingdom. (Even the Chinese provide more detailed information on small-arms exports than does a Labour government supposedly committed to transparency in arms sales; Amnesty International UK, 1999.) The EU arms sales code of conduct, which Labour cites as one of the main achievements of its ethical arms sales policy, is, in large part, more restrictive than Labour's own national criteria upon which the EU agreement is supposed to be modelled (see the appendix to this chapter). For instance, under the UK criteria, the commitment not to export equipment for internal repression is qualified by a statement effectively exempting equipment judged to be for the legitimate protection of a country's security forces from violence, a qualification that has been criticised by the arms control lobby (Chalmers, 1997: 22). During the negotiations over the EU code of conduct, a similar loophole was deleted (Amnesty International, 1998). The government is considering whether to adopt a single set of criteria based on the EU code. Officials, however, are currently working on the basis of the more permissive UK criteria (Trade and Industry Committee, 1998: para. 32).

The EU code itself is flawed in a number of ways that undermine the government's attempt to claim it as a major step forward in the promotion of an ethical arms policy: it is not legally binding; the section governing the export of arms to repressive regimes and a no-undercutting requirement were watered down largely at French insistence; there is no requirement that annual reports on defence exports, to be provided by states, will be published; and the annual review of the code's implementation remains confidential (Foster, 1998; O'Callaghan, 1998). The rationale underlying the code is not necessarily ethical: the increasing use of collaborative weapons procurement and the rationalisation of the European defence industrial base (which is bringing about the creation of pan-European defence companies) necessitates the development of standardised, EU-wide principles on arms exports. Without the code of conduct the export of defence equipment that incorporates substantial sub-components from countries with differing arms export criteria is problematic. The EU code is as much about making it easier for European defence companies to export in the future as it is about developing the building blocks with which to make arms sales more ethical. Two months after the unveiling of the code, six of the EU's largest arms exporters, including the United Kingdom, pledged to co-ordinate methods of bolstering arms exports (*Defense News*, 5–11 October 1998).

Labour might complain that the relevant criteria against which to judge current policy are those of the previous government, an administration that failed to give due weight to human rights considerations when licensing arms exports. Even set against this rather low standard, however, Labour's record is mixed. There have been changes to the language used in judging applications for export licences. Most notably, the guidance issued to Foreign Office desk officers used to note that restrictions should be placed on the export of equipment *likely* to be used for internal repression. In contrast, Labour has lowered the standards of proof required on this issue by substituting the word 'might' for 'likely' (*Hansard*, 31 July 1997: cols 65–6). Notwithstanding such changes, however, the House of Commons Trade and Industry Committee concluded that 'Comparison of the new criteria with their predecessors suggests ... that the July 1997 criteria represent a rather less radical break with past policy than is sometimes represented to be the case' (1998: para. 28).

Thus, if one accepts Wheeler and Dunne's contention that language is constitutive of action, then current policy looks remarkably unethical. Indeed, the two-stage framing process noted above has resulted in a 'double whammy' effect whereby the wider arms control agenda has been de-prioritised in the first stage and the pariah agenda has been substantially weakened in the second stage. Moreover, the pariah agenda pursued by Labour and the manner in which it has been articulated have, ironically, had the effect of legitimising both the large space in which most arms exports fall and the huge subsidies thrown at the so-called 'legitimate' defence trade by government. At its worst, as in the case of landmines (see below), the pariah agenda represents little more than a totemic displacement activity, which has the effect of obscuring the continued attempt to maximise arms sales and so avoiding debates about the real economic and security benefits to be derived from such sales. For instance, Stephen Martin (1999) has suggested that the net direct cost to the government of subsidising arms exports amounts to £228 million per year. This raises questions about the claimed economic benefits to be derived from arms exports yet the government seems uninterested in seriously addressing this debate. Moreover, the huge government marketing apparatus that such subsidies underpin breeds a culture of export permissiveness that consistently erodes attempts to apply the pariah agenda to export licensing decisions, particularly given that many of the same organisations responsible for maximising 'legitimate' exports are also responsible for restraining 'pariah' exports.

Pariah weapons

Labour has focused on four categories of pariah weapons: landmines, weapons of mass destruction, torture equipment and, to some extent, small arms and light weapons. I will concentrate here on landmines and on Labour's approach to the missile technology control regime (MTCR). Landmines have been the most prominent item on Labour's pariah weapons agenda (Bowers and Dodd, 1998: 15). The MTCR is of interest because it straddles the interface between the pariah weapons agenda and the government's pursuit of 'legitimate' arms sales.

Labour's policy on landmines neatly illustrates the principal flaws in the pariah weapons agenda. First, Labour has failed to go beyond the commitments it signed up to in the Ottawa convention. It has proceeded with the procurement of a vehicle-launched scatterable anti-tank mine ordered by the last government. The failure to include anti-tank mines in the Ottawa convention has come under criticism from NGOs which argue that it is a loophole that arms manufacturers can exploit to get round the agreement (Atwood, 1998: 10). More pertinently, the United Kingdom continues to use cluster bombs, such as the BL755, which was deployed in Kosovo (*The Guardian*, 20 April 1999). Unexploded cluster bombs pose much the same risks to civilians as landmines. Kosovo is estimated to be littered with some 11,000 unexploded NATO ordnance, the vast bulk of which are the small 'bomblets' released from cluster bombs (US State Department, 1999). Labour could justifiably argue that it has gone further than many governments (the United States, for instance) in signing up to the Ottawa convention at all. Critics could equally argue that a government that has given such prominence to the landmines issue might have been expected to go beyond a minimalist adherence to the convention. This is to the miss the point of the pariah agenda. The precise effect of the pariah agenda, particularly in relation to conventional weapons, is to marginalise the control agenda, so that it focuses on a narrow category of armaments while leaving a legal and normative space for the prosecution of the vast majority of arms sales. By definition, the pariah weapons agenda will always be minimalist and by definition it will frequently be marked by 'orphan weapons' that are excluded from treaties and government arms control initiatives, despite apparently strong claims for their inclusion in the same family of arms being controlled.

Second, the combined phenomenon of globalisation and weak states with porous borders means there is little guarantee that explosives exported from the United Kingdom will not end up in landmines. The United Kingdom has weak end-use controls and the culture in Whitehall emphasises the maximisation of arms sales, not their rigorous control.

Third, Labour qualified its commitment to destroy landmines by noting that this would not occur until 2005. It qualified the ban on their use by promising a moratorium only until 2005 or until the Ottawa convention entered into force. Until this point, the government retained the right to use them, albeit in exceptional circumstances. The Ottawa convention came into force in February 1999: in the same month Labour announced it had destroyed the landmines. However, the delay in the destruction of these stocks was widely interpreted as a concession to the military, who were worried that alternative weapons, such as more advanced conventional bombs, would not be available earlier (*The Guardian*, 22 May 1997). For instance, in 1996 the MoD ordered the Conventional Armed Stand-Off Missile (CASOM) to replace the JP233 airfield denial weapon (now banned under the Ottawa convention) but this is due to enter service only in 2001. The delay thus reduced the gap between the phasing out of the JP233 and its replacement with CASOM.

This illustrates a further deficiency in the pariah weapons agenda, namely that, given the inertia in the arms dynamic, the effect of banning the market in one weapon is simply to create a market in another, albeit one that has managed to avoid being labelled inhumane. Indeed, one of the ironic codicils to Labour's policy on landmines is that the United Kingdom will provide 100 Paveway III laser-guided bombs as a 'gift' to Saudi Arabia so that it can replace the JP233s it received from the United Kingdom in the mid-1980s (*Jane's Defence Weekly*, 3 March 1999: 5). The MoD estimates the cost to the British taxpayer at £15–17 million (*Hansard*, 15 March 1999, col. 506w). Thus Labour's pariah weapons agenda has not been allowed to undermine the broader arms trade relationship with the United Kingdom's biggest single customer. Indeed, it has become part of the process by which the government subsidises arms exports to that state.

The limits of the pariah agenda are also apparent in Labour's approach to the MTCR, a supplier-based regime designed to limit the spread of missile technology. Labour has placed special emphasis upon this regime; a paper produced by the government notes 'international efforts to constrain the spread of missile technology are an important priority needing urgent attention'. It gives three reasons. First, there are concerns over the potential delivery of weapons of mass destruction by missile; second, the spread of missile capabilities can be destabilising in regions where it occurs; and third, their spread stimulates the development of defences against ballistic missiles. The last has the potential to destabilise efforts to limit strategic nuclear forces (FCO, DTI and MoD, 1999).

Labour's ethical stance on this issue becomes less clear when the definition of weapons is muddied and when commitment to the MTCR conflicts with the aim of maximising arms sales. In particular, the government (albeit against the reported wishes of Robin Cook) has authorised the sale of the Black Shahine missile to the United Arab Emirates, despite protests from the United States that this breaches the terms of the MTCR. The debate between the United States and the United Kingdom centred on whether the missile is a category 1 system (with a range of over 300 kilometres and a payload of 500 kilograms) or a category 2 system (with a range over 300 kilometres but a payload less than 500 kilograms). The former are automatically banned from export. Transfers of the latter are at the discretion of national governments

(*Defense News*, 14–20 September 1998). The point about this debate is not whether the missile actually falls into category 1 or 2 but that a government supposedly concerned about the uncontrolled transfer of missile technology and supposedly committed to an ethical arms sales policy should choose to abide by a debatable interpretation of the letter of its international commitments, rather than their spirit. The episode demonstrates a consequence of the pariah weapons agenda. By legitimising non-pariah exports, it acts to reduce the debate about the transfer of arms to a technical debate about the capacity and function of the technology under consideration (whether the technology is pariah or not) rather than one about the general effects of arms supplies. The fact that the United Arab Emirates ranks as the eleventh largest importer of arms in the world (Stockholm International Peace Research Institute, 1998: 300) and the effect this may have on the country's development or on stability in the Middle East is downplayed in favour of a technical discussion about missile range and missile loads. The fact that that the deal has been underpinned by a defence co-operation agreement with the United Arab Emirates which commits the United Kingdom to assist in deterring threats or preventing aggression against it (Cooper, 1997: 148) raises little concern as it does not fall within the remit of the pariah agenda.

Pariah states

At the heart of Labour's formal policy with respect to pariah states is its commitment, as expressed in Robin Cook's new arms sales criteria, not to approve export licences for arms that might be used for internal repression, or where there is a clearly identifiable risk that the intended recipient would use the proposed export aggressively against another country. However, the promise not to export equipment for internal repression is qualified by the exemption of equipment for the legitimate protection of a country's security forces. The restrictions on exports to countries that might use them aggressively against another country are watered down by the assertion that 'a purely theoretical possibility that the items concerned might be used in the future against another state will not of itself lead to a licence being refused' (FCO, DTI and MOD, 1999: 3–6).

Such qualifications would be of little significance if there existed a real commitment on the part of government to constrain arms sales through a serious consideration of their ethical implications. The evidence for such a commitment is weak. The United Kingdom abides by international arms embargoes, although these do not always apply either to so-called non-lethal or dual-use defence equipment, or to equipment for which contracts are already in place. Both exemptions apply to the United Kingdom's interpretation of the EU embargo on China applied after the Tiananmen Square massacre in 1989. Thus announcement of an arms embargo does not necessarily signify that the door to defence equipment sales has been totally closed. Even when the door has been closed, the horse has often bolted (or at least been supplied with the necessary equipment to blow up the stable), as was the case with Argentina, Iraq and now Serbia (Phythian, forthcoming). Given Labour's support for the maximisation of arms sales, these problems are likely to persist. Indeed, the House of Commons International Development Committee has already rebuked the DTI for approving two export licences to Eritrea despite objections from the DFID (International Development Committee, 1999: xlixx). Eritrea has subsequently become the subject of an arms embargo because of its conflict with Ethiopia.

Many pariahs escape formal international arms embargoes (partly, of course, as a result of the influence their arms acquisitions give them with the major arms exporters). In theory, this does not represent a problem given the constraints in the UK export criteria and the EU code against exporting arms that might be used for the purposes of internal repression or international aggression. In practice, such provisions represent another twist (albeit a more long-standing one) on the pariah weapons agenda. These provisions are predicated on the assumption that it is possible to make a distinction between, for instance, equipment that might be used in repression and that which is for 'legitimate' defence needs. It is this distinction that explains why, between 2 May 1997 and 8 June 1999, the government could issue some 101 standard individual export licences for goods on the military list to be exported to Indonesia (including communications equipment, aircraft spares, aircraft machine gun spares, communications encryption equipment, naval electronics, radar spares, pilot displays and components, spares for aircraft engines and body armour). In contrast, just eight licences were refused (FCO, DTI and MOD, 1999: 49; *Hansard*, 2 July 1999, col. 314). The same distinction explains why, despite this record, Robin Cook could tell the 1999 Labour conference: 'Let's put a myth to rest. Your government has not sold weapons that would suppress democracy or freedom. We rejected every licence to Indonesia when weapons might have been used for suppression' (Cook, 1999).

In reality, the distinction between equipment that is used for repressive or aggressive ends and that used for 'legitimate' defence is difficult to uphold. Even the government (implicitly) recognised the problems with the distinction during NATO action against Serbia. Attacks on purely civil targets were justified on the grounds that they either represented important instruments of state repression and control or contributed to the war-making capacity of the Serbs. Ministers, however, seemed impervious to the irony involved in justifying the bombing of television make-up ladies in Belgrade because of their role in government repression while also insisting that the export of Hawk jets to Indonesia did not contribute to repression in East Timor. Only after the mass killings and expulsions that accompanied the UN-organised referendum on independence in East Timor, as well as persistent reports of intimidatory over-flights by Hawk aircraft, did the government reluctantly, and belatedly, concede this was fiction by announcing the suspension of

Hawk deliveries and its support for an EU embargo on further arms sales: a case of shutting the stable door once the crimes against humanity had been perpetrated.

The government's attempt to distinguish between legitimate and illegitimate arms would arguably be less problematic if its definition of repressive or destabilising equipment was an expansive one. The opposite is the case. The proportion of all export licence applications that have been refused has fallen from 1 per cent under the Conservatives to just 0.7 per cent under Labour (Defence, Foreign Affairs, International Development and Trade and Industry Committees, 1999). Even where pariah states have been concerned, Labour's approach to arms exports has been largely permissive. Labour's record on Indonesia, referred to above and well documented elsewhere, needs little elaboration. Unfortunately, Indonesia is not the only example of the permissive approach. Turkey's poor human rights record, as well as continuing tensions with Greece, did not stop Labour approving 101 standard individual export licences to the country and rejecting just one between 2 May and 31 December 1997 (FCO, DTI and MoD, 1999: 87). The Defence Export Services Organisation reportedly has a goal of achieving $200 million a year in defence sales to the country (*Defense News*, 21–27 September 1998: 10), which, if realised, would place Turkey among the United Kingdom's leading arms customers.

Thus Labour's rhetoric on the restriction of defence equipment to pariah states has been translated into formal commitments that are shot through with qualifications. In a bureaucratic milieu that places an emphasis on maximising arms exports, these qualifications have then been exploited to produce an export licensing process in which ethical concerns have been allowed to intrude only at the margins.

The pariah agenda and the post-Cold War security discourse

The key point regarding Labour's pariah agenda on arms sales is not only that it acts to create a legitimised space for the prosecution of the vast majority of UK arms sales but that it is rooted in a post-Cold War Western security culture which itself legitimises continued high levels of defence expenditure and new weapons developments. As a number of commentators have noted, the post-Cold War era has been characterised by the evolution of a new discourse of threat in the West, one that emphasises the dangers posed not by the Soviet Other but by a range of actually or potentially hostile rogue or pariah actors (Latham, 1999: 222; Klare, 1995). These include revisionist or pariah states (particularly, but not exclusively, those that possess, or aspire to possess, weapons of mass destruction) and pariah non-state actors such as 'warlords' in Afghanistan or Colombian drug cartels. The latter, for instance, are represented as constituting a threat not only to regional and global order but also to Western values and Western society as a result of their trade in illegal drugs or weapons; hence the development of a control agenda on the issue of light weapons that has a 'drugs and thugs' focus (Dyer and O'Callaghan, 1999: 4).

This 'new imaginary', as Latham terms it (1999: 223), is not necessarily grounded in any objective reality. For instance, the representation of the Afghan 'warlords' has been transformed from a Cold War image that emphasised their role as freedom fighters against Soviet communism to one that emphasises their role as agents of fundamentalist intolerance and drug running. As Keith Krause and Andrew Latham have argued, the constitution of this new threat discourse can, at least in part, be explained by reference to the need of the military and the defence industry to establish a new self-justifying mantra to replace that of the communist threat (Krause and Latham, 1998: 36–7). Defence from rogue actors, be they state or non-state, has become the new catch-all with which to defend military budgets under threat from national treasuries looking for peace dividends. Ironically, this also provides a rationale for the maximisation of arms exports and a minimalist approach to the restriction of supplies to pariahs: we have to supply arms to odious actors, the argument goes, because otherwise we would be unable to generate the economies of scale necessary to pay for the arms we need to defend ourselves from odious actors.

Furthermore, in tandem with the development of the rogue or pariah doctrine has gone a return to Western values. A corollary of the rogue doctrine has been to elevate the principles of Western civilisation as a standard against which to judge the threat posed by these new enemies to the international order in general and to Western society in particular (Krause and Latham, 1998: 43–4). The contrast with the Cold War is marked. It was represented as a confrontation between the West and communism. It was not the standard of civilisation that was the reference point for the determination of threat but the ideology of the actors concerned. Consequently, standards of good governance, human rights and democracy were of less relevance in determining whether actors received arms or were denied them than whether they came within the Soviet or Western sphere of interest. Similarly, to quote Krause and Latham, 'the "totality" of the struggle with the Soviet Union ... encouraged Western policy-makers to emphasize the utility of weapons (such as napalm or carpet bombing in Vietnam) rather than their putative humanity (or lack thereof)' (1998: 44). In contrast, the emphasis on Western standards of civilisation has encouraged a return to a concern with the inhumanity of weapons. For Krause and Latham, it is this shift in the West's security culture in the early 1990s that established the terrain upon which national and international NGOs (and certain states) were able to campaign for tighter regulation of particular weapons, notably landmines.

This is not perhaps the whole explanation for the current focus on inhumane weapons. The new 'smart' technologies associated with the revolution in military affairs have been hyped as providing the capability to effect the delivery of military force with minimum loss of life. The question of discrimination between combatants and non-combatants that was at the heart of the landmine debate has been utilised as a major selling point for the current generation of smart weapons. The extent to which the revolution in military affairs actually exists, and the extent to which the claims made for it can be justified, is arguable. More pertinently, however, the very same discourse that has brought renewed salience to the question of inhumane weapons has also been deployed to legitimise the latest generation of weapons programmes. Of course, it could be argued that the development of smart weapons has been undertaken in direct response to this new concern with inhumane weapons and that it thus represents a positive and progressive event. Given that many of these technologies were under development before the end of the Cold War, this interpretation is difficult to sustain. What seems more likely is that there has been an interacting dynamic: that the nature of the new security discourse has encouraged manufacturers to posit their claims for new technology less in terms of the way in which arms contribute to deterrence and more in terms of their qualities as civilised weapons for civilised societies. At the same time, public relations for the new technologies has contributed to and reinforced the emphasis on Western values. Similarly, it can also be argued that while landmines have become an unintended victim of the defence industry's own propaganda, it is also the case that the NGO community, which has campaigned so strongly on this issue, has unwittingly contributed to a discourse that legitimises current high-tech weapons. Moreover, the rising real-terms costs of such programmes, coupled with declining post-Cold War defence budgets, has meant that these same programmes are economically viable only if they are supported by large export orders from abroad.

Thus Labour's ethical arms sales policy is rooted in a wider Western security discourse, which has mobilised the threat from pariah actors to justify the maintenance of relatively high defence budgets and the development of new weapons technologies. The concern with pariah weapons, and in particular their indiscriminate effect, is located in the same discourse from which springs the legitimisation of supposedly accurate smart weapons.

The problems of technology denial in a globalised world

The pariah agenda is peculiarly ill suited to the development of effective strategies aimed at preventing the proliferation of weapons. It emphasises strategies of technology restriction. However, the globalising dynamic inherent in the contemporary international defence industry, the increasingly porous nature of national borders (particularly but not exclusively in weak states) and the commercial imperatives created in an industry suffering from reduced demand and over-capacity all place question marks over the effectiveness of strategies of technology control.

Of particular note in this respect is the problem of licensed production agreements – where one company enables another company to manufacture its product under licence in a second country. Such agreements represent an increasingly significant component of the global arms trade (Held *et al.*, 1999: 119–20). Under the current export licensing system in the United Kingdom, once goods are licensed for production in another country the government has little control over the use to which this technology is put, for instance over whether the goods produced are re-exported to a third country. Thus the company Heckler & Koch (a British Aerospace subsidiary) has established licensed production deals for the manufacture of small arms with, among others, Turkey, Pakistan and Iran. Heckler & Koch small arms produced in these countries have reportedly been exported to countries such as Indonesia, Myanmar and Sudan. Indeed, in the case of Iranian supplies to Sudan this would appear to have taken place after the licence for production ran out and thus without even the consent of Heckler & Koch. The United States, in contrast, attempts to place limitations on the export of goods produced under licence (Oxfam, 1998) but even this approach does not prevent abuses, particularly given that at present there is little end-use monitoring of onward transfers by a licensee, nor of production that occurs after a licensed production agreement has ceased.

It should also be noted that for pariah control strategies to be effective one has to be assured that most actors in the market will implement them and that arms transferred to so-called legitimate states will not simply be re-transferred to pariahs. As the arms-to-Iraq scandal demonstrated, this is not the case. The proliferation of weak states with porous borders, limited state authority and poor control over weapons stores has turned a number of regions into major centres for the black market trade in weapons.

The emphasis on technology denial in pariah strategies presumes a division can be made between categories of weapons or technology that can be used to promote internal repression or international aggression and those that are legitimate. This distinction has always been a spurious one, but the growing role of civil and dual-use technology in the military equipment of both state and non-state actors is making this distinction harder to operate at all levels of the technology spectrum. For instance, both US troops in Somalia and Russian troops in Chechnya found themselves confronted with warlords who used cellphones to warn each other of enemy movements (Gray, 1997: 20) while remotely piloted vehicles designed for crop spraying are capable of being used as delivery or reconnaissance vehicles of the kind that proved so useful in the conflict in Kosovo (Smith and Udis, 1998). Even the US military is now having to buy into civilian satellite projects while simultaneously expressing concern that the prospective availability of commercial satellites with high-resolution imaging systems will negate the military advantages the United States enjoys as a function of its superior space capabilities (*Defense News*, 22 March 1999).

The scale and intensity of the information revolution have also meant that knowledge transfers have become easier and more difficult to restrict. Equipment designs can simply be downloaded by computer and transmitted anywhere in the world via the Internet. Indeed, the Iranians have reportedly paid money to scientists working in Russia to solve over the Internet problems related to their programmes for weapons of mass destruction.

Globalisation and the information revolution have meant that Labour's pariah control strategy, with its emphasis on the elimination or the restriction of technology, is an increasingly ineffective tool with which to prevent arms proliferation. For a party that has made such play of the need to adjust to both the information revolution and the reality of globalisation this is particularly ironic.

Towards a structural arms control agenda

What this implies then is the need for a far more innovative approach to the problems of weapons proliferation than has traditionally been operated by the international community. For instance, it needs to be recognised that the components of what the Carnegie Commission on Preventing Deadly Conflict (1997) has referred to as 'structural prevention' or what the European Commission (1996) refers to as 'structural stability' (for example democracy, good governance, civic society and equitable development) are essential prerequisites for sustainable peace. There is also an important role for conflict resolution programmes designed to encourage actors to develop non-violent mechanisms for resolving disputes. However, for these initiatives to work they also need to be complemented by the adoption of 'structural arms control' strategies aimed at either raising the cost of acquiring and retaining arms or enhancing the economic benefits to be derived from the pursuit of non-military security strategies (see Cooper, 1999). Such strategies are based on recognition of the fact that the key constraint facing actors concerned to acquire arms is no longer the difficulty of obtaining them on the international market but rather the availability of funding to pay for them. They are also aimed at complementing (indeed in some cases they overlap with) strategies of structural prevention/stability and are designed to supplement (and to some extent replace) pariah control strategies that focus on restricting the availability of particular technologies.

A key element in this approach is the need to reduce or eliminate the subsidies made available for arms exports by all suppliers, including the United Kingdom, and also to take action against companies found guilty of bribing foreign officials to place arms orders. In particular, Labour should advocate international agreements designed to restrict or eliminate the use of export credits and offsets to lubricate arms deals. In September 1997, the UK government made a token gesture on the issue when Gordon Brown committed the United Kingdom not to provide defence-related export credits to highly indebted poor countries (HIPCs), although this was only for two years. The gesture should not be overestimated as many HIPCs are likely to have poor credit ratings anyway, thus reducing their chances of receiving credit. Between 1990 and 1997, for instance, the United Kingdom extended export credits for defence-related business to just three HIPCs (India, Pakistan and Zimbabwe). Together these accounted for just 0.15 per cent of all export credits furnished to defence buyers in this period by the United Kingdom (*Hansard*, 5 May 1998: col. 263wa). However, the government is also pressing for an agreement on this issue in the Organization for Economic Cooperation and Development (OECD). Such an agreement should be widened to include states other than the HIPCs and should be pursued within the framework of the Wassenaar arrangement. If meaningful agreements were to be achieved, they could significantly raise the economic and political costs of arms acquisitions for states.

More radically, the United Nations Development Programme (UNDP) has called for a global tax on all arms sales (1994: 57). The receipts from such a tax could fund demobilisation, disarmament or conversion programmes. A modified version of this proposal could be operated on a unilateral basis by the United Kingdom. The MoD currently places an export levy on the sale of arms that have been developed with government funds. The levy is often either waived or reduced by the MoD in order to facilitate exports; it nevertheless brings in an income of roughly £50 million per year (*Hansard*, 22 June 1998: col. 375wa). Compared with the funding for defence research and development provided by government to UK companies, this is a derisory sum. If the levy were raised and if the receipts were hypothecated either to fund demilitarisation initiatives or to finance a rigorous end-use inspection regime, then the United Kingdom could argue it was putting the receipts from arms sales to an ethical purpose consistent with the polluter-pays principle.

Restrictions on the provision of export credits, offsets and other forms of subsidy would have to be part of a wider deal in which developed states committed themselves to bringing down their own levels of defence expenditure and to pursuing conversion strategies designed to reduce the dependence of their national economies on defence production. In addition, Western states could reward states with low levels of militarisation. Some states have already undertaken, in principle at least, to make aid conditional upon low levels of defence expenditure. To date, however, the actual implementation of such commitments has been weak. Other incentives to be offered could include either agreements to transfer civil technology or more favourable treatment in trade negotiations.

Additionally, arms embargoes should be extended to include restrictions on banks and counter-trade houses to prevent them assisting the financing of arms deals through either the extension of export credits or through the management of barter or offset deals associated with a banned export. Wolfgang Reinicke has argued that such organisations should be required to furnish regular data on the arms deals they have financed, thus opening up a further avenue by which governments could monitor and prevent illegal arms sales (1993: 205). This is relevant given that financing or offset brokering may be performed by companies resident in a country other than that from which the buyer, seller or arms originate.

In the current international climate, defence companies have little incentive to enforce embargoes rigorously and every incentive to break them: the chances of detection are small and, given the symbiotic relationship that exists between governments and defence companies, any breaches of formal policy are often overlooked. Even where they are not, the punishment for illegal arms exports may not represent a substantial deterrent. Therefore mechanisms are required to tag arms at the point of export and import and to ensure tighter end-use controls, such as the imposition of regular checks to establish that equipment is being used for its stated purpose and not being transferred to unauthorised destinations. In contrast, New Labour has backed off from its commitments to introduce tighter end-use controls, arguing instead that the best way to reduce the diversion of arms is to restrict their export to legitimate end users in the first place (Lloyd, 1998). Such initiatives need to be coupled with the introduction of significant sanctions against actors trading in pariah weapons or to pariah states. Sanctions are likely to be pursued with greater vigour if a right of redress is provided to the victims of illegitimate arms exports. For example, where companies or states are found to have knowingly breached an arms embargo then the government or the citizens of the state to which arms have been supplied should have the capacity in international law to sue the firm or state responsible and to claim substantial reparations, which could be put towards the costs of demilitarisation and peace-building. Of course, it can be argued that such a proposal is unrealistic given that weapons often change hands a number of times before ending up in a particular conflict. However, the tagging of arms should make the monitoring of weapons flows easier. Moreover, it is not uncommon for other industrial sectors to be fined for failure to implement government policy even where they are not at fault, the assumption being that the onus is on them to develop the systems necessary to ensure policy is implemented. In the United Kingdom, ferries, airlines and road hauliers face fines of £2,000 for every illegal immigrant they bring into the country, even if the person discovered is a stowaway whose presence was not detected by the carrier (*The Guardian*, 7 December 1998).

There is also a strong case for providing support to states to improve security at weapons depots, to fund conversion and demobilisation programmes, and to improve the capacity of the authorities to patrol national borders. Some initiatives already exist but have either yet to go beyond promises of assistance or remain under-funded. Moreover, such initiatives tend to focus on eliminating pariah weapons (Shields and Potter, 1997) or on providing help to states experiencing a proliferation of arms within their own societies or regions, generally after civil conflicts (Greene, 1998). To be effective they need to be extended to those states that are centres of black market arms trading but not necessarily contiguous to centres of conflict. For instance, such initiatives could usefully be adapted and extended to cover all the states of Central and Eastern Europe, to address the problem of security at arms depots holding conventional arms and to promote conversion across the defence sector.

Conclusions

Labour's ethical arms sales policy has given particular emphasis to control strategies that focus on restricting exports to pariah states and/or restrictions on pariah weapons. At the same time, the language adopted in formal policy documents has meant that even this agenda has been framed in a manner that implies a largely permissive attitude to UK arms exports. Judged solely on its own language, Labour's arms sales policy is less ethical than its own policy in the 1980s, less ethical than that of a number of other states, less ethical than the EU code and little different from the ethically challenged approach of its Conservative predecessors. Thus, at least as far as arms export policy is concerned, Wheeler and Dunne's argument that Labour's language marks a shift on to a new ethical plane is wrong. Indeed, while Labour's policy on arms sales is not particularly ethical it does do what it says it will do, albeit sometimes in the small print.

Labour's ethical arms sales policy is rooted in a post-Cold War security discourse that legitimises both relatively high levels of defence expenditure on the part of Western states and the current generation of high-tech weapons developments. To pile irony on top of irony, Labour's pariah control agenda depends for its effectiveness on the ability to abolish or restrict the flow of technology. Yet the twin forces of globalisation and technological revolution, two phenomena Labour claims to have embraced, have substantially undermined this ability. Indeed, the reality today is of a global defence market in which the major challenge for arms buyers is not obtaining the weapons they want, but obtaining the finance to pay for them. Given this constraint, existing control strategies need to be augmented (and in some cases replaced) by a structural arms control approach designed to raise the costs of arms and reduce the price of non-military security strategies. Unless Labour is prepared to embrace this agenda its ethical arms sales policy will continue to be, at worst, an undertaking quite deliberately confined to the margins of the United Kingdom's arms trade or, at best, a pointless exercise.

Note

The research for this chapter was funded by grants from the Trust for Research and Education on the Arms Trade and the Joseph Rowntree Charitable Trust.

Appendix. A comparison of the UK arms export criteria and the EU code of conduct

UK criteria	EU code of conduct
will take into account respect for human rights and fundamental freedoms in the recipient country	having assessed the recipient country's attitude towards relevant principles established by international human rights instruments
will not issue an export licence if there is a clearly identifiable risk that the proposed export might be used for internal repression	not issue an export licence if there is a clear risk that the proposed export might be used for internal repression
equipment which might be used for internal repression will include: equipment where there is clear evidence of the recent use of similar equipment for internal repression by the ... end-user ... Equipment which has obvious application for internal repression in cases where the recipient country has a significant and continuing record of such repression, unless the end use of the equipment is judged to be legitimate, such as protection of members of security forces from violence	equipment which might be used for internal repression will include ... equipment where there is evidence of the use of this or similar equipment for internal repression by the ... end-user
In some cases the use of force by a government within its own borders does not constitute internal repression. The use of such force by government is legitimate in some cases e.g. to preserve law and order against terrorists or other criminals. However force may only be used in accordance with international human rights standards	No equivalent
No equivalent	The internal situation in the country of final destination ... Member States will not allow exports which would provoke or prolong armed conflicts or aggravate existing tensions or conflicts in the country of final destination
will not issue an export licence if there is a clearly identifiable risk that the intended recipient would use the proposed export aggressively against another country ... However, a purely theoretical possibility that the items concerned might be used in the future against another state will not of itself lead to a licence being refused	will not issue an export licence if there is a clear risk that the intended recipient would use the proposed export aggressively against another country

The need not to affect adversely regional stability in any significant way will also be considered. The balance of forces between neighbouring states, their relative expenditure on defence, and the need not to introduce into the region new capabilities which would be likely to lead to increased tension, will all be taken into account	EU Member States will take into account ... the need not to affect regional stability in any significant way
In assessing the impact of the proposed export on the importing country ... the following will be considered ... the technical capability of the recipient country; whether the purchase would seriously undermine the economy of the recipient country	The compatibility of the arms exports with the technical and economic capacity of the recipient country, taking into account the desirability that states should achieve their legitimate needs of security and defence with the least diversion for armaments of human and economic resources ... whether the proposed export would seriously hamper the sustainable development of the recipient country
The risk of the arms being re-exported or diverted to an undesirable end-user, including terrorist organisations	The existence of a risk that the equipment will be diverted within the buyer country or re-exported under undesirable conditions [the following will be considered] ... the capability of the recipient country to exert effective export controls; the risk of the arms being re-exported or diverted to terrorist organisations

Source: *Annual Report on Strategic Export Controls* (London: TSO), 1999. See Foreign and Commonwealth Office (FCO) website at: http://www.fco.gov.uk.

References

Amnesty International (1998), memorandum in Trade and Industry Committee, *Strategic Export Controls*, second report, minutes of evidence (London: TSO).

Amnesty International UK (1999), memorandum in Defence, Foreign Affairs, International Development and Trade and Industry Committees, *Committees' Inquiry into the 1997 and 1998 Annual Reports on Strategic Export Controls*, fifth special report, HC540 (London: TSO).

Atwood, D. C. (1998), 'Tackling the problem of anti-personnel landmines: issues and developments', paper presented at the third International Security Forum, 19–21 October, Kongresshaus, Zurich.

Bowers, P. and Dodd, T. (1998), 'Anti-personnel mines and the policies of two British governments', *RUSI Journal*, vol. 143, no. 1, 11–17.

Brown, C. (1999), 'On the relationship between ethics and foreign policy', paper presented at Ethics and Foreign Policy Workshop, University of Bristol, 8–9 June.

Carnegie Commission on Preventing Deadly Conflict (1997), *Preventing Deadly Conflict: Executive Summary of the Final Report* (Washington, DC: Carnegie Corporation of New York).

Chalmers, M. (1997), *British Arms Export Policy and Indonesia* (London: Saferworld).

Cook, R. (1997a), 'British foreign policy', statement, 12 May.

Cook, R., (1997b), 'Human rights into a new century', speech, 17 July.

Cook, R. (1997c), 'Britain's new approach to the world', speech, Labour party conference, Brighton, 2 October.

Cook, R. (1999), speech, Labour party conference, Bournemouth, 28 September.

Cooper, N. (1997), *The Business of Death: Britain's Arms Sales at Home and Abroad* (London: Tauris Academic Studies).

Cooper, N. (1999), 'Arms sales and nano-ethics: New Labour in office', paper presented at the Annual Meeting of the American Political Science Association, Atlanta, 2–5 September.

Defence, Foreign Affairs, International Development and Trade and Industry Committees (1999), *Committees' Inquiry into the 1997 and 1998 Annual Reports on Strategic Export Controls*, fifth special report, HC 540 (London: TSO).

Dyer, S. L. and O'Callaghan, G. (1999), *One Size Fits All? Prospects for a Global Convention on Illicit Trafficking by 2000*, BASIC Research Report 99.2 (London: BASIC).

European Commission (1996), *The European Union and the Issue of Conflicts in Africa: Peacebuilding, Conflict Prevention and Beyond* (Brussels: European Commission).

FCO, DTI and MoD (1999), *Second Annual Report on Strategic Export Controls* (London: TSO).

Foreign Affairs Committee (1981), *Overseas Arms Sales: Foreign Policy Aspects*, session 1980–81 (London: HMSO).

Foreign Affairs Committee (1998), *Foreign Policy and Human Rights*, first report, session 1998–99, HC 100-II (London: TSO).

Foster, E. (1998), 'Ethical? Effective? The EU's arms export code', *Newsbrief*, vol. 18, no. 7, 1–3.

Gray, C. H. (1997), *Postmodern War: The New Politics of Conflict* (London: Routledge).

Greene, O. (1998), 'Tackling illicit arms trafficking and small arms proliferation', paper for the BISA conference, University of Sussex, 14–16 December.

Held, D., McGrew, A., Golblatt D. and Perraton, J. (1999), *Global Transformations. Politics, Economics and Culture* (Oxford: Polity Press).

International Development Committee (1999), *Conflict Prevention and Post-conflict Reconstruction*, vol. I, session 1998–99, HC 55-I (London: TSO).

Klare, M. (1995), *Rogue States and Nuclear Outlaws: America's Search for a New Foreign Policy* (New York: Hill and Wang).

Krause, K. and Latham, A. (1998), 'Constructing non-proliferation and arms control: the norms of Western practice', in K. Krause (ed.), *Contemporary Security Policy, Special Issue. Culture and Security: Multilateralism, Arms Control and Security Building*, vol. 19, no. 1, 23–54.

Labour party (1997), *New Labour Because Britain Deserves Better* (London: Labour party).

Latham, A. (1999), 'Re-imagining warfare: the revolution in military affairs', in C. A. Snyder (ed.), *Contemporary Security and Strategy* (Basingstoke: Macmillan), 210–35.

Lloyd, T. (1998), speech, Council for Arms Control Seminar, Developing Arms Export Controls: Progress and Priorities, King's College, London, 11 November.

Martin, S. (1999), 'The subsidy savings from reducing UK arms exports', *Journal of Economic Studies*, vol. 25, no. 4, 15–37.

O'Callaghan, G. (1998), 'EU pays high price for French support on code of conduct', *BASIC Reports*, no. 64 (see http://www.basicint.org).

Oxfam (1998), *Out of Control: The Loopholes in UK Controls of the Arms Trade* (Oxford: Oxfam).

Phythian, M. (forthcoming), *To Secure Our Rightful Share: The Politics of British Arms Sales* (Manchester: Manchester University Press).

Reinicke, W. H. (1993), 'Cooperative security and the political economy of non-proliferation', in J. E. Nolan (ed.), *Global Engagement: Cooperation and Security in the 21st Century* (Washington, DC: The Brookings Institution), 175–234.

Shields, J. M. and Potter, W. C. (eds) (1997), *Dismantling the Cold War: US and NIS Perspectives on the Nunn–Lugar Cooperative Threat Reduction Program*, CSIA Studies in International Security (Cambridge, MA: MIT Press).

Smith, R. and Udis, B. (1998), 'New challenges to arms export control: whither Wassenaar?', discussion paper, Department of Economics, University of Colorado at Boulder.

Stockholm International Peace Research Institute (1998), *SIPRI Yearbook 1998: Armaments, Disarmament and International Security* (Oxford: Oxford University Press).

Trade and Industry Committee (1998), *Strategic Export Controls*, second report (London: TSO).

UNDP (1994), *Human Development Report 1994* (Oxford: UNDP/Oxford University Press).

US State Department (1999), *Special Briefing on Kosovo*, 26 July 1999: See http://www.fas.org/man/dod-101/ops/docs99/990726-kosovo--usia3.htm.

Wheeler, N. J. and Dunne, T. (1998), 'Good international citizenship: a third way for British foreign policy', *International Affairs*, vol. 74, no. 4, 847–70.

Wickham-Jones, M. (1999), 'New Labour and ethical foreign policy', paper presented at Ethics and Foreign Policy Workshop, University of Bristol, 8–9 June.

10

Exporting the Third Way in foreign policy: New Labour, the European Union and human rights policy

Angela Bourne and Michelle Cini

Introduction

Two policy priorities advanced by New Labour after the May 1997 general election have characterised government thinking on foreign affairs. The new government had committed itself to a first priority of engaging constructively with its fellow EU member states in its election manifesto. This was to be an approach that would henceforth allow the United Kingdom to play a leading role in Europe. Second, the government (and particularly the Foreign Office) stated its intention to inject a human rights component into the United Kingdom's international policy, to forge a foreign policy with an 'ethical dimension'. This too was to mark the beginning of a new approach to foreign policy for the United Kingdom. Thus far, however, these two priorities have been treated as discrete, unconnected policies, rarely mentioned together in speeches, documents, media reports and academic studies. This chapter draws together these two strands of New Labour's international policy in order to question whether the Labour government has sought to export its 'ethical' foreign policy to the EU as part of its agenda of 'constructive engagement' with Europe.

Labour came to office promising an improvement in the United Kingdom's relations with its European neighbours. This not only meant the adoption of a more positive line on European integration but also the forging of bilateral and multilateral alliances (or 'axes'), particularly with the larger EU member states. The Franco-British 'St Malo declaration' of December 1998 (*Financial Times*, 5 December 1998), which dealt with the thorny issue of Europe's defence identity, was perhaps the most high-profile example of this new foreign policy approach, but other such agreements, particularly with the German government on 'Third Way' issues, are also worthy of mention.

Under the Conservative governments of Margaret Thatcher (and perhaps to a lesser extent John Major) the United Kingdom had confirmed its reputation as the EU's 'awkward partner' (George, 1999). This was as much about the spirit in which UK governments engaged in European affairs as it was about policy substance. Tony Blair promised that under a Labour government this would change. More controversial was the new government's leadership ambitions, which some within the EU looked upon with a degree of scepticism. This is hardly surprising given that Blair's predecessor, Major, rather similarly talked of placing the United Kingdom 'at the heart of Europe'. Moreover, complaints about the prime minister's preaching on such topics as labour market flexibility have continued to plague Blair even if they have not stopped him striving to shape the EU's agenda on economic reform, which was to become a central plank of the Labour government's European policy.

Since 1997, the Labour government's relations with its fellow EU member states have been subject to the usual peaks and troughs that characterise EU politics. On some issues, such as on EU enlargement, institutional reform and defence co-operation, constructive engagement has developed into something more than mere rhetoric. On other issues, not least beef exports and tax harmonisation, intra-EU relations have been tense, if not acrimonious. Neither has the government's reluctance to take a firm stand on euro-zone membership helped to prove its European credentials and allay continental European suspicions that little in UK European policy has actually changed. Yet, while it is not clear that there is much to separate the Blair government from that of his Conservative predecessor when it comes to policy substance, there has been a marked change of tone under New Labour. And if this has done nothing to affect British public opinion, it has in general made for more cordial meetings of the European Council and Council of Ministers.

Before addressing in more detail New Labour's European policy, this chapter begins by considering the ethical (or human rights) dimension of international policy in both the United Kingdom and within the EU, questioning what is meant by an ethical dimension in the context of UK foreign policy and how this concept has been operationalised. The chapter moves on to look at the second strand in the United Kingdom's international policy – that of its relations with the EU. Here, we analyse New Labour's approach to early challenges, paying particular attention to the UK government's presidency of the EU, which it held in the first half of 1998. We argue that while the United Kingdom has not played a leadership role as such, it has nevertheless sought to influence the EU's policy agenda, especially on issues like employment. However, we find little evidence that it has used the issue of human rights and ethical foreign policy to a similar end. Elsewhere, we have reviewed UK and EU policy towards China (Bourne and Cini, 1999) and the evidence that we outline briefly towards the end of this chapter confirms this conclusion.

New Labour and the ethical dimension

In the Foreign Office's mission statement issued on 12 May 1997, and in Robin Cook's subsequent foreign policy speeches, a new British approach towards international policy was outlined (FCO, 1997). In a now much quoted statement, Cook asserted that the United Kingdom's foreign policy must have an 'ethical dimension' and support other people's demands for the rights which British people insist upon for themselves. To these ends, human rights would be 'put at the heart' of the United Kingdom's foreign policy (Cook, 1997a).

Underpinning this new approach was an acknowledgement by the government of its 'moral responsibility' for human tragedy overseas and recognition that the objectives of Labour's foreign and domestic policies should be consistent. However, morality and consistency were not the only aspects of the 'ethical dimension' to be emphasised. The new approach, it was often repeated, would also allow the United Kingdom to determine foreign policy events rather than simply react to them (Symons, 1997). It would place the United Kingdom at the heart of the international community rather than on the sidelines and it would allow the government to play a leadership role, whether through the Commonwealth or the EU (Cook, 1997a). While, externally, the ethical dimension would affect how the United Kingdom was perceived abroad (Cook, 1997a), internally it would become a new source of pride for the British people, one which was based neither on being feared nor on the past (Cook, 1997d). Thus the ethical dimension was tied, among other things, to contemporaneous debates about British identity at the end of the twentieth century.

Although there is debate on how much the broad brush of UK foreign policy objectives changed with the New Labour government, Cook's statement and events played out in subsequent episodes pointed to significant differences with the line taken by the previous Conservative administration. As Wheeler and Dunne emphasise, New Labour's language of 'internationalism' and the explicitness of its moral purpose on the issue of human rights were in sharp contrast with the Conservatives' pragmatist approach, and with its emphasis on 'sovereignty' and the principle of 'non-intervention' in states' internal affairs (1998: 850–1).

Cook spelt out the means by which the policy would be pursued. Twelve strategies were identified: support for the international community and condemnation of regimes violating human rights; full support of sanctions (including those on Iraq); refusal to supply equipment/weapons to regimes denying human rights; ensuring that trade does not undermine human rights; support for human rights in multilateral fora; bilateral dialogue and support for NGOs; support for a permanent international criminal court; more resources for international criminal tribunals; a review of the Military Training Assistance Scheme; support for the media when under threat; publication of an annual report of activities on the promotion of human rights; and concern for domestic human rights issues (Cook, 1997c; see also Foley and Starmer, 1998). Moreover, Cook explicitly committed himself to new initiatives on the death penalty and on torture. He stressed the importance of bringing external human rights experts into the Foreign Office and introduced new guidance on human rights issues for British ambassadors.

Blair acknowledged that his government's universalistic conception of human rights would be controversial for some countries but believed the 'dialogue' and 'partnership' strategies privileged in the new approach could nevertheless achieve results (Blair, 1998c, see also Cook, 1997c; FCO and DFID, 1998: 4). As Cook put it, 'We have emphatically not sought to lecture or hector. We have instead built genuine partnerships that make a practical difference in improving the observance of human rights' (Cook, 1998a). This involved a commitment by the government to integrate human rights issues into all aspects of international policy, with the Foreign Office and the DFID both having a central role to play. As the *Annual Report on Human Rights* (FCO and DFID, 1998: 5) stressed, human rights 'is not an add-on or a sidelined appendage, but an integral part of the way we see the world', even if little mention is ever made of the DTI's role and support for this ethical policy.

In many ways, the contours of the 'ethical dimension' of the government's foreign policy are still being drawn. On the one hand, the United Kingdom's active support for the March 1999 NATO intervention in Kosovo, a defining moment for the administration's foreign policy, was justified according to the logic of the policy's 'ethical dimension'. More than a strategy 'for the sake of the future safety of our region and the world', the achievement of NATO's aims were, as the prime minister stated, 'for the sake of humanity' (*The Times*, 27 March 1999). However, in terms of the means used to pursue its humanitarian objectives, military intervention in Kosovo was a clear departure from the conciliatory tenor of the above-mentioned emphasis on 'partnership' and 'dialogue'. Indeed, the Kosovo crisis inspired Blair to call in a Chicago speech for a 'new doctrine of international community' where 'the West was to identify the circumstances in which we should get actively involved in other people's conflicts' (*The Times*, 23 April 1999).

On other issues, translating ethical principles and strategy into effective policy has been, in practice, far from easy and the government has frequently been criticised (Driver and Martell, 1998: 146). While this is not least a consequence of raising expectations, the critical attention paid to the arms export issue has frequently led to accusations of inconsistency in the application of the policy, for example in the case of arms exports to Indonesia (*Financial Times*, 29 July 1997) and Sierra Leone (*Financial Times*, 4 May 1998). More generally, the strategy has frequently been deemed little more than an exercise in public relations.

Yet for Wheeler and Dunne, the injection of an ethical dimension into UK foreign policy does not imply that human rights concerns must take priority over all other governmental objectives. Rather, it implies 'good international citizenship' and the 'Sacrificing [of] the pursuit of narrow economic and political advantages in the cause of promoting international standards of human rights'. It does not mean sacrificing security or relinquishing the use of force (Wheeler and Dunne, 1998: 868–9). Thus Wheeler and Dunne, after Cook himself, talk of the government's approach to the ethical dimension as the equivalent of a Third Way in foreign policy (Lloyd, 1998; illustrated in Wheeler and Dunne, 1998).

While human rights and economic development are deemed to go 'hand in hand' as only one of four policy objectives spelt out in the Foreign Office mission statement, 'choices still have to be made in uncertain circumstances' (FCO and DFID, 1998: 8–10). Thus adding ethical content to foreign policy involves the government in confronting a number of dilemmas and constraints (*Financial Times*, 13 May 1997). First, the United Kingdom's dependence on trade makes the disentangling of 'ethics' from 'commercial self-interest' taxing and yet extremely important. Second, as the *Financial Times* pointed out, 'Britain's capacity to effect international change [on the human rights front] depends heavily on securing the backing of other European Union governments. The Labour government's more positive approach to its EU partners promises to win it a sympathetic hearing' (13 May 1997). At the very least, the impact of the EU on UK trade with third countries and the importance of multilateral human rights initiatives point to a compatibility between the pursuit of an ethical foreign policy and a pro-European agenda of constructive engagement. Before addressing the extent of the interface between these two policy strands, however, we turn to the EU's own 'ethical foreign policy'.

The European Union's 'ethical foreign policy'

While there was no mention of human rights in the founding Treaty of Rome, the Treaty amendments of the 1980s and 1990s allowed for the introduction of a human rights dimension in the EU's international policy. However, flimsy legal sources constrained its development and the horizontal or 'transversal' character of the policy (Brandtner and Rosas, 1998) has meant that policy coherence has been somewhat illusive. Adherence to the principles of universality and indivisibility (Commission of the European Union, 1995) and a commitment externally to the defence of minority rights as well as to individual rights (Biscoe, 1999) do, however, offer a foundation upon which the EU's multifarious human rights strategies are constructed. Moreover, the Commission has committed itself to a flexible approach in this area, which means making 'due allowance for the cultural sensitivities and specific needs of the countries concerned' (Commission, 1995), a policy which rests on 'continuous dialogue', that is, 'a positive, practical and constructive approach based on the concepts of exchange, sharing and encouragement' (Commission, 1995).

In translating such principles into practice, the EU is constrained by its own institutional structure. Thus there are two main components to the EU's human rights policy. Under pillar one of the Maastricht Treaty, the European Community pillar, human rights have become an element of the EU's development and external trade policy. While in this pillar the EU has the wherewithal to act coherently, it lacks instruments that would allow for the prioritisation of human rights concerns. By contrast, under the intergovernmental second pillar of the Treaty, which covers the EU's common foreign and security policy (CFSP), the instruments are potentially powerful but coherence is more problematic. Here, the near monopoly of CFSP decisions by European Council summits of EU leaders and the General Affairs Council of Ministers vests decisions with the political authority required to tackle this sensitive policy area. However, the unanimity decision rule in all aspects of CFSP (except on some aspects of implementation) takes the bite out of many decisions, despite the escape clause introduced in the 1997 Amsterdam Treaty article on 'flexibility' (article J.13), and encourages member states to use alternative international arenas for more contentious foreign policy issues.

Nevertheless, CFSP was established to reinforce co-operation among the EU member states, bringing economic sanctions under the CFSP's remit and establishing new foreign policy instruments (joint actions and common positions). CFSP certainly offers a repository for human rights policy, but one which remains far from fully developed. Human rights, however, is one of those foreign policy areas in which both common positions, which define strategies to be pursued, and joint actions, which commit member states to concrete actions, have been taken. For example, in 1996 a common position was adopted on the human rights situation in East Timor (decision 96/477/CFSP, 6 July 1996) and in the same month a joint action appointing a special envoy to the African Great Lakes was agreed (decision 96/441/CFSP, 24 July 1996). Perhaps more importantly, though, the introduction of CFSP has facilitated common declarations, explanations of vote and joint resolutions in international fora (especially the UN). And while 'political dialogue' is only an implicit element of the CFSP framework, it is clear that high-level discussion between the EU presidency (or a 'troika' of past, present and future presidencies) and third countries may be used to raise human rights concerns (Fouwels, 1997: 299–302).

Within the European Community pillar there are a number of ways in which the EU has been able to use its economic power to inject a human rights component into external trade and development policies. The importance of taking positive steps in this respect was emphasised in the Council's 1991 resolution on human rights, democracy and development and has been reiterated ever since (Napoli, 1995: 303; see *Bulletin of the EU*, 1991, no. 11, point 2.3.1; and Commission, 1998a: 146). All new external economic agreements are now conditional upon a respect for human rights and since May 1995 a model clause, drafted to ensure consistency, has been applied. The inclusion of human rights clauses (including suspension clauses) in bilateral trade and co-operation agreements with third countries has been applied more or less systematically since the early 1990s, even though, as Smith observes, in practice the clauses have not yet been invoked to denounce or suspend such agreements (1999: 11).

Human rights policy in the European Community pillar is also pursued through special incentive measures included in unilateral agreements, such as the scheme of generalised tariff preferences, and through conditions included in technical assistance programmes. The latter have been most apparent in the EU's dealings with the Central and East European states in the Phare and Tacis programmes and in the EU's pre-accession strategy (Mayhew, 1998: 162). However, suspension of such agreements for human rights reasons is likely to occur only where breaches are extreme (Fouwels, 1997: 309). Also under the European Community pillar, the European Initiative for Democracy and Human Rights, with a budget, established in 1996, of 90 million ecu, provides financial support for projects with a human rights dimension.

The Treaty also allows for the adoption of economic sanctions, a decision that cuts across the European Community and CFSP pillars and one that is a long-standing policy instrument of the Community. By contrast, it is only since the early 1990s that arms exports and the arms trade in general have become a matter of EU involvement. The prospect of a common arms export policy has been hindered by article 223 of the Treaty, which prevents member states from supplying information 'the disclosure of which it considers contrary to the essential interests of its security'. However, it has become apparent in recent years that if the EU is to claim to have a coherent human rights policy it must 'control and regulate the transfer of military, security and police equipment, technology, personnel and training, including logistical and financial support for such transfers' (Amnesty International, 1996). During the United Kingdom's presidency of the EU, member states deepened their commitment to make approval of licences for arms exports conditional on respect for human rights by approving an EU code of conduct on arms exports (see *Bulletin of the EU*, 1998, no. 5, point 1.3.6).

More recently, the EU played an important, if auxiliary, role in international intervention in Kosovo. With NATO, the EU took the view that the intervention was necessary for humanitarian reasons: 'to stop the [Serbian government's] brutal campaign of forced deportation, torture and murder in Kosovo' (General Affairs Council conclusions, Luxembourg, 26 April 1999, C/99/118). Kosovo was NATO's war but it had the support, in general terms at least, of the EU, most of whose member states were part of both organisations (see, for example, General Affairs Council conclusions, Luxembourg, 26 April 1999, C/99/118). Its forums provided the principal arena outside NATO for EU members to air their not inconsiderable differences over the course the war should take and especially tensions over the issue of ground troops in Kosovo (see for instance *The Times*, 26 March 1999 and 15 April 1999). In addition, the EU mobilised the full gamut of its foreign policy instruments, including economic sanctions on the Serbian government, financial support for neighbouring countries affected by the war, assistance to refugees and the diplomacy of Finnish president Martti Ahtisaari in negotiations to end the conflict.

In the search for a coherent human rights policy the European institutions have played a pivotal role, as Fouwels attests (1997: 316–18). By issuing resolutions on human rights issues the European Parliament has put its moral influence to excellent use, while the Commission has been pushing for a more positive and a more coherent approach to the policy. The European Court of Justice, too, has contributed by delivering numerous judgements and rulings on human rights issues (Fouwels, 1997). While there is still a gap between the increasingly coherent rhetoric espoused by the EU on the one hand and the *ad hoc* and piecemeal policy practice on the other, there is no doubt that the EU's international policy does have an explicit 'ethical dimension' of its own.

Labour's new European policy?

While foreign policy with an ethical dimension forms one strand of New Labour's international policy, European policy (that is, policy on the EU) forms a second. Over the course of the 1980s the Labour party's policy on Europe underwent a dramatic 'U-turn'. From a policy of withdrawal early in the decade, Labour had become, by 1989, the party of Europe (Daniels, 1998). The 1997 general election manifesto emphasised the party's pro-Europeanism, even if 'Europe' as an issue was played down during the election campaign itself (Driver and Martell, 1998: 146). Nevertheless, by the time the Labour government took office in May 1997 the party leadership had committed itself to a policy of 'constructive engagement' within the EU. With emphasis placed on intergovernmental co-operation and 'constructive partnership', however, the government was clearly rejecting both the supra-national and the regulatory methods of integration conventionally associated with the EU (Hughes and Smith, 1998). And while the positive yet reformist tone adopted by the government was well received, there were (as there would continue to be) doubts as to whether there was in fact any substance behind the pro-European rhetoric (Barber, 1998: 54).

Indeed, the line taken by Blair looked very much like old wine in new bottles. When the new government was thrown into the final stages of the Amsterdam Treaty negotiation, Blair took on key aspects of the Major government's general policy orientation and its strategy of positive caution. At Amsterdam Blair refused to lift the veto the Conservatives had placed on plans for a European defence union, reiterated support for the UK fishing industry and kept the Conservative preference to remain 'outside the European consensus' when immigration and borders were discussed (Hughes and Smith, 1998: 101). Blair also took on Major's 'wait and see' policy on economic and monetary union. In contrast, New Labour's commitment to sign the Social Chapter and its support for an increase in the European Parliament's powers and the extension of qualified majority voting were important departures. By late 1998 Blair had also capitulated on defence, ending the United Kingdom's long-standing reluctance to give the EU a defence capability (*European Voice*, 16–22 September 1999). While it would be an exaggeration to characterise these moves as a new 'maximalist' position on Europe, the

United Kingdom under New Labour has gone a long way towards weakening the tint of the Conservatives' 'minimalist' stance.

As early as 1994 the Labour party had signalled its European leadership aspirations when it stated that a 'Europe guided by Labour's values of community, opportunity, and justice will benefit Britain, her people and her children' (Labour party, 1994, quoted in Holden, 1998: 7). By 1997, leadership in Europe was a prominent if somewhat under-defined theme of the party's manifesto. In the manifesto, leadership was mostly pitched as a strategic device by which Labour would pursue British 'interests' in its new pro-European policy. However, there were important hints that 'leading from the front' in Europe would involve the export of key Labour values, principles and models of the kind featured above. Although 'preference shaping was rejected' on economic and monetary union (Holden, 1998: 8), there was clearly an attempt to shape preferences along the lines of Blair's Third Way in domestic economic policy, something made more feasible as the number of social democratic governments within the EU grew.

Blair described this Third Way in domestic economic policy – the Third Way which put the 'new' in New Labour (Blair, 1998a) – as the middle ground between the 'unbridled individualism and laissez-faire' of the Anglo-Saxon model on the one hand and 'old-style Government intervention [and] ... corporatism' of the European social model on the other (Blair, 1998a; see also Blair's Paris speech, 1998b). This Third Way in economic policy 'combin[es] economic dynamism with social justice' through government involvement to ensure flexible labour markets (Blair, 1998a). To improve the economy, 'active governments' address supply-side factors like education, skills, technology and infrastructure; they would provide job security through education programmes and an employment service helping people to re-train and get jobs (1998a).

The model was clearly for export. It is no coincidence that one of Blair's key European speeches on this subject was made to the Congress of the Party of European Socialists in Malmo, Sweden (Blair, 1997). According to Blair, there was a need 'to reform the European social model' whose foundations the United Kingdom could 'take a lead in helping to create' (1998a). While Holden (1998) claims that Blair's efforts to offer an 'alternative vision of society' limited his European options, there is no doubt that such an approach gave him the potential to marry domestic political priorities and concerns with a commitment to 'leadership' in Europe. While this left the door open for eventual membership of economic and monetary union, it did not necessarily imply that either his domestic or his European constituencies would automatically be convinced. As Barber puts it, 'the Labour government should not kid itself that the British model in toto is for export' (1998: 10).

Indeed, the leadership aspirations of the new government suggested at best a certain naïveté and at worst an arrogance that proved irritating to fellow EU leaders. Blair was much criticised for 'preaching' to his European colleagues about the merits of labour market flexibility and 'employability' (Barber,

1998: 13–14). This criticism meant that in future Blair would have to adopt a more sensitive and 'humbler' approach (*The Guardian*, 2 December 1998), built initially on co-ordination, consultation and the sharing of best practice (Barber, 1998: 50–1). Moreover, preference-shaping would be important at home. As Hughes and Smith put it, 'it is relevant to ask to what extent Labour's initial European policy approach reflects caution and the aim of slowly building up a new consensus on European issues' (1998: 102). From this perspective, and in the light of Blair's positive yet cautious stance during Amsterdam Treaty negotiations, the New Labour government's European policy may be much more subtle than a face-value overview might suggest.

The United Kingdom's presidency of the European Union

After only eight months of the Labour government the presidency of the EU passed to the United Kingdom. Holding the six-month presidency means performing a wide range of functions on behalf of the EU. But while some governments are also keen to use the presidency to push their own domestic agendas, in practice this is not always easy to do (Hayes-Renshaw and Wallace, 1997: 146). Before the start of the presidency the government set out its objectives in the form of a list of priorities, overlain with the commitment 'to give Europe back to the people' (Cook, 1997e). According to the former minister for Europe, Doug Henderson, 'That meant breaking a corrosive pattern of sterile debate and empty caricatures in the UK, and working with our partners to show how the Union serves the interests of ordinary people' (Henderson, 1998: 564). The government also committed itself to playing a leadership role in the EU, though this, it has been claimed, was more about normalising the United Kingdom's relations within the EU than about actually taking the lead (Lloyd, 1998).

Alongside preparing for enlargement and the euro, jobs appeared as one of the government's main priorities. Once again the emphasis was placed on using the EU as 'a clearing house for innovation' (Cook, 1997e), promoting and sharing best practice on employability, flexibility, entrepreneurship and equal opportunities within the single market. Other priorities were also mentioned in speeches and in the presidency work programme: for example, institutional and policy reform, stressing the reform of the Common Agricultural Policy and the EU budget; and the role of the EU in the world. Cook even mentioned in the very last paragraph of his key November 1997 speech, 'We will use our Presidency to develop an EU Code of Conduct on arms exports. We shall ensure that human rights remain a key factor in the EU's relations with the rest of the world' (Cook, 1997e).

While there is an element of continuity in all of these presidency priorities, it is the 'jobs' objective that the government made its own. While predating the UK presidency, the saliency of the issue (at EU level) coincided with the election of both the Labour government in the United Kingdom and the

Socialist government in France. While the French prime minister set the agenda by arguing for some form of 'economic governance' at EU level to balance the euro zone's single monetary policy, this (with Blair's help) was watered down to the inclusion of an employment chapter in the Amsterdam Treaty, a jobs summit to be held in November 1997 and a commitment to co-ordination of and co-operation on national employment policies across the EU. This ultimately reflected more of the Blair agenda than that of the French Socialists, with whom relations were strained.

Yet Blair's active advocacy of his Third Way in domestic economic policy during the UK presidency was still treated with either scepticism or hostility within many EU states. Ludlow (1998: 580–1) comments on an interview with *The Guardian* given in Washington in February 1998 in which the British prime minister claimed that his mission was to create an international consensus on the centre-left for the twenty-first century, bringing together Anglo-Saxon and European ideas. According to Ludlow, the reaction in Europe was hostile. Although Blair was in a sense a role model for centre-left political leaders owing to his electoral success and popularity at home, Ludlow claims that it was his 'methods more than his message which interested those who wanted to emulate him'. His Third Way, flexible market agenda was either conceived of as mystifying and unoriginal (Ludlow, 1998: 582) or simply as alien (Barber, 1998). At a high point, Blair appeared to find a soul mate in German chancellor Gerhard Schröder, with whom he published the joint statement called 'Europe: The Third Way/Die Neue Mitte' (Blair and Schröder, 1999). But, by the October 1999 Socialist International Conference in Paris, tensions between Blair and French Socialist prime minister Lionel Jospin and the apparent dilution of the German chancellor's enthusiasm for Blair's position showed just how little progress Blair had made in convincing his European partners to take up his Third Way in domestic economic policy (*The Times*, 9 November 1999).

While labour market reform sat high on the government's European agenda during the presidency, the same cannot be said for human rights concerns. The mention of external human rights and the government's unequivocal commitment to securing agreement on an EU code of conduct for arms exports does suggest a seeping of Labour's international policy at home on to the EU agenda (see the press statement from the meeting of the General Council of Ministers of 25 May 1998). However, these objectives seemed rather modest given the interest in the 'ethical dimension' at home preceding the start of the presidency and the potential for consensus on this issue within the EU.

For Cook (1998b), the agreement on arms stands outs as a key human rights achievement of the United Kingdom's EU presidency, an interpretation not without support in the broadsheet press (see, for instance, Neal Ascherson in *The Observer*, 2 August 1998). Yet the aims embodied in the code build upon an existing agreement which itself is still very much 'work in progress'. Eight common criteria for arms exports, for example, had been agreed by the European Council in 1991–92, in which member states also agreed to respect human rights in the country of final destination. The lack of agreement on how these criteria were to be interpreted and implemented had led to calls (especially from NGOs) for the EU code of conduct eventually agreed during the United Kingdom's EU presidency. The practical achievements of the agreements continue to be questioned in the press and criticised by groups like Amnesty International (*The Observer*, 2 August 1998). Moreover, continuing pressure to strengthen the code prompted Germany, during its presidency of the EU, to propose controls on EU arms brokers who bought weapons outside the EU and an upgrading of the non-binding code to a CFSP common position (Smith, 1999: 10).

The government's first *Annual Report on Human Rights*, published around the end of the presidency, identified a number of areas, beyond the code of conduct, that involved a European dimension. Mention is made of an EU visit to East Timor by the EU troika; the EU mission to Algeria to build upon the ongoing political dialogue; a common position on Afghanistan proposed by the United Kingdom and adopted on 26 January; efforts to construct a coherent EU human rights policy on Rwanda; use of the presidency to make representations to Albania and South Korea on the death penalty; support for the use of qualified majority voting for the suspension of trade agreements on account of human rights breaches; support for development regulations proposed by the Commission, which would channel more funds into human rights projects; and an effort to encourage fellow EU member states to support the UK line on Myanmar (Burma) (FCO and DFID, 1998: 13, 18, 37, 42, 46). At the end of the presidency, Robin Cook highlighted how the previous six months had been used to re-invigorate the EU's dialogue with China, conclude the code of conduct and make 'slow but steady progress' in Bosnia and Kosovo (Cook, 1998b). However, although this list is impressively long, the substance is somewhat thin. Nevertheless, we consider it prudent to explore the question of the UK government's 'export' of its ethical dimension to the EU further. We do so by taking one of the cases that Cook himself highlighted, that of China.

Labour, the European Union and human rights in China

China is emerging as a major economic and political power, exciting the interest of the developed world, but it is also routinely accused of being out of step with international human rights norms. The Hong Kong handover in June 1997 was one of the earliest tests of the Labour government's ethical foreign policy. It was the first real taste of the tensions inherent in a policy that aimed to balance the United Kingdom's commercial interest in China with a desire to bring China's government into line on human rights. From our perspective, an interesting feature of the handover is the early indication that the United Kingdom's policy on China was to have an EU dimension.

In this episode, the government looked for and received the moral support of other EU member governments in its gestures of protest against China's decision to appoint rather than hold popular elections for representatives to Hong Kong's new legislature when China resumed rule in 1997. Indeed, as the Blair government settled into office it very quickly became apparent that a key element in the United Kingdom's ethical or human rights policy on China was to consist of EU initiatives and European policy co-ordination.

The advantages of such a strategy are not too difficult to deduce. As the prime minister emphasised during his visit to China in autumn 1998, 'In China, just as in the USA, our bilateral relations are stronger if reinforced by strength in Europe. That message has been put to me as clearly by the leadership in China as by the leadership in the US and other leading powers' (Blair, 1998e). Similarly, achievements in the human rights field at EU level that are broadly compatible with national priorities can be usefully appropriated for consumption at home. This was particularly in evidence during the UK presidency, when a number of important EU–China initiatives were undertaken.

Considered against the government's desire to play a 'leading role' in Europe and the probable advantages of an EU-level human rights strategy, the pivotal place of the EU within the government's China policy makes one wonder whether, in this case at least, the government might indeed be seeking to export its ethical foreign policy to Europe. In order to examine whether the Blair government had tried to export its Third Way in foreign policy on China with the same vigour it had sought to export its Third Way in domestic economic policy, we address two key questions. The first queries the extent to which EU policy on China resembles its UK counterpart, particularly in terms of the principles, objectives and strategies. The second question we focus on explores whether the United Kingdom's policy on China has influenced the EU's approach or, more specifically, whether the 'ethical foreign policy' pursued by the United Kingdom in relation to China has in some way altered the EU's line on human rights in China. To answer these questions we draw on empirical evidence that we have expanded upon elsewhere (Bourne and Cini, 1999).

The heavy imprint of EU-level initiatives on the Labour government's China policy make it difficult to untangle the role of the Labour government in the EU sphere. The EU dimension now forms a major element of the United Kingdom's approach to human rights in China, to the extent that it is often impossible to identify an exclusively domestic policy (though Hong Kong is of course the exception to this). To hammer home this point, in a summary of government policy towards China delivered in the House of Commons towards the end of the UK presidency of the EU, all nine of the UK policy successes mentioned involved, whether explicitly or implicitly, some degree of European policy co-ordination (see Derek Fatchett, Foreign Office minister, *Hansard*, 1 April 1998, cols 1236–9). There are no equivalent statements highlighting purely UK policy successes since mid-1997. In this sense we might talk of the interpenetration of UK and EU policy on China.

An assessment of the UK government's influence on EU policy is further complicated by the similarity of EU and UK policies on China, policies which resemble one another in terms of principles, strategies and practice. In the first place both emphasise a strategy of 'constructive relations' or 'constructive engagement' with a country emerging as a world political and economic power of considerable commercial and strategic interest to the West (see for instance Derek Fatchett, *Hansard*, 10 June 1997, col. 932; Commission, 1998b). Furthermore, human rights objectives were to be pursued, principally by means of 'dialogue' based on open exchanges of views between leaders but also direct expressions of concern to Chinese leaders on key human rights issues (FCO and DFID, 1998; Commission, 1998b). In line with the Third Way model in foreign policy suggested above, demands that China adhere to human rights norms were to be balanced against the United Kingdom's and the EU's commercial interests and sensitivity to China's prominence in the international security order (see for example Cook, 1997b; Blair, 1998d; Commission, 1998b). It is also reasonable to claim that both the UK and the EU policies towards China as they have been played out in practice tend to be 'all carrot and no stick', with a reluctance at both a national and European level to apply a heavy-handed approach to the sensitive issue of human rights breaches in China. The EU, for example, stopped its practice of presenting draft resolutions on China in the UN Human Rights Commission when China's 'fierce reaction' to the practice disrupted the process of EU–Chinese dialogue taking shape in the mid-1990s (Fouwels, 1997: 319).

Similarly, the UK government took particular care to shield the Chinese president from protests by human rights demonstrators during his state visit in October 1999. Against the background of president Jiang's comments that the Swiss had 'lost a good friend' when demonstrators dogged his visit there earlier in the year and warnings from Beijing that 'anti-Chinese protests ... would undermine relations' (*The Times*, 20 October 1999) the government appeared to go out of its way to keep protesters from the president's sight. At one stage the police parked vans directly in front of demonstrators to 'screen them from Mr Jiang's view' (*The Times*, 23 October 1999) and the Chinese leader was ushered into Downing Street by a back route, avoiding demonstrators gathering in Whitehall (*The Times*, 22 October 1999). When the time came to tackle the thorny question of human rights president Jiang began the session by restating his government's preference to deal with human rights in the context of the wider relationship between China and the United Kingdom (*The Times*, 22 October 1999).

In contrast to the influence of the EU on UK policy towards China, we have found no evidence to suggest that the Labour government has been able as yet to influence substantively the EU's policy on China. The EU's agreed strategy and, in particular, the Commission's preference for dialogue and partnership date from well before the election of the Labour government, and while the revitalisation of EU–China relations occurred after the arrival in office of New Labour there is nothing to suggest any direct agenda-setting by the UK government. Rather, it is more likely that it is the European Commission that has been pro-active in setting the EU's agenda on relations with China over this period. This is particularly appropriate given the underlying EU-wide consensus on the general principles and norms that would underpin such a policy, ideas clearly reflected in Cook's take on the foundations of the United Kingdom's China policy described above.

However, the UK government was effective in using its presidency to follow through on the Commission's initiatives and priorities, and the compatibility between EU and UK approaches would have been helpful in this respect. Yet even if the Labour government did take the credit for certain successful policy changes, such as China's reception of EU troika ambassadors (high-level EU representatives) in Tibet in May 1998 and its invitation to the UN Commissioner for Human Rights to visit China (Cook, 1998b), many of these changes arose out of inherited EU business which any government holding the presidency would have had to pick up. While we would not wish to understate the importance of 'following through', and would agree with Robin Cook that the presidency was indeed used to 're-invigorate the EU's dialogue with China' as was reported above, the role played by the UK government should not be overstated.

Conclusions

This chapter has looked at the United Kingdom's European policy and at the EU's human rights agenda through the lens of the Labour government's 1997 commitment to pursue a foreign policy with an ethical dimension and to follow a policy of 'constructive engagement' in European affairs. When the Labour government came to office in May 1997, it did so with the express intention of changing both the substance and the tone of UK European policy. The test of this new approach to European politics by the government came almost immediately with the UK presidency of the EU in the second half of 1997. At the same time the government was also putting into effect its new approach to foreign policy, an approach which would have at its centre an ethical dimension. In tying these threads together, we questioned whether the New Labour government had sought to export its Third Way in foreign policy to the EU as a means of operationalising its commitment to play a more positive role in this forum.

A number of factors suggested the government might indeed attempt to promote its Third Way in foreign policy among its European partners. In the first place, Cook's early speeches suggested the government would actively pursue the 'ethical dimension' of its foreign policy with a strategy of leadership in international organisations, which included the EU (Cook, 1997a). Additionally, the government had actively sought to export its other Third Way, or its domestic economic policy preference for labour market flexibility. This Third Way in domestic economic policy occupied much of the prime minister's attention in relations with other European states and topped the government's priorities when the United Kingdom held the EU presidency. Furthermore, our comparison of the United Kingdom's and the EU's 'ethical' foreign policies and our case comparing their policies on China showed a marked approximation in both policy thinking and practice, suggesting possible foundations for a deeper European dimension in the United Kingdom's human rights policy.

Contrary to such expectations, we identified no evidence to support the view that the UK government used human rights as a hook upon which to hang its European policy. While the Labour government had certainly sought to build coalitions with its European neighbours as a way of enhancing its agenda-setting influence within the EU – notably with the Germans on the jobs issues – there is nothing to suggest that ethical foreign policy has been dealt with in anything like the same way. Human rights items like the code of conduct on arms exports and relations with China were far from prominent features of the United Kingdom's EU presidency agenda and even though the government did try to take the credit for some developments in this field most built on existing EU commitments and inherited business.

The government's reluctance to bring the 'ethical' and 'European' strands of its international policy together in practice and the limited impact of its Third Way in foreign policy at the EU level have left some of its key aspirations on the 'ethical dimension' unfulfilled. There is little to suggest that the United Kingdom used the EU to try to determine, rather than simply react to, foreign policy events or to situate itself at the heart of the international community (Cook, 1997a). Nor is it clear that the foreign policy's 'ethical dimension', trumpeted as a feature of a new image of the United Kingdom abroad (Cook, 1997a, 1997d), has contributed to any significant change in the perceptions of its European partners about the United Kingdom or its role in the processes of European integration.

References

Amnesty International (1996), *Memorandum Proposals for a Strengthened Protection of Human Rights by the European Union in the Context of the Intergovernmental Conference 1996* (London: Amnesty International).

Barber, L. (1998), *Britain and the New European Agenda* (London: Centre for European Reform).

Biscoe, A. (1999), 'The European Union and minority rights', in P. Cumper and S. Wheatley (eds), *Minority Rights in the 'New' Europe* (The Hague: Kluwer Law International), 89–103.

Blair, T. (1997), speech, Congress of the Party of European Socialists, Malmo, Sweden, 6 June.

Blair, T. (1998a), speech, Annual Friends of Niewspoort Dinner, The Ridderzaal, The Hague, The Netherlands, 20 January.

Blair, T. (1998b), speech, French National Assembly, Paris, France, 24 March.

Blair, T. (1998c), speech, Congress of European Socialists, Malmo, Sweden, 6 June.

Blair, T. (1998d), 'A British–Chinese partnership', *People's Daily*, Peking, 6 October (also available on the FCO website).

Blair, T. (1998e), 'The patriotic case for internationalism', speech, Hong Kong, 9 October.

Blair, T. and Schröder, G. (1999), 'Europe: The Third Way, Die Neue Mitte', Labour party website.

Bourne, A. and Cini, M. (1999), 'Exporting the Third Way in foreign policy: New Labour, the EU and human rights', paper presented to the Political Studies Association Conference, Nottingham, 23–25 March.

Brandtner, B. and Rosas, A (1998), 'Human rights and the external relations of the European Community: an analysis of doctrine and practice', *European Journal of International Law*, vol. 9, no. 3, 491–509.

Commission of the European Union (1995), *The European Union and the External Dimension of Human Rights Policy: From Rome to Maastricht and Beyond*, communication from the Commission to the Council and European Parliament, Brussels, 22 November 1995, COM (95) 0567.final.

Commission of the European Union (1998a), *Democratisation, the Rule of Law, Respect for Human Rights and Good Governance: The Political Issue of the Partnership of the European Union and the ACP States*, Brussels, 12 March 1998, COM (98) 0146.final.

Commission of the European Union (1998b), *Building a Comprehensive Partnership with China*, communication from the Commission, Brussels, 25 March 1998, COM (98) 181.

Cook, R. (1997a), 'British foreign policy', statement, 12 May.

Cook, R (1997b), 'A bridge, not a wall of China,' *The Times*, 13 June (also available on the FCO website).

Cook, R. (1997c), 'Human rights into a new century', speech, Locarno Suite, FCO, London, 17 July.

Cook, R. (1997d), 'Britain's new approach to the world', speech, Labour party conference, 2 October.

Cook, R. (1997e), 'The British presidency: giving Europe back to the people', speech, Institute for European Affairs, Dublin, 3 November.

Cook, R. (1998a), 'The first year', speech, Mansion House, 23 April.

Cook, R. (1998b), speech, Royal Institute for International Affairs, Chatham House, 25 June.

Daniels, P. (1998), 'From hostility to "constructive engagement": the Europeanisation of the Labour party', *West European Politics*, vol. 21, no. 1, 72–96.

Driver, S. and Martell, L. (1998), *New Labour: Politics after Thatcherism* (Oxford: Polity).

FCO (1997), 'Mission statement', 12 May.

FCO and DFID (1998), *Annual Report on Human Rights* (London: TSO).

Foley, C. and Starmer, K. (1998), 'Foreign policy, human rights and the United Kingdom', *Social Policy and Administration*, vol. 32, no. 5, 464–80.

Fouwels, M. (1997), 'The European Union's common foreign and security policy and human rights', *Netherlands Quarterly of Human Rights*, vol. 15, no. 3, 291–324.

George, S. (1999), *An Awkward Partner: Britain in the European Union*, 3rd edn (Oxford: Oxford University Press).

Hayes-Renshaw, F. and Wallace, H. (1997), *The Council of Ministers* (Basingstoke: Macmillan).

Henderson, D. (1998), 'The UK presidency: an insider's view', *Journal of Common Market Studies*, vol. 36, no. 4, 563–72.

Holden, R. (1998), 'Confronting the European challenge – New Labour and the development of a clear strategy for integration', paper presented to the UACES Research Conference, University of Lincoln and Humberside, 9–11 September.

Hughes, K. and Smith, E. (1998), 'New Labour – new Europe?', *International Affairs*, vol. 74, no. 1, 93–103.

Lloyd, J. (1998), 'A very British lead', *New Statesman*, 2 January, 10–12.

Ludlow, P. (1998), 'The 1998 UK presidency: a view from Brussels', *Journal of Common Market Studies*, vol. 36, no. 4, 573–83.

Mayhew, A. (1998), *Recreating Europe* (Cambridge: Cambridge University Press).

Napoli, D. (1995), 'The European Union's foreign policy and human rights', in N. Neuwahl and A. Rosas (eds), *The European Union and Human Rights* (The Hague: Martinus Nijhoff).

Smith, K. (1999), 'Foreign policy with an ethical dimension? The EU, human rights and relations with third countries', paper presented to the UACES Research Conference, University of Sheffield, 8–10 September.

Symons, Baroness (1997), 'New government, new foreign policy', speech, Canadian foreign service, Ottawa, Canada, 10 October.

Wheeler, N. J. and Dunne, T. (1998), 'Good international citizenship: a Third Way for British foreign policy', *International Affairs*, vol. 74, no. 4, 847–70.

11

British foreign policy, human rights and Iran

Davina Miller

Introduction

This chapter discusses the extent to which human rights are now, as the Labour government claims, a new consideration in the United Kingdom's bilateral relationships. It is only by examining those relationships in some detail that an accurate assessment can be made of New Labour's assertion that it has embarked on a foreign policy with an 'ethical dimension'. As such, a case study approach is adopted here. Iran seems an obvious candidate in this respect for the following reasons: its appalling human rights record extends to infringing the rights of a British citizen (Salman Rushdie); it has undergone a recent rapprochement with the United Kingdom; and the seven-year policy of EU engagement offers some evidence of the effects of dialogue, the government's preferred mechanism for effecting improvements in human rights.

The chapter begins by describing the 'ethical dimension' of foreign policy – the new human rights agenda – and sets out some criteria for assessing whether or not this stated agenda has changed policy. Using these criteria, the chapter examines the Labour government's policy towards Iran, concluding that, far from being motivated by human rights, the government made concessions on human rights. The chapter then examines the efficacy of the government's preferred approach to human rights, that of dialogue with the countries concerned. It concludes that dialogue is ineffectual in the case of Iran. The chapter ends by assessing UK interests in the pursuit of human rights improvements in Iran and elsewhere.

The ethical dimension: Labour's human rights agenda

The 'ethical dimension' of its foreign policy means that the United Kingdom 'must support the demands of other peoples for the democratic rights on which we insist for ourselves'. It is a universal commitment by New Labour and, as such, human rights are to be placed 'at the heart of our foreign policy' – 'an integral component'. The foreign secretary seems to have dispensed with the argument that the one true morality in international relations is prudent self-interest, speaking instead in terms of 'duty', 'responsibility' and 'integrity'. However, the promotion of human rights is spoken of in terms of both duty *and* self-interest in that the United Kingdom is 'better able to trade with countries that are stable and free' (Cook, 1997a, 1997b, 1998c).

Human rights strategies have been devised, the foreign secretary assures us, for over seventy countries. The overarching strategy, however, will be to 'seek dialogue on the observance of human rights wherever we have cause for concern' (Cook, 1998c, 1997b). The choice is not one of convenience: 'Long-term engagement provides the best means to secure sustained change' (Foreign Affairs Committee, 1998: 40).

This, then, is the Third Way in foreign policy, illustrated, the foreign secretary argued, by the case of China, which 'has proved that it is possible to have a constructive dialogue on human rights and also strengthen, not damage, our economic links' (Cook, 1998b). The Foreign Office does not rule out other measures in pursuit of human rights. The United Kingdom will support international criticism 'of those regimes who grotesquely violate human rights and repeatedly fail to respond to demands for an improvement in standards'; and will consider trade sanctions in 'extreme cases' where there is 'no prospect of progress through dialogue' (Cook, 1997b; Foreign Affairs Committee, 1998, 49; FCO and DFID, 1998: 46).

Assessment

If we are to assess whether or not human rights are an 'integral component' of foreign policy – that they are 'one of the legs upon which foreign policy stands' (Foreign Affairs Committee, 1998: 162) – we need to set forth some criteria for judging these claims. If human rights are one of the objectives of the United Kingdom's external relations, then we can speak of a human rights policy in the same way we speak of the United Kingdom's security policy or trade policy. We need to specify what it means to have an external human rights policy. This is a somewhat different task from simply asking whether or not the Labour government's foreign policy has an ethical dimension.

The Labour government's stated commitment to human rights, although more explicit perhaps than that of other governments, does not constitute an external human rights policy, unless one wants to argue that virtually all governments have human rights policies. As Amnesty International points out, 'All governments of the UN are bound to work for the protection and promotion of human rights' (1998a: 10); and as Donnelly puts it, human rights are 'treated as an ordinary part of international relations' (1998: 15).

Apart from the promise to raise individual cases with other states (in any case, something many governments do fairly routinely), the changes to the policy process merely increase information about human rights within government – although the Foreign Affairs Committee was sceptical that that information was circulating properly (1998: 165). An act of political will is required to translate knowledge into action.

The two *Annual Reports on Human Rights* (FCO and DFID, 1998, 1999) outline many worthy projects, for example funding twenty Indonesian students to attend British courses on good government, or a children's rights 'infobus' in the Ukraine. The Human Rights Projects Fund spent £5 million in its first year on 200 programmes in over sixty countries. The *Annual Reports* also discuss many initiatives, including the ban on the export of torture equipment and support for the proposed international criminal court. But such initiatives do not constitute an external human rights policy. An external human rights policy means that the objective of promoting human rights becomes incorporated into bilateral relations. Sikkink argues: 'A country can be said to have an external human rights policy when it has explicit mechanisms for integrating human rights concerns into foreign policy, and when those mechanisms have modified foreign policy in some cases' (1993: 143). Luard makes a similar point: 'No foreign policy objective can be achieved without a price' (1980: 589). If a country has an external human rights policy, it ought to be possible to delineate the sacrifice – or modification – it has made in its pursuit.

This does not mean that a state has to sacrifice its security. While some have argued that an external human rights policy entails consistency, Sikkink rejects that as too stringent given the many considerations that must be taken into account in any foreign policy decision (1993: 143). Nor does it mean that governments apply trade sanctions to every state that violates human rights – assuming that one could get agreement on their usefulness or, indeed, their morality. As Luard argues: 'The breaking-off of trade relations is the most serious step of all that can be taken ... It will only be considered in the most extreme cases ... On the other hand, investment in a country with a bad record could be prevented or at least discouraged at a much earlier stage' (1980: 601). Having an external human rights policy means the government has 'take[n] into account our own responsibility for creating or fostering rights-repressive policies or regimes' (Donnelly, 1998: 161–2). Or, as Wheeler and Dunne put it: 'Sacrificing the pursuit of narrow economic and political advantages in the cause of promoting international standards of human rights is the most important principle of good international citizenship' (1998: 868).

There is a general scepticism about the effectiveness of both dialogue and participation in international criticism in promoting human rights. The use of weak instruments, Donnelly argues, is 'clear evidence of the low value placed on human rights' (1998: 90). As Luard points out, governments 'have come to expect comment on human rights affairs by other states' (1980: 586–7). As such, dialogue has very few, if any, costs attached to it.

A separate question is the *effectiveness* of both dialogue and criticism. Here, the major problem lies in *assessing* that effectiveness. The government argues that not only is dialogue effective in changing human rights practices but that it represents the best method available except in certain extreme cases. Amnesty International and the Foreign Affairs Committee point out that the government provides no criteria for determining when dialogue or engagement should govern policy and when other measures are more appropriate (Amnesty International, 1998a: 18; Foreign Affairs Committee, 1998: para. 124). Furthermore, as Wheeler and Dunne argue, the difficulty in evaluating the Third Way is that 'we cannot know how much more might be achieved by adopting a tougher stance' (1998: 864). In addition, in qualifying both 'engagement' and 'change' with 'long-term', the government makes an assessment even more problematical.

It is not necessary here to attempt an evaluation of the utility of sanctions, first, because the foreign secretary has accepted their usefulness in some circumstances and, second, because the issue does not form part of the criteria for judging whether or not an external human rights policy exists. The modification of policy entails the promotion of human rights above 'narrow economic and political advantage'. It lies not in what states do but in what states refrain from doing in respect of countries that abuse human rights, that is, not undertaking new investment, not providing aid and not exporting arms. As such, one would expect to find a consistency in the treatment of all countries, unless *raison d'état* intervened.

The government states that human rights are an 'integral component' of foreign policy. If that is the case – if this represents an external human rights policy rather than simple and rather old rhetoric – then one would expect to find a modification of policy in all cases, except where British security is at stake. This modification should take the form of an avoidance of those actions that might buttress policies or states that abuse human rights. It might also include contact with opposition groups. However, the government, in insisting that 'long-term engagement provides the best means to secure sustained change', allows itself to invest, to provide aid and to export arms since these are all part and parcel of 'engagement'.

Policy towards Iran

In examining policy towards Iran, one does not find any modifications in pursuit of human rights. Indeed, one finds that ethical considerations, including human rights, have been sacrificed in order to effect engagement. Two questions then arise. The first is whether the means justify the ends: whether the price paid for engagement with Iran will bring improvements in human rights or prolong violations. As such, the construction of current Iranian politics is important. The second is whether the government was in any way motivated by human rights in addition to narrow national interest.

Of course, Robin Cook did state that the promotion of human rights is but one of four foreign policy goals (1997a), listing it last, behind security, prosperity and quality of life, although the foreign secretary has not explicitly prioritised these objectives. If, as he says, 'a top priority' is to be the promotion of exports (Cook, 1997a), we are back where we were when the Conservative government exported arms and defence technology to Iraq. Human rights were then a part of the many considerations that affected such decisions but they were overwhelmed by short-term considerations of trade – a policy which the then shadow foreign secretary critiqued most effectively. In spite of the rhetoric, and the 'new constituency of human rights' (Foreign Affairs Committee, 1998: 36) that the present foreign secretary has alluded to as supporting his policy, the privately ordered national priorities of Whitehall will continue to prevail.

Throughout its years in opposition, the Labour party maintained a consistent policy towards Iran. Conference habitually adopted resolutions condemning human rights abuses, including, after 1989, the *fatwa* on Salman Rushdie, and offering support to the National Council of Resistance of Iran (NCRI), which it typically described as 'the democratic, progressive opposition'. Frontbench spokespersons met with leaders and representatives from the NCRI. The foreign secretary was in the chair at conference for the 1997 resolution, later endorsed by the party's NEC, which condemned Iran's human rights violations and called upon the newly elected government to support the Iranian people's resistance.

By January 1998, as the United Kingdom assumed the presidency of the EU, diplomats were speaking of a 'big shift' in British thinking about Iran, with the foreign secretary reportedly looking for an alternative to both the suspended 'critical dialogue' and US sanctions against Iran. The main stumbling block for improved relations with Iran was the *fatwa* imposed on Salman Rushdie in 1989. On 30 March 1998 the (General Affairs) Council of the EU decided to renew dialogue with Iran, suspended following the verdict of a German court that the Iranian government, at the highest levels, had orchestrated the murder of four Kurdish dissidents in Berlin in 1992. The Foreign Office minister of state noted the 'positive signs' in Iran's ratification of the Chemical Weapons Convention and condemnation of terrorist attacks by Islamic groups in Algeria and Egypt. However, the minister stated: 'As we have said on many occasions, we are prepared to judge the new regime not by the rhetoric of the past, but by its record and what it achieves and sets out to do in future.' The government wanted 'more concrete and positive indications' in respect of weapons of mass destruction and the sponsorship of terrorism (*Hansard*, 18 March 1998: cols 1267–8) and was most stringent in its demands vis-à-vis the *fatwa*. In January, as the review of policy towards Iran got underway, the foreign secretary stated that 'Britain would remain resolute in our demand that Iran must lift the *fatwa* against Salman Rushdie' (Cook, 1998a). In February, Baroness Symons said that the issue was 'non-compromisable' (*Hansard*, 10 February 1998: col. 993).

Once the threat of US sanctions against European countries investing in Iran was lifted in May 1998, both the United Kingdom and the EU moved to speed the process of rapprochement. EU officials had two days of talks in Iran in July, with the British official remaining for further discussions. In August, the United Kingdom restored short-term cover for exports to Iran through the ECGD. In early September, the most senior Iranian diplomat to visit the United Kingdom in a decade spent two days in talks with Derek Fatchett, a foreign office minister, and civil servants from both the FCO and the DTI.

UK concessions on human rights

The Labour government changed policy in two respects to reach an accommodation with Iran. First, it abandoned its relationship with the NCRI, condemning and circumscribing its activities. Second, it accepted the Iranian position on the *fatwa*, a position that the Iranian government had held since 1993. At a meeting with the NCRI in July 1996, Derek Fatchett had assured those present that a Labour government would not change the party's policy of dialogue with the NCRI and would maintain policy towards the Iranian regime, upholding Labour's principles in defence of human rights. He had known and supported the resistance for years and promised that, once Labour was in power, the NCRI would enjoy regular contact with the Foreign Office (Mohaddessin, 1998: 15).

The NCRI asserts that, at a meeting of the Iranian Supreme National Council in June 1998, three conditions for the United Kingdom's expansion of economic ties with Iran were set. First and foremost, the United Kingdom must condemn and restrict the People's Mujahedin Organisation of Iran, the largest contingent of the NCRI. The second was that the United Kingdom must shelve its demands vis-à-vis the *fatwa*. The third was that the United Kingdom must make some financial concessions, including the provision of credit, to Iran (Mohaddessin, 1998: 3–4). In July 1998, Fatchett, speaking to the Iranian News Agency, pledged to limit the activities of the Mujahedin and its front organisations. Two days later, the Charity Commission froze the bank accounts of Iran Aid, a charity connected with the Mujahedin.

The Mujahedin insists that it has a right to resist a regime that has executed thousands of its members and that refuses to allow free elections. It also insists that its military operations are conducted in the context of the Geneva conventions and that it attacks only military targets (Mohaddessin, 1998: 33). The former Iranian president, Hashemi Rafsanjani, speaking in June 1998, said of the Mujahedin, 'From day one, they were opposed to the Islamic system; they talked about a democratic system' (Tehran Radio, 27 June 1998).

It is possible that, on assuming power, the Labour government was given information about the Mujahedin and the NCRI that seventeen years of contacts had failed to reveal. However, the coincidence of the government's circumscribing the NCRI at the very point when it sought a rapprochement cannot be overlooked, even if one dismisses the NCRI's claim that this was one of Iran's preconditions. (According to the Tower Commission investigating the Iran–Contra affair, US condemnation of the Mujahedin was part of the hostage deal with Iran in 1985.) Whatever the charges against Iran Aid, British governments had fifteen years to observe and therefore fifteen years in which to close down its operations. While the Conservative government did not recognise the NCRI, it took no action against Iran Aid. Whatever the true nature of the Mujahedin and the NCRI might be, the Labour government has seemed anxious to be *seen* to condemn.

In March 1998, the minister of state at the Foreign Office said of the *fatwa*: 'It is totally alien to our values for one state to declare what is in effect a death sentence against a citizen of another country. It is wholly alien for us to negotiate in any way or conciliate about our own basic values ... We know what the regime has said in the past and it has not gone far enough' (*Hansard*, 18 March 1998: col. 1268).

The agreement reached with Iran in September 1998 comprised this assurance by the Iranian foreign minister: 'Senior Iranian officials have previously made clear our position on this issue. I reaffirmed that position' (Embassy of the Islamic Republic of Iran, 1998: 3). This, then, was no more than a restatement of a five-year-old policy that the Iranian government would not take action, nor encourage anyone else, to threaten the life of Salman Rushdie and, as such, did not support the bounty on his head. Assurances, which in the spring had 'not gone far enough', were welcomed in the autumn as new and acceptable.

The Iranian government presented the agreement in somewhat different terms. Dr Kharazzi, Iran's foreign minister, said Iran had taken no new stance (Iranian State Television, 3 October 1998). The chargé d'affaires, Mr Ansari, asserted that, in the September meeting, 'The *fatwa* was not essentially raised in negotiations ... for it was obvious that it could not be rescinded' (Iranian News Agency, 1 October 1998). Mr Ansari boasted: 'When you have such a big government, one of the pioneers of so-called freedom of speech backing down and accepting that the *fatwa* cannot be withdrawn or weakened it is a clear triumph' (*Q News*, October 1998: 16).

The United Kingdom and the EU presented the agreement as new in that it offered a 'clarification' of previous assurances (EU, 1998b). What signal this sent to Iran, given the previous demands of both the United Kingdom and the EU for the lifting of the *fatwa*, the removal of the bounty or written assurances of Rushdie's safety, is important in terms of human rights. The EU had previously declared that 'the *fatwa* remained null and void because it violated the Universal Declaration on Human Rights' (EU, 1998a). In effect, the EU and the United Kingdom had sacrificed the human rights of a citizen of the EU. This appears to send a signal to Iran (and other states) that whatever might be said about human rights in the course of dialogue will not be supported by an active commitment.

However, as the government says, 'choices still have to be made in uncertain circumstances and between sometimes unwelcome options' (FCO and DFID, 1998: 10), and it might be argued that the government has had to adapt itself to the reality of the *fatwa*'s permanence. But the Labour government also asserts that, 'We have learnt the vital lesson of the twentieth century: when we appease in the short-term we pay an even greater price in the longer term' (Fatchett, 1997b). If one is to accept that the sacrifice of Salman Rushdie's human rights and the circumscribing of the most vocal and effective critic of Iran's violations of human rights were not simple acts of appeasement but choices in uncertain circumstances, then one needs to be able to demonstrate a principled end. More importantly, if Iran is to take seriously European concerns about its human rights situation, Iran needs to see these concessions as not simply motivated by the pursuit of narrow political and economic advantage.

Means and ends: dialogue

The government's case for engagement with Iran rests on two premises. First, the Foreign Office 'believe[s] that the improvement in our bilateral relationship ... offers the best forum to address [human rights] concerns' (Fatchett, 1998). This echoes the general case the government makes for a policy of engagement or dialogue towards those states that abuse human rights. The second premise is that Iran has embarked, under president Khatami, on a process of moderation, which the UK government 'must do all [it] can to encourage' (Cook, 1998a). An assessment is therefore necessary of the state of Iran's human rights and the effect dialogue, the EU's policy since 1992, has thus far had. The US State Department, Amnesty International and the UN all paint a similar picture of the human rights situation in Iran, noting extrajudicial execution, 'disappearances', torture and ill-treatment, cruel and unusual punishments, including stoning to death, detention without trial and unfair trials. Amnesty International described the situation in its 1998 report as one consisting of 'patterns of serious and widespread human rights violations' (Amnesty International, 1998b: 203). Iran has not signed the Protocol on the Abolition of the Death Penalty, the Convention against Torture and Other Cruel, Inhuman or Degrading Treatment or Punishment, or the Convention on the Elimination of All Forms of Discrimination against Women. The special representative of the UN Commission on Human Rights reported in 1998 that the situation of women had deteriorated (Reuters, 8 October 1998).

The UK government, however, was quick to draw attention to the small improvements noted by the UN and by the US State Department (1999). 'There is a lively political debate in Iran's media', argued the government. In addition, citing the appointment of the first four women judges and a female vice-president, 'there have also been some modest improvements in the situation of women'. Ministers also stressed that local elections were held for the first time since the revolution and that officials were arrested after the murders of intellectuals (*Hansard*, 11 November 1998: col. 832; 14 July 1999: cols 337–8).

The United Kingdom and the EU issue declarations and sponsor international resolutions about human rights in Iran. The EU sponsored the UN resolution on human rights in Iran passed on 18 November 1998 (Reuters, 18 November 1998). A further, EU-sponsored resolution at the UN Commission on Human Rights on 23 April 1999 expressed concern at continuing religious persecution, harassment of journalists, the lack of transparency in the judicial process and the high number of executions and cases of torture (FCO and DFID, 1999: 70; Hoon, 23 June 1999). Derek Fatchett argued, 'We know from our contacts with the UK Baha'i community that external pressure of this kind has an effect on Iran', even if progress was 'frustratingly slow' (Fatchett, 1999).

The minister of state asserted that the United Kingdom and the EU give human rights violations in Iran 'a high priority in our dealings with the Iranian government' (Fatchett, 1999). Yet the evidence that engagement or dialogue is effective in bringing about change in Iran's domestic behaviour is scant. In the choice between policies, the government has argued that, 'The key consideration is the extent to which constructive engagement is likely to bring real human rights improvements on the ground, including over the long-term' (FCO, 1998: 46). While the then chargé d'affaires (now the ambassador) has approached parliamentarians since the mid-1990s with the message that Iran has been moderating its policies, when members of the House of Lords have, on various occasions, approached him about human rights issues they have received no response. A political prisoner whose offence was to criticise the 'Butcher of Evin', Assadollah Lajevardi, was dismissed by the ambassador as 'a criminal'. When Lords Ahmed and Clarke asked that access to members of the Jewish community, arrested in early 1999, be granted, they 'were told quite firmly that the Iranian government would not tolerate any outside interference'. On another occasion, Lord Avebury raised the persecution of the Baha'is. The ambassador in response spoke about the Diplock courts in Northern Ireland (*Hansard*, 14 July 1999: cols 331; 22 June 1999: cols 861, 867).

The minister of state at the Foreign Office admitted that while the issues of Jewish detainees and the persecution of the Baha'is had been raised with the ambassador, 'It is often difficult to raise individual cases with the authorities in Iran due to a reluctance on their part to grant appointments to discuss such issues' (Hoon, 1999). It therefore remains to be seen whether engagement with Iran was chosen on the grounds of effecting change in the human rights situation. When asked to assess the results of the EU's 'critical dialogue' in securing anything other than trade, the then German foreign minister conceded that 'they have not been phenomenal' (Lane, 1995: 86).

Means and ends: encouraging moderation

In 1989, Ayatollah Ali Khamenei succeeded Ayatollah Ruhollah Khomeini as the supreme leader, *velayat-e faqih*, and as chief of state and commander-in-chief. Sayyid Mohammed Khatami was elected president in 1997. While there are regular elections for the presidency, parliament and now local government, the Council of Guardians, appointed by the government, vets all candidates and all legislation for adherence to Islamic law.

The UK government argues that there are 'significant changes' in Iran, pointing to 'a commitment to develop an Islamic civil society based on respect for the rule of law' and 'greater freedom of expression' (*Hansard*, 11 November 1998: col. 832). One needs to make explicit the premises underpinning the current construction of Iranian politics. The main supposition is that president Khatami's moderate pronouncements can be taken at face value and the intemperate ones can be dismissed as insincere, as attempts to manage the power struggle. Second, and underpinning the first, is the assumption that Khatami's personal history can be ignored for he has undergone a trans-formation from radical cleric to liberal reformer. Third, it is assumed that, although very limited, reforms thus far implemented represent the first steps towards meaningful change in both the domestic and international spheres, with the bitterness of Khamenei's opposition to Khatami indicating the extent of the latter's reforming intentions.

While it might be possible that such a construction of Iranian politics is valid, it is worth exercising some academic scepticism. European governments and media seem unwilling to do so, instead defining the debates and protagon-ists in Western terms, which might or might not be appropriate. This is important for human rights. Donnelly distinguished three levels of political progress: liberalisation, democratisation and a rights-protective regime. He argued that they are not all phases of a single, continuous and linear process of development. European governments speak of Iran as if it had embarked on just such a process. Speaking generally, Donnelly argues that, 'Such an overly convenient assumption ... poses risks to effective and sustained inter-national human rights policies' (1998: 158).

Khatami was one of only four presidential candidates chosen from a field of 238. In the eyes of the ruling elite, therefore, he was seen as having excellent revolutionary credentials. Khatami was forced to step down as minister of Islamic culture and guidance in 1992 as part of Rafsanjani's purge of the radical Line of the Imam faction. In 1991, Khatami said that, 'We are fundamentally and profoundly opposed to Western civilisation and culture' (*Ressalat*, 7 July 1991). In 1989, he called for the execution of Salman Rushdie (*Kayhan*, 7 March 1989).

At face value, Khatami's current words – freedom, participation and accountability – can be recognised as belonging to a Western liberal tradition. However, in the context of Islamic clerical government, they might have very different meanings. Even though he might disagree with the choice of Khamenei, Khatami has repeatedly emphasised the centrality of *velayat-e faqih*, the rule of the jurisprudent, most recently in July 1999 (Agence France Presse, 29 July 1999). When the president speaks of 'freedom', it is always within the context of clerical rule. For example, he has said: 'Freedom must not undermine the tenets of Islam'; 'the clergy should be the true and natural representatives of [the] people'; and 'the government is obligated to provide a safe environment for the exchange of ideas and views within the framework of the criteria set by Islam and the Constitution'. Whether or not Khatami wishes to change the present system of government, which he calls 'cherished' and 'democratic' (1997a, 1997b, 1998), is at best an open question. It is possible that, by addressing the rule of law, his central concern, he seeks to strengthen clerical power.

The limited liberalisation so far falls short of even a minimum standard of respect for human rights. The limited freedom of the press is only the freedom to echo the debates between clerical factions. It could be argued that such freedom results, as it did immediately after the revolution, 'not from the dominance of a liberal value system, but only from the balance of hostile and rival forces' (Salehi, 1988: 158).

The warnings not to treat Khatami as essentially different to Khamenei come from the mouths of decision-makers. As the foreign minister, Dr Kharazzi, remarked, 'when it comes to fundamental issues, there are no differences between them' (Iranian State Television, 22 January 1998). Indeed, Khatami was as quick to move against the student demonstrators in July 1999 as was Khamenei. The recurring theme in the West's relations with the Islamic Republic is the belief that liberalism on economic issues translates into moderation in foreign and domestic policy. It is worth remembering that Khomeini could also be pragmatic in the face of domestic or international pressure as well as moderate, or thoroughly disingenuous, in his rhetoric. Khatami, like Khomeini and Rafsanjani, continues the practice of confusing the West. Alternatively, it is not that Europe allows hope to lead to expectation but that the EU simply desires a stable government and a stable economic system. Respect for human rights would be a bonus of course, but not essential to good relations.

Means and ends: UK interests

As to British interests in rapprochement with Iran, the foreign secretary said that the United Kingdom was able to find common ground with Iran on Iraq and on Afghanistan (Embassy of the Islamic Republic of Iran, 1998: 2). The United Kingdom has yet to make the argument for engagement from security. While it would no doubt be beneficial to be on good terms with the most powerful actor in the Middle East and the country with the second largest reserves of gas and the fourth largest reserves of oil, the fact that the United Kingdom has survived quite well for nine years, and perhaps more, without those good relations with Iran would make such an argument very difficult to sustain.

Before turning to the issue of trade, it is worth setting this in the context of the Foreign Office's general ethos and its current priorities. Vincent outlined the natural resistance of diplomats to raising human rights issues in bilateral relations. Their 'seeming gutlessness' is a result of two factors: first, the diplomat's primary concern with communication; and second, 'clientism'. The outcome is that good relations become an end in themselves, diplomacy's primary objective, rather than one objective among many (Vincent, 1986: 137; 1989: 55–6). Ted Rowlands, MP, remembered from his time at the Foreign Office how, if policy was 'post-driven ... there would be a tendency ... for the post to offer a suggestion that further constructive engagement will help ... where in fact there is a wide abuse of human rights' (Foreign Affairs Committee, 1998: 54).

The foreign secretary, however, has said that, generally, he has not found any resistance from Foreign Office officials to his external human rights policy, arguing that they appreciate 'clear, lucid direction from the top' and understand the 'priority and significance' the minister attaches to the policy (Foreign Affairs Committee, 1998: 46). However, the Conservative government made the Foreign Office shift from 'diplomacy to trade promotion' (Clark, 1993: 56) and the Labour government has maintained that change in priorities. The minister of state asserted that commercial work is the Foreign Office's 'largest single activity', and went on, 'We are in the business of helping British business' (Fatchett, 1997a). In its *Annual Report on Human Rights*, the government argued that, 'Britain is one of the world's largest investors and traders, a position the government wishes to sustain and promote' (FCO and DFID, 1998: 46).

The 1979 revolution in Iran cost the United Kingdom £500 million a year in lost exports. Since then there has been a continuous effort to regain the United Kingdom's position in the Iranian market. UK exports to Iran in 1996 and 1997 were just under £400 million. In February 1997, Salman Rushdie complained about the Conservative government's initiatives to encourage investment. The Foreign Office argued, in a comment that presaged the Labour government's policy of engagement, that there was 'no contradiction' between trade and claims that more pressure must be brought to bear on Tehran (*The Guardian*, 14 February 1997).

The Iranian chargé d'affaires attributed the UK government's change in policy to 'its recognition of commercial realities' (*Q News*, October 1998). Iran noted that, after the United States lifted the threat of sanctions, the EU 'set about improving trade ties with the Islamic Republic of Iran and one trade delegation after another began to visit Tehran' (Embassy of the Islamic Republic of Iran, 1998: 2). The United Kingdom adopted a number of measures to promote trade and investment in Iran, supporting the formation of the British-Iranian Chamber of Commerce, restoring short-term ECGD cover and sponsoring outward trade missions and exhibitions.

UK oil companies were enthusiastic: even with depressed crude prices, 'there was a significant volume of Iranian reserves with a low cost base for development' (Steve Lowdon, Premier Oil, quoted in Embassy of the Islamic Republic of Iran, 1998: 8). The Foreign Office minister of state noted that there was 'a great deal of interest among Britain's financial sector to expand co-operation with Iranian firms, especially at a time when Iran is considering ways to absorb foreign investment' (Iranian News Agency, 21 July 1998).

The NCRI argues that the Iranian government held the auction to the overseas rights to forty-three oil exploration and drilling projects specifically in London 'to encourage the acceptance of Tehran's terms for normalising relations' (Mohaddessin, 1998: 3–4). Certainly Iran has used access to its market as a lever in relations with the United Kingdom on a number of occasions in the past (Miller, 1996).

The government has argued that, 'If we do not engage with the Iranians, then we cannot hope to influence their thinking or behaviour' (Fatchett, 1999). The notion that free trade is 'the conduit for the transference of civilised values' is as old as it is uncertain. As Vincent said, 'trade can as easily buttress uncivilised values as carry civilised ones' (1989: 56, 60). The argument has been made that exposure to the outside world can foster democratic values and that, as such, 'the voice and influence of business can often be so useful' (Howe, 1996: 3). However, a new 'political crimes' bill in Iran will make contact between foreigners and Iranians illegal and those companies that are permitted to invest in Iran will be strictly controlled by the government (*The Guardian*, 5 August 1999). Thus, as Lord Avebury argued, whatever the United Kingdom's interests in Iran, 'The human rights case for supporting President Khatami is not yet proven' (*Hansard*, 22 June 1999: col. 867).

Conclusions

If a state is to claim that human rights are an integral part of foreign policy, then one would expect to find a change, a modification of policy. This modification of policy entails, to reiterate, the promotion of human rights above 'narrow economic and political advantage'. It lies not in what states do but in what states refrain from doing in respect of countries that abuse human rights, that is, undertaking new investment, the provision of aid or the export of arms. As such, one would expect to find a consistency in the treatment of all countries, unless *raison d'état* intervened. The Foreign Office has not claimed *raison d'état* in its rapprochement with Iran. Instead it has claimed that engagement represents the best means of securing improvements in human rights in Iran. In order to get that engagement, it sacrificed human rights considerations. This might strike one as a case of throwing the baby out with the bathwater.

The government has tacitly accepted that its policies could be responsible for fostering particular regimes. Its second premise for engagement with Iran, that it must support president Khatami, acknowledges this. The Third Way means furthering human rights for others while furthering prosperity at home through the dual-purpose policy of engagement. But it is not possible to have a cost-free human rights policy. The four objectives of UK foreign policy will inevitably conflict. It is the government's job to decide where the balance of interests lies. On the evidence from this case, the balance of UK interests are adjudged to lie with prosperity, in spite of the Foreign Office having described the promotion of human rights as 'crucial to UK interests'.

The foreign secretary has variously said that he wishes to 'make Britain once again a force for good in the world', that 'Britain is the champion of the oppressed', and that it has 'provided leadership in the international community on human rights' (Cook, 1997a, 1997c, 1998c). If that is the case, something more than business as usual is required. However, concrete UK interests are also at stake. What is gained in the short term might be lost in the long term if the government's assessment of a country's human rights situation is wrong. To what extent any state can influence the course of political events in another is a moot point. However, the Foreign Affairs Committee argued that the government had appeared to legitimise the Suharto regime in Indonesia shortly before it fell and that, 'if the policy of constructive engagement is to be meaningful', the government needed to learn from its failure of judgement in this case (Foreign Affairs Committee, 1998: para. 126).

If the unrest in Iran in the summer of 1999 is indicative of a widespread desire for meaningful political change, then the UK government is risking its long-term interests in being seen to support the current ruling class. 'Encouraging moderation' can come close to offering an apologia for the regime. For example, asked about Iran's scud attacks on opposition forces in June 1999, Baroness Symons argued that the attacks followed the assassination of lieutenant-general Shirazi. She wanted to 'make the point that this was the sequence of events' (*Hansard*, 22 June 1999: col. 874). The closure of publications, new press restrictions and the arbitrary detention and ill-treatment of students who took part in the July demonstrations might all be seen merely as 'retrograde steps' (*Hansard*, 14 July 1999: col. 338), as detours on the road to liberalisation. Similarly, Khatami's condemnation of the demonstrations as 'an insult to the political system' (Agence France Press, 29 July 1999) might be seen as merely an attempt to negotiate the power struggle with Khamenei. And it might also be the case that the main opposition force, with which Labour enjoyed a dialogue of some seventeen years' standing, 'is despised by many Iranians' (*Hansard*, 22 June 1999: col. 874). However, if this construction of Iranian politics is wrong, the UK government has much more to lose than the moral high ground.

References

Amnesty International (1998a), *Human Rights Audit 1998: UK Foreign Policy and Human Rights* (London: Amnesty International).

Amnesty International (1998b), *Amnesty International Report 1998* (London: Amnesty International).

Clark, A. (1993), *Diaries* (London: Weidenfeld and Nicolson).

Cook, R. (1997a), 'British foreign policy', statement, 12 May.

Cook, R. (1997b), 'Human rights into a new century', speech, Locarno Suite, FCO, London, 17 July.

Cook, R. (1997c), 'Britain's new approach to the world', speech, Labour party conference, 2 October.

Cook, R. (1998a), 'Europe and America: the decisive partnership', speech, European Institute, Washington, DC, 15 January.

Cook, R. (1998b), 'Annual foreign policy report', speech, Mansion House, London, 23 April.

Cook, R. (1998c), 'Human rights: making the difference', speech, Amnesty International, London, 16 October.

Donnelly, J. (1998), *International Human Rights* (Oxford: Westview Press).

Embassy of the Islamic Republic of Iran, Press Department (1998), *Persia Update*, vol. 10, no. 3.

EU (1998a), *Declaration by the Presidency on Behalf of the European Union*, 16 February (see http://uc.eu.int/).

EU (1998b), *Declaration by the Presidency on Behalf of the European Union*, 28 September.

Fatchett, D. (1997a), 'The Foreign Office in export promotion', Institute of Exports Partnership 2000 conference, London, 13 November.

Fatchett, D. (1997b), 'British policy towards the Middle East', Washington Institute for Near East Policy, Washington DC, 26 November.

Fatchett, D. (1998), letter to Sir Sydney Chapman, MP, 22 October.

Fatchett, D. (1999), letter to Ruth Kelly, MP, 1 February.

FCO (1998), *First Report from the Foreign Affairs Committee, Foreign Policy and Human Rights, Response of the Secretary of State*, cm 4229 (London: TSO).

FCO and DFID (1998), *Annual Report on Human Rights* (London: TSO).

FCO and DFID (1999), *Human Rights Annual Report for 1999*, cm 4404 (London: TSO).

Foreign Affairs Committee (1998), *Foreign Policy and Human Rights*, first report, HC369 (London: TSO).

Hoon, G. (1999), letter to Hazel Blears, MP, 23 June.

Howe, G. (1996), *Human Rights in China* (London: Amnesty International).

Khatami, M. (1997a), Inauguration speech to the Majlis, 4 August (see http://www.persia.org.khatami).

Khatami, M. (1997b), speech to Friday prayer leaders, 27 December.

Khatami, M. (1998), speech, Tehran University, 23 May.

Lane, C. (1995), 'Germany's new *ostpolitik*', *Foreign Affairs*, vol. 74, no. 6, 77–89.

Luard, E. (1980), 'Human rights and foreign policy', *International Affairs*, vol. 56, no. 4, 579–606.

Miller, D. (1996), *Export or Die: Britain's Defence Trade with Iran and Iraq* (London: Cassell).

Mohaddessin, M. (1998), *Unethical Policy* (Auvers-sur-Oise: NCRI).

Salehi, M. M. (1988), *Insurgency Through Culture and Religion: The Islamic Revolution of Iran* (New York: Praeger).

Sikkink, K. (1993), 'The power of principled ideas: human rights policies in the United States and Western Europe', in J. Goldstein and R. O. Keohane (eds), *Ideas and Foreign Policy: Beliefs, Institutions and Political Change* (London: Cornell University Press), 139–72.

State Department (1999), *Iran Country Report on Human Rights Practices for 1998* (Washington, DC: US Government Printing Office).

Vincent, R. J. (1986), *Human Rights and International Relations* (Cambridge: Cambridge University Press).

Vincent, R. J. (1989), 'Human rights in foreign policy', in D. M. Hill (ed.), *Human Rights and Foreign Policy: Principles and Practice* (London: Macmillan).

Wheeler, N. J. and Dunne, T. (1998), 'Good international citizenship: a Third Way for British foreign policy', *International Affairs*, vol. 74, no. 4, 847–70.

12

New Labour and the politics of Kashmir

Vernon Hewitt and Mark Wickham-Jones

Introduction

In October 1997, Robin Cook, entering his sixth month as foreign secretary, suffered one of the most significant setbacks of what proved to be a difficult and fractious first year in government. On the eve of a state visit by Queen Elizabeth II to India, he was reported as offering the 'good offices' of the UK government to negotiate a solution between India and Pakistan to the long-running conflict over the disputed territory of Kashmir (Kampfner, 1999: 175). Cook's comments were made during the first leg of the Queen's trip, in discussions with Nawaz Sharif, the Pakistani prime minister. Reportedly, he repeated the proposal in informal remarks to a journalist (*The Times*, 12 October 1997).

The proposal was seized upon by the Pakistani government and widely publicised: it was perceived to match a desire by Pakistan to internationalise the dispute. Reaction in India was much less favourable: the government argued that the Kashmir dispute was an internal matter. Indian politicians concluded that the British foreign secretary had articulated a straightforwardly pro-Pakistani standpoint. I. K. Gujral, the prime minister, was alleged to have exploded, describing the United Kingdom as a meddlesome 'third rate power', though the comments were later denied (*Financial Times*, 18 October 1997). Cook's protestations about the innocence and informality of his comments amounted to little as Indian displeasure at his stance became manifest during the Queen's visit. The band of the Royal Marines accompanying her was prevented from playing, the invitations to all but one of the British diplomats expected at a banquet were withdrawn and an after-dinner toast by the Queen was cancelled. Hostility was not confined to the government: the Indian press was acerbic in its analysis of Cook's intentions. The reaction to Cook's performance in the United Kingdom was equally scathing: he was perceived to have broken protocol and unnecessarily dragged the head of state into a political dispute. The foreign secretary alone did not contribute to the problems surrounding the trip: the visit was already a controversial one because of the Queen's visit to the Jallianwala Bagh in Amritsar, site of a notorious massacre of Indian protesters against British rule in 1919. Matters here were not helped by Prince Philip's blunt contestation of the numbers who had died. By the end of the trip, few commentators in either India or the United Kingdom doubted that relations between the countries were extremely strained. Most concluded that the reputation of the Foreign Office had been damaged. Considerable blame for that state of affairs was laid at the British foreign secretary's feet. According to *The Times* the tour was characterised by 'friction, embarrassment and ineptitude' (17 October 1997).

Before coming to power in the 1997 general election, Labour had already reviewed its policy on Kashmir and had adopted a more pro-active stance over the fate of the former princely state. This policy emerged within the party from 1995 onwards: its aim was to try to resolve the Kashmir dispute by committing a future Labour government to provide direct mediation between India and Pakistan. Mediation would also include a series of broad-based (if ill-defined) Kashmiri representatives. It was believed that, through such a strategy, the crisis could be peacefully resolved either by making Kashmir an integral part of India or Pakistan or by creating it as an independent state in its own right. Labour had no pre-conceptions over the solution but its willingness to condone the possibility of an independent sovereign state (illustrated by its interest in canvassing Kashmiri opinions) was unprecedented in the context of its previous South Asian foreign policy, and of Labour's close links with the Indian National Congress. It was this possibility, an utter anathema to the Indian government, which contributed greatly to the disastrous outcome of the October 1997 trip.

The difficulties encountered by Cook in India had not been expected by most observers in the United Kingdom. Kashmir was not a prominent issue for the vast majority of the British electorate. It had not figured in Labour's manifesto at the 1997 general election. There was little media interest in the territory. Yet not only did Labour undergo a notable political reverse on the matter, it did so on an issue of its own choosing. Cook's comments on Kashmir were neither a reaction to events nor a reflection of a subject being forced upon him without warning. Far from it: they reflected the considerable interest and attention that had been given by Labour, partly in private, to the politics of Kashmir before the 1997 general election. That the new British administration could alienate the Indian government on a topic of its own choosing to which it had given much thought was all the more remarkable. In this chapter we look at Labour's policy towards Kashmir during the 1990s and explain why Cook found himself in such trouble in October 1997. We examine how Labour studied the Kashmir conflict and discuss what the party hoped to achieve in its policy. In charting the course taken by policy-making on the issue, we assess the eventual outcome of Labour's attitude to Kashmir. These issues raise significant questions about the nature and coherence of New Labour's foreign policy. There is also a wider dimension at stake here. The case provides an illustration of one of the means by which New Labour has made foreign policy and of the way in which its commitments abroad have been shaped, in part at least, by domestic concerns.

The evolution of Labour's policy towards Kashmir

The background to Labour's review of its policy towards Kashmir is complex, a reflection of the issues involved, and space precludes any detailed examination here. The party's interest in India has been as much historical as ideological. It had, after all, been the 1945–51 Labour government that presided over the independence of the sub-continent, including its partitioning into India and Pakistan. The confusion over the fate of the then princely state of Jammu and Kashmir (excluded, as was all princely India, from the pains of the Boundary Commission) left a bitter legacy in South Asia. Many in the Labour party genuinely believed it was the United Kingdom's responsibility to help solve that legacy. This point was to be reiterated in full in Labour's NEC statement of 1995, wherein it was stated that 'Britain must accept its responsibility as the former imperial power' (Labour party, 1995c).

Although predominantly Muslim, Jammu and Kashmir was ruled by a Hindu maharaja. Located on the north-west marches of the Punjabi plains, the maharaja's kingdom could have gone to either India or Pakistan in 1947. Supporters of Pakistan's claim to it argued that the decision to place the state within India went against both the logic of the terrain and the religious make-up of the population. To Pakistan, the maharaja Hari Singh's decision to join India did not reflect the wishes of the people of Kashmir. A subsequent Indian undertaking offered to settle the matter through a plebiscite. But attempts to ascertain public opinion within Jammu and Kashmir in 1947 were deeply flawed (and have remained so – a point which appeared continually to elude Labour's grasp in the 1990s) and came to little (see Hewitt, 1995).

Tensions between India and Pakistan over the issue (among others) gave way to open conflict and, following a brief war in 1947–48, Pakistan gained a small but significant area of Kashmir, delineated by a cease-fire line. India referred the matter to the UN, wherein there was much debate over how any plebiscite to ascertain public opinion over the region's future was to be held. No agreement could be reached and debates became bogged down. British interest in the dispute declined: politicians merely encouraged dialogue between the Indian and Pakistani governments. Significantly, at no time did British policy-makers entertain the idea of establishing an independent Kashmiri state. Instead, two UN resolutions (supported by the British delegation) called for the holding of a plebiscite to determine whether the people of Kashmir wished to join India or Pakistan. No one contemplated the formation of a third sovereign successor state to the British Raj, especially one so strategically located (see Lamb 1991; Hewitt, 1997).

By the early 1960s, in tandem with US thinking, the British urged India and Pakistan to undertake the partition of the disputed territory along the lines of the 1948 cease-fire. The only concession to Kashmiri sensibilities was that assured access should facilitate the unhindered movement of Kashmiris across their own state. Although the notion of self-determination was absent from British government policy, that of mediation was not and various offers were made. They came to little. Significantly, the British were aware that mediation would work only if accepted by the Indians. Sir Morrice James (British high commissioner to Pakistan during much of the 1960s) noted of one initiative: 'It was apparent to both of us [the United States and the United Kingdom] that many Indians would regard our action in promoting Kashmir talks as one more proof of our partiality for their Pakistani rivals' (James, 1993: 103).

Following the third Indo-Pakistan war, of 1971, India pressurised the Pakistanis at Shimla to moderate the cease-fire line and convert it to the so-called line of control. The Shimla accord was, in effect, the conclusion of the logic of partition, without any reference to the use of a plebiscite. More critically, the accord sought to supersede the UN resolutions and to curtail further international interest in the dispute. Under duress, Pakistan agreed, a decision it soon regretted. It did not accept that the UN resolutions were irrelevant: by the mid-1980s the Pakistani government sought support to bring Kashmir to the attention of the international community (Hewitt, 1995).

A changed context: Jammu and Kashmir into the 1990s

By 1989, the situation within Jammu and Kashmir had been transformed by the emergence of a series of organisations pressing for independence. The surfacing of these groups, such as the Jammu and Kashmir Liberation Front (JKLF), was intimately linked to a breakdown in law and order within Indian-administered Kashmir, especially around Srinagar, the capital, and resulted in the deployment of a large number of Indian security forces by 1990. The response to the situation was perceived by many as repressive and there were allegations of widespread human rights abuses (often on religious grounds). The genesis of the situation lay both in the mismanagement of Kashmir by the Indian political centre and in the rise of powerful Islamic sentiments, linked to wider events throughout the Muslim world. The insurgency was not monolithic, however, in its make-up or in its political demands. By the early 1990s, a whole plethora of groups had sprung up, some in association with Pakistan, while others demanded an independent state. From 1995 onwards, the situation on the ground became further complicated by the emergence of pro-Indian militants.

For Pakistan, the crisis within Indian-administered Kashmir was an opportunity because it gave Islamabad a chance to renew calls for international mediation in the dispute. The crisis was also a warning in that, while some Kashmiri insurgents were pro-Pakistan, many were not. Pakistan remained as unwilling as India to entertain the idea that the state could become independent. Unlike India, however, Pakistan was prepared to risk flirtation with the idea of 'self-determination', as this was outweighed by the advantages of internationalising the issue.

The increasing crisis took place in a radically changing international context. International opinion appeared no longer willing to condone state violence on the simple grounds of either national security or state sovereignty. Self-determination was placed on the global agenda in a prominent fashion by events in Yugoslavia and the former Soviet Union. Both India and Pakistan were aware of these changed circumstances (as were Kashmiri organisations themselves). Pakistan's initial success in adding a human rights spin to the predicament was matched by India's attempts to link Pakistan's support for the Kashmir 'insurgency' into a wider Islamic conspiracy linked to international terrorism. Many Kashmiri groups made use of both claims to secure for themselves the notion of an independent state. Their offensive was aimed, in part, at a strategic audience of Muslims resident in other countries, including, critically, in the United Kingdom.

Labour's policy towards Kashmir

The strategic location of this audience, both in terms of its ethnic attachments to Kashmir and its electoral significance to the British Labour party in the run-up to the 1997 general election, must be noted. Throughout the 1950s, many Kashmiris settled in the United Kingdom, the United States and Canada. Many of these immigrants, known as Mirpuris, came from areas occupied by Pakistan in the 1947–48 war. Settling in urban conurbations such as Birmingham, Bradford, Leeds and Luton, they were initially identified as Pakistanis. Subsequently, they became increasingly self-identified as Kashmiris and sought recognition as such. By the mid-1970s, much of the Kashmiri diaspora had mobilised in support of separatist organisations, primarily the JKLF. Formed in the United Kingdom, it came to the attention of both the British and Indian authorities following the kidnapping of the Indian deputy high commissioner in 1974 from the Birmingham consulate office.

Significantly for Labour, many Kashmiris were active members of the party. Although ethnic members of Labour comprised a small proportion of the total membership, they were often concentrated in particular ward branches of constituencies. An extreme example was Manchester Gorton, with a Mirpuri population of fifteen per cent. In 1993 alone more than 600 Asians applied to join Labour (twenty-eight per cent of applications were rejected). This matched the number that had joined in the years after 1987 in the same constituency (Shukra, 1998: 129; Geddes, 1998: 162). In the late 1980s, Mirpuri members of the party began to raise Kashmir as a political issue to which the party should respond. In the 1980s, the matter was neither debated by the Labour party conference nor raised in the annual report of the ruling NEC. When the crisis in Kashmir escalated from 1989 onwards, elements within the party were well placed to react. Constituencies in which self-identified Kashmiris enjoyed a significant presence were able to make their views known to local MPs. Such MPs, including Derek Fatchett, were later to emerge as key figures in driving a review of Labour's policy on Kashmir.

Labour did not refer to Kashmir in the party's policy documents in the 1980s. It was not mentioned in the stream of publications produced during the formal review of policy following the 1987 election defeat. The manifesto for the 1987 general election did not refer to the matter. In 1990, Labour's NEC endorsed a resolution from the Socialist International aimed to promote dialogue between India and Pakistan over Kashmir (Labour party, 1990: 30). It offered the Socialist International as a mediator, mentioned the UN resolutions and the Shimla accord, and gave no hint of self-determination. Little came of the initiative. The party's 1992 manifesto offered to make a Labour government 'available to our friends in India and Pakistan to assist in achieving a negotiated solution to the problem of Kashmir that is acceptable to all the people of Kashmir' (Labour party, 1992: 27). The NEC report the following year brought up briefly the troubles in Kashmir. More significantly, the 1993 parliamentary Labour party report within the NEC document expressed 'concern for democracy in India', in a rather sweeping and vague fashion, a statement unlikely to commend Labour to the New Delhi authorities (Labour party, 1993: 64).

In 1994 two motions were submitted to the Labour conference. The Conference Arrangements Committee tabled one, though it was not debated and so subsequently remitted by the party. In 1995, five motions and two amendments were tabled. The motions from nine constituency parties (including Bradford West, which had sponsored a motion the previous year, Luton South and Manchester Gorton) included calls for self-determination for the people of Kashmir (Labour party, 1995a: 82–3). An amendment from Ealing Southall (a constituency with a high proportion of voters of Indian descent) proposed that Labour should not offer a solution to the problem. The interest generated in the matter was sufficient to get the Conference Arrangements Committee to table a composite motion on the subject. (The Conference Arrangements Committee worked in a relatively open and straightforward fashion, reflecting the concerns of party members.) This motion, composite 53, sponsored by the Bradford West and Luton South constituency parties, called for self-determination. It was striking that it made no reference to the Shimla accord, emphasising instead the UN resolutions (Labour party, 1995b: 36–7).

At the 1995 party conference, Labour's NEC tabled a statement on Kashmir. The statement was a reflection of the anticipated difficulties into which the party might get should composite 53 be adopted. The composite's call for Labour to 'prepare principles of policy for an incoming Labour government, building on United Nations Security Council resolutions based upon the principles of self determination for the people of Kashmir' would manifestly be unacceptable to the Indian government and would be taken as improper interference by the United Kingdom in Indian affairs. The statement also gave Cook the opportunity to clarify his own position. He had been cheered at a meeting earlier in 1995 for stating that 'Kashmir is part of the Indian state', only for his qualification that any settlement be negotiated to be drowned out by applause (Kampfner, 1999: 174).

Introducing the NEC statement to the Labour conference, Cook offered Labour's 'good offices to end the violence and to seek a solution acceptable to all parties and all the peoples of Kashmir' (*LPACR*, 1995: 190). His comments were concise; he did not mention either the UN resolutions or the Shimla accord and he did not use the term self-determination. Composite 53 was introduced with an emphasis on self-determination and human rights abuses in Indian Kashmir. Moving it for the Bradford West constituency party, Mukhtar Ali stated, 'There can be no settlement that does not include the right of the people of Kashmir to choose independence if they so wish ... Comrades, since when is the Labour party afraid to oppose tyranny?' (*LPACR*, 1995: 200). The debate that followed was brief, with few speakers on Kashmir (it covered several other international issues as well). Labour's NEC called on the movers to remit composite 53, on the grounds that seven of the constituency parties had agreed to do so: no substantive reason was given. The effect of remitting the motion was to place it to one side on the understanding that the NEC would look into the issues during the ensuing year. Stating that he was prepared to trust the Labour leadership, Mukhtar Ali agreed, the composite was remitted without a vote and did not become party policy. The NEC statement on Kashmir was carried without a vote.

The two-page NEC statement reiterated the salient facts of Kashmir as a disputed territory containing a majority Muslim population, with significant Hindu and Buddhist minorities. The statement went on to say:

> Conference is deeply concerned by the continuing conflict in Kashmir, which has involved the considerable suffering for all the peoples of the region. Thousands of people have been killed over the last five years alone ... The peoples of Kashmir have also repeatedly experienced violations of their human rights and acts of terrorism. (Labour party, 1995c)

Labour offered to negotiate a solution through its close relationship with India and Pakistan. The statement was more modest than composite 53. It did not mention self-determination. It drew attention to the UN resolutions of 1948–49 and the Shimla accord of 1972, stating, 'Conference believes that the United Nations resolutions on Kashmir are of equal validity to all other UN resolutions'. This more moderate stance was itself controversial because New Delhi's interpretation of the Shimla accord was that the bilateral agreement superseded the earlier UN resolutions. The Shimla accord, unlike the UN resolutions, makes no call for a plebiscite to resolve the crisis. In effect, Labour had resurrected the UN resolutions and the notion of a referendum. The party, albeit perhaps unintentionally, appeared to side with the long-standing Pakistani position of trying to unravel the Shimla accord to which the Pakistanis had agreed so unwillingly. *The Times* commented later, 'Indian politicians maintain [the NEC statement] strongly favoured the Pakistani position' (14 October 1997).

The involvement of British Kashmiris in Labour's 1995 decision is telling: the party's statement was a direct response to their concerns. The shift reflected their views. Labour politicians were also deeply concerned with human rights violations throughout Jammu and Kashmir on both the Indian and the Pakistani side. But the party failed to comprehend the disproportionate make-up of the British Kashmiri population in relation to that of Kashmir itself. Over eighty per cent of all self-identified Kashmiris derive (either originally or as second-generation British Kashmiris) from so-called Azad Kashmir (the area administered by Pakistan since 1947–48). The emphasis placed upon their views did not in any way discredit the concerns that the relevant groups expressed. It did, however, allow Labour's opponents (in particular, the Indian government) and others to claim that the soon-to-be elected government was siding with what were, in effect, Pakistani-inspired allegations against India's human rights record (see *Financial Times*, 18 October 1997). Stephen Grey, for example, commented in *The Times*: 'It was as a result of Pakistani lobbying that the 1995 Labour conference urged the implementation of a United Nations resolution which backed Pakistan's call for a plebiscite to decide Kashmir's future' (19 October 1997). The assertion was untrue given the JKLF's call for an independent state of Jammu and Kashmir. It could be made because the Indian government characterised British Kashmiris as 'Pakistanis' and therefore as part of the pro-Pakistani lobby. According to *The Times*, 'India has been wary of any Labour initiative on Kashmir, believing that it is bound to be partisan' (14 October 1997). Indeed, as the 1997 UK general election neared, the Indian government sought to organise pro-Indian senti- ments among British Asians. During the campaign, it complained that the use by Labour of the Jammu and Kashmir crisis was a cynical electoral ploy. A *Times* leader remarked later: 'Labour's policy is deeply suspect in Delhi, with politicians quick to seize on party policy documents which they say are intended to woo Muslim voters in Britain' (14 October 1997). At the same time, Labour accused John Major of a 'cynical ploy for the "Asian vote"' during a trip to India (Labour party press release, 20 January 1997).

The adoption of the 1995 statement by the Labour conference did not in itself commit the party to the active pursuit of a settlement in Kashmir. Kashmiri elements within the party had succeeded in placing the issue on the party's conference agenda and they had catalysed the NEC into the drafting of its statement. The party was not by any means committed to placing that statement at the forefront of policy. Many other issues were raised during Labour's years in opposition between 1992 and 1997, only to be quietly buried by the party's leadership. Had the Labour leadership wanted to drop its approach to Kashmir, there would have been little difficulty in doing so, even though some Kashmiri members of the party might have been dissatisfied. At Labour's 1996 conference three motions were submitted along with two amendments. One composite was tabled but was not debated. In 1997 no motions were submitted. The remitted composite 53 from the 1995 conference had little impact on the party: Labour's NEC report in 1996 stated 'the points made [in composite 53] have been taken into account in drafting the foreign policy paper to be presented to conference this year' (Labour party, 1996b: 40). The document concerned referred briefly to Kashmir. It was rather more tentative about British involvement than had been the NEC statement. It noted that 'Britain would be well placed to help facilitate' a settlement (Labour party, 1996a: 13). By contrast, the NEC statement had included the passage, 'Labour in government must use its influence to bring about genuine initiatives'. The Kashmir dispute was mentioned in the party's *Policy Handbook* (Labour party, 1996c: section 5.3.4).

That there might be electoral benefits from the approach the party had taken was apparent: many commentators concluded that Muslim voters were more sympathetic to Labour than to the Conservative party (see, for example, *The Times*, 19 October 1997). Survey evidence suggested that around eighty per cent of British Pakistanis voted Labour while under three per cent supported the Conservatives (Saggar, 1998: 36). Of course, some constituencies enjoyed concentrated populations of ethnic voters. *The Times* described the Kashmir dispute as being of 'vital electoral importance' for Labour (14 October 1997). Luton South, co-sponsor of composite 53, was a marginal Conservative seat with an ethnic population of nearly thirteen per cent (Saggar, 1997: 149). Labour took it easily at the general election. British Indians also supported Labour for the most part but a significant number, nearly fifteen per cent, were perceived to be orientated towards the Conservatives. Mirpuri members of the party had not in some sense or other either captured or determined Labour's policy agenda. The leadership might, however, have electoral and other reasons to pursue Kashmir as a political issue. Public debate within the party over Kashmir had been put on hold following the 1995 conference: new approaches were not mentioned in any documents before the general election. The NEC statement remained party policy in an unobtrusive manner. The issue was not raised openly by Labour's frontbenchers, let alone given any emphasis by them as a priority matter. Privately, however, Kashmir remained on Labour's foreign affairs agenda.

Labour's review of policy on Kashmir, 1996–97

In the autumn of 1996, the Labour party approached a London-based think-tank known as the Next Century Foundation. It had worked on conflict resolution in the Middle East, where it had specialised in bringing different factions together in informal surroundings to brainstorm their differences and try to work towards mutually acceptable resolutions. For the next six months, in the run-up to the 1997 general election, the Foundation organised a series of sessions, roughly once a month, based on a core group of specialist academics and a series of invitees representing specific Kashmiri groups. The nature of the latter was uneven and in some cases rather obscure. While some represented a sizeable following, within both the Kashmiri diaspora and the disputed territories, others were less representative bodies run by idio-syncratic individuals. An emergent document formed the basis for each session, with the academic participants and the director of the Foundation, William Morris, seeking to provide continuity. The document was provisionally entitled *A Report into the Current Kashmir Dispute: The Way Ahead*. Derek Fatchett, a member of Labour's frontbench team for foreign affairs, attended one of the later meetings and liaised frequently with the director.

Drafting a report proved difficult given the differences between those present over the interpretation of particular events and germane issues. Two partici-pants, for example, disagreed over the precise meaning of the Shimla accord and the reference within it to the UN. This disagreement was to have serious consequences with regard to the Indian reaction once the report was eventually leaked. The Shimla accord of 1972 stated that India and Pakistan should seek to reach a bilateral agreement over Kashmir in line with the charter of the UN, to which both states were signatories. For the Indian delegation, this reference was meant to stress the need to find a peaceful solution and did not refer to the specific resolutions on Kashmir itself. Yet several anti-Indian groups that attended the meetings of the Next Century Foundation argued aggressively that the reference to the charter was inclusive of all UN resolutions, specifically the reference to a referendum. The Shimla accord was drafted to preclude this option once and for all (Wirsing, 1998).

Two other areas of heated controversy are worth noting in that they dominated discussion and led to endless argument and amendment. One concerned the genesis of the 1989 crisis itself and the other the degree of human rights abuses by the Indian authorities. Both topics resulted in the report undergoing numerous and substantial rewrites, culminating in a series of appendices being added to convey 'dissenting opinion'. Many representatives attending the meetings argued that the crisis in 1989 was in large part an insurrection. They pointed to the extensive abuses of Kashmiri rights on both sides of the divide, going back to the early 1950s. Others – including the sole pro-Indian representative throughout – argued that the causes were linked to an insurgency, that is, the deliberate infiltration into the Kashmir valley of militants from Afghanistan and the North-West Frontier Province by the Pakistani authorities. The situation was, in reality, a complex pastiche of both, with the success of the latter largely dependent on the degree of the former. Delineating the two processes was a difficult, painful process and the meetings of the Foundation did not provide the most suitable framework for this to take place. The failure to do so jeopardised the success that the subsequent recommendation for mediation would have on the conflict itself.

Not surprisingly, the issue of human rights abuses remained controversial throughout. Significant evidence emerged throughout the 1990s cataloguing violent actions by the Indian Border Security Force against Kashmiri civilians

(Hewitt, 1995). Yet evidence of human rights abuses in Azad Kashmir was largely neglected because, having occurred over a lengthy period, they were relatively unspectacular. It was pointed out that a majority of Kashmiris from the 'Pakistani side' had migrated to the West because the economic and social conditions in Azad Kashmir were so dire and opportunities in Pakistan so limited. It was also noted that, until very recently, Kashmiris resident in Gilgit and the Northern Territories had been denied any rights to vote in either Pakistani national elections or elections to the Azad Kashmir assembly in Muzaffarabad. The Indian member was outraged at these inconsistencies and yet, given the nature of the groups at the meetings, often found little support.

The result of these and other controversies was a time-consuming process that led to the report undergoing complex amendments, often by the core members, including William Morris, who devoted considerable time and intellectual energy to the project. The end product in early 1997 was, however, despite such tireless dedication, an uneven, largely imprecise document outlining what was dimly perceived by participants to be a radical departure from official UK policy. Interestingly, the document identified a role that a Labour government might have as a potential mediator in the crisis, not simply because of British involvement in its Empire, but because of the significant Kashmiri population now resident in United Kingdom, residents who continued to be interested in the fate of Kashmir.

Significantly, the document discussed the various claims advanced by the Indian and Pakistani governments as to why the issue of a 'three way' referendum could not be allowed. Throughout the 1950s, the prospects for the right to determine a separate Kashmiri state (as opposed to one joined to either India or Pakistan) had not been entertained. Now it was. The report concluded that the central issue was effectively one of self-determination. British mediation was designed to assist in determining what were the wishes of the Kashmiri people. The available options would include, if necessary, the establishment of an independent state. The position adopted was close to that taken in composite 53 at the 1995 Labour conference. The final report was completed on the eve of the 1997 general election. Although neither part of Labour's official programme nor the result of its formal policy-making process, the document was well received by senior figures within Labour, including Robin Cook, the shadow foreign secretary.

News of the document was leaked to India House in London in the run-up to the 1997 general election. The high commissioner was an intelligent, conservative man closely related to Hindu nationalist sentiments (and was subsequently nominated to the Indian Rajya Sabha, the upper house of parliament, by the BJP prime minister, Atal Vajpayee, in 1999). As a former human rights lawyer, the high commissioner was 'utterly bemused' by the timing of the report and its contents. One source close to India House stated that the response of the high commissioner to the report was to offer mediation in the Northern Ireland dispute, on the grounds that such a policy would be 'equally offensive and inappropriate to the British government as this [one] is to mine'. Various allegations were made in both the British Asian press and the Indian English press that Labour was adopting a pro-Pakistan policy by explicitly internationalising the Kashmir issue. In the context of already frosty Indo-Pakistan relations, India reacted immediately and strongly to Labour's overtures. By the time of the 1997 general election many Indian commentators were deeply suspicious of Labour's intentions towards Kashmir. In January 1997 *The Times* reported that *The Times of India* and *The Hindustan Times* were both hostile to Labour (11 January 1997). By contrast, many Indian commentators and politicians were favourably disposed towards John Major's Conservative government. Reportedly, one Conservative foreign secretary, Douglas Hurd, had commented that the UN resolutions were too dated to form the basis for future policy, a stance in accordance with that of the Indian government (see *The Times*, 14 October 1997).

Surprisingly, given Labour's internationalism and its long-standing connections with South Asia, in the formation of its policy the party had failed to appreciate the complex changes that had occurred to political identities since 1947. The Kashmiri identity within the British Asian diaspora had diverged from the identities that persisted throughout the disputed area itself: a point not registered by Labour. This failure was partly to do with the absence within the British Kashmiri diaspora of a significant Pandit (or Hindu) element. Neither it nor a Buddhist nor even a Shiite Muslim element was present to challenge the prevailing interpretations of the causes and solutions to the crisis. Only when Labour's policy process was well underway was the panel of experts widened to include representatives from such organisations as Panun Kashmir, the Kashmir Front and other representatives from Jammu and Ladakh. At this point, Labour confronted the difficulties of mapping on to a disputed territory a consistent and universally acceptable image of cultural nationalism and identity. It continued to articulate a solution orientated towards self-determination.

This process of policy formation was extraordinary. In opposition (and, later, in power) Labour appreciated the complexities of the Bosnian situation, in which territory and ethnic identities did not match and in which ethnic aspirations to nationhood configured different and competing images of statehood. In such circumstances, the party took great care over the way in which it articulated causes and issues. Over Kashmir, Labour would have had access to well established UN archives, including the Dixon report. This report comprehended plainly the contradictions inherent in viewing competing ethnic identities as monolithic in structure or, worse still, as mapping neatly on to contiguous territorial areas. Yet the party persisted in adopting a trajectory acceptable to a significant element of the British Asian electorate, one that was utterly intolerable to the Indian government.

Labour in office

On coming to power, the Next Century Foundation report was handed over to civil servants in the Foreign Office, following the appointments of Robin

Cook as foreign secretary and Derek Fatchett as minister of state. At this stage, Labour's rethink on Kashmir might have been subsumed within the administration's wider claims to have initiated an ethnical dimension to foreign policy. Kashmir was not mentioned on 17 July 1997 when Cook gave his much-noted set-piece address on human rights in the recently refurbished Locarno suite at the Foreign Office (Cook, 1997). In the speech, Cook reiterated the centrality of human rights as part of the proper conduct of nations both domestically and within the international system. His support for Amnesty International was read in New Delhi as an oblique reference to the Kashmir crisis, as India had recently banned the organisation from sending a team into the troubled area. The Indian government had heavily criticised an Amnesty report on human rights violations in Jammu and Kashmir in 1997, which had misrepresented the situation by several inaccuracies, including a photograph of a woman mourning her husband at a Muslim burial which later transpired to have been taken in Tamil Nadu, a southern state in India.

India signalled its disquiet both in London and in New Delhi, where the administration pressed the British high commissioner for clarification over Labour's position on Kashmir. The desk officers in the Foreign Office in London and the High Commission in New Delhi were, however, not in a position at this stage to offer any explanation. On receiving the Next Century Foundation's report, following the 1997 general election, the permanent secretary in the Foreign Office was reportedly incredulous at its contents and unclear as to whether it was to be treated either as a background paper or as a serious proposal for policy. Apparently, staff in the research unit at the Foreign Office initially returned the document to Cook on the grounds that it was self-evidently the wrong brief: an internal party paper, not designed to direct policy. Following clarification that, in fact, it was intended to be the basis of a rethink over Kashmir, the research unit tried to remind the foreign secretary that Labour's initiative, containing as it did the notion of in- dependence, would re-open the controversy surrounding the deployment of a plebiscite. After all, India had clearly and definitively rejected such a course ever since 1972. Moreover, it might be presumed to question the legitimacy of India's administration of the territory. Such an initiative would inevitably provoke India into the kind of hostile response that had occurred from government and press alike when a senior US spokesperson in the State Department had referred to Kashmir as 'a disputed territory' in 1995.

Despite persistent rumours in the press, the Foundation's document continued to drive policy formation, although it was not explicitly mentioned in public. Within weeks of taking office, Derek Fatchett visited India and Pakistan (between 11 and 18 June 1997). Before his departure from London, Fatchett noted, 'I am delighted to be making an early visit to India and Pakistan ... I wish them luck in their talks next week, which I hope will make progress over Kashmir and the other issues that divide them' (FCO press release). In marked contrast to a favourable reception in Pakistan, the Indian government was unambiguous in reiterating to Fatchett that any offers of mediation were inappropriate, all the more so since they came from the former colonial power. It stated that a suggestion that independence was an acceptable option for Kashmir would be considered a grave and un- warranted intrusion into the internal affairs of the Indian state. It was intimated to Fatchett that such an intrusion would not only prejudice Indo- Pakistan relations over Kashmir but would severely undermine Anglo-Indian relations as well.

At the 1997 Labour conference – a post-victory gathering in Brighton – however, Fatchett told a meeting sponsored by Justice for Jammu and Kashmir that he favoured a referendum to determine the territory's future (*The Hindustan Times*, 3 October 1997). He endorsed self-determination and the UN resolutions without mentioning the Shimla accord. The next night, at a predominantly British Indian meeting, Fatchett reportedly arrived late and departed without taking questions. (Later Fatchett became the first British minister to meet official representatives from Azad Kashmir.) He made several visits to the area and on one occasion was accompanied by William Morris himself.

Despite warnings from Foreign Office researchers and patent opposition from the Indian government, Labour persisted in its policy. It avoided any public statement acknowledging either the policy review document or the content of its various bilateral talks with the Indian and the Pakistani governments, despite India's growing irritation. *The Times* commented later that Indian government sources claimed Labour had a secret agenda to create an independent Kashmir: 'the unnamed sources said Mr Cook had told Indian authorities that Kashmir was an article of faith within the Labour party' (17 October 1997). Lukewarm attempts to placate Indian domestic opinion were not helped by the style of the British high com- missioner, Sir David Gore-Booth, known in Delhi as Gore-Blimey, whom the New Delhi elite disliked and who was associated with an overbearing, incompetent attitude. However arbitrary this attribution was, Gore-Booth was responsible for defending Labour's policy; more critically, he was involved in preparing the schedule for the Queen's disastrous visit to India in October 1997.

It is clear that both Gore-Booth and the Foreign Office significantly underestimated the political mood in the Indian capital. The Queen's visit was an opportunity, in the minds of several senior advisers to India's United Front government, for a sustained political embarrassment of the British government, as a means to draw attention to the folly of its policy review on Kashmir. *The Times* noted bluntly that the row 'has its origins in Labour party politics and intense Indian suspicions of the government' (14 October 1997). The deep resentment felt by the Indian establishment, otherwise as anxious as any British government to avoid politicising the protocol of a royal visit, can also be gauged by prime minister Gujral's remark about India suffering the unwelcome interferences of a 'third rate power'. I. K. Gujral was – and remains – the perfect example of a dedicated politician with great warmth and genuine affection for Britain and British culture. The Queen's programme was interrupted on five separate occasions. The target of such interventions was not the monarch as much as her foreign secretary.

This extraordinary situation attracted considerable adverse media comment in the United Kingdom and India, much of it directed at Robin Cook. It led to a critical rethink about policy both within the Foreign Office and within the prime minister's Downing Street policy unit, which effectively pulled the report and realigned Labour's stance on Kashmir. The British government ensured that the newly appointed British high commissioner to India would seek to placate the Indians by assuring them that UK policy on Kashmir remained unchanged from that of previous administrations. Tony Blair took care to inform Gujral that Labour accepted Kashmir was a bilateral issue, a stance he has since repeated (*The Hindustan Times*, 25 October 1997). In 1999 Cook told the House of Commons that the parties to the dispute should negotiate a solution to the problem. He went further than Blair in emphasising the importance of public opinion. But it is noticeable that he neither offered to mediate nor referred to self-determination (*Hansard*, 20 July 1999, cols 956–8). In effect, the party had distanced itself from the document it had sponsored and resorted to advocating bilateral talks between India and Pakistan.

In 1998 both India and Pakistan carried out nuclear tests, refocusing international attention on Asian politics. This was followed by renewed and severe tensions, including overt conflict, over Kashmir during 1999. Quite what was the long-term damage done by Labour's initiative in 1997 either to British–Indian relations or to the United Kingdom's influence in the region more generally remains to be seen.

Conclusions

Several points can be noted from this discussion about Labour's policy towards Kashmir. The party's review of policy over the dispute failed because of the unorthodox nature of the review process and the extent to which this route was dominated by well meaning, well organised but nonetheless partisan sections of the United Kingdom's Asian population. Such dominance came about not just through the disproportionate make-up of British Kashmiris but also through the way in which the Next Century Foundation think-tank sought representation by a plethora of Kashmiri groups at its meetings and went on to incorporate their views into its final report. The weaknesses of the document were disguised both by the enthusiasm of the individuals involved (reinforced by their own constituency links with some of the Kashmiri groups present at the meetings) and by the general climate of the times, which emphasised human rights as an input into the foreign policy process, at the expense of how such a policy might be implemented in the face of overt hostility from one of the key states involved. The emphasis on the Mirpuri standpoint may explain, in part, Cook's apparent failure to grasp the complexities of the issues involved.

Labour's 'Kashmir fiasco' illustrates the dangers inherent in the evolution of foreign policy by think-tanks in a closed and private process. It also demonstrates the weakness of an overtly ideological approach to international affairs, which must run the risk of offending and undermining states that have formerly been the United Kingdom's friends. While Labour appears to have backed away from further involvement in the Kashmir situation, both the New Delhi government and the Indian media remain suspicious about the British government's intentions.

The question remains as to why Labour embarked on the trajectory it did concerning policy towards Kashmir. Its formal policy processes allowed British Kashmiris to place the issue on the party's agenda. That in itself did not ensure that Labour would take up the issue: the party's formal process was by-passed from 1996 onwards. Many opportunities existed for Labour's leadership to jettison the commitment made at its 1995 conference. There were undoubtedly electoral dividends for the party in offering international negotiations and hinting at self-determination for Kashmir: it was a policy that was attractive to British Muslims, especially those from the Kashmiri diaspora. It cost few votes among British Hindus. There was, in part, a straightforward domestic electoral imperative to Labour's initiative. Stephen Grey, writing in *The Times*, concluded: 'For Labour, there appeared to be domestic political advantages in even such a veiled reference [as contained in Cook's comments in Pakistan] to the future of the [Kashmiri] state. More than 350,000 voters of Pakistani origins are scattered across Britain and many have made Kashmir a weekly headache in the surgeries of Labour MPs' (19 October 1997).

Such an explanation is, however, incomplete, given the secret and un-publicised way in which policy was developed under the auspices of the Next Century Foundation during 1996 and 1997. This approach paid few electoral dividends. Labour politicians may have hoped that mediating a solution in Kashmir might provide a new administration with a quick and relatively easy triumph in foreign affairs, one through which they could demonstrate their credentials as actors on the world stage. Equally, policy may have been driven by a determination that the United Kingdom did have a genuine obligation to help resolve such a long-running and seemingly intractable dispute, both for historical reasons and for existing cultural links. The intensifying crisis of the 1990s and the allegations about human rights abuses fuelled Labour's resolve that any policy must adopt the notion of self-determination and accept the full range of solutions. The late Derek Fatchett in this regard was driven by a concern over the crisis and a desire to grasp what was perceived to be the moral solution, however thorny it might prove to be. Labour's policy may have been designed, in part at any rate, within an explicitly ethical framework. More instrumentally, a solution to one of the last great territorial disputes of the twentieth century would have generated considerable inter-national kudos. In that regard, the risks of failure were outweighed by the possibility of an extraordinary foreign policy achievement in the first term of a Labour government. In the event, however, the implementation of such a strategy proved much tougher than its architects anticipated.

Note

This chapter draws on extensive fieldwork by Vernon Hewitt in India throughout the 1990s. He also participated in several meetings of the Next Century Foundation, beginning in the autumn before Labour's May 1997 election victory.

References

Cook, R. (1997), 'Human rights into a new century', speech, Locarno Suite, FCO, London, 17 July.

Geddes, A. (1998), 'Inequality, political opportunity and ethnic minority parliamentary candidacy', in S. Saggar (ed.), *Race and British Electoral Politics* (London: UCL Press), 145–74.

Hewitt, V. (1995), *Reclaiming the Past* (London: Portland Press).

Hewitt, V. (1997), *The New International Politics of South Asia* (Manchester: Manchester University Press).

James, Sir M. (1993), *Pakistan Chronicle* (ed. P. Lyon) (London: Hurst and Co.).

Kampfner, J. (1999), *Robin Cook* (London: Phoenix).

Labour party (1990), *NEC Report* (London: Labour party).

Labour party (1992), *It's Time to Get Britain Working Again* (London: Labour party).

Labour party (1993), *NEC Report* (London: Labour party).

Labour party (1995a), *Agenda* (London: Labour party).

Labour party (1995b), *Conference Arrangements Committee Report* (London: Labour party).

Labour party (1995c), *NEC Statement on Kashmir* (London: Labour party).

Labour party (1996a), *A Fresh Start for Britain. Labour's Strategy in the Modern World* (London: Labour party).

Labour party (1996b), *NEC Report* (London: Labour party).

Labour party (1996c), *Policy Handbook* (London: Labour party).

Lamb, A. (1991), *Kashmir, a Disputed Territory* (Hartingfordbury: Roxford Books).

Saggar, S. (1997), 'The dog that didn't bark? Immigration, race and the election', in A. Geddes and J. Tonge (eds), *Labour's Landslide* (Manchester: Manchester University Press), 147–63.

Saggar, S. (1998), *The General Election 1997. Ethnic Minorities and Electoral Politics* (London: Commission for Racial Equality).

Shukra, K. (1998), 'New Labour debates and dilemmas', in S. Saggar (ed.), *Race and British Electoral Politics* (London: UCL Press), 117–44.

Wirsing, R. (1998), *India, Pakistan and the Kashmir Dispute* (Basingstoke: Macmillan).

13

Labour's defence policy: from unilateralism to strategic review

Darren Lilleker

Introduction

Between 1945 and 1989 (and arguably beyond), the Cold War was fought out in minutia within the Labour party. Debate centred upon the issues of how the United Kingdom should be defended and against whom that defence should be orientated. Policy formulators constantly attempted to appease the party ideologues while following the role expected of the United Kingdom by its NATO allies. Many left-wingers projected an idealistic image of how the world should be: they subscribed to a notion of peaceful coexistence, which was propounded, to a much greater extent, by the Soviet leadership than their Western counterparts. Leading figures on the left argued that the United Kingdom should stand as an example to the world by implementing a policy of unilateral nuclear disarmament and by reaching agreements with those states perceived as enemies. For examples of these views see Zilliacus (undated) and Foot (1999: 61–91) (Zilliacus was a Labour MP 1945–50 and 1955–67). Frank Allaun, Labour MP 1955–83, produced a myriad of pamphlets between 1955 and 1989 through the UDC and later CND. Though pamphleteering maintained constant pressure on Labour and Conservative governments alike for much of the post-war period, unilateralists were unable to change the consensus surrounding British defence.

The rationale for this consensus was grounded on the notion of responsible governance. It built on the policies enacted by Ernest Bevin as foreign secretary between 1945 and 1951: these measures, devised as a reaction to international events immediately following the Second World War, led the United Kingdom into anti-communist alliances and to become a participant in the arms race. The adoption of an independent nuclear deterrent became the cornerstone of British defence and an important indication of the country's perceived status as a world power. Proponents held it to be necessary given the supposed nature of communist aggression and the realities of world politics. In the 1960s and 1970s, Labour governments argued that nuclear weapons should be decommissioned, but only as part of an international process. It was only during Michael Foot's brief spell as leader of the party that unilateralism was adopted as the central goal of the party's defence policy. The unilateralists held that the United Kingdom's nuclear deterrent was an indication of its failure to come to terms with its declining power within world politics. Much more than that, it entrenched the country in an expensive and unstable arms race. As well as ending that arms race, unilateralism would permit a Labour government to emphasise the internationalist element of its foreign policy, an issue long of concern to the left within the party.

The underlying principle behind the United Kingdom possessing nuclear weapons, according to the inter-party consensus, was to deter attack from the Soviet Union. Following the Gorbachev–Reagan initiatives of the mid-1980s, this threat was perceived to reduce exponentially, and all but disappear in 1989 as the communist regimes imploded. Amid talk of a 'new world order', it was expected that the arms race would not only end but that existing arsenals would be significantly reduced. While only an extra-parliamentary minority actively campaigned into the 1990s for this development, some of those who had subscribed earlier to the arguments of CND held private hopes that a Labour government would remove weapons of mass destruction from British shores. Their expectations were based normatively on the belief that there was something inherently anti-socialist and anti-humanist in the destructive potential of nuclear weapons. It was not to be. The Blair government's defence review of 1998 affirmed the continued reliance on such weapons as a deterrent. In so doing it emphasised arguments long associated with the Conservative party. As a major world power, it was claimed, the United Kingdom should retain nuclear armaments while others did likewise.

The only element of New Labour's approach that had the appearance of innovation was the attachment of an ethical notion to foreign and defence policy. On taking up the post of foreign secretary, Robin Cook stated that there must be an 'ethical content to foreign policy' (Cook, 1997), defining this as a move away from the concerns of *realpolitik* and a concentration on establishing the United Kingdom as a 'force for good in the world'. This ill-defined but far-reaching goal is claimed to be the guiding principle behind policy formulation. Whether this fully corresponds to the organisations and tools that have been chosen as the cornerstones of British defence is questionable, particularly given the continued reliance on the 'unethical' nuclear deterrent.

In this chapter, I explore Labour's journey from unilateralism of the 1980s to the 1998 strategic defence review and ask what has been the justification for New Labour's defence policy. Critics argue that policy relies heavily upon past traditions, making no significant break with either the Cold War rationale or the policy of the previous Conservative governments. New Labour has, in this regard, failed to come to terms with the United Kingdom's past. Those supportive of the Blair administration argue that its defence policy has allowed the party finally to put to rest the ghost of unilateralism and to adopt an appropriate strategy for the United Kingdom. They argue that the interventionism of the Labour government, as evidenced in Kosovo in 1999 and elsewhere, is compatible with the historic internationalism of the left. It represents a new means to secure a long-held objective. I explore these arguments by examining the nature of the party Blair leads and analysing how it differs from that led by Foot. I ask how the process of modernisation, so associated with Blair's project to reform Labour, has affected the way the party views the United Kingdom's role in the world. I detail the strategic review carried out by the Blair administration, assess its ethical content and discuss New Labour's abandonment of yet another central tenet of the party's left wing: its acceptance of Trident as a tool for national defence.

The break with unilateralism

It was the triumph of the idealists over the realists that led to unilateralism becoming Labour party policy, so turning defence into one of the key issues of the 1983 general election. The party followed the arguments propounded over the previous thirty years by the left-wing ideologues of the Victory for Socialism group, CND and the broader peace movement. (Victory for Socialism was a group founded in 1946 and re-established in 1957 to counter the party's right-wing leadership. Its ideas, including support for non-nuclear defence, continued into the Tribune group.)

Put starkly, left-wingers argued that the United States had subjugated the United Kingdom to its own foreign policy. To remedy this state of affairs, Labour should reassert the United Kingdom's influence on the world stage by leaving the 'nuclear club' and persuading other nations to follow the example.

This was first put on to the agenda at the 1980 annual conference, but was formally ratified by delegates the following year, by 3,433,000 to 3,401,000 votes – a majority of only 32,000 votes (*LPACR*, 1981: 279). The unilateralist policy had far-reaching implications. The proposals demanded the closure of all US bases on British territory, the termination of agreements to upgrade the United Kingdom's nuclear weaponry and the nationalisation of the armaments industry. It was recognised that this could cause job losses; Labour proposed that those displaced would be retrained to manufacture 'useful products such as artificial limbs' (*LPACR*, 1982: 279). This idealism captured little support either within the Atlanticist strand of the party or with the electorate.

This lack of widespread support for the policy led to a growing fissure dividing the left from the centre and right within the party. Denis Healey, as deputy leader and shadow spokesperson on foreign affairs, remained hostile to unilateralism, as did many leading members of the shadow cabinet, who made little secret of their dissatisfaction with the policy. The formal adoption of unilateralism proved intensely problematic for the party. It illustrated the far-reaching extent of the split within Labour over defence issues and it contributed directly to the bitter internal disputes that charac-terised the party's politics in this period. The highpoint of the clashes over defence came early in 1981 when four senior figures deserted the party to found the Social Democratic party. The motivation for their decision was their belief that the party had moved much too far to the left, a shift evidenced by its articulation of unilateralism. The formation of the Social Democratic party did not resolve disputes within the Labour party over defence. Indeed, the whole period between 1980 and 1984 saw what was called the 'hard' left reach its zenith of power within Labour.

Labour itself came to represent an ever-decreasing minority of the electorate and in June 1983 suffered a crushing defeat in the general election. The outcome was catastrophic: Labour only narrowly escaped being pushed into third place by the Alliance between the Liberal party and the newly founded Social Democratic party. It was the result, according to Philip Gould, later one of Neil Kinnock and Tony Blair's most influential strategists, of Labour's policy proposals being 'completely divorced from what the British people wanted from a government' (Gould, 1998: 50). Unilateralism was only one part of this package that the electorate had rejected so decisively. Some commentators attributed the Conservative victory to the 'Falklands factor': Margaret Thatcher's administration had organised a successful expedition to recapture the Falklands in 1982, following an Argentine invasion. Others blamed Labour's manifesto. In a caustic sound bite, Gerald Kaufman, a senior figure within the party, called the party's manifesto 'the longest suicide note in history'.

It can be argued that both interpretations are correct and that it is on the issue of defence policy that the election defeat can be centred. The electorate backed the Falklands War with jingoistic enthusiasm and revelled in the image of a renewed, stronger United Kingdom. Labour could not have chosen a worse juncture at which to advance a controversial policy, one that would apparently strip what was perceived to be a vital part of the country's existing armoury. Ruthlessly, the Conservatives used this perception as a potent vote-winning weapon, one that would haunt the party until the 1997 general election campaign. Conservative politicians questioned both the wisdom (in the face of external aggression) and patriotism of unilateralism. Though many within Labour remained committed to the unilateralist goal in the long term, in the aftermath of 1983 some accepted that in electoral terms it was an immensely problematic policy. However, changing policy without appearing utterly pragmatic and unprincipled was also difficult. From the mid-1980s onwards, as right-wingers slowly won back ground, Labour came to reassert an Atlanticist stance and reforge the party's image to be in line with both its members' principles and the electorate's desires.

Labour's transition from a party with a unilateral defence policy was neither easy nor smooth. It was, however, facilitated by developments in the Strategic Arms Limitation Talks (SALT) in 1987, which placed the issue of disarmament on the political agenda. Neil Kinnock, once a fervent unilateralist, who became Labour's new leader in October 1983, was able to appease both strands within the party by linking a unilateral policy with Soviet disarmament promises. Between 1983 and 1987 progress was slow and the party reaffirmed its support for unilateralism. A 1986 policy document called for the United Kingdom to become a non-nuclear nation similar to Denmark and Norway, retaining NATO membership and protection under the US 'nuclear umbrella' (Labour party, 1986). This, however, did not conform to the Conservative government's policy of strengthening the Anglo-American alliance, or the agreement to buy Trident to replace the redundant Polaris.

During the 1987 general election, the Conservatives once again mercilessly exploited Labour's defence policy, most notably in a poster of a soldier surrendering that was underwritten with the slogan, 'Labour's policy on arms'. Kinnock's attempts to defend unilateralism and to expound his party's policy in an interview with David Frost ran into difficulties and were ridiculed in the popular press. Differences of interpretation between Healey (still foreign affairs spokesperson) and leading unilateralists were manifest. While this was most evident in the run-up to the 1983 general election, it remained a constant feature that leading defence spokesmen such as Healey, John Silkin and Gerald Kaufman, alongside other leading figures such as ex prime minister James Callaghan, would propound the notion that the United Kingdom's nuclear deterrent should not be given up without a *quid pro quo* agreement (Young, 1997: 147). Equally the party's commitment to expanded conventional defence forces as a replacement for nuclear weapons did not appear a viable deterrent in an atmosphere of bipolarity and nuclear standoff.

Kinnock later regretted that he had not moved more decisively against Labour's unilateralism between 1983 and 1987. After the 1987 election defeat the opportunity to redesign the party's defence policy was apparent, as part of the wide-ranging reassessment of its programmatic commitments that comprised the 1987–89 policy review. In June 1988 Kinnock claimed there was 'no need for a something-for-nothing unilateralism'. This rather cryptic phrase combined leftist aspirations with Atlanticist caution and an attempt to build a national consensus (Keohane, 1993: 116). The Labour leader's efforts at keeping the party united on the issue failed. Within ten days of the introduction of a 'something-for-something' disarmament policy, and as Kinnock sought to move towards a multilateralist disarmament policy, Denzil Davies, Labour's defence spokesperson 1981–82 and 1983–88, resigned. There followed a further period of confusion about party policy and Kinnock's intent. In the circumstances of the 1980s, less idealistic but no less committed disarmers were able to put forward the plausible argument that Labour's defence policy should work in conjunction with international disarmament. The United Kingdom could use Cruise and Trident missiles as a bartering chip. It was recognised that as the Cold War drew to an end (a development characterised by much improved US–Soviet relations) the United Kingdom could gain nothing by disarming overnight, but should do so as part of a larger process. In effect, unilateralism was dead in the water by the summer of 1988. It was finally rejected by the 1989 Labour party conference when the trade union NUPE withdrew the support of its 600,000 block vote (Rikihisa, 1991: 74).

Labour remained firmly committed to the removal of nuclear missiles. A Labour government would carefully negotiate reductions in nuclear weapons multilaterally. *Meet the Challenge: Make the Change* stated that only 'negotiation[s] with and between nuclear armed powers, are the best way of achieving nuclear disarmament' (Labour party, 1989: 86). Writing in *Labour Party News*, Kinnock stated clearly his own case: 'Britain can't afford them, we can never use them, why have them'. His answer was 'for the purposes of participation in the disarmament process ... to clear the world of nuclear weapons' (Keohane, 1993: 119). Kinnock appeared no less committed than members of the hard left to disarmament (he was after all long associated with the unilateralist cause). What he sought was a viable strategy that would combine the idealists' aims with electoral success. This strategy was in tune with the international mood: US, Russian and European leaders, the last of whom were especially influential upon Kinnock, had begun to talk the language of nuclear arms limitation, which was facilitated by SALT II and the ratification of the Strategic Arms Reduction Treaty (START) and START-2 in 1987–89. NATO allies reached agreement that no one nation should act alone in disarming. This goal could be reached only if all parties involved worked from a position of parity (Keohane, 1993: 121–2; MacDonald, 1989). This proposal would be the basis for Labour's defence policy from 1989 until the early stages of the 1997 general election campaign. It was at this point that the last sacred cow of the party's once entrenched commitment to disarmament was sacrificed at the altar of consensus politics.

New Labour and defence

John Smith's short term as Labour leader between July 1992 and May 1994 was dominated by a reform of the party's machinery. Defence issues were placed on the backburner. Labour adopted a largely bipartisan and consensual approach, committed to multilateral disarmament and the maintenance of conventional armed forces. Gerald Kaufman, shadow foreign secretary 1988–92, neatly outlined the party's stance in 1991, stating that Trident would be retained with the current warheads and would be decommissioned only when agreement had been reached between 'all thermonuclear powers completely to eliminate these weapons' (Kaufman, 1991). Meanwhile, within the party the last remnants of hard-left influence were eroded.

There remained some uncertainty about policy. There was debate surrounding which of the supranational organisations should be the cornerstone of future defence, either the EU or NATO, both of which had lost their status as anathemas to Labour. NATO was recognised to be undergoing a process of reformation following the end of the Cold War and it was argued that this had led it to adopt Labour's programme of 1989 (Labour party, 1991: 51). This had outlined the adoption of no first use, the development of strategies for nuclear arms limitation and the adoption of flexible or rapid response forces to deal with destabilising elements. Spending cuts were recognised as necessary: party documents suggested that this could be achieved by defence diversification (Labour party, 1990: 47–8; 1991: 57–8). This clashed with the notions of *It's Time to Get Britain Working Again* (Labour party, 1992) because it had the potential to undermine the UK armaments industry: 'one in ten manufacturing jobs [are] dependent on defence' (Labour party, 1991: 58). However, cuts had become a reality of government and no longer a subject of contention. The Conservative government had recognised the need to reduce defence spending and did so effectively during 1992–97 (MoD, 1999: 6).

This pragmatic but indefinite policy continued after Tony Blair was elected party leader in July 1994 with few changes to existing commitments being enacted in the run-up to the 1997 general election. New Labour policy documents reinforced the position that nuclear weaponry would be retained: 'A new Labour government will retain Trident', a promise symbolically printed in bold in the pre-election policy manifesto (Labour party, 1996b: 8). The party affirmed its commitment to multilateral negotiations, establishing that there would only be something-for-something decommissioning. This document also introduced the notion that Labour would reassert the United Kingdom's position in the world, stating that under Labour it would become 'a leading force for change in the world' (Labour party, 1996b: 8). Defence became an issue, though not an especially important one, as soon as it became apparent that Labour's opportunity to form a government might finally have arrived. At the first available opportunity, Blair removed the spectre that had haunted Labour since 1983: that in power the party would leave the United Kingdom undefended. In 1996 he told the press that a leader of the United Kingdom must 'envisage circumstances in which your nuclear deterrent can be used' (*Daily Telegraph*, 26 June 1996).

Unlike Neil Kinnock after his rejection of unilateralism in the late 1980s, Blair was straightforward and categorical. Nuclear weapons were to be retained for the foreseeable future and a Labour government would be prepared to use them should the appropriate circumstances arise. Attempts by Michael Portillo, the Conservative defence secretary, to raise the issue of defence as an obstacle to voting Labour fell flat. The party went into the election campaign for the first time since 1979 with a responsible image in defence policy.

The opportunity for a new and radical approach remained: once in government Labour could re-evaluate its position and decide against the conservative statements of the pre-election period. In its election manifesto, Labour promised to 'conduct a strategic defence and security review to reassess our essential security interests and defence needs' (Labour party, 1997). Quite what such a review entailed remained obscure. Within the party there still existed members who had campaigned for a nuclear-free United Kingdom, one of whom, Robin Cook, became foreign secretary. Equally the rhetoric of ethics and essential security underlined the fact that changes were to be made. However, the party maintained a firm distance from ideological issues. Blair insisted that 'outdated dogma' should be abandoned in favour of responsible governance, an image Labour had been seeking to re-attain since the 1983 election debacle. It was within this context that Labour's defence policy would be formulated: it would be orientated around an independent nuclear deterrent and strong conventional forces.

Labour took office with a landslide majority following the May 1997 general election. The commitment to a bipartisan defence policy remained undiminished and at odds, potentially at any rate, with the ethical dimension to foreign policy that was enunciated by Cook at the same time. The strategic review was designed to meet the needs of the international order in which it was formulated, with the United Kingdom maintaining a leading role in that order. The review was presented to the House of Commons by defence secretary George Robertson on 8 July 1998 and was received favourably, in evidence of its consensual nature. The only real dissent came from a Labour backbencher, John McAllion, who accused the government of having 'missed an unique opportunity to give a lead on nuclear disarmament' (*Hansard*, 8 July 1998). It can be noted that Labour need not have followed a consensual and orthodox trajectory in its defence policy. Members of the party's left, such as Ken Livingstone, had long argued that substantial cuts in defence spending were necessary (given constraints on spending commitments elsewhere) and feasible (given the proportion of national incomes that other countries spent on defence).

Such left-wingers were not alone. Years earlier, as prime minister in the 1960s, Harold Wilson had maintained that defence cuts were simply a realistic reflection of the resources available to the United Kingdom and the constraints that then existed. Wilson, of course, had to contend with the perceived threats posed to British interests by the dynamic of the Cold War. By 1997 there were few such threats, on anything like the same scale, to the United Kingdom. The United States had taken on the role of 'watchdog'. A UK government had the option of taking a backseat, one where it might concentrate more on European strategic co-operation and less on pursuing leadership responsibilities within the world order. Such a course was unacceptable to those framing New Labour's trajectory. Through his close personal friendship with Bill Clinton, Tony Blair had deepened the United Kingdom's 'special relationship' with the United States. He appeared committed to a hawkish line in foreign policy, one which defended a variety of military operations during 1997–99. The strategic review supported this stance and offered little by way of significant change to the orientation of UK defence policy.

The strategic defence review

The strategic review was a long time in the making. As John Maples, shadow defence spokesperson, observed, it was 'intended to take six months but it

has taken fourteen' (*Hansard*, 8 July 1999). It was foreshadowed by considerable press speculation and a plethora of leaks about its content. Such reportage
concentrated on the proposed cuts in personnel and budget. This highlighted
the fact that the criticisms were more likely to come from the right and would
be limited in scope. In the event it was something of a damp squib. The review
(MoD, 1998) offers the United Kingdom the opportunity to act as a world
leader within an ethical framework, defined in the phrase a 'force for good'.
The organisations that are the keystones to collective security remain NATO
and the UN, while the transatlantic alliance is prioritised over Europe. The
United Kingdom will retain a nuclear capability, but will work towards
multilateral negotiations. Alongside this, conventional forces will be ration-
alised and rapid response units developed to prevent destabilisation to the
global order.

Its production followed the familiar Blair rhetoric about open and responsive government. There is little evidence of transparency in the final product.
The review boasts an extensive consultation process. However, those included
in consultations are described as representing the MoD, the armed forces
and 'elsewhere'. The last are listed as academics, journalists, opposition MPs
and members of unspecified NGOs. It appears that the participants in the
review were directly involved in the defence business and not commentators.
Equally apparent is the significance attached to the views of Tony Blair and
George Robertson, the defence secretary. These can be encapsulated in the
phrase 'Britain cannot be strong at home if it is weak abroad' (Labour party,
1996b: 8).

Therefore the review is predicated on the premise that there will be no
significant reductions in defence capabilities. This is reinforced by the spending
forecasts published in the Foreign Office expenditure plans. These set the
threshold for departmental expenditure as relatively unchanged from the
levels for 1996–97 (FCO, 1999, Part 5: 6). Furthermore, defence expenditure
decreased by only 0.1 per cent in the two years after Labour came to power,
compared with a seven per cent reduction between 1991/92 and 1995/96
(MoD, 1999: 6). The review persists in obliging the United Kingdom to take
on a wide role in the international order as a 'force for good' rather than
one which might be defined by narrow self-interest alone, a position that
is often described as a commitment to 'punching above our weight' (*The
Economist*, 11 July 1998: 35). Robertson quotes the UN secretary-general,
Kofi Annan, as saying the United Kingdom will offer the world 'diplomacy
backed up with firmness and force' (MoD, 1998: 201).

It is also stated that a nuclear arsenal would be retained while offering
a commitment to arms control, thus taking Kinnock's reluctant advocacy of
nuclear weapons in the face of failed multilateralism one stage further. New
Labour has retained the full compliment of Trident submarines, a departure
from the party's 1992 general election manifesto. Arguably, the review ties
the United Kingdom to the continuance of a world order reliant on nuclear
weapons to sustain peace. The strategy is, of course, not without difficulties.

The alternative to a world role is characterised by the review as isolationist. It is considered in stark terms and rejected out of hand:

> We could of course ... choose to take a narrow view of our role and responsibilities which did not require a significant military capability. This would mean that we would not wish and would not be able to contribute effectively to resolving crises such as Bosnia ... This is indeed a real choice, but not one the Government could recommend for Britain. (MoD, 1998: 59)

The desire to meet such commitments effectively decides the course steered by the review. Defence strategy will be determined by the government's foreign policy, which includes in its mission statement a much quoted ethical dimension. This, though innovative in comparison with the strategic review, furthers the notion of a wider responsibility for the United Kingdom as a force for good. The issue of how practicable such a policy is remains unresolved.

The extent of Labour's ethical dimension is probed by the retention of a nuclear arsenal. Out of office, US president Reagan admitted subsequently that he could never have authorised the use of nuclear weapons (Foot, 1999: 45). By contrast, New Labour appears to have no such qualms. They expound the stock argument in the strategic review that 'while nuclear arsenals and risks of proliferation remain, our minimum deterrent remains a necessary element of our security' (MoD, 1998: 60). To reinforce their case, they use economic determinism. The cost of decommissioning outweighs maintenance; thus as other nations have chosen to retain or develop similar weapons, the responsible course is retention. William Peden, CND's parliamentary researcher, countered this by claiming 'Labour are quite clearly embarrassed to have inherited Trident yet have done nothing to get rid of it, so they decided instead to make it look expensive' (*The Independent*, 17 August 1998). A further voice of dissent came from Michael Clarke, director of the Centre for Defence Studies, King's College, London. He argued that there is a 'profoundly dangerous' element in using Trident as a purely defensive weapon, pertinently asking from whom it is to defend us (*The Guardian*, 10 July 1998). He notes the existence of 'rogue states' that refuse to conform to the established rules of the international order. However, to use Trident against Milosevic's Serbia or Hussain's Iraq would plainly undermine Labour's pursuit of the 'force for good' image. Furthermore, Labour's support for NATO's 'no first use' policy concentrates on the use of conventional military defence (British–American Security Information Council, 1997). We should ask, therefore, are there other reasons for maintaining a nuclear arsenal? It can be argued that nuclear weapons have become a badge denoting superpower status: to lose that emblem would be to abandon a role in world affairs. Blair appears to aspire to the role of world leader that is associated with the United Kingdom's status as a nuclear power. Kinnock argued that you have to be 'in the club' to have a say in the future of international nuclear policy.

The policy continuities of the strategic review question New Labour's promise of 'radicalism' in 'achievement', given in the 1997 general election manifesto (Labour party, 1997). Continuity is most pronounced in the alliance chosen as the cornerstone of British security. It was equally hoped and feared by many commentators and participants that European states collectively would become the key partner for the United Kingdom in the future, particularly given the rhetoric employed as the United Kingdom took over the presidency of the EU in January 1998. Both Cook and Blair spoke of providing leadership of and deepening partnership with the European collective (Labour party, 1996a, 1996b, 1997: 7; Cook, 1997). Instead, New Labour has reaffirmed and sought to entrench the special transatlantic relationship between the United Kingdom and the United States. This association has long been viewed as an anathema to the party's left-wingers, who perceive it to represent the utter subordination of UK interests to those of the United States. Years ago, Frank Allaun, the veteran ideologue and former MP, perceived Labour to be 'on our knees licking [the president's] boots' (*Morning Star*, 28 December 1970). (A similar line was taken by *Private Eye* in characterising Blair as Clinton's dog during Operation Desert Fox against Iraq in 1998.)

The effect of such an alignment may be to place the United Kingdom in limbo, given that the current special relationship relies heavily on the close personal friendship of Blair and Clinton. In the longer term, the result may be to locate a rudderless United Kingdom in an indeterminate space, one that is neither European nor American. In the strategic review, New Labour concludes that 'membership of NATO will continue to provide the UK with its best insurance against all ... risks' and goes on to claim that the organisation has 'shown it is highly relevant to the specific circumstances of Europe today' (MoD, 1998: 37–8). In an indication of the importance of the US–UK partnership, it is striking that the government asserts that the effectiveness of NATO 'depends on the transatlantic relationship and the continued engagement in Europe of the United States' (MoD, 1998: 18). NATO was dominated by this axis during the 1990s, a situation Blair has no desire to change.

The character of the United Kingdom's special relationship with the United States, especially Blair's endorsement and support for external US military interventions (often in the face of European opposition), has led to challenges to the ethical dimension of New Labour's policy. Jeremy Corbyn, MP, reiterated the argument of the late Konni Zilliacus (1949), a strong supporter of the UN, stating 'the UN will feel that it is impossible to intervene ... [as] NATO will act unilaterally and ignore its views' (*Hansard*, 25 March 1999). The effect of NATO involvement has been to undermine more peaceful action on the part of the UN. For example, in December 1998, ignoring a Security Council resolution, the United States and the United Kingdom bombed Iraq. Under New Labour, the United Kingdom remains tied to alliances synonymous with the politics of the Cold War. It is unable to break with the long-established high-spending, nuclear-reliant, world role. The continuity with Cold War policies was highlighted in Robin Cook's 1999 Ernest Bevin memorial lecture, in which the foreign secretary praised Bevin in laying the groundwork for current security policy. However, in noting the importance of NATO during the Cold War, Cook stated 'no such arrangement ... would have been found necessary ... if the effectiveness of the Security Council ... had not been undermined by the Soviet use of the veto' (Cook, 1999a). The foreign secretary did not explore the possibility that the end of the Cold War and the collapse of the Soviet Union might, as Corbyn argues, provide the basis for a stronger and more active UN, one able to engage effectively with some of the difficulties of world politics. Given that Russian leaders mistrust NATO, greater stability might well be offered by developing a more inclusive organisation.

It can be concluded that the review is no more than a restatement of the bipartisan policy that emerged during the 1990s. This consensual approach has led critics to accuse New Labour of abandoning principles purely for electoral success. This does appear accurate in the case of defence policy. As Rikihisa explains, consensus was reached in the late 1980s by 'virtually unilateral concession from Labour' (1991: 68). This has continued with Labour in power and thus there seems little chance for Labour to break with policy traditions.

George Robertson described the review as 'one of the most radical and fundamental reshapings of Britain's defence'. He argued that the government's reforms would allow a global role to be sustained and that the administration's policies could provide the potential to extend national capabilities (Robertson, 1999). Some commentators have questioned the alignment of resources and objectives under New Labour, arguing that the available armed forces do not match the goals that the Blair administration has set itself. Cook noted at the 1999 Labour party conference that 'no other nation has a higher proportion of its armed forces active on peace-keeping measures around the globe' (Cook, 1999b). Observers conclude that such commitments are un-sustainable, given the demands on the United Kingdom's defence forces and the resources available. The argument that the United Kingdom can be a 'force for good' in the world has been applied selectively: intervening in Kosovo to protect Albanians in the face of Serbian opposition but waiting for Indonesian assent before sending troops to East Timor. In the case of Sierra Leone, the United Kingdom chose not to be directly involved in the first instance. It can be asked whether its role in such situations has a substance independent of other forces (namely the United States) in the world. Any failure to act unilaterally and consistently begs the question of why New Labour has adopted an interventionist rhetoric if, in the end, all the United Kingdom will do is follow the lead of other, stronger forces. This is controversial given that Labour projected an image of itself as the force that shaped the Kosovo campaign. Overall, this gives the impression that Labour's attempt to reassert the national kudos is being enacted selectively: seeking to demonstrate the nation's capacity, but avoiding taking an independent stance in case of failure. The fact that the United Kingdom feels unable to take a stand without support brings into question the reality of the ethical principle. Equally, the retention of status or kudos appears in conflict with the Blairite modernising style. This point is illustrated succinctly by Lord Wallace, Liberal Democrat defence spokesperson, who described the United Kingdom's world role as belonging to 'the country of Rule Britannia, rather than the rebranded Cool Britannia' (Wallace, 1998).

Conclusions

The strategic review can be characterised as containing little that is substantially new. It represents a continuation of tradition and consensus. Was there an alternative strategy that New Labour might have adopted? Might any other approach have been electorally successful? The lessons of 1983 remain fundamental to the modernisers within the party, reinforcing the view that neither its embedded ideology nor its idealism has a place in the formation of strategy. For the Labour party, the review is new in the positive direction and clarity it gives to defence. It demonstrates that the party can form a responsible and co-ordinated government, an indication of the break between 'Old' and 'New' Labour. A contrast can be made with the dissent and conflict that characterised policy between 1980 and 1989. Also, on defence matters, dissident MPs within the parliamentary Labour party number no more than twenty out of 419, so the appearance of cohesion can be easily maintained. (This at least was the number of supporters claimed by George Galloway, MP, when arguing that participation in Operation Desert Fox should be put to a vote: *Hansard*, 17 December 1998: col. 1160.) Labour's approach attracts little criticism either from the Conservative opposition or from the armed services. Furthermore, membership of the peace movement has long since declined to small numbers and, as such, receives little press attention.

The consensual direction of the review designates a strengthening of the growing political bipartisanship that characterised defence policy between 1989 and 1997. Labour spent much of this time trying to bury the spectres of 1983. By the time of the 1997 general election, unilateralism had been substituted by multilateralism, which in turn had been replaced by an endorsement of the nuclear deterrent, including the Trident programme. In its affirmation of a world role synonymous with that adopted by the Conservatives under Margaret Thatcher, New Labour had abandoned many socialist principles about defence and foreign policy that had once been deeply embedded within the party. I conclude that little of any significance has changed in defence policy with the change in government. The 1997 Conservative party manifesto equally talks of national strength, the spreading of ethical notions of democracy and providing leadership (Conservative party, 1997). Labour's rhetoric is significantly stronger and more evocative; however, the substance does not follow the rhetoric. The administration has not gone beyond those policies that were enacted under John Major. While this is not a new phenomenon of British politics, it appears as a failure on the part of a political party that declared it should be judged on 'radicalism ... not that of doctrine ... but of achievement' (Labour party: 1997).

The perceived requirements of electoral success were a central motivating element in this transformation for Labour. As Philip Gould testifies, the party's much-used focus groups associated the policies of the Foot-led party with a 'loony left' image: they were unpopular and undesirable. It can be noted, however, that defence currently lacks public priority: opinion polls taken in 1996–97 indicated that domestic issues held public priority. Defence issues and nuclear weaponry were seen as a priority by only one per cent of those polled. Options remained open for the Blair government. Fear of electoral rejection led the new Labour leadership not to explore such paths. The determination to be elected meant no risks could be taken. As such, old Labour ideals and commitments had to be replaced with a commitment to nuclear weapons. Labour's shift was not purely electoral. It can be viewed as a response to a changing world order. As more nations seek to join the nuclear club, the maintenance of some form of deterrent can be defended. The reliance of economic growth upon international stability means that to prevent destabilisation any so-called 'rogue nations' need dealing with swiftly and decisively. However, nuclear weapons cannot be used against the present 'rogue' actors. Therefore it is necessary to have a diverse range of resources that are able to meet any threat to the international community and ensure the integrity of the nation. From this viewpoint the strategic review can be seen as a product of Labour's new-found maturity, a reflection of the responsibilities of government.

Finally, Tony Blair's ideology must be considered. The cataclysmic events of 1989 liberated the world from the parameters of the Cold War; many commentators concluded that they demonstrated the redundancy of dogmatic socialism of the kind so often associated with the old left. It is debated whether the break-up of the Soviet Union and the collapse of communism had any real effect on Labour. Tony Wright argues it liberated socialism (Wright, 1997). Tony Blair's adoption of a Third Way brought a new focus for policy formulators. Two aspects that can be identified as especially relevant to defence policy are the concepts of 'community responsibility' and 'pragmatic realism' (Shaw, 1999). For New Labour, community responsibility is not just a domestic perspective but contains an international dimension covering such matters as crimes against humanity, for example the Kosovo crisis, terrorism, drug trafficking and, to a lesser extent, environmental damage. A recurrent theme in Blair's speeches is that to enjoy rights in the international arena the relevant actors must demonstrate the necessary responsibilities within that community. This formulation lends a strongly interventionist ideal to defence policy. When actors fail to articulate their duties, those who are able must be prepared to take the necessary steps. Although Blair's position might be characterised as projecting the United Kingdom as a 'force for good' or 'punching above our weight', it is one that potentially goes well beyond the existing trajectory of foreign policy in justifying interventionist action. New Labour's position has been governed so far by the administration's pragmatism in answering questions about the viability and necessity of any possible involvements.

From these perspectives, the strategic defence review can be portrayed as being founded on a mixture of ideological and electoral motives. In the late 1980s, Neil Kinnock buried the spectre of 1983's general election defeat. He laid much of the groundwork for the policies adopted by New Labour. In capitalising on Kinnock's work, Tony Blair has created a new alignment for the party's external outlook. It is not one built on the ideals of Keir Hardie, Sidney and Beatrice Webb, G. D. H. Cole or Richard Crossman, all of whom were firmly committed to an internationalist orientation in social democratic foreign policy. New Labour's commitments reflect the electoral and governmental situation in which policy will be developed and the dictates of Blair's vision of rights and responsibilities. New Labour has been designed as a 'catch-all' party, one that is designed to appeal to all. So too is the defence review in attempting to combine electoral preferences with the wishes of the armed services and the perceived needs of the international community.

The future is by no means certain: New Labour's leaders have projected an ambitious image of the United Kingdom as a world leader. Whether this stance can be sustained is an open question. The United Kingdom's position in global politics hinges, in part, upon the special relationship, which in turn is based largely on close personal affinities between the relevant leaders. Such affinities may not persist. In any case, whether the role projected for the United Kingdom can be sustained, given the available resources, is by no means certain. Any downturn in the currently buoyant economy would raise serious problems for funding the kind of commitments into which New Labour has entered. The issue of whether New Labour should consign the role of world leader to British posterity and adopt a less grand role in world politics may well re-emerge.

References

British–American Security Information Council (1997), *Nuclear Futures: Western European Options for Nuclear Risk Reduction* (London: British–American Security Information Council).

Conservative party (1997), *You Can Only Be Sure with the Conservatives* (London: Conservative party).

Cook, R. (1997), 'British foreign policy', statement, 12 May.

Cook, R. (1999a), Ernest Bevin memorial lecture, Rochford Hall, Lincolnshire, 22 January.

Cook, R. (1999b), speech, Labour party conference, 28 September.

FCO (1999), *The Government's Expenditure Plans 1999–00 to 2001–02*, cm. 4209 (London: TSO).

Foot, M. (1999), *Dr Strangelove, I Presume* (London: Victor Gollancz).

Gould, P. (1998), *The Unfinished Revolution: How the Modernisers Saved the Labour Party* (London: Little, Brown).

Kampfner, J. (1999), *Robin Cook: The Life and Times of Tony Blair's Most Awkward Minister* (London: Phoenix).

Kaufman, G. (1991), 'Leading the way to peace', *The Guardian*, 10 July.

Keohane, D. (1993), *Labour Party Defence Policy Since 1945* (Leicester: Leicester University Press).

Labour party (1986), *The Power to Defend Our Country* (London: Labour party).

Labour party (1989), *Meet the Challenge: Make the Change* (London: Labour party).

Labour party (1990), *Looking to the Future* (London: Labour party).

Labour party (1991), *Opportunity Britain* (London: Labour party).

Labour party (1992), *It's Time to Get Britain Working Again* (London: Labour party).

Labour party (1996a), *A Fresh Start for Britain: Labour's Strategy for Britain in the Modern World* (London: Labour party).

Labour party (1996b), *New Labour: New Life for Britain* (London: Labour party).

Labour party (1997), *New Labour Because Britain Deserves Better* (London: Labour party).

MacDonald, C. (1989), 'Changing times mean changes in the means to achieve disarmament', *Tribune*, 17 March.

McInnes, C. (1998), 'Labour's strategic defence review', *International Affairs*, vol. 74, no. 4, 823–45.

MoD (1998), *The Strategic Defence Review*, cm. 3999 (London: TSO).

MoD (1999), *Shaping the Future Together: Annual Report on Defence Activity 1997– 98* (London: TSO).

Rikihisa, M. (1991), *Labour's Nuclear Defence Policy: The Rise and Fall of Unilateralism 1945–91*, unpublished MA dissertation, University of Sheffield.

Robertson, G. (1999), transcript of press conference, MoD, London, 4 August.

Shaw, E. (1999), 'Which way New Labour?', unpublished paper for the conference New Labour: Two Years In Power, University of Birmingham, 8–9 May.

Wallace, W. (1998), 'Spent force', *The Guardian*, 9 July.

Wright, T. (1997), *Who Dares Wins: New Labour – New Politics* (London: Fabian Society).

Young, J. W. (1997), 'Foreign, defence and European affairs', in B. Brivati and T. Bale (eds), *New Labour in Power: Precedents and Prospects* (London: Routledge), 137–55.

Zilliacus, K. (1949), *Dragon's Teeth: The Background, Content and Consequences of the North Atlantic Pact* (London: Narod Press).

Zilliacus, K. (undated), *Home on the Bomb and Labour's Alternative to Genocide* (London: New Gladiator Press).

14

Reforging the 'special relationship': Blair, Clinton and foreign policy

Richard Hodder-Williams

Introduction

Reference to a 'special relationship' between the United States and the United Kingdom stems from the alliance that provided the basis for a victory over Hitler's Germany in the Second World War. Its continuing vigour has widely been associated with another war, the Cold War, between a democratic and capitalist alliance led by the United States and an authoritarian and communist alliance led by the Soviet Union (though there is a case to be made that a special relationship existed earlier; see Dobson, 1995). John Baylis reflected the views of most commentators when he argued that 'the end of the Cold War threatened to undermine the whole basis of the "special relationship" [since] the absence of a clear and identifiable enemy meant that the close military partnership which had been at the core of the "special relationship" was no longer regarded as being of such crucial importance' (1997: 223; a powerful version of this argument is Dickie, 1994).

This seemed a plausible position to hold at a time when the relations between Bill Clinton and John Major showed little sign of being special (Coker, 1992). Tensions were sparked when the United Kingdom's Conservative government helped the Republican candidate in the 1992 US presidential election. (The Home Office 'inadvertently' revealed that it had checked its files to see whether Clinton had applied for UK citizenship in an effort to avoid the draft, while he was a student at University College, Oxford.) Clinton consciously shunned the government when he made his first visit to the United Kingdom after his electoral victory, to receive an honorary degree from Oxford University. The contrast with Tony Blair was striking. Although relations with Major improved, they remained essentially workmanlike, in the way that leaders of any countries thrown together must learn to operate. By contrast, Clinton made a special visit to London soon after Tony Blair's decisive electoral victory in May 1997 and met the full cabinet. Immediately, journalists began to talk about the reforging of the 'special relationship', despite the end of the Cold War.

This chapter focuses on such a view. It needs, however, to be placed in both a historical and a conceptual framework. It is obvious that the idea of a special relationship, whether as ideal or as description, has a much wider currency in the United Kingdom than in the United States. Nevertheless, it has proved difficult, if not impossible, to examine relations between the two countries without, in the end, even the Americans having to acknowledge that there is something of significance in this 'special relationship'. When the Ditchley Foundation and the Woodrow Wilson International Center for Scholars established a collaborative series of seminars, alternately held in the United States and the United Kingdom between September 1984 and May 1985, the organisers deliberately eschewed any mention of a 'special relationship', since that focus was thought to prejudice and distort a wide-ranging debate on the contexts and actions involved in the relations between the two countries after the Second World War. But, as William Louis observed in the preface of the book to which the seminars contributed: 'Yet the idea of an intimate connection, a "Special Relationship", would not go away. Indeed it haunted the discussions. Eventually it was referred to as the ghost, ever present yet elusive, derided by some but acknowledged by all' (Louis, 1986: vii). Recognised, yet indefinable, the special relationship has much in common with Justice Potter Stewart's conception of obscenity: 'I cannot define it, but I know it when I see it' (*Jacobellis v. Ohio*, 378 US 184 (1964), 197).

This is not the place to define the indefinable, but discussion at least of some aspects of the term's usage is essential. Each relationship is special in a trivial sense. But some relations are clearly more special than others. There is no denying that there are unique characteristics that are far from trivial that distinguish the United States' relationship with, say, Israel or Canada or Japan. What we need to do is identify those unique characteristics (which are assumed, *sub silentio*, more often than not) that mark out the relationship between the United States and the United Kingdom. It is essential at the outset to stress that the concept is an evaluative tool, not a causal force. Many factors contribute to the precise nature of a relationship at any one moment and we should, therefore, expect the strength of that relationship to alter over time. There will, nevertheless, be consequences that flow from a particular relationship (of trust and understanding, for example), which will contribute to a full explanation of events. It is important, however, to see the special relationship primarily not as a causal force but as a shorthand expression to encapsulate a unique set of relationships. The literature rarely seems to conceive of the concept in this way. In an influential article Alex Danchev has developed three categories, but they relate overwhelmingly to those who write about or are active in pursuing the special relationship, rather than an evaluation of the nature and intensity of the relationship itself (Danchev, 1996).

In this chapter I take a different perspective. Relationships of any kind, when they function well, are based upon shared expectations. This is as true of nations as of individuals. The closest, the most special of relationships seem to require no words, no reminders, no pressures for the partners to operate in harmony. Each expects the other to behave in a particular way and these expectations are usually fulfilled. Because the implications behind the phrase 'special relationship' suggest something akin to familial intimacy, I conceive of it as being composed of three sets of expectations. Danchev does note, 'As in life, so in international relations: expectations are crucial' (1996: 748). However, my approach, while embracing some of his concerns for transparency, is significantly different.

The first set I have characterised as the expectation of policy agreement. This reflects one view about the 'special relationship', namely that there is a natural affinity of interest between the United States and the United Kingdom. Perhaps Winston Churchill was the classic exponent of such a view but others, on both sides of the Atlantic, have suggested that, for historical and cultural reasons, there will be a congruence of interests on the great issues of international import between the United Kingdom, as the begetter of democracy and capitalist industrialisation, and the United States, as the promulgator of modern democracy and the major capitalist industrialised nation on earth.

The second set I have characterised as the expectation of information. This reflects the habit among particularly close friends that their thoughts and plans are largely shared; they are not all shared, for there is always a degree of privacy and secrecy in even the closest of relationships, a reality that Winston Churchill found hard to accept. In the context of relations between states, there is likely to be a set of institutionalised structures that survive over time through which the parties share information. A set of bilateral arrangements, between security forces or military analysts, ensures a ready, although never complete, interchange of communications.

The third set I have characterised as the expectation of friendship. In a sense, this is tautologous when applied to relations between individuals. But in the context of international relations, where the unit of inter-relationship is usually 'the state', a depersonalised organisation with positions filled over time by different people, there can be no automatic assumption that leaders will be personally attracted. Indeed, history has shown that this expectation has not always been fulfilled and analysts have tended as a consequence to note how the special relationship under these circumstances was under some strain.

The historical analyses of special relationships as a class of international relationships can be fitted into this conceptual framework. When all three expectations are largely fulfilled, the relationship will be close and 'special'; when all three expectations are uncertain, the relationship will be weak. In this format, then, we do not need to ask what *is* the 'special relationship', expecting an answer that would cover all the vicissitudes of the relations between the two countries over the last half century or more; it acknowledges the ebb and flow, the peaks and troughs, of that relationship. One of the weaknesses of virtually all the literature on the 'special relationship' is the assumption that a definition must be able to cover, without exception, the changing relationships across many arenas for nearly sixty years. My framework enables a judgement to be made about the *degree* to which an 'ideal' is achieved.

This framework provides the basis for an exploration of the distinctiveness of the special relationship between the United States and the United Kingdom. Each set of expectations will vary in intensity and extent over time. But, taken together, the dimensions indicate an overall level of congruence in the special relationship that is closer than that for any of the United States' relations with other states. Consider the relationships between the United States and Germany or Japan, or even the United States and Israel, along each distinct dimension. They do not demonstrate the same breadth, the same intensity and the level of congruence to be found between the United States and the United Kingdom. Such extensiveness and concentration in different aspects make the relationship special. The framework also permits us to mark high and low points in the relationship. This chapter is intended to do precisely that for the period since the Labour party's electoral victory in May 1997.

The expectation of policy agreement

Policy agreement had its roots in war, hot and cold, and was most obviously, and explicitly, true of the Second World War. Harry Hopkins in 1941 was happy to quote from the Bible to reflect this unity of intentions: 'Whither thou goest, I will go, and where thou lodgest, I will lodge: thy people shall be my people, and thy God my God ... even to the end' (cited from Lord Moran by Danchev, 1996: 752).

Some observers, those more interested in actions than rhetoric, tend to argue that the congruence of behaviour is merely the obvious consequence of similarity of interests. When the interests diverge, the congruence ends. There is, in effect, therefore no special relationship. What is problematic with this view is that states other than the United Kingdom have a major interest in a world economy safe for capitalism and a commitment to the democratic project, but their relations are, over time, nowhere nearly as close.

It is, of course, easy to identify several occasions over the last fifty years when the interests of the two countries did not coincide and when this expectation was not fulfilled. Decolonisation, the Suez affair and the invasion of Grenada are examples. Of particular significance for this chapter is the early period of president Clinton's first administration. These were not happy days for the special relationship. Take just two instances. How to deal with the Bosnian crisis was a cause of deep disagreement – see the account by Raymond Seitz (1998: 327–30) of the 1993 visit by US secretary of state Warren Christopher to the United Kingdom, the career diplomat who represented the United States at the Court of St James from 1991 to 1994. The readiness to grant Gerry Adams a visa to visit the United States was deeply wounding; it 'overturned a 50-year hegemony over Irish policy that the British government had exercised through [sic] the State Department' (Guelke, 1996: 533). The special relationship need not indicate unanimity of policy positions.

The Balkans regularly led to divergences of opinion, both within Washington and London and between the two governments. Blair and Clinton have been able, for the most part, to resolve their differences. The Kosovo conflict in 1999 sparked serious behind-the-scenes tension between the two countries, especially over the use of ground troops. The feeling among Blair's aides seems to have been that Clinton was not fully engaged with the issue; Charles Grant, director of the Centre for European Reform, claimed that there had 'hardly been inspired leadership' (Godmin, 1999). Clinton was in some difficulties domestically. Senator John McCain criticised what he saw as the administration's tendency to be drawn into conflicts in the Balkans by NATO allies, without ensuring that such missions conformed to US interests; at the same time senator Dick Lugar maintained that the United States had 'a special responsibility of leadership in NATO' (Congressional Quarterly Weekly, 20 March 1999).

The two heads of government conversed regularly about their respective positions. The UK view did not prevail initially. When president Clinton sent US troops to Bosnia in 1995 as part of a NATO-led peacekeeping force, he had to convince a reluctant Congress. In June 1998, important elements within Congress were pushing him to deploy troops as part of a NATO-led force to contain ethnic violence in Kosovo. Even though Clinton's national security adviser, Samuel R. Berger, had asserted that the use of US troops was not viable, government officials indicated that they would support a UK resolution at the UN calling for the use of 'all necessary means' to end the fighting, including military force (Congressional Quarterly Weekly, 13 June 1998). The resulting NATO policy was very much a compromise agreed between the two partners in the special relationship. And, when Sir Michael Jackson, the British commander of the ground troops that were ultimately sent into Kosovo, clashed with the US supreme commander of NATO, general Wesley Clark, Clinton backed the British view.

Northern Ireland provides another example of mutual co-operation, one in which Clinton's contribution should not be underestimated. Clinton had originally seen Gerry Adams as rather akin to Nelson Mandela or Yasser Arafat, terrorist leaders who represented a potential majority and could be corralled into negotiations and peaceful solutions (Stevenson, 1996–97). His initial approach, to grant Adams a visa against British wishes and nominate ambassador Smith to Dublin, undoubtedly ruffled feathers in London. But he soon learned that his original analogy was false and that the host government needed to be appreciated. Clinton became a major and active player in the negotiations and the St Patrick's Day celebrations became a significant date in the Northern Ireland calendar. Such intimate involvement contravened the traditional understanding of the special relationship, that the issue should be left exclusively to the United Kingdom; moreover, the issue was not forced upon the White House, as involvement in the Middle East was, by the power of a domestic lobby (Evans, 1998; MacGinty, 1997).

In part, the explanation may be presented as no more than the concentration of several individual interests. Clinton sought a 'success', stymied by a Republican Congress and hounded over his affair with Monica Lewinsky; Blair sought external influence to bring Sinn Fein to the negotiating table; Gerry Adams needed his position to be legitimised. All are true. But the time Clinton spent in person in Northern Ireland itself (he need not have visited Omagh) and on the telephone to Blair (at the very time he was to go before the Grand Jury to testify about his relationship with Monica Lewinsky) was not driven by imperatives of national interest. He chose to prioritise the issue. And he did so because of the special relationship, in part to recognise Blair's loyalty to him and in part, as Sir Kenneth Bloomfield (the former head of the Northern Ireland civil service) put it, to 'remove once and for all what in the past has proved a major irritant in Anglo-American relations' (*Financial Times*, 11 April 1998).

Deciding what is 'pure' national interest and what is special relationship is difficult. Some analysts maintain that the special relationship is of minimal importance to the United States but essential to the United Kingdom, as the only way to preserve the appearance of a world power. The United Kingdom is effectively Washington's poodle. To strengthen the argument about the asymmetrical nature of the power relationship, they observe that the United Kingdom is prepared to do Washington's bidding, sometimes on occasions when it is not in the interests of the United Kingdom. This argument can be self-fulfilling. Take, for example, some of the major moments of Blair's support for Clinton's foreign policy in a context in which common interests are not immediately manifest. These would cover the military action against Iraq and the bombing of Afghanistan and Sudan in August 1998. In both cases officials within the Foreign Office had doubts about the wisdom of the rapid support. In neither case did European allies (or indeed other developed states) come quickly to the United States' cause. If it is assumed that the United Kingdom's role, epitomised by its ambivalence over Europe, is to be seen as a stalwart ally of the United States, the United Kingdom's actions are self-explanatory. But that assumption is, at the very least, questionable.

The United States, as do most states, prefers to act unilaterally; but this is increasingly impossible. Particularly in the aftermath of the Cold War, interventions have increasingly needed a moral justification and a multinational presence. The United States has had to build coalitions – in the UN on some matters, in a less structured form on others – before acquiring the legitimacy for employing its military muscle in distant lands. The first, seemingly the most natural, and the most reliable, partner has been the United Kingdom. The United States, in other words, has *needed* British assistance. This mutuality of interest is at the heart of any special relationship but it does not, and rarely does, have to involve parity. What is perhaps more striking is the readiness, at the margin when an issue has little resonance in the home capital, for one leader to identify with the policy preferences of the other and then lend what might, from a *realpolitik* perspective, be reasonably termed unnecessary support. (Support from one side in one area may, of course, be exchanged for support from the other on a different issue.) Such behaviour encapsulates the ideal of a 'special relationship'.

The points of unity have increased over the period of Clinton's presidency, most sharply after the Labour party's success in the May 1997 general election. When the enlargement of NATO was being discussed in Madrid in July 1997, president Chirac of France wanted the expansion to include not only Poland, Hungary and the Czech Republic but also Romania and Slovenia. President Clinton favoured the inclusion of fewer states. With a strong assist from Blair, he succeeded in limiting the initial round of invitees to three (*Congressional Quarterly Weekly*, 12 July 1997). The special relationship has not prevented profound, and litigated, differences on trade matters between the United States and Europe. Yet it is interesting that the sanctions imposed in Washington bore less heavily on the UK economy than might have been produced by an entirely even-handed policy. What is important about this expectation is that a *divergence* of policy causes the raised eyebrows, not the consistency.

The post-war alliance was (and is), of course, much wider than the United States and the United Kingdom; NATO involves additional states but at its heart is the especially close relationship between the United Kingdom and the United States. As NATO develops in the post-Cold War period, one of the strongest links between the United States and the United Kingdom will be put under considerable strain but, already, the two countries are trying to co-ordinate their approach. Whether the policies of the other states in the alliance were dominated by rebuilding domestic economies and societies (or protecting an integrated empire), both Washington and London felt impelled to consider, and become involved in, the management of foreign relations where they had no direct involvement.

Getting the balance right between the United Kingdom and Europe is difficult. From the London end, there are two distinct perspectives and even perhaps antagonistic ones, such that the closer one gets to one party the further one gets necessarily from the other. From Washington, the perspective is more focused, more overlapping. Margaret Thatcher never truly grasped this position. An integrated Europe, strong militarily and politically, was the ideal and the United Kingdom, it was hoped, would play a leading role both in guiding Europe towards the sort of international perspective Washington had and in linking Washington to important players in Europe. But there was, and still is, little doubt that the United Kingdom is envisaged as the major player. No other country has come forward so willingly and so quickly to support the United States in its military adventures; Blair recognised this over Iraq and deliberately, despite holding the presidency of the EU at the time, lent his immediate support to the United States. George Robertson, the defence secretary at the time, claimed bizarrely to be 'flying the European flag in the Gulf'. This reflected the crippling paralysis of much of Europe's collective policy-making. The United States needed allies and the United Kingdom leapt readily into the breach, while France was determined, as usual, not to be seen to support any policy that could be interpreted as dancing to Washington's tune. This has been an ongoing expectation. Unsurprisingly, therefore, no other country has received the sort of preferential treatment offered to the United Kingdom, epitomised perhaps by the United States offering Trident when it was its most advanced strategic nuclear system.

The closeness is not based upon a 'natural' similarity of conception of the national interest. The Second World War and the Cold War – and, perhaps, a more recent concern for political and economic stability – were likely to create a high degree of commonality. But this would apply to all capitalist liberal democracies, which are likely in any case to have a high coincidence of interests. It arises out of specific needs: the Americans for an ally where contemporary conventions require multilateral action, the United Kingdom for the military support to offset its diminished post-imperial power. (Those Eurosceptics who suggest that the United Kingdom could emulate Norway successfully forget that Norway has few aspirations to play a global role.) But this, again, could apply to other countries. The simple, but overwhelming, point is that no other country, whether a former imperial power or an aspiring international actor, enjoys such a relationship with the United States. The curve of congruence of policy agreement, although never touching the ceiling of complete agreement, is permanently higher for this ally than for any other. That is what makes it special.

The expectation of information

At the heart of the special relationship, one British ambassador to the United States has recently written, 'lay the privileged collaboration, dating from the [Second World] war, which the British enjoyed on defence, nuclear and intelligence issues' (Renwick, 1996: 272). Kissinger noted that he kept the United Kingdom better informed and more closely engaged than he did the State Department (Renwick, 1996: 275)! By the early 1950s, representatives of the CIA's Office of National Estimates worked with the British Joint Intelligence Staff on a daily basis (Aldrich, 1998: 337). US code-breakers will be found in Cheltenham at the Government Communications Headquarters, while their British counterparts appear in Langley. The FBI, the Drug Enforcement Agency and US Customs, recent arrivals within the American embassy in London, share information with their British counterparts. David Newsom has noted that the United Kingdom was always the first country to be informed of US policy decisions, a habit which did not always endear it to Europe (Newsom, 1986). Former foreign secretary Douglas

Hurd observed that the practical meaning of the 'special relationship' was that the British were involved in US thinking 'at an earlier stage than most people, and that is crucial' (cited in Baylis, 1997: 226). It did not mean, however, that the advice was followed. And there are ongoing meetings and collaborations on military matters, most obviously in the case of the two navies (Eberle, 1986).

While there has been a long and continuing tradition of sharing information, there has not been a shared interpretation of that intelligence. Indeed, most of the disagreements arising between the two countries can be traced to sharply different conclusions drawn from this information. Covert actions, to which the Americans were much more attracted than the British, were a constant source of aggravation (Aldrich, 1998). In an important sense, this epitomises a relationship between comparative equals. While there is an exchange of plans and information, each is free to act independently; in the context of the relationship between the United States and the United Kingdom, those actions are not always (although they are usually) similar.

Sharing intelligence could be a dangerous matter. The high-profile defections of British intelligence officers to the Soviet Union created noise in Washington, but it disturbed the professionals less than might be imagined. The awareness that there were defectors within the American ranks reminded both sides that this was an occupational hazard (Aldrich, 1998). The heart of the matter was that both countries needed the other's assistance. The British position is simply understood: the size and technical sophistication of the Americans are obvious. But the Americans not only respected some of the particular skills of the British, most notably in code-breaking; they were also aware of the privileged position the British intelligence had in some parts of the globe. This was manifestly the case in the People's Republic of China, where the Americans had no embassy within which to conceal operatives; but it was also true of much of the Commonwealth, especially Cyprus and Hong Kong, where British access to information was better (Grasselli, 1996: 104).

The Soviet invasion of Afghanistan provides ample evidence of the extraordinarily open sharing of secret information (Grasselli, 1996). The linkage went further than information-sharing, however. In the dying days of the Carter presidency, he decided to provide substantive support for the Mujahedin. Assistance, however, had to be covert and the principle of 'plausible deniability' had to be buttressed. The CIA turned instantly to the British secret service to help get arms into the country. Thereafter, the British were further involved. Training of Mujahedin leaders took place in the Scottish borders under the careful tutelage of the SAS. When Soviet helicopters dominated the air space and steadily destroyed the insurgents' forces, the United States turned to a British weapon, the blowpipe hand-held missile, since it was sufficiently available on the open market to disguise the central role of the CIA. It was only when that weapon proved incapable of reaching its goals that the Americans, discarding the whole principle of clandestine action, came into the open to provide stinger missiles, which ultimately proved decisive.

The Falklands War provides perhaps the most striking instance of the value of this relationship to the United Kingdom. At the beginning of the crisis, the United States sought publicly to act as a mediator between Argentina, a valued ally in its own hemisphere, and the United Kingdom. Jeanne Kirkpatrick, the US ambassador to the UN, was a firm believer in prioritising Latin American links and was openly critical of any knee-jerk support for British military activity. However, the personal intelligence networks were immediately activated and critical information fed through to London. With the British ambassador, Sir Nicholas Henderson, using his access and personal connections to obtain privileged influence within the White House, it was not long before the public face of US policy shifted from benevolent neutrality to substantive assistance (Bartlett, 1992: 154–5). Given the multidimensional nature of the foreign policy process in the United States, supportive linkages can continue at one level (normally between officials from the Foreign Office and the State Department) when disagreements occur at another (normally between the White House and Downing Street) (Grasselli, 1996: 195).

What we find, as Henry Kissinger observed, was a pattern of consultation 'so matter-of-factly intimate that it became psychologically impossible to ignore British views. There evolved a habit of meetings so regular that autonomous American action somehow came to seem to violate club rules' (1991: 90). This was an impression that ambassador Raymond Seitz shared almost two decades later. Having come to London determined not to think in terms of a 'special relationship' and acutely aware of the divergences of views and priorities between the two countries, he nevertheless observed it daily:

> For almost any diplomatic initiative in Europe, London is customarily the first port of call, and it's a rare British initiative that isn't first aired in Washington. The integration of operations and personnel between the respective military services is legendary. We exchange sensitive intelligence with each other by the bucketful. (Seitz, 1998: 337)

Even the best of friends do not share all their thoughts and all their information. But there has grown up a web of expectations that ensures a high level of shared information and a degree of trust that enables knowledge to be contained. The British were aware, for example, of what was going on in the Iran–Contra affair, but kept a discrete and loyal silence.

What has developed has been the institutionalisation of information-sharing, which is unique. The standing committees, the regular meetings within the military hierarchies and in the embassies, the assumptions of actors in the intelligence world, the informal friendships that endure over time together have created a system that outlives presidents and prime ministers. Notwithstanding the occasional failure to communicate or consult, it is this structural permanence, so hard to dismantle, that surely makes the relationship special and provides the enduring basis for its continuation.

The expectation of friendship

Much of the literature on the special relationship focuses upon prime ministers and presidents, upon Churchill and Roosevelt, upon Macmillan and Kennedy, upon Thatcher and Reagan, contrasting these personal chemistries with more troubled relations, Eden and Eisenhower, or Heath and Nixon. What caught the imagination of the media in the late 1990s was the apparent personal attraction of the two leaders, and their wives, to each other. On the American side, reference was early made to their 'much ballyhooed simpatico', while British journalists were making the same point in more restrained language (*US News & World Report*, 7 July 1997). In many ways, the two men are not very similar at all but, as politicians, they saw not only that they had problems in common but that they each had potential answers to offer.

It misses an important dimension, however, merely to focus on heads of government. Beneath them in the political hierarchy there developed a host of reinforcing personal links, which ensured that the relationships between the two countries never deteriorated too far and which were always ready to encourage a closer association. Sometimes this was at the level of secretary of state and foreign secretary. David Owen and Cyrus Vance provide perhaps the most obvious instance at this level but there have been many genuine friendships, often some quite unlikely ones, over the years (see Owen, 1992; Seitz, 1998). Robert Reich, Clinton's labor secretary, who (along with Larry Sumners, a Clinton economist) taught Ed Balls (chancellor Gordon Brown's economic adviser), is a contemporary example. Reich praised the 'intellectual excitement about public policy in London' (*Financial Times*, 11 November 1997).

The media emphasis upon heads of government and personal diplomacy has the danger that the daily working out of disagreements and establishing shared positions is downgraded. Embassies remain important places, especially in the major cities of the world. No account of the 'special relationship' would be complete without mention of the ambassadors from the two countries who played major roles not only in interpreting one country to the other but in building trust and understanding. Following the self-confident involvement of Oliver Franks, UK ambassadors to the United States Sir Oliver Wright, Ormsby-Gore (with Kennedy) and Sir Nicholas Henderson (at the time of the Falklands War) had close working relations with very senior members of the administration. Robert Renwick had built up a relationship with Clinton before he ever reached the White House (Renwick, 1999: 6). Similarly, US ambassadors have been well received in the Court of St James, especially when some of them have had direct lines to the president. This is not accidental. Within the patronage culture that colours ambassadorial appointments, presidents tend to reward with the London posting people whose judgement they have come to know personally and trust. It is no surprise, therefore, that critical negotiations concerning Northern Ireland in October 1999 should have taken place within the American embassy in London.

The linkages between London and Washington since May 1997 reflect the depth and variety of the personal connection. Blair is not an Americophile. He looks to Europe for his cultural relaxation, to France and Italy. Gordon Brown, by contrast, holidays regularly in the United States, knows many of the major political figures there and is regularly invited to chair important meetings of the International Monetary Fund (IMF) or G8. Jonathan Powell, chief of staff to the prime minister, completed an MA at the University of Pennsylvania and was posted, when in the Foreign Office, to Washington from 1991 to 1995. Somewhat surprisingly, Robin Cook and Madeleine Albright are also close and Cook, again, is asked to chair many meetings in the US secretary of state's gift. Careers regularly bring Americans to the United Kingdom, as Rhodes scholars, perhaps, or on official business, just as careers carry Britons to the United States, through Fulbright scholarships or professional associations. The policy-making and administrative elites have a great deal in common. Glance through the memoirs of recent presidents and secretaries of state in search of alternative 'special relationships' and they are noticeably absent. Although there is a major imbalance in the emphasis given to the special relationship by leaders on the different sides of the Atlantic, there is nevertheless a powerful sense of commonality that seeps out of these recollections. George Ball was conscious in the 1960s of the United Kingdom's strained circumstances and weakened economic and military power and was intellectually convinced that UK interests lay in a wholehearted involvement in the creation of a new Europe (which too close an emotive attachment to the United States harmed); but he was also convinced of a special bond between the two countries.

Such closeness is not serendipitous. It is built into the career patterns of politicians, military leaders and senior administrators. Historically based and reinvigorated by tradition (as well as conscious planning), the strength of personal associations is undoubtedly helped by a common language. With that common language, however differentially nuanced, goes a propensity to visit, to read the same books and watch the same films; so long as presidents continue to reflect the British fragment of the United States' immigrant community, the awareness of common historical ties of origin remain strong. A plethora of reinforcing factors ensure that no other country comes remotely close to the special relationship that the leading political players of the two countries have enjoyed in the past and still enjoy. This expectation is, however, the most contingent. Language will almost certainly maximise the closeness of leaders; but the heterogeneous ethnic composition of the United States will surely over time bring into leadership positions fewer and fewer individuals with direct ancestors to be sought in the United Kingdom.

Is there currently a special 'special relationship'?

In this chapter I have not been concerned with whether there is a special relationship (there unquestionably is) but with what form it currently takes.

Nor is it concerned with the normative argument about whether the interests of the United Kingdom or the United States would be better advanced through different, and less privileged, relationships. It has accepted that the special relationship is multidimensional and that it has waxed and waned over the years as its various components have been more or less strong. In short, this chapter has tried to 'take the temperature' of the special relationship in the three years since Tony Blair's Labour government took office in May 1997.

So far as the first expectation is concerned, a simple functionalist view, that policies coincide exclusively when national interests *happen* to coincide, is not fully adequate. The ending of the Cold War was not followed by an obvious dividing line that drew countries together into alliance blocs. The new threat to the nation-state could be seen partly as internally generated – the mismatch between social security expectations, the growth of an under-class and taxpayers' propensity and ability to fund them – and partly as externally generated – the tensions of an international underclass. Such a perspective drew Clinton and Blair together. The unwritten assumption of international relations in the modern age is that, except in self-defence, states do not act unilaterally. This is true even for the United States outside its hemisphere. It needs partners and allies to establish any pretence of legitimacy. (See Cox, 1995, for an account of the international and national constraints that prevent the United States, even as the sole superpower, from acting unilaterally.) The *Financial Times* suggested that it was *Clinton* who 'deliberately revived the idea of a special relationship' (6 February 1998). Hence a common interest to which Winston Churchill drew attention still exists, but it has been dramatically redefined in both form and content. The United Kingdom still counts in Washington just as it still depends upon US assistance to project its power globally.

One must not get dewy-eyed. There have been plenty of occasions when these expectations were not fulfilled. The early days of the Clinton admini-stration were quintessentially so. But the latter days have been very different. One can see this in the Balkans and in Northern Ireland. One can see it also in the way a moral dimension has permeated the rhetoric and sometimes the practice of both countries. (The North Atlantic Treaty actually speaks of 'strengthening their free institutions, by bringing about a better understanding of the principles upon which these institutions are founded'.) There is an enduring logic at work. So long as the United Kingdom wishes, in Douglas Hurd's words, to 'punch above its weight' and so long as the United States needs the cloak of multilateral support for actions outside its sovereign auth-ority, the current tendency to policy congruence will continue to be high.

The second expectation, almost by its very nature, is impossible to evaluate with confidence at this time. The papers, memoirs and recorded telephone calls (and probably reconstituted e-mails) are still to be plotted, both to clarify the sequence of actions and to weigh the relative degree of attention given to various countries (Aldrich, 1994). But somebody who had as good a view of the multiple relationships as anybody was Raymond Seitz. 'The collaboration between London and Washington', he wrote in 1998, 'does put the relationship in a league by itself ... One thing is sure: neither nation could possibly replicate the relationship with any other country' (Seitz, 1998: 337, 338). The evidence for an institutionalised privileged position is strong. If this had been de-institutionalised – if the intelligence links or the naval co-operation had been significantly reduced – it is likely that this would have seeped out into the public domain through the leaky portholes of Washington, and increasingly London, public officials.

The third expectation is the most random one. While there are clear reasons why the relationships on policy and information matters might be close over a period of time, there are no such forces undergirding a personal rapport. Indeed, unlikely friendships have been struck up. Nobody would have been very surprised if the southern Clinton with an easy sense of morality might have grated on the Scot with genuine attachment to so-called 'family values'. Similarity in age and political achievements might establish mutual admiration but it would not necessarily be sufficient to kindle human warmth. But observers from both sides of the Atlantic attest to a genuine bond of support and affection between the two heads of government. This, however, is only a partial view. What is critical is the aggregation of personal links, between the military and officials as well as politicians, and this is likely to be uniquely strong while current career patterns continue. On the curve of congruence, the personal relationship dimension is distinctly high.

The reason for the high level of overall congruence is linked directly to the nature of the three types of expectation. While they are analytically separable and indeed operate to some extent independently, they are in fact closely inter-related and they tend to converge towards congruence over a presidential or prime ministerial period of office. It is important to note, however, that the relationship does not rely on the expectation of personal friendship alone. The enduring networks of meetings and committees continue regardless of the changes of heads of government, pulling the two countries and their leaders towards accommodation. The myriad of individual fiefdoms, on both sides of the Atlantic, enabled specialist intelligence links, for example, to endure, even when disagreements were rife among the major politicians (Aldrich, 1998). In most cases, this is strengthened by a growing sense of personal trust, helped greatly by a regularity of private meetings and by a common language in which nuances and a common intellectual heritage play a major supporting role.

That, however, is not the end of the matter. One whole dimension of the relationship has barely appeared in the discussion so far. Even before Tony Blair became prime minister, US intellectuals had become fascinated both by his apparent success in shifting the ideological centre of gravity within the Labour party decisively to the centre-right and also by his own vision of a 'Third Way' (see Applebaum, 1997; Stelzer, 1996). At the same time, Blair had been fascinated by the transformation of the Democratic party by Bill Clinton and had, while in opposition, consciously and seriously sought to learn from his electoral triumphs and his success in party transformation. (Labour as a whole was fascinated by the measures used by the Democrats to re-establish themselves electorally: the party adopted many of these techniques.)

Links between the Labour party and the New Democrats go back to the early 1990s. Tony Blair paid a high-profile visit to Washington in April 1996. This visit was part of a project to sell him, and New Labour, as a party 'of the centre', with which business could do business. While much of the visit was devoted to speaking to major industrial and financial figures, he also spent time – indeed, the 'main focus' as he told reporters – in discussing solutions to problems of social and economic insecurity (*Financial Times*, 13 April 1996). Blair's own testimony had been thin to the point of non-existence on foreign and defence matters. Even when the Foreign Policy Centre was established as a think-tank, with a director drawn from New Labour's favourite think-tank Demos, it was concerned more with presentation than substance. What did interest him were the consequences of globalisation. Over the years, this became virtually an obsession.

For a year or so after Labour's victory in May 1997, top officials from both countries met to devise domestic policies that would transfer to public–private partnerships much of what the state traditionally did. This concern reflects two fundamental changes. First, it emphasises a new conception of national security and defines it, in part, in terms of the dangers facing the developed nations from unsustainable expectations for social welfare in an ageing population and from internal tensions emanating from a growing, and unintegrated, underclass. Second, it sees, for the first time, the special relationship sharing ideas and investing effort in common domestic, rather than foreign policy, issues.

The first visit when both Clinton and Blair were heads of government took place in May 1997. The symbolic event of inviting Clinton to a meeting of the cabinet was accompanied by very real progress on a shared domestic policy strategy. Officials hailed this as the start of a new chapter in the special relationship. The meeting had been requested by Washington and it was extended on the initiative of the Americans. A joint initiative on job creation was launched and this was to be advanced through their consecutive presidencies of the G8 (*Financial Times*, 30 May 1997). This was followed by a series of regular, timetabled meetings in which domestic politics were paramount.

In February 1998, a return visit was paid. This was a critical event. To some extent, the closeness of Thatcher and Reagan had owed a great deal to a common set of ideological beliefs, but the acceptance of monetarism, the rolling back of the state and privatisation was not consciously enforced after mutual intellectual discussion. There had been no structures or formal arrangements for deliberations and analyses of common policy frameworks. For Clinton and Blair, the search for a special ideology was an active and ongoing enterprise. With Blair that February were a veritable gaggle of gurus:

David Miliband from the prime minister's office, Geoff Mulgan (the founder of Demos), Gavin Davies (economic adviser from Goldman Sachs) and Professor Tony Giddens (social theorist and newly appointed director of the London School of Economics and Political Science). In September, the meeting moved up the hierarchy but repeated a US location. On this occasion, New York University hosted a seminar on the 'Third Way', to which not only Blair and Clinton came but also several social democratic leaders from Europe (with the notable exception of French prime minister Lionel Jospin). (The seminar coincided with the publication of Blair's pamphlet setting out the 'Third Way'; Blair, 1998.) This signalled both the unique nature of part of the current relationship between London and Washington, but also the determination of Blair to keep his European ties strong while simultaneously deepening his friendship with Clinton. A further meeting was held in Florence in the autumn of 1999. To some, these political links might amount to a new fourth dimension of the special relationship, one based on an expectation of ideological affinity. (A dimension that Thatcher and Reagan had hinted at but never fully realised.)

Conclusions

How, then, should we see the 'special relationship'? The first requirement is to cast away the simple Aunt Sally of Churchillian aspiration against which too much contemporary scholarship, for example Danchev (1997), takes unnecessary issue. By measuring the relationship against the ideal of Aristotle's conception of friendship, Danchev has little difficulty in showing that the special relationship cannot match what I consider to be wholly unreal expectations: to be special is not to be perfect.

We need a different approach with which to conceptualise. The special relationship is not an absolute, something that either exists or does not. It is a constantly changing sum of several parts, marked – to make it special – by the uniquely high level of congruence between the United States and United Kingdom along three dimensions. In this chapter, I have set out a framework that enables us to calibrate that relationship and I have judged that it is currently strong in the sense that scores along the three dimensions will be high. Of course, the context and agenda of the relationship have altered since the apogee of 1942; but the specialness will continue for some time and will outlive Blair. There remains a logic for this relationship at a policy level, institutionalised networks at the informational level, and career patterns and cultural affinities at the personal level. One particular aspect of the contemporary relationship, however, is likely to be relatively brief and peculiar, rather than special: after Bill Clinton has left the White House, it is highly unlikely that the regular meetings devoted to domestic policy issues and ideology will continue with such intensity. To that extent, we are currently witnessing a 'special' special relationship.

References

Aldrich, R. J. (1994), 'Never-never land and Wonderland? British and American policy on intelligence archives', *Contemporary Record*, vol. 8, no. 2, 133–50.

Aldrich, R. J. (1998),'British intelligence and the Anglo-American "special relationship" during the Cold War', *Review of International Studies*, vol. 24, no. 3, 331–51.

Applebaum, A. (1997), 'Tony Blair and the New Left', *Foreign Affairs*, vol. 76, winter issue, 45–60.

Bartlett, C. J. (1992), *'The Special Relationship': A Political History of Anglo-American Relations since 1945* (London: Longman).

Baylis, J. (ed.) (1997), *Anglo-American Relations since 1939: The Enduring Alliance* (Manchester: Manchester University Press).

Blair, T. (1998), *The Third Way: New Politics for the New Century* (London: Fabian Society).

Coker, C. (1992), 'The special relationship in the 1990s', *International Affairs*, vol. 68, no. 3, 407–22.

Cox, M. (1995), *US Foreign Policy After the Cold War* (London: Pinter for RIIA).

Danchev, A. (1996), 'On specialness', *International Affairs*, vol. 72, no. 4, 737–50.

Danchev, A. (1997), 'On friendship: Anglo-America at *fin de siecle*', *International Affairs*, vol. 73, no. 4, 747–59.

Dickie, J. (1994), *'Special' No More: Anglo-American Relations: Rhetoric and Reality* (London: Weidenfeld and Nicolson).

Dobson, A. P. (1995), *Anglo-American Relations in the Twentieth Century: Conflict and the Rise and Decline of the Superpowers* (London: Routledge).

Eberle, J. (1986), 'The military relationship', in W. R. Louis and H. Bull (eds), *The Special Relationship* (Oxford: Clarendon Press), 151–60.

Evans, E. (1998), 'The US peace initiative in Northern Ireland: a comparative analysis', *European Security*, vol. 7, summer issue, 63–77.

Godmin, J. (1999), 'Continental drift', *New Republic*, 28 June.

Grasselli, G. (1996), *British and American Responses to the Soviet Invasion of Afghanistan* (Aldershot: Dartmouth).

Guelke, A. (1996), 'The United States, Irish Americans and the Northern Ireland peace process', *International Affairs*, vol. 72, no. 4, 521–36.

Kissinger, H. (1991), *The White House Years* (London: Weidenfeld and Nicolson).

Louis, W. R. (1986), 'Preface', in W. R. Louis and H. Bull (eds), *The Special Relationship: Anglo-American Relations since 1945* (Oxford: Clarendon Press).

MacGinty, R. (1997), 'Bill Clinton and the Northern Ireland peace process', *Aussenpolitik* (English edition), vol. 48, no. 2, 237–44.

Newsom, D. (1986), 'US–British consultations: an impossible dream?', *International Affairs*, vol. 63, no. 2, 205–25.

Owen, D. (1992), *Time to Declare* (Harmondsworth: Penguin).

Renwick, R. (1996), *Fighting with Allies: America and Britain in Peace and War* (London: Macmillan).

Renwick, R. (1999), *Can the 'Special Relationship' Survive into the 21st Century?* (London: British Library).

Seitz, R. (1998), *Over Here* (London: Weidenfeld and Nicolson).

Stelzer, I. M. (1996), 'Christian socialism in Britain', *The Public Interest*, no. 124, summer issue, 3–11.

Stevenson, J. (1996–97), 'Northern Ireland: treating terrorists as statesmen', *Foreign Policy*, no. 105, winter issue, 125–40.

15

Conclusions: the ethics and the strategy of Labour's Third Way in foreign policy

Richard Little

Introduction

The aim of this book has been to provide a preliminary assessment of how UK foreign policy has evolved since May 1997 when New Labour came into office after eighteen years languishing in the political wilderness. Unsurprisingly, the contributors do not speak with a single voice. One point they do agree on, however, is that there has been an active and persistent attempt to identify 'clear blue water' between New Labour's approach to foreign policy and the measures adopted by both Conservative and Labour administrations of the past. There is much less agreement about whether talk of following a 'Third Way' and imbuing UK foreign policy with an 'ethical dimension' represents a significantly new way of approaching foreign policy. There is disagreement too about whether it has given rise, in practice, to a meaningful shift in the orientation of foreign policy. There are two difficulties in trying to adjudicate on whether or not New Labour has been successful in resetting the foreign policy compass. The first is that New Labour is still at the stage of clarifying how it intends to operationalise foreign policy. As a consequence, Dunne and Wheeler, who have produced one of the seminal discussions on the Third Way as a foreign policy strategy (Wheeler and Dunne, 1998), are required to adjust their position in their contribution in this book (chapter 4) in order to accommodate the arguments made by Blair in his Chicago speech, given during the Kosovo crisis, when he endeavoured to explain why and when force can justifiably be used for humanitarian purposes (Blair, 1999). The second difficulty is that it takes time to identify the full effects of any foreign policy and it is too soon to make any categorical judgements about whether or not New Labour will be able to chart a distinctive, new approach. Our aim, however, is not to make categorical judgements: rather it is open up this crucial area of policy for discussion.

The very claim to be re-orientating UK foreign policy, however New Labour's approach is eventually evaluated, is worthy of investigation. It is the first time since the end of the Second World War that a British government has claimed to be adopting a new kind of foreign policy. This is not to say that there have been no new developments in UK foreign policy in the past. On the contrary, it is often argued that for most of the twentieth century governments were constantly making very significant changes to foreign policy in the process of managing the United Kingdom's slow but inexorable political and economic decline. In 1945 the United Kingdom was still regarded as a Great Power; now it is seen to be a middle-ranking power. In the intervening years the country has had to accommodate to this new status. And major foreign policy adjustments have been required, as a consequence: dissolving the empire at one extreme and becoming a member of the EU at the other.

Both Labour and Conservative governments were intimately involved in the tasks of managing these dramatic changes in the United Kingdom's international position and they did so, for the most part, on a highly consensual basis. But the United Kingdom's realignment was made in the context of the Cold War, which represented an unchanging background for over forty years after 1945. The key elements of the UK response to the Cold War – membership of NATO and the development of nuclear weapons – remained the same throughout this period. Neo-realists would consider the continuity to be predictable because their theory presupposes that during the Cold War states were constrained by the bipolar structure of the international system to pursue policies that had the effect of reinforcing the structure of the system (Waltz, 1979). Foreign policy analysts, however, find this structural argument unpersuasive. They note that in the case of nuclear weapons, bipartisanship between the Conservative and Labour parties broke down and it was the electorate that ultimately ensured that the United Kingdom persisted as a nuclear state by consistently voting down the policy of unilateral nuclear disarmament propounded during the 1980s by the Labour party. In contrast to neo-realists, moreover, foreign policy analysts do not necessarily consider that Labour was pursuing an irrational strategy. What they find intriguing is the failure of the party to convince the general public that the nuclear deterrence was not a rational strategy for the United Kingdom to be following.

Neo-realist theory runs into even greater problems when attention is focused on the post-Cold War period. It predicts that key allies of the United States, such as Japan, Germany, France and the United Kingdom, should pull away from that alliance, asserting their independence now that the Russian threat has diminished (Layne, 1993). Instead, US alliances established during the Cold War have persisted into the post-Cold War era, with the United States continuing to exert considerable influence over its partners.

It is against this background that New Labour's call for the pursuit of a Third Way in foreign policy needs to be examined. In this conclusion, I reassess the idea of the Third Way in terms of continuity and change in foreign policy. Discussion of the Third Way has almost invariably been restricted to the ethical dimension of foreign policy. Undoubtedly, this aspect of New Labour's foreign policy has been thrust into the foreground. And it is this aspect that has occasioned most debate because critics of New Labour argue that the expectations raised by promises of a new 'ethical dimension' to foreign policy have not been fulfilled. But the emphasis on the 'ethical dimension' has tended to overshadow other aspects of New Labour's foreign policy associated with defence that must presumably also form part of the Third Way. Here we find much more evidence of continuity with the past and, it has been suggested by Lilleker in chapter 13, potential tension with the 'ethical dimension'. It is, I think, no accident that New Labour has chosen to highlight the 'ethical dimension' because by this means it has tended to obscure a fundamental ambiguity in New Labour's approach to foreign policy generated by the decision to maintain the nuclear deterrent.

In the next section of the chapter I explore the way in which the 'ethical dimension' of foreign policy was emphasised by New Labour and then linked to the Third Way. In the following section I go on to look at the significant elements of continuity that can be observed in New Labour's Third Way. I then re-examine the evidence that suggests that New Labour is interested in or intending to bring about fundamental change in UK foreign policy. Finally, I assess briefly the relationship between principles and pragmatism in foreign policy.

The ethical dimension of the Third Way

New Labour's conception of the Third Way was initially examined within a primarily domestic context, where it is seen to form a more acceptable economic strategy than either the new right's enthusiasm for unfettered market forces or the old left's pre-occupation with public ownership. Despite the importance attached to the idea by New Labour, however, Wickham-Jones finds it 'frustratingly elliptical and vague' (chapter 1). And, more important for our purposes, Wheeler and Dunne (1998) argue, in an early and rare systematic application of the term to international relations, that New Labour simply failed to 'think through the implications of the Third Way in foreign policy'. Vickers (chapter 2) goes further and argues that it is not readily apparent how the Third Way can be applied to foreign policy although, like Dunne and Wheeler (chapter 4), she goes on to acknowledge that an explicit link has been made between the Third Way and an ethical approach to foreign policy. As Dunne and Wheeler (chapter 4) note, however, Robin Cook had been in office for a year before making the connection.

Before exploring the Third Way, however, it is important to note how and why New Labour harnessed the ethical dimension to its approach to foreign policy. During the 1997 election scant attention was paid to either foreign or defence policy. This is not, of course, unusual. Parties generally do focus on domestic issues in elections. It meant that the announcement by Robin Cook that in future UK foreign policy was to be guided by an 'ethical dimension' was unheralded and unexpected. The announcement was given extensive publicity because it was seen to represent a significant, indeed a radical, development that could place the government at loggerheads with the Foreign Office. Despite later denials, Cook was, from the start, widely interpreted as proposing to implement 'an ethical foreign policy': expectations were immediately raised that the orientation of UK foreign policy was about to undergo a seismic shift. Although retrospectively it can be seen that many commentators over-reacted to Cook's announcement, it is significant that there was no attempt at the time to contain these reactions. Indeed, Cook invited the over-reaction by describing the announcement in terms of 'new directions'.

More astute observers recognised that Cook had made no undertaking to pursue a full-blown and transformative ethical foreign policy. As Neal Ascherson (1997) noted in the immediate wake of the election, 'Robin Cook is a prudent man. Offering hostages to fortune is not his style.' Ascherson stressed that providing an 'ethical dimension' to foreign policy was not the same as pursuing a 'moral crusade' and that, far from couching the new approach to foreign policy in terms of altruism, it was being presented in terms of 'enlightened self-interest'. Ascherson could have gone further and suggested that the idea of an 'ethical dimension' in foreign policy in practice represented no more than a particular 'spin' on New Labour's established commitment to promote human rights and good governance while regulating the sale of weapons to regimes that might use them for internal repression or international aggression. Such an outlook reflected a long-established desire within sections of the party to promote a moral foreign policy. The only surprise was to see this feature expressed so explicitly when the party was in office rather than in opposition (Vickers, chapter 2).

Despite Ascherson's reference to Cook's prudence, the announcement of an 'ethical dimension' to foreign policy proved to be a hostage to fortune. Wickham-Jones (chapter 6) suggests that the initiative had a political objective – that of maintaining Cook's profile within the party. But it is unlikely that he could have launched such a policy without either the approval of the prime minister or the agreement of Labour's spin doctors. All must have accepted that it was possible and desirable to sell foreign policy in ethical terms. Of course, the mission statement itself (FCO, 1997) is open to interpretation and it may be that Downing Street came to disagree with the spin placed by Cook on the document (and the fanfare that surrounded the launch), rather than the contents.

Nevertheless, it is far from clear that Labour's decision was just a consequence of election euphoria. There were two good reasons for highlighting foreign policy in ethical terms. First, it helped to assuage the feelings of those in the electorate who were deeply unhappy about the retention of nuclear weapons. Although the government was committed to a fundamental defence review, New Labour had agreed to maintain the nuclear deterrent. Second, there were good reasons for thinking that the public would welcome the spin. As Ascherson noted, there has been a sea-change in the opinions of the general populace, with public support ebbing away from a *realpolitik* and nationalistic approach to foreign policy and flowing towards one that expressed solidarity with other people in the world. By promoting an 'ethical dimension' to UK foreign policy, therefore, New Labour could also fortuitously strengthen its own domestic political position.

Perhaps the best evidence for this supposition was the scale of Labour's electoral victory. Of course, it was seen to be a product of confidence in New Labour as a responsible party, but no one doubted that its scale demonstrated a deep-seated disaffection with both the image and policies of the outgoing Conservative government. The nature of the problem was illustrated a year before Labour's victory by the response to the report published by Sir Richard Scott into the arms-to-Iraq affair. Intimations of the Conservatives' crushing defeat were foreshadowed in comments made at the time in the broadsheets. *The Independent* (16 February 1996: 18), for example, described the report as 'damning' and it observed that the Conservatives had 'grown so complacent by their years in power that they regard the electorate as a hostile force that can be easily duped'. The report made it clear that although Foreign Office officials had warned ministers that they were licensing British machine tools that could assist Iraq's nuclear programme, members of the government had 'deliberately' withheld this information from parliament and that the 'over-riding and determinative reason was fear of strong public opposition' (cited in Robertson, 1996).

Highlighting the ethical dimension of foreign policy provided a distinction between the way the Conservatives had conducted foreign policy and the way that New Labour intended to do so. Foreign policy was one area where New Labour could, with relative ease, distance itself from the policies of the former government. But this move could be effective only if, eventually, significant policy differences were opened up. Detailed analyses in some of the earlier chapters express serious doubts about whether the present signs on this score are at all promising. Miller (chapter 11) concludes that an investigation of the United Kingdom's policy towards Iran does not reveal 'any modification of policy in pursuit of human rights'. Bourne and Cini (chapter 10) demonstrate that although New Labour committed itself to an 'ethical dimension' through its membership in international organisations, there is 'no evidence to support the view that the UK government used human rights as a hook upon which to hang its European policy'. Cooper (chapter 9) reaches a similar conclusion after an investigation of New Labour's arms sales policy, which he finds 'little different from the ethically challenged approach of [Labour's] Conservative predecessors'. After a year in office, Ann Clwyd, a Labour MP, made a similar assessment. She argued that the arms trade 'continues with only limited regard for the effects it has in increasing violence or the impact on human rights'. She saw Indonesia as a fundamental case and concluded that the government had failed the test; 'not a lot has changed' (Sengupta, 1998).

Critics insist, moreover, that the manner in which New Labour has associated the 'ethical dimension' with the Third Way actively discourages any significant changes in policy. Cook explicitly identified the Third Way with a policy of 'constructive engagement' around the globe in order to promote reform. It is argued that 'Long-term engagement provides the best means to secure change', so that the United Kingdom must 'seek dialogue on the observance of human rights wherever we have cause for concern' (cited in Miller, chapter 11). Dialogue is postulated as a Third Way between 'kow-towing' to another regime and 'rowing'. Miller argues, however, that the effect of such a strategy is business as usual, with the Third Way sanctioning the extremely sanguine belief in a 'dual-purpose strategy' that makes it possible to further 'human rights for others while furthering prosperity at home'. Cooper (chapter 9) demonstrates that New Labour's response to arms sales has remarkably similar consequences, with the language in policy documents suggesting 'a largely permissive attitude to UK arms exports'. Buller and Harrison (chapter 5) make a similar point when countering Wheeler and Dunne's (1998) argument about the impact of New Labour's change of rhetoric.

From Cooper's perspective, moreover, the capacity to implement a more effective strategy to regulate arms sales has largely been undermined by the forces of globalisation. But this is not the implication that New Labour has drawn from the growth of globalisation. In New Labour's outlook, globalisation means that it is no longer possible for any state to pursue a wholly independent foreign policy that fails to take account of what is happening to others. Economic and environmental problems in one corner of the world, for example, are now seen to have consequences that spread inexorably across the globe. It is in the long-term interest of us all, therefore, to acknowledge that we are part of an international community and to frame our foreign policy accordingly. As Ascherson (1997) noted, soon after New Labour came into office, it is this perspective that encourages a belief in the importance of enlightened self-interest. This idea underpinned Gareth Evans' argument that Australia had a vested interest in becoming 'a good international citizen'. Dunne and Wheeler, Vickers, and Buller and Harrison all consider this idea to be central to New Labour's Third Way. As Buller and Harrison (chapter 5) observe, the idea of the 'good international citizen' rejects the traditional dualism between national self-interest and a collective international interest that underpins the familiar debate between realism and idealism. But if we accept Cooper's point, then globalisation needs to be seen as a Janus-faced concept. It may well have created an environment where it is easier, in practice, for Iraq, for example, to acquire the necessary machine tools to produce nuclear weapons but, at the same time, the forces of globalisation ensure that such an outcome is not in anyone's self-interest. Dialogue can help, presumably, to promote an awareness of enlightened self-interest. The difficulty with this line of argument, as Miller makes clear, is that it encourages the erroneous belief that an ethical foreign policy can be cost-free. It is difficult, however, to contest the argument that human rights and ethical arms export policies that do not entail costs become indistinguishable from the absence of such policies. New Labour's critics fear that the change of rhetoric from national self-interest to ethical and enlightened self-interest has not resulted in any practical changes in policy. Below, I draw a balance sheet that attempts to assess whether New Labour has, in fact, redirected UK foreign policy.

The strategic dimension of the Third Way

Within weeks of announcing that UK foreign policy would now embrace an 'ethical dimension', the new government also launched its promised review of UK defence policy. The initial signs were that this would be the most fundamental review that any government had undertaken since that of 1966 which led Denis Healey, the then defence secretary, to eliminate UK commitments 'East of Suez'. George Robertson, New Labour's new defence secretary, insisted that the review was not a cost-cutting exercise: it provided an opportunity for building a national consensus around defence that would make it possible for the United Kingdom to pursue its future role in the world (Bellamy, 1997).

There has been surprisingly little debate about the United Kingdom's role in the world since the end of the Second World War. The starting point has always been Churchill's speech to the Conservative party conference in 1948, when he argued that the United Kingdom was located at the 'point of conjunction' of three interlocking circles that described global, Atlantic and European relationships (cited in Shlaim, 1975). Dean Acheson, a US secretary of state, generated a much less flattering image in 1962 when he suggested that the United Kingdom had 'lost an empire and has not yet found a role' (*Keesing's Contemporary Archives*, 1963–64: 19181). New Labour acknowledges that 'Acheson's barb', as Blair calls it, struck home at that time, with successive generations of politicians endeavouring, but without success, to formulate a new role for the United Kingdom (Wickham-Jones, chapter 1). Blair went on to argue that there is no point in hankering after a superpower role and that there will always be distinct limits to what the United Kingdom can do in the international arena. But he insisted that the United Kingdom does still have what he refers to as a 'pivotal role' because of the strength of its relations with Europe and the United States. As he put it: 'We are stronger with the US because of our strength in Europe and we are stronger in Europe because of our strength in the US' (cited in Vickers, chapter 2).

In developing this conception of the United Kingdom's pivotal role, Blair did not reflect upon the obvious commonalities with Churchill's assessment of UK foreign policy made fifty years earlier. Churchill failed, Blair claimed, to find a role for the United Kingdom in his three interlocking circles. Yet there is less than a hair's breadth separating Blair's 'pivot' from Churchill's 'point of conjunction'. In both images the United Kingdom has the potential to co-ordinate the actions of two of the crucial centres of world power – Europe and the United States. Less clear is whether there is or ever has been any substance to these images. Blair clearly thinks that the potential contained in the image has not been realised and to play this pivotal role, he insists, involves 'charting a new course for British foreign policy' (cited by Wickham-Jones, chapter 1). Quite what such recharting involves is much less apparent. Hodder-Williams (chapter 14) suggests that ever since the Second World War there has been something 'special' about Anglo-American relations and that this is reflected in the expectations of friendship and the way that the relationship is structured by embedded organisational and linguistic links.

But it is by no means obvious either that the United States needs an intermediary to co-ordinate relations with Europe or, if it does, that the United Kingdom represents the natural choice. After all, the United States has close and long-standing links with Germany and it could well see that country playing a more effective pivotal role than the United Kingdom.

One area where the United Kingdom does have a comparative advantage over Germany, however, is in defence. There is no doubt that New Labour has ascribed considerable importance to its strategic defence review. The government was determined that whatever changes were made as a consequence of it should be 'foreign policy led', so that the United Kingdom could be 'a force for good in the world' (Lilleker, chapter 13; McInnes, 1998). In assessing the strategic defence review, however, Lilleker insists that it 'represents a continuation of tradition and consensus'. McInnes agrees, arguing that key assumptions about British defence were left unchallenged, so ensuring 'continuity with previous Conservative policies'. It was taken for granted that the United Kingdom's armed forces would be sufficient to guarantee that the country could play a leading role in world politics. In particular, it was acknowledged that the United Kingdom must retain its nuclear deterrent, preserve the centrality of NATO in its defence posture and maintain the strength of its conventional forces. Because these issues were not open to discussion the scope of the debate was severely circumscribed.

The scale of continuity is not, of course, surprising, particularly on the issue of nuclear weapons. Labour had come to the conclusion in the late 1980s that attempting to challenge the United Kingdom's defence posture in any radical way was to invite electoral suicide. Blair made his position on nuclear weapons unequivocal, insisting that any national leader must 'envisage circumstances in which your nuclear deterrent can be used' (Lilleker, chapter 13). The importance attached to the use of conventional weapons also remains unquestioned and it can be argued that this combined posture poses problems for the ethical dimension of the Third Way.

Evidence of change

Critics of New Labour's foreign policy have argued that the government has been long on rhetoric and rather short on the delivery of any significant foreign policy changes. As a consequence, it is argued that there is much more evidence of continuity than change in the United Kingdom's foreign policy orientation. Theakston (chapter 7) suggests that this represents a familiar pattern because politicians in opposition often fail to anticipate the constraints that exist in the foreign policy arena. Hewitt and Wickham-Jones (chapter 12) provide an excellent illustration. While in opposition, members of the Labour party succeeded in getting Kashmir on to the party's political agenda. By the time New Labour came into office it had a commitment to self-determination for Kashmir. The position not only reflected a one-sided assessment of a complex situation but it also led to a serious deterioration in relations with India that quickly forced the government to abandon the policy.

It is easier to make the argument in favour of continuity than change at this stage because evidence of substantial change usually takes time to emerge. New Labour acknowledges that a permanent transformation may require the creation of new institutions and the transformation of old ones. The DFID with Clare Short as the secretary of state was formed in order to foster Labour's intention to introduce policies that would eventually eliminate international poverty. But it is recognised that are no quick or easy solutions to the problem of poverty, though Short did indicate when the DFID was established that she hoped that 'within 25 to 30 years both the aid programme and my department will be closed down because our basic task has been accomplished' (Crawshaw, 1997). Transforming established bureaucracies is also seen to be significant: Theakston notes that in the past Labour governments 'have usually been institutionally conservative' and they have been reluctant, in particular, to contemplate a radical overhaul of the diplomatic service. But he believes that Cook has been willing to grasp this particular nettle and that, whatever the fate of ethical foreign policy, he is likely to succeed in ensuring that the Foreign Office is 'up to date, well managed, efficient and properly resourced' (Theakston, chapter 7).

But to introduce a radical shift in foreign policy requires more than institutional change within the Foreign Office. There is increased sensitivity to the impact that bureaucratic politics (Allison, 1971) can have on attempts to pursue a consistent and coherent foreign policy. Inter-departmental conflicts can frequently stand in the way of change and reform. Wickham-Jones (chapter 1) details disagreements, for example, between Cook and the DTI over the question of arms sales. Cook eventually succeeded in having arms to Indonesia suspended in September 1999, but only because the United Kingdom was, by that stage, out of step with the rest of the international community. Promoting exports has been given priority in the United Kingdom for many years and it is inevitable that there will be considerable institutional resistance to policies that require the systematic imposition of restrictions on trade. This is only an illustration of a more general problem whereby attempts to introduce change in one area of government get systematically blocked by other sectors of government. As Theakston notes, this problem highlights the need for 'joined up foreign policy', a concept that draws on the now familiar idea of 'joined up government' (chapter 7).

Institutional resistance to change can certainly help to explain why it may take some time for clear-cut evidence of a reformed foreign policy to emerge. But friction of this kind is also being reinforced by a general policy to use the promise of British reforms to help bring about multilateral reform. Such a strategy reverses the Labour party conviction in the 1980s that the United Kingdom should carry out a policy of unilateral disarmament. By the end of the 1980s, the party had shifted ground and acknowledged that there was no point in giving up something without receiving anything in return. Now New Labour is committed to the position that the United Kingdom will renounce nuclear weapons only in the context of a comprehensive and all-encompassing multilateral disarmament agreement. The logic of this position has been generalised. Clare Short, for example, who is known to be very opposed to the principle of 'tied aid' (requiring an aid recipient to use the aid to purchase goods from the aid donor), is nevertheless committed to the position that the United Kingdom will move away from such a principle only on a multilateral basis. New Labour is pushing for a multilateral deal on tied aid, but progress on this front is proving difficult. A plan put to the OECD countries at the end of 1999 to 'untie' aid failed because both France and Japan refused to sign up. A spokesperson for DFID said afterwards, 'Personally Ms Short is very much against tied aid but she knows it is no good doing something unilaterally and by their very nature multi-lateral arrangements take time' (Carr-Brown, 1999). A similar approach has been taken to arms sales in the development of the European code of conduct.

New Labour has acknowledged that unilateral initiatives can sometimes be used in conjunction with more extensive multilateral moves. Gordon Brown, the chancellor of the exchequer, developed this argument in the context of his decision in December 1999 to write off the debt incurred on bilateral loans made by the United Kingdom to forty-one of the poorest countries in the world. It is a relatively modest gesture, amounting to only £640 million to be realised over a twenty-year period, but it builds on a multilateral agreement brokered through the IMF and the World Bank that has established a target of ninety per cent debt relief. In announcing the unilateral move, Brown argued that 'Britain has played a leading part in securing a multilateral deal on debt relief that will reduce these debts by two-thirds. The time is now right to take the extra step on our own and to lift the burden of the remaining debt to us'. He went on to argue that 'This is a pledge with a purpose, because we want other states to follow our lead' (Schaefer, 1999: 10). Leaders of NGOs that have been pushing governments for some time to waive third world debt put a rather different spin on the move. A spokesman for the coalition that launched the Jubilee 2000 campaign argued that Gordon Brown 'knew his announcement would tap into public opinion. Debt is quite a difficult issue, but it's become a popular issue and politicians must respond' (*The Independent*, 19 December 1999: 13). This line of argument, however, corresponds to New Labour's belief that there is a widespread popular desire to see the introduction of an ethical foreign policy.

Principles and pragmatism

A recent analysis argues that, although it is generally assumed that UK foreign policy since the end of the Second World War has been designed to promote peace, democracy, human rights and economic development in the third world, in fact its central features included 'brutal military interventions, large-scale abuse of human rights, and opposition to economic development benefiting the poor' (Curtis, 1995: 1, 6). It is impossible to deny that there is a widespread tendency to view the United Kingdom as a benevolent state and to overlook some of devastating consequences of UK foreign policy for third world countries. It is much more debateable whether, as Curtis suggests, some of the highly undesirable outcomes were deliberately intended. However, what we should not be willing to entertain, Michael Doyle (chapter 3) argues, is the idea that foreign policy is conducted in a milieu that renders it either unnecessary or inappropriate to embrace an ethical dimension when making foreign policy decisions. New Labour has unequivocally acknowledged the validity of this position: it is taken for granted that the United Kingdom should not abuse human rights, prohibit economic development or engage in brutal military interventions. Such actions would be without any doubt unethical. Indeed, for New Labour the ethical problem is the second-order one of how far the United Kingdom should be responsible for preventing the abuse of human rights carried out by other states or promoting their economic development. The Third Way is premised on the assumption that it is necessary to carve a route between the extremes of indifference to the plight of others and a moral crusade to put the wrongs of the world to right.

So far, however, New Labour has failed to establish a consistent and coherent approach to this task. In Kosovo, Blair took the moral high ground, his rhetoric proclaiming a crusade; elsewhere critics have claimed Labour has been slow to act, if not indifferent. As Dunne and Wheeler demonstrate (chapter 4), pursuing a policy of dialogue or engagement with Indonesia rather than withholding military equipment failed to achieve the objective of protecting human rights in East Timor. On the contrary, the weapons were used to suppress the East Timorese. If the aim was genuinely to improve the situation, then the best that can be said of the policy was that it was self-defeating. Dunne and Wheeler respond more favourably to New Labour's response to the Kosovo crisis and acknowledge that Blair's checklist of five 'new rules' opens the way to establishing a Third Way on humanitarian intervention. But the rules are both too narrow and too wide. They are too narrow because Blair indicates that the United Kingdom should be prepared to resort to force only when our national interests are at stake. This argument suggests that the United Kingdom would not be prepared to bear any unnecessary costs in the pursuit of international justice. Dunne and Wheeler imply that this position is unacceptable. But they also argue that Blair fails to accommodate the idea of proportionality, which is central to any discussion of a just war. Doyle (chapter 3) and Bartlett (chapter 8) agree. The problem with this provision is that we can count the costs of war only after the fighting is over. Doyle indicates that although the United States endeavoured to minimise the costs incurred by the Serb population, these costs are proving to be very much higher than was ever envisaged.

It is possible to query Dunne and Wheeler's belief that problems associated with the ethics of foreign policy can be resolved by means of a more explicit conceptual framework. More explicit principles do not resolve the ambiguity and uncertainty that so often bedevil foreign policy and one perceptive observer has been led to conclude that 'the unqualified identification of principled behaviour with morality requires sceptical appraisal' (Claude, 1993: 219). Moral crusades (and it is possible to view the NATO response to Kosovo in this light) do not necessarily bring about moral outcomes. Gladstone is often regarded as the last British statesmen to have conducted UK foreign policy as a moral crusade and far from enhancing his reputation it led Disraeli to taunt that he was 'inebriated with the exuberance of his own verbosity' (cited in Jenkins, 1997: 405). Vickers (chapter 2) suggests that Harold Wilson suffered from a similar weakness. The war over Kosovo illustrates very clearly that principles need to be balanced with both prudence and pragmatism.

References

Allison, G. T. (1971), *The Essence of Decision* (New York: Addison-Wesley).

Ascherson, N. (1997), 'After 18 years of national egoism, the world has a chance to like us again', *The Independent*, 1 June, 22.

Bellamy, C. (1997), 'Biggest defence review for decades', *The Independent*, 29 May, 6.

Blair, T. (1999), 'The doctrine of the international community', speech, Economic Club of Chicago, United States, 22 April.

Carr-Brown, J. (1999), 'Buy British if you want aid, Short tells world's poor', *The Independent*, 19 December, 11.

Claude, I. L. (1993), 'The tension between principle and pragmatism in international relations', *Review of International Studies*, vol. 19, no. 3, 215–26.

Crawshaw, S. (1997), 'Short spells out mission to cut poverty', *The Independent*, 29 May, 6.

Curtis, M. (1995), *The Ambiguities of Power: British Foreign Policy since 1945* (London: Zed Books).

FCO (1997), 'Mission statement', 12 May.

Jenkins, R. (1997), *Gladstone* (Basingstoke: Macmillan).

Layne, C. (1993), 'The unipolar illusion: why new great powers will rise', *International Security*, vol. 17, no. 4, 5–51.

McInnes, C. (1998), 'Labour's strategic defence review', *International Affairs*, vol. 74, no. 4, 823–46.

Robertson, G. (1996), 'Ministers must be sacked', *The Independent*, 16 February, 19.

Schaefer, S. (1999), 'Brown challenges West to write-off poor nation loans', *The Independent*, 22 December, 10.

Sengupta, K. (1998), 'Cook takes ethical Third Way on policy', *The Independent*, 22 April, 8.

Shlaim, A. (1975), 'Britain's quest for a world role', *International Relations*, May, 835–56.

Waltz, K. N. (1979), *Theory of International Politics* (New York: Random House).

Wheeler, N. J. and Dunne, T. (1998), 'Good international citizenship: a Third Way for British foreign policy', *International Affairs*, vol. 74, no. 4, 847–70.

Appendix

A chronology of Labour's foreign policy, 1983–2000

Igor Cusack

1983

June
9 At the general election the Conservatives are re-elected with a majority of 144 seats. Labour, under Michael Foot, wins 209 seats. Tony Blair is first elected to the Commons.

October
2 Neil Kinnock is elected leader and Roy Hattersley deputy leader by the electoral college at the Labour party conference.
22 Kinnock speaks at CND anti-cruise missile rally in London.

November
8 Kinnock warns that British lives will be put at risk if the United States retaliates for the bomb attack on marines in Beirut.
14 First cruise missiles arrive at Greenham Common.

December
6 Kinnock urges withdrawal of British troops from Lebanon.

1984

January
5 Kinnock, on an official visit to Greece, promises the Greek culture minister that the Elgin marbles will be returned to Greece if Labour comes to power.

February
13 In Washington Kinnock criticises US policy in Latin America, telling George Shultz, US secretary of state, that the United States was supporting 'government by death-squad in El Salvador'. Meets president Reagan and discusses Labour policy on cruise and Trident missiles.

May

1 Kinnock calls for independent inquiry following the shooting of a policewoman in London from Libyan People's Bureau in April.

October

3 Labour conference endorses NEC statement on defence committing a Labour government to 'effective non-nuclear defence' within NATO. Conference calls for the removal of US nuclear bases and weapons from the United Kingdom.

November

26 Kinnock visits Moscow to discuss Soviet intentions on arms talks. He is told by president Chernenko that Russia is ready to talk to the United States without preconditions and will reduce missiles proportionately to unilateral reductions by the United Kingdom.

1985

January

6 Kinnock is critical of US policy at the start of a tour of Central America, which includes the inauguration of Daniel Ortega, Nicaraguan president, and a meeting with Fidel Castro.

7 Press reports that Kinnock is angry over the slow response of the Soviets on thirty human rights cases raised during his visit to the Soviet Union.

March

6 Kinnock reaffirms commitment to NATO and a non-nuclear policy during a visit to NATO headquarters, Brussels. He expresses hostility to 'star wars' technology research but notes that the United States is 'a cherished and permanent ally'.

July

30 Kinnock, in Nairobi at the end of an eleven-day visit to Africa, promises increased aid under a Labour government.

August

16 Kinnock urges the United States and United Kingdom to introduce tough sanctions against South Africa.

September

18 At a meeting with the Argentine president in Paris, Kinnock says he is willing to have open talks over the Falklands Islands, but stresses the importance of the wishes of the islanders. He is criticised by Margaret Thatcher for holding the meeting.

October
1 At the party conference Kinnock quotes field marshal Lord Carver that
   the United Kingdom should give priority to 'our conventional forces ...
   not delusions of nuclear grandeur'.

1986

March
15 Kinnock criticises the US air raid on Libya, which included planes based
    in the United Kingdom.

May
27 Kinnock, in Chandigarh in India, urges more joint action between the
    UK and Indian governments to deal with Sikh extremism.

September
23 On the BBC's *Panorama* programme, Casper Weinberger, US defence secret-
    ary, states that Labour's defence policy would mean the break-up of
    NATO. Denis Healey, Labour's foreign affairs spokesperson, hints that US
    bases might be able to remain in the United Kingdom.
30 At the party conference Kinnock insists he is still a unilateralist: 'I would
    fight and die for my country, but I tell you I would never let my country
    die for me'. He insists that president Reagan is wrong to arm the Contra
    forces in Nicaragua and calls for tough sanctions against South Africa.

December
1 On a visit to the United States, Kinnock calls on the UK government to
   ban America's Poseidon submarines in response to president Reagan
   breaching SALT 2 by arming B52 bombers with cruise missiles.
10 Labour launches the document *Modern Britain in the Modern World: The
    Power to Defend Our Country*. It reaffirms unilateralism. Savings from the
    abandonment of nuclear defence would be spent on conventional forces.

1987

March
26 Kinnock begins a 'disastrous' visit to the United States. He describes the
    Thatcher government as a 'poodle' in its relationship with the United States.
28 Kinnock sees Reagan at the White House for less than the allotted half
    hour and the president's staff give a dismissive press briefing. The president
    says Labour's defence policy would seriously damage NATO and undercut
    'our' negotiating position in Geneva. Reagan mistakes Healey for the
    British ambassador.

May

25 Kinnock gives a television interview with David Frost that exposes some implications of the non-nuclear defence policy, including a suggestion of 'guerrilla warfare' against an occupying Soviet force.

June

11 General election. Conservatives returned with a majority of 102 seats. Labour wins 229 seats.

July

21 The United Kingdom is ready to 'reflag' Kuwaiti oil tankers in the Persian Gulf to protect them during the Iran–Iraq war. Gerald Kaufman, foreign affairs spokesperson, warns of the grave and incalculable consequences of such action.

September

27 A wide-ranging policy review is launched at the Labour party conference, including defence and foreign affairs.

1988

May

11 At a Socialist International meeting in Madrid, Kinnock calls for NATO to declare a 'no first use' policy on nuclear weapons.

June

 5 Kinnock gives a confusing interview to the BBC that is widely interpreted as a change in defence policy. He says there is no need for 'something-for-nothing' unilateralism.

14 Denzil Davies, defence spokesperson, resigns in protest at Kinnock not keeping him informed about policy changes.

20 Kinnock tells *The Independent* that he remains a unilateralist – he 'stands by pledge to scrap Polaris and Trident on coming to power'.

July

 7 Kinnock leaves for an eleven-day tour of front-line states, where he presses for comprehensive sanctions against South Africa.

17 Kinnock's party held at gun-point in Zimbabwe after plane lands at wrong airport on return from Mozambique.

18 Iran agrees to cease-fire in Gulf War.

October

 4 Kinnock's speech to the Labour party conference is pro-European and opens doors to a change in policy, speaking of the need to be 'serious' about defence.

6 Conference votes for a commitment to unilateral disarmament by a large majority.

1989

January
31 Publication of the Fabian pamphlet *Working for Common Security*, presenting the case for multilateralism.

February
 3 Kaufman returns from Moscow with the party's defence review team, which had explored bilateral and multilateral defence options with the Soviets.
 9 In an interview Kinnock confirms that Labour's unilateralist policy would be dropped at the next general election. It is seen as the first clear break with unilateralism.
14 Armed guards are provided to Salman Rushdie after the Ayatollah Khomeini, the Iranian leader, urges Muslims to kill him in response to the publication of *The Satanic Verses*.

April
 8 Kinnock tells Kaufman that he accepts the report abandoning unilateralism.

May
 9 Meeting of Labour's NEC agrees policy review. Kinnock firmly rejects unilateralism. Polaris and Trident missiles would be put into the START 2 disarmament talks.
18 *Meet the Challenge, Make the Change: A New Agenda for Britain* is published. Unilateralism is abandoned.

June
15 In the European elections Labour wins forty-five out of the seventy-eight seats – its first nationwide election win since 1974.
22 Following the violent suppression of the pro-democracy student demonstrators in Tiananmen Square, China executes more people for pro-democracy protests; the Thatcher government refuses Kinnock's proposal to implement economic sanctions.

July
23 The *Sunday Times* reports that Kinnock has secretly met with Salman Rushdie at Michael Foot's house. Kinnock, in response to criticism by Keith Vaz, MP (who was concerned that the controversy was generating feelings against ethnic minorities), is reported as saying that he did not know that Rushdie was going to be there. Kinnock regrets the offence caused to Muslims but defends Rushdie's right to publish.

October
2 Unilateralist motion defeated at the Labour party conference with over sixty per cent of the vote.

November
10 Demolition of the Berlin Wall begins. This is later seen as a symbol of the end of the Cold War.

1990

May
24 Launch of a campaign document, *Looking to the Future*. Labour promises to play an active role in achieving a deeper and wider EU and supports arms diversification.

July
17 Kinnock welcomes the thawing of White House hostilities as president Bush expresses confidence that the special relationship between the two countries would continue if Labour came to power.

August
2 Iraq invades Kuwait.

September
6 In the Commons, Kinnock stresses that the UN, not the United States, must be supported in the Gulf crisis. This 'must be a victory for the international community'.

October
3 Kinnock disowns a Labour party conference resolution calling for deep cuts in defence. He says that Labour's policy would remain to seek gradual reductions in defence spending in step with multilateral arms negotiations.
4 Kinnock says that if force is needed to implement the UN resolution on the Iraqi seizure of Kuwait then Labour will not demur.

November
22 Margaret Thatcher resigns following her poor showing against the leadership challenge made by Michael Heseltine.
28 John Major becomes prime minister.
29 Speaking at the North Atlantic Assembly, Kinnock backs the UN resolution authorising the use of force to expel Iraq from Kuwait. He says that even Saddam in 'his cocoon of tyranny' would understand the implications of the resolution setting a deadline of 15 January.

1991

January

15 Kinnock argues for more time for sanctions and the naval blockade against Iraq to work but accepts that force may have to be used.

21 Labour backs the Conservatives in their refusal to contemplate a cease-fire to allow time for talks on a peace settlement. Kinnock argues that when Iraqi aggression had been reversed, the international community should return with renewed vigour to resolving the wider problems of the Middle East.

February

28 Kinnock stresses that the victory of the allies in the Gulf War has enhanced the authority of the UN.

1992

April

9 Conservatives under John Major win the general election with a majority of twenty-one seats. Labour wins 271 seats.

13 Kinnock resigns as Labour party leader.

May

29 John Smith, favourite to win the party leadership, stresses his personal commitment to development as a priority in foreign policy: 'development should be promoted on ethical grounds'.

July

18 Smith elected Labour party leader.

August

19 Smith supports the Major government's decision to send 1,800 troops to Bosnia.

November

4 Bill Clinton elected US president.

9 The Matrix Churchill executives, who had been accused of illegally exporting arms-making equipment to Iraq, are acquitted as the prosecution case at their trial collapses. Labour MPs demand a judicial enquiry.

December

15 In the Commons, Smith presses the prime minister, John Major, to join the United States and France in pressing for a new UN resolution to allow the use of military force to halt flights of Serbian military aircraft over Bosnia.

1993

April

21 Labour MPs back the party leadership's call for air strikes on Serbian supply and communications lines in Bosnia. Fifty MPs urge the UN to issue an ultimatum to the Serbs and if necessary take decisive military action.

29 Jack Cunningham, shadow foreign secretary, welcomes the tightening of sanctions against Serbia and repeats Smith's support for air strikes.

June

27 Foreign affairs spokesperson George Robertson expresses 'grave doubts' about the US missile attack on Baghdad: any action against Iraq should be governed by the UN.

November

 6 Smith signs the European Socialists' manifesto for the next European elections, including support for a common immigration policy and a single currency that all member states can join.

1994

May

12 Death of John Smith.

June

 9 Labour wins landslide in European elections with sixty-two seats; Conservatives take eighteen.

July

21 Tony Blair elected Labour leader.

October

20 Robin Cook appointed shadow foreign secretary.

1995

January

30 Press reports of Cook's intention to set out a fresh approach to foreign affairs by focusing on five main issues: reforms of international organisations like the IMF; agreements to resolve environmental problems; reform of the UN so that there are sufficient troops for peacekeeping; shake-up of Foreign Office to give support to British industry; and finally reform of the EU.

March

29 Cook scorns the government's vision of a global role for the United Kingdom as a substitute for a strong relationship with its continental partners.

April

5 At a speech at Chatham House, Blair urges enthusiastic UK participation in the EU.

May

31 Labour front bench give full support to the government's decision to send 6,000 troops to Bosnia. There is widespread unease among backbench Tory MPs.

July

20 Labour broadly supports the government's handling of the UN safe-haven crisis in Bosnia and argues against the withdrawal of troops unless military commanders say it is too dangerous.

October

3 Cook is given a standing ovation at the party conference for calling for a more positive approach to the EU.

November

21 Agreement is reached over Bosnia after peace negotiations at Dayton, Ohio, United States.

December

20 NATO-led multinational Implementation Force (IFOR) commences mission as part of the Dayton peace agreement for Bosnia.

1996

February

15 Publication of the Scott report on the arms-to-Iraq affair, which is highly critical of the government's approach to the arms trade with Iraq and which concludes that the trial of the Matrix Churchill executives 'ought never to have commenced'.

April

11 Blair speaks to the British–American Chamber of Commerce in New York and says that a Labour government would be of the 'radical centre'. Cements close relationship with Bill Clinton.

May

1 Cook supports the government's line on Hong Kong but may be prepared to offer Hong Kong's ethnic minorities a right of abode in the United Kingdom.

28 Cook promises that Labour will take a positive approach to the EU at the launch of a party document, *A Business Agenda for Europe*.

June

25 Blair launches the foreign affairs and defence policy document *A Fresh Start for Britain*, drawn up by Cook. Labour will promote UK trade and put human rights and developmental issues at the forefront of its diplomacy.

September

3 Press reports that Labour's forthcoming document *Vision for Growth* will contain a claim by Cook that international trade should have a moral aspect.

November

5 In the United States Clinton wins the presidential elections for the second time.

20 In Bosnia the NATO-led Stabilisation Force (including 5,000 British soldiers) takes over officially from the Implementation Force.

1997

February

12 *The Times* reports that Cook will make human rights central to its foreign policy, with a tougher stance on Nigeria and Myanmar (Burma).

26 Cook vows to make the environment central to a Labour government's foreign policy as he launches a 'Green Globe Task Force'.

March

18 Major announces the date of the general election.

May

1 Labour wins the general election, gaining a record number of seats (419 including the speaker).

4 In an interview with *The Observer*, Cook places no emphasis on a turn to ethics in foreign policy. His priorities are to take a leading role for the United Kingdom in Europe, to encourage trade, to promote human rights and environmental issues, and to integrate foreign and domestic policies.

7 Cook visits Paris and Bonn: he hopes for 'a triangular' leading role in

Europe and indicates the United Kingdom's firm intention of reaching agreement at the intergovernmental conference in Amsterdam in June.

12 Cook launches a mission statement for the Foreign Office, arguing that the government's foreign policy must have an ethical dimension.

21 Cook announces a ban on the import, transfer and manufacture of anti-personnel mines, including a moratorium on their use by UK forces.

24 Cook promises 'searching questions' on arms sales to Indonesia.

29 Clinton addresses Labour cabinet in London.

June

17 The Amsterdam treaty is agreed by the fifteen member states of the EU. Its measures include a new employment chapter and common foreign and security policy. Member states fail to agree the significant institutional reforms thought to be necessary for enlargement.

30 Hong Kong is returned to China.

July

1 Clare Short, secretary of state for international development, attends a ceremony at the UN as the United Kingdom rejoins UNESCO.

17 Cook stresses the administration's commitment to human rights in a set-piece speech. His proposals include the setting up of an international criminal court.

28 Cook announces new guidelines for the awarding of arms export licences but states that these will not be backdated. The sales of sixteen Hawk fighters and 100 Scorpion tanks to Indonesia will proceed. The government will publish an annual report on arms exports.

29 On a visit to Bosnia, Cook bluntly warns his hosts about corruption and about the lack of a free press: 'neither our patience nor our resources are unlimited'.

September

1 Cook completes a visit to South East Asia (Malaysia, Indonesia, Singapore and Philippines) claiming to have established a better balance between morality and commerce in the United Kingdom's relationship with the region. British police officers will address their Indonesian counterparts on 'modern policing methods'. Books on political science worth £2,000 are donated by Cook to the Jakarta Human Rights Commission.

23 Cook addresses the General Assembly of the UN and calls for reform of the Security Council to include Germany and Japan.

26 The *Financial Times* reports that the UK government has blocked the sale of some arms to Indonesia.

October

2 At the Labour party conference, Cook gives support to a proposal from the French prime minister, Lionel Jospin, for a European code of conduct

to regulate the arms trade. Cook notes, 'we have a duty to the 400,000 people who work in our defence industries'. Press reports suggest that Cook has been told by Blair to moderate his policy of blocking arms sales to countries accused of human rights violations.

12 The Queen, accompanied by Robin Cook, arrives in India to a hostile reception because of Cook's recent comments in Pakistan, where he had said that the United Kingdom would help to find a just solution to the disputed territory of Kashmir.

13 Inder Kumar Gujral, the Indian prime minister, denies a report that he called the United Kingdom a 'third-rate power'.

26 Cook announces some flexibility with Libya over the siting of the Lockerbie trial.

November

10 Blair gives his only speech on foreign policy during his first year of office: reportedly, a section on the ethical dimension is added at the last moment.

December

11 The United Kingdom breaks rank with other permanent members of the UN Security Council to back the setting up of a strong international court of justice to try war criminals.

1998

January

5 The United Kingdom formally takes over the presidency of the EU from Luxembourg.

16 The United States and the United Kingdom step up pressure on Iraq after Iraqi objections to US and UK participation in UNSCOM weapons inspection teams. HMS *Invincible* is to be sent to the Gulf region.

20 During a visit to China by Cook, representing the EU, the Chinese foreign minister, Qian Quichen, announces that he would welcome a visit by the UN Commissioner for Human Rights.

February

5 Blair and Clinton meet in Washington and have a 'brainstorming session' on the future of the centre-left. Clinton revives the idea of a special relationship.

17 In a debate in the Commons, Cook defends his hard line on Iraq, threatening aerial bombardment if UNSCOM is not allowed to carry out effective inspections.

March

10 Customs is asked by the Foreign Office to investigate a report that a UK company, Sandline International, a mercenary firm, had arranged for

weapons to be flown from Bulgaria to Sierra Leone to support the deposed president, Ahmed Tejan Kabbah, contrary to UN guidelines.

12 Foreign Office minister Tony Lloyd speaks in the Commons but has not been told of the arms supply to Sierra Leone.

17 Israeli prime minister Benjamin Netanyahu cancels dinner and cuts short a meeting with Cook, after the latter, representing the UK presidency of the EU, had met Palestinians at Har Homa, the site of a new Jewish settlement in Arab East Jerusalem.

24 Blair gives a speech in French to the French national assembly: he appeals to political leaders to embrace the Third Way.

April

2 The 'Good Friday' agreement is reached on the peace process in Northern Ireland.

12 The first human rights report (fifty-six pages) is presented by Cook; it claims that through 'practical partnerships' and dialogue there have been improvements in China, Indonesia and the Philippines but little change in Nigeria.

23 Cook makes a speech on the Third Way in foreign policy that reflects on the first year in office.

24 Cook makes a speech on the Third Way in domestic politics. Later press reports indicate that it was on this date that defence ministers first heard the allegations that Sandline had broken the arms embargo. Sandline faxes a copy of a letter sent to the Foreign Office claiming that it had acted with government approval.

28 Cook first hears about the Sandline affair.

May

1 Cook, in a *New Statesman* interview, argues that ethical objectives in foreign policy are an indication of the Third Way at work.

2 During a visit by the Chinese prime minister, Zhu Rongji, Blair and EU partners praise China for economic reform but add that they want an improvement in human rights. China has given permission for three EU ambassadors to visit Tibet.

3 Arms-to-Africa story breaks. *The Observer* reports that Sandline has broken the UN embargo on arms sales to Sierra Leone and that the Foreign Office had given approval for this in February. Cook says ministers were not involved and that a customs investigation will be given full support.

6 Cook announces an independent inquiry into the supply of arms to Sierra Leone.

12 In an emergency statement to the Commons, Cook states that he has found no evidence that Foreign Office officials had approved the sale of arms to Sierra Leone.

14 The Foreign Office's permanent secretary, Sir John Kerr, retracts evidence

that he has given earlier in the day to the Foreign Affairs Committee that Lloyd had been briefed in March about the customs investigation.

17 There are reports in the press that customs has found that Sandline did breach the UN arms embargo but has decided that it would not be prosecuted.

21 The Foreign Affairs Committee demands that the Foreign Office hand over telegrams about the Sandline affair.

June

9 MPs are told that Baroness Symons, a Foreign Office minister, had been briefed on 10 March about the investigation into arms to Sierra Leone.

22 An EU summit is held in Cardiff.

July

7 Cook agrees to hand over summaries of telegrams about the Sandline affair to the Foreign Affairs Committee.

10 A bill to ban anti-personnel landmines is rushed through the Commons.

17 In Rome, 160 countries meet and agree to set up an international court of justice. The United Kingdom is joined by France in supporting the treaty.

27 A report by Sir Thomas Legg on the arms-to-Africa affair is published: ministers and officials are cleared of conspiracy to supply arms to Sierra Leone.

August

20 The United States launches missiles against Sudan and Afghanistan in response to terrorist attacks on US embassies in Nairobi and Dar es Salaam.

27 There are press reports that the Foreign Office is increasingly concerned that Blair has given support too quickly to Clinton over the US military attacks, which have destroyed a pharmaceutical factory in Sudan.

September

11 Blair supports Clinton following the latter's domestic difficulties over the Starr report into the president's relationship with Monica Lewinsky.

21 A meeting in Washington between Blair and Clinton furthers discussion of the Third Way.

24 The United Kingdom and Iran agree to restore diplomatic relations after the Iranian foreign minister says that his government will not threaten the life of Salman Rushdie.

October

16 General Augusto Pinochet is arrested in London in response to an extradition request from Spain. Cook announces that staff from Amnesty International and Save the Children will be seconded to the Foreign Office.

25 Cook urges NATO allies not to soften the threat of military action against
Yugoslavia.

November

13 In an interview in the *New Statesman* Cook distances himself from an
'ethical foreign policy'.
18 The Global Citizenship Unit is launched in the Foreign Office. This is to
advocate that companies should act responsibly overseas, shun child
labour and give priority to environmentally friendly business practices.
25 The Lords rules that Pinochet does not have immunity from prosecution
as a former head of state.
27 The Chilean foreign minister visits London and says that Pinochet should
be freed. The Foreign Office announces an increase in the number of
diplomats to be sent to the EU and eastern Europe and a doubling of
its representation in countries around the Caspian Sea. Six new embassies
would be opened, including in Guinea, Mali and Gabon in West Africa.

December

4 An Anglo-French summit in St Malo produces a Franco-British declaration
on a common defence policy. The British and French also agree on
diplomatic co-operation in Africa.
6 Blair arrives in China for a six-day visit accompanied by senior business
executives from the United Kingdom. Trade is high on the agenda but
the prime minister promises that human rights will also be discussed.
10 Baghdad bars UN weapons inspectors from entering a Ba'ath party office.
15 UNSCOM weapons and International Atomic Energy Authority inspectors
withdraw from Iraq.
16 Cook appears before the parliamentary inquiry into the arms-to-Africa
affair and says it has produced no new evidence. The United States and
United Kingdom launch Operation Desert Fox, a four-day cruise missile
and bombing attack on Iraq. UN personnel are hurriedly evacuated from
Baghdad to Bahrain.
21 The Foreign Affairs Committee presses Cook to take firmer action to promote
human rights. Cook is criticised for shaking hands with president Suharto
in Indonesia in August 1997. Cook argues for 'constructive engagement'.

1999

January

8 In a speech in Cape Town, Tony Blair argues that the Third Way is not
just a domestic issue but concerns international matters.

February

3 The opening of the Rambouillet conference on Kosovo is chaired by Cook
and Hubert Vedrine, the French foreign minister.

9 Blair and Cook claim that the critical report of the Foreign Affairs Committee on the arms-to-Africa affair has uncovered nothing new.

15 In a speech by Cook to the 'Green Alliance', he says he has pushed the environment up the Foreign Office's agenda.

March

1 The UK government promises £200 million of aid to fund the building of a dam in Ilisu, Turkey. The project is controversial because of the number of people who would be displaced, its impact on the environment and the disruption to water supplies in Iraq and Syria.

23 NATO secretary-general Javier Solana authorises (at 23.30 Brussels time) general Wesley Clark to 'initiate air operations' against Yugoslavia. Blair says there is no alternative to military action.

25 Publication of the first annual report on strategic export controls. Campaigners for the control of arms sales are concerned at the granting of export licences to Singapore and Jordan, both suspected of re-exporting arms.

April

18 Clinton, writing in the *Sunday Times*, and Blair, speaking on the US CBS network, present a united front on action in Kosovo.

22 In Chicago, Blair speaks about the doctrine of the 'international community' and justifies NATO's action in Kosovo. He suggests ground rules for action against regimes perpetrating 'barbarous acts' on their own people.

23 Russia refuses to attend the NATO summit in Washington in protest at the bombing campaign in Kosovo.

May

1 Part of the Amsterdam treaty, the strengthening of EU foreign policy, comes into force.

13 Blair is awarded the Charlemagne prize in Aachen. He wants the United Kingdom to be a leading player and to resolve once and for all its ambivalence towards Europe.

18 Blair is feted on a visit to Albania.

June

3 EU summit in Cologne. Yugoslav government accepts peace plan brought to Belgrade by the Finnish president, Martti Ahtisaari, and the Russian prime minister, Viktor Chernomyrdin. A UN Security Council resolution will be drawn up authorising the creation of the international security force.

10 UN Security Council approves Kosovo peace plan. Javier Solana announces a halt to the seventy-nine-day NATO bombing of Yugoslavia.

22 Cook sees 'not the slightest prospect' of the EU having its own army.

He states that Western aid to Serbia would only follow the overthrow of Slobodan Milosevic.

23 Cook visits the sites of atrocities in Kosovo and speaks of 'a vision of hell'.

25 The United Kingdom informs Kofi Annan, the UN secretary-general, that it will put up to 8,000 troops on permanent standby for UN peacekeeping operations.

27 Cook meets his Cuban opposite number, Felipe Perez Roque, in Rio at a summit of the EU, Latin American and Caribbean nations. He is the first foreign secretary to do so since Fidel Castro came to power.

July

  5 Cook gives an interview in the *New Statesman*: 'the place where human rights, democracy and freedom have been challenged over this past year has been Kosovo, and we've asserted these values'.

15 The ban on Argentines visiting the Falkland Islands is lifted.

29 Baroness Scotland of Asthal joins the Foreign Office as the United Kingdom's first black female minister.

August

  4 George Robertson, the defence secretary, is appointed secretary-general of NATO.

30 The people of East Timor vote overwhelmingly for secession from Indonesia in a UN-organised referendum. Pro-Indonesian militias take to the streets of Dili and begin a campaign of terror.

September

11 Under intense pressure, the United Kingdom suspends arms sales to Indonesia in response to Indonesian and militia violence in East Timor.

20 Following intense diplomatic activity, an Australian-led UN multinational force arrives in Dili, East Timor, charged with restoring peace and security.

23 Amnesty International publishes *Human Rights Audit of UK Foreign and Asylum Policy*: it commends the government for its 'genuine and active commitment to human rights in a number of areas' but concludes that the DTI is out of step by 'not meeting its responsibility to promote trade in a manner not harmful to human rights'.

October

12 General Parvaiz Musharrah leads to a military coup in Pakistan.

15 Cook, speaking at an EU meeting in Finland, announces that the United Kingdom is to suspend development aid to Pakistan and will be recommending that Pakistan is suspended from the Commonwealth.

22 President Jiang Zemin of China ends a four-day visit to the United Kingdom. The police are accused of over-zealous control of human rights demonstrators.

24 Cook begins a visit to Israel and offers to raise with Iran the case of a missing Israeli airman shot down over Lebanon in 1986. Cook and the Israeli prime minister, Ehud Barak, wish to emphasise friendship.

November
3 Publication of the second annual report on strategic export controls. The government is shown to have approved export licences for military equipment to countries with poor human rights records, such as Turkey, China, Bahrain, Algeria and Indonesia. Over 10,000 licences had been granted during 1998.

December
13 *The Guardian* reports that Tony Blair has ruled that the Elgin marbles will not be returned by Labour to Greece.
21 Chancellor Gordon Brown announces that the United Kingdom will waive all bilateral debt owed by the world's poorest forty-one countries.
22 *The Guardian* reports that Tony Blair has approved aid for the Ilisu dam project in Turkey, against the opposition of some cabinet colleagues. Conditions are to be attached to the aid.

2000

January
12 Jack Straw, home secretary, rules that general Pinochet is unfit to stand trial and will not be extradited to Spain. *The Guardian* reports that the government is split over the unfreezing of export licences to Pakistan. The MoD and the DTI want to renew arms sales; the Foreign Office and DFID oppose the move. A junior minister is quoted: 'this is the filthy end of foreign policy'. *The Guardian* also reports that the United Kingdom will ban the use of export credits for arms sales to sixty-three of the world's poorest nations.
14 The government announces that the EU arms embargo on Indonesia will be lifted.
17 EU embargo on arms sales to Indonesia imposed four months earlier in response to atrocities in East Timor lapses.
27 Press reports suggest that Blair has over-ruled Cook to sanction the sale of spare parts for fighter jets to Zimbabwe. Zimbabwe has sent troops to fight in the civil war in Congo/Zaïre.

February
16 The Defence, Foreign Affairs, International Development and Trade and Industry Committees report that there has been no radical shift in the pattern of arms sales to Indonesia under Labour. No licences granted by the Conservatives to Indonesia have been revoked.

28 The government announces that a bill to regulate the arms trade will
   be introduced in the autumn. The ECGD will also be restructured.

March
  6 John Pilger's television documentary blames the tough sanctions employed
    by the UK and US governments for the suffering of the Iraqi people.
16 Government reports that the defence diversification agency budget, at
   £1.1 million, is a fraction of that for the defence export services organisation (at £45 million).

April
  3 Following criticism about UK policies towards Iraq and Russia, Peter
    Hain, Foreign Office minister, tells the *New Statesman* that 'The phrase
    "ethical foreign policy" was never used – it was "ethical dimension". But
    in a sense it was a hook on which we found ourselves, and I think it
    has obscured the very big advances we have made.'

May
  3 The United Kingdom suspends arms sales to Zimbabwe following attacks
    on white farmers and opposition parties.
  9 UK troops are deployed in Sierra Leone following worsening of civil war
    there.
17 The government checks its support for the Ilisu dam project in Turkey
   as the Turkish government fails to meet Labour's conditions for agreeing
   to fund the project with £200 million of aid.
19 An article in *The Guardian* suggests that defence spending under Labour
   is too low for the kind of overseas operations to which the armed forces
   have been committed by the Blair administration.

June
27 In a speech to the German parliament, Jacques Chirac, the French
   president, quickens the pace of European integration, suggesting that a
   core group move together without other members of the EU. The United
   Kingdom is perceived to be outside this core group, largely because of
   Labour's ambivalence to membership of the euro (the single European
   currency).

July
  5 The UK ban on arms exports to Pakistan is partially lifted.

Index